P9-CKX-835

Let's Get a Divorce!

AND OTHER PLAYS

Nous naissons toutes soucieuses
De garder l'honneur de l'époux
Mais des circonstances fâcheuses
Nous font mal tourner malgré nous.
Témoin l'exemple de ma mère:
Quand elle vit le cygne altier
Qui (vous le savez) est mon père
Pouvait-elle se méfier?
Dis-moi, Vénus, quel plaisir trouves-tu
A faire ainsi cascader la vertu?

— Helen of Troy
in *La Belle Hélène.*

ERIC BENTLEY
Editor

DISCARD

Let's Get a Divorce!

AND OTHER PLAYS

A MERMAID DRAMABOOK

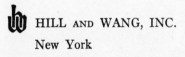 HILL AND WANG, INC.
New York

Copyright © 1958 by Eric Bentley

Library of Congress Catalog Card Number: 58-6065

Inquiries about permissions for any kind of performance should be addressed to Samuel French Inc., 25 West Forty-fifth Street, New York 36, New York, unless otherwise stipulated on the title page of the play concerned.

Manufactured in the United States of America by The Colonial Press Inc.

842.0108
L649

ACKNOWLEDGMENTS

Permission to print was kindly provided by the following:

A Trip Abroad: Mr. R. H. Ward
Célimare: Mrs. Lynn Hoffman
Let's Get a Divorce!: Mr. Robert Goldsby
Keep an Eye on Amélie!: Dr. Jan Van Loewen and Mr. Brainerd Duffield
A United Family: Mr. J. D. Allen
Marcel Achard's essay on Feydeau: Dr. Jan Van Loewen and Mrs. Mary Douglas Dirks

A word of thanks should go to the translators who worked on commissions for this volume under considerable pressure of time: Mr. and Mrs. Hoffman, Mr. and Mrs. Goldsby, and Mrs. Dirks; and also to those whose translations delightfully descended upon me, unsolicited: Mr. Duffield and Mr. Allen. Mr. Ward's translation was thoughtfully brought to my attention by Mr. John Wardle.

Parts of "The Psychology of Farce" have appeared in *The New Republic. These Cornfields* has appeared in *Chrysalis*.

E. B.

CONTENTS

THE PSYCHOLOGY OF FARCE

> "Be friends, be lovers, be what you will, but
> as for being husband and wife, God in heaven!"
>
> *Count Almaviva*

IDEALLY a compendium of exact information and intelligent opinion, an encyclopedia addresses itself, in fact, to the codification of current prejudices. The article on farce in the only encyclopedia of theatre in our language starts out this way:

> *Farce,* an extreme form of comedy in which laughter is raised at the expense of probability, particularly by horseplay and bodily assault. It must, however, retain its hold on humanity, even if only in depicting the grosser faults of mankind; otherwise it degenerates into travesty and burlesque.

After remarking, *en passant,* that farce died out before Molière, the writer winds round to this conclusion:

> In modern usage, the word farce is applied to a full-length play dealing with some absurd situation hingeing generally on extra-marital relations—hence the term bedroom farce. Farce has small literary merit, but great entertainment value, and owing to its lack of subtlety can be translated from one language to another more easily than comedy.

An extreme form. The tone is patronizing. Why? Is extremity bad? And if farce is already an extremity, how can it further *degenerate into travesty and burlesque?* And why does the writer have it in for travesty and burlesque? Or is it just that everything is a degenerate something else: burlesque is degenerate farce, farce is degenerate comedy, comedy is degenerate tragedy . . . ? *At the expense of probability.* And why not? Why should not probability have its price? *Even if only in depicting the grosser faults of mankind.* Why "even if only"? Is this such a contemptible or easy thing to do? Why be hoity-toity about gross faults? *Owing to its lack of subtlety it can be translated . . . more easily.* Not "its lack of subtlety of language," please note, but its "lack of subtlety," *tout court.* That farce has subtlety in other spheres than dialogue is nowhere intimated, and that even its dialogue often has subtlety of a kind (I am thinking not only of the obvious case of Wilde but of the more orthodox farceurs like Labiche and Feydeau) is completely overlooked. *Small literary merit but great entertainment value.* In the middle of this phrase the subject switches abruptly from the inherent qualities of the work to the response of an audience. And are we to understand that a work pleases an audience by its lack of merit? Merit apart, it would seem psychologically necessary to attribute pleasure to the presence, not the absence, of something. But, of course, the whole article is based on the opposite assumption—that farce consists of defects without qualities.

What we uncover, then, in this guide to theatre is a massive prejudice against one of the most honorable and remarkable forms of dramatic art. It is not a new prejudice. The comment was made on Labiche's admission to the Academy that it was farce, the first of theatre arts in France, that was now being honored—last. The "literature" of the subject is, accordingly, very slender, and in fact the only thorough descriptions of farce are to be found in works on comedy or laughter. There is, for example, no better account of the mechanisms of farcical plot than Bergson's famous essay; references to Labiche abound in it; but Bergson's subject is laughter, and even life, in general. Most dramatic critics assume that the farcical bag of tricks was easy to amass and is even easier to use. Once there is a bed on stage, and some confusion as to its proper occupancy, no difference is noted between the clumsiness of a tyro and the virtuosity of a master. The craftsmanship of Feydeau is as complex and, yes, as subtle as any in the whole history of drama, yet when one of his plays is done in Anglo-Saxon countries we inevitably have to hear it talked down to as a quaint period piece.

If farce is more readily acknowledged as an ingredient in higher comedy, it has not always been welcome even there. Molière has been scolded for using farce by generations of critics, beginning with his own generation. He would certainly have roused more enthusiasm in Anglo-Saxon countries had he left farce entirely alone. Confronted with Molière, the young American asks: "If he wants to be taken seriously, why isn't he serious?" Conversely, a playwright of half Molière's talent could secure a reputation for twice as much by replacing the farcical elements with what might be called certified seriousness, that is, currently fashionable psychology and sociology.

Melodrama—the counterpart of farce on the tragic side—

is in similar disrepute. The term, like the term farce, is used to show contempt for something admirable or admiration for something contemptible. Yet just as the supreme master of comedy, Molière, was an incorrigible farceur, the supreme master of tragedy, Shakespeare, was an incorrigible melo-dramatist. Explaining this away has provided employment for generations of scholars. They have advanced such arguments as these: Shakespeare wasn't as great as he is cracked up to be, and melodrama is one of his many Gothic mistakes of taste; Shakespeare was so great he could get away with anything, even melodrama; Shakespeare may have been melodramatic, but he wasn't as melodramatic as Marlowe or Webster; Shakespeare wasn't melodramatic, there's a consistent and naturalistic psychology to him, once you find out how many children Lady Macbeth had. . . . And to this day, it is impossible to stage a Shakespearean tragedy without inviting, from the press in general and *The New Yorker* in particular, a lot of heavy irony on the subject of stage villains, the pile of corpses in the last scene, or some other melodramatic item. If a bit of melodrama actually takes a critic's fancy, he will hasten to assure you that this is not Shakespeare at his best: it is a case of *small literary merit but great entertainment value.*

The words farce and melodrama are now so devalued that one would wish them discarded like farthings and one-lira bills, were it not that they would then have to be speedily replaced because what they refer to—in Elizabethan tragedy, the comedy of Molière, or even the classic American novel—is central to literature and drama. And it is not a defect but a quality. The "absurd" plots of tragedies from *Oedipus Rex* to *King Lear* represent, not a failure of primitive man to be mature, but the refusal of tragic man to limit himself to naturalism. The feeling one had as a child that the "absurd" opening scene in *Lear* was supremely right is justified. The "absurdity" expresses the real absurdity of life, of which our encyclopedist's "probability" is a misleading mask. If art imitates life, it should be added that while naturalistic art imitates the surfaces, "melodramatic" art imitates what is beneath the surface. It is a matter, then, of finding external representation—symbol—for what cannot be photographed or described. As such symbols, the plots of the masters are apt, expressive, economic, and amazing. Aristotle, who has more often been thought too rational than not rational enough, put the plots of the Greek tragedies before all their other attributes, and made a special favorite of *Oedipus Rex,* which has the "absurdest" plot of any.

It may be that the principle of the primacy of plot holds for all drama. It certainly holds for melodrama and farce. Here in the action lies that subtlety which is sometimes and notoriously absent from dialogue and even character. The enacted story is itself a language. And this is to say that it is symbolic. Like dreams, farces show the disguised fulfill- ment of repressed wishes. That is a Freudian formula, but not, surely, one that only Freudians can accept. For one thing, the comparison between farce and dream is a matter, up to a point, not of analogy but identity. Examining my own dreams, I have been not a little surprised to discover how many affinities they show with Chaplin films—in ideas for a whole sequence of action (chases in automobiles, "routines" of dressing or moving furniture) or in characteri- zation (heroes and villains, "chickens" and bullies) or even in style of performance (large grimaces and gesticulation being very much in order).

The word *repressed* brings us back to our encyclopedist's remarks about grossness. Repressed wishes find an outlet, surely, in all drama; many repressed wishes are gross ones; and if we take the family to be the very center of culture, we should not be surprised that gross wishes are mainly, if not exclusively, desires to damage the family, to desecrate the household gods. Consider the Greeks, who had just created the family. They naturally found the supreme virtue in the pious and loyal relation of husband to wife, or child to parent, of sibling to sibling. The subject of tragedy is the violation of this piety. What, then, would be the worst con- ceivable violation of both the marital and filial pieties? Why, the double crime of Oedipus. And the phrase "some absurd situation hingeing on extra-marital relations" is richly sug- gestive of tragic plot—the plot of *Othello,* for example.

But what situation "hingeing on extra-marital relations" is not full of absurdities and therefore potentially melodramatic or farcical, tragic or comic, according to the temperament, state of mind, and view of life of the witness? Outrage to family piety and propriety is certainly at the heart of farce— "hence," as the book says, "the term bedroom farce." Indeed, the fearsomeness of the enterprise might explain why people prefer either to brush farce off as totally meaningless or as- sign it a meaning that could never explain its prodigious energy. For example, the great dramatic critic Sarcey, noting that serious plays about adultery were unsavory, concluded that playwrights should get a little fun out of the subject instead: he justified farce on grounds of its triviality, and one is surprised, perhaps, to find Labiche agreeing with him.[1]

If Sarcey's view—though preferable to the Anglo-Saxon notion that adultery should be banished from the drama altogether—is one that skims the surface, there is a more widely current view that is merely an error—the idea that "wicked" comedy, farce or otherwise, French or English-Restoration, is amoral. It is hard to imagine what true indifference to morals could produce, if anything at all. Comedy and farce presuppose accepted standards, and when the playwrights don't respect those standards, they resent them. If English Puritanism were ever totally forgotten, it could still be deduced from Restoration comedy, which was born under the sign of Oliver Cromwell. And it is interesting that the word we today apply to bawdy farces is "naughty"—a word that belongs essentially to the vocabulary of mothers and nursemaids, the appointed deputies of the superego. Where there is no established virtue, there can be no sense of outrage, and farce, as we have seen, is no less "outrageous" than tragedy.

The marriage joke, then, exists only for a culture that knows itself committed to marriage. But is the joke necessary or even salutary? There is a growing tendency in modern civilization to think that it is neither. Only the other day, I happened upon a magazine headline: "Don't Let Them Scoff at Marriage," which turned out to be the title of an article blaming "the moral crisis of today" on the marriage joke and attributing that joke to the post–1945 generation as if it had not been told through the centuries.[2]

It is true, however, that the marriage joke could be abolished if the family were the unmixed blessing that many of our contemporaries take it for. In another recent article, the chief of the Division of Social Medicine at an important American hospital writes as follows:

[1] The passage mentioned here is quoted below, page 346.
[2] The author does not use the *term* "marriage joke" but does describe the *thing:* "The gross libel on marriage is the notion that the chase, the allure is the goal. Marriage is seen as a dull aftermath." Gross libel it may be; it is certainly a perennial fantasy of mankind, and therefore no good pretext for a gross libel on the present generation. The article, by Howard Whitman, appeared in *Better Homes and Gardens,* August, 1957.

The family is central to the development of humanity not only for the perpetuation of the race but because the proper psychological development of an individual can only occur within the warm circle of the nuclear family. Social and psychological studies indicate quite clearly that a strong family structure helps to develop and maintain a personality free of dangerous (to self and society) characteristics.

The author draws the conclusion that sexual deviation and juvenile delinquency can be prevented by closer, warmer family relations, and no doubt there is some truth in this. Unhappily there is evident truth in precisely the opposite proposition. The close, warm family is also a seedbed of neurosis, vice, and crime. About the same time as this article appeared,[3] a newspaper picture caught my eye. It showed a beaming public relations executive with his good-looking wife and three attractive children. They seemed a model American family in a model American home, and one could imagine the picture passing in triumph around the public relations office. The caption underneath, however, reported that the mildest and most candid-looking of the boys had just killed the mother and sister and told the police that he had planned to kill the rest of the family as well. It would be comforting to think that such a shocking event could be declared irrelevant to the experience of normal folk. But, however psychotic that poor lad's behavior, the fact remains that neurosis and psychosis are extensions of patterns present in us all. The understanding attitude to Hitler's massacres is not: "How could he ever dream of such a thing?" but: "How could he ever have done what others only dream of?"

The cruelty of sick behavior and healthy fantasy is found also in farce. In Charlie Chaplin's film farces, for instance. Though what we consciously remember from them may be Chaplin's incomparable delicacy, they are for the most part taken up with violent pursuit and violent combat. Fantasy multiplies movements and blows by a thousand. The villain is a giant whose strength passes the limits of nature. He can bend lampposts with his bare hands. Since the "little man's" revenges have to be more than proportionate to the provocation (as with Brecht's Jenny the Pirate's Bride), he can drop a cast-iron stove on the villain's head and ram that head inside a street lamp with the gas turned on. Another symptom of cruelty is the abstractness of the violence. Prongs of a

[3] May 25th, 1957, in *The Nation*.

rake in the backside are received as pin pricks. Bullets seem
to pass right through people, sledge-hammer blows to produce
only momentary irritation. The speeding up of movement
contributes to the abstract effect. So, even more, does the
silence proper to the screen of those days, many of the effects
being lost when a sound track is superimposed. The cops
shoot, but there is no noise. Heavy objects fall, but there is
no crash. Gruesome infighting has the air of shadowbox-
ing. . . . All of which signifies that, in farce, as in dreams,
one is permitted the outrage but is spared the consequences.
Chaplin's delicacy of style is actually part of the pattern:
he parades an air of nonchalance when acting in a manner
that, in real life, would land him in Bellevue or Sing Sing.

But while dreams are ignored or forgotten, farces incur
the censure of professional moralists and amateur psycholo-
gists. The thought arises: "The theatre is inciting my children
to hate the home, if not to commit murder and arson. We
must have more censorship!" It is overlooked that such fantasies are kept for dreams and pictures and plays just because
each of us already has within him so strong a censorship,
and it is wrongly inferred from the power of the fantasies
that people are likely to fail to distinguish between fantasy
and reality. On a person who could not distinguish between
fantasy and reality, Chaplin movies might well have a disastrous effect *except that such a person is already too far
gone to go much further.* Though, from the devil's standpoint,
Hitler excels the rest of us in having the courage to do what
we all dream of doing, from the standpoint of mental hygiene,
the Satanic superman must simply be adjudged a lunatic,
while those who refuse to act out their morbid fantasies are,
in that respect at least, sensible and sane.

The function of "farcical" fantasies, in dreams or in plays,
is not as provocation but as compensation. The violent release is comparable to the sudden relieving hiss of steam
through a safety valve. Certainly, the mental energies involved are destructive, and in all comedy there remains
something of destructive orgy, farce being the kind of
comedy which disguises that fact least thoroughly. But the
function of orgies is also that of a safety valve. An orgy—as
still practiced in the Munich Carnival, for example—is an
essentially temporary truancy from the family pieties, and,
like farces, if it has any appreciable effect at all, it helps
those pieties to go on existing. The main point of Freud's
Civilization and its Discontents is pertinent here: when we

buy civilization, as we do, at the price of frustration, the frustrated impulses become a potential source of trouble. The pressures are enormous and perpetual. We ought to welcome any relief from them, however slight or trivial, provided it is harmless. Dreams are the commonest relief but are usually unpleasant. The most pleasurable relief is to be found in the arts, for one of which I am staking out a claim in this essay.

In his book on jokes, Freud explains in effect that he would "let them scoff at marriage" not only because he would never be able to prevent them but also because a safety valve is a good thing. It is a sort of open secret, he says on one page,[4] that marriage does not satisfy the sexual demands of men and that this secret is half-kept, half-told in marriage jokes. I would add that the classic form of the marriage joke takes a couple of hours to tell and has a cast of three characters known as *le mari, la femme, et l'amant,*—"hence," again, "the term bedroom farce." Just as Restoration comedy was provoked by the Puritans and is, so to speak, forever dedicated to them, the farce of adultery has been provoked by married men and is dedicated to them. Farce in general enables us, seated in dark security, to enjoy the delights of complete passivity while watching on stage the most violently active creatures ever imagined by man. In that particular application of the general formula which is bedroom farce, we enjoy the adventure of adultery, ingeniously exaggerated to the nth degree, without incurring the responsibilities or suffering the guilt, without even the hint of an affront to the wife at our side.[5]

---

[4] The exact words are: *"Dass die Ehe nicht die Veranstaltung ist, die Sexualität des Mannes zu befriedigen, getraut man nicht laut und öffentlich zu sagen . . ."* The familiar English title of the book is *Wit and its Relation to the Unconscious,* but *Der Witz,* here translated as wit, is also the ordinary German word for a joke; and Freud's book is all about jokes, though it has implications for wit and humor in general. Incidentally, *Civilization and its Discontents* is another misleading title, though there may be no perfect substitute for it. "Discontents" suggest political grievances ("Thoughts on the Present Discontents") whereas the original title, *Das Unbehagen in der Kultur,* connotes stress and strain, discomfort, uneasiness, malaise.

[5] I refer those who find Freudianism newfangled to Gilbert Murray's Norton lectures of 1925 (reprinted as *The Classical Tradition in Poetry*) for some fine remarks, albeit not always fair to psychoanalysis, about the "close similarity . . . between . . . Aristotle and Freud." Murray applies to the whole of comedy

In speaking of exaggeration, it is important to see what is exaggerated in farce and what is not. While, certainly, the external facts are distorted, the inner experience is so wild and preposterous that it would probably be impossible to exaggerate it. To the inner experience, the farceur tries to be utterly faithful. This fact raises the question whether farce is as indirect a form of literature as it is commonly assumed to be.

What kind of literature is direct? I have addressed the question to well-read persons, and have sometimes received the answer: Jane Austen's novels. For they are straightforward in style and crystal clear in tenor. But is not this limpidity the last effect of indirectness? It is Jane Austen's strategy, surely, to pretend to accept the surfaces of life at what is well called face value, then, in highly indirect ways, to enable us to sense how much happens beneath those surfaces. An open breach of the surface would be an unthinkable breach of decorum.

Farce, on the other hand, while it begins by accepting the bland, placid, imposing façade of life, proceeds to become farcical by knocking the façade down. The farceur, like the lunatic and the unruly child, flies in the face of decorum. Harpo Marx is the supreme case in point. For him, there is nothing to do with clothes but take the scissors to them, nothing to do with a façade but throw a bomb at it. Many other comedians destroy things. Few manage so impressively as Harpo to convey the idea of human nature as in itself destructive. It is the impishness, the quasi innocence, the complication of aggression with bizarre fantasy; and the dumbness helps, both as a psychological trait (suggestive of a general deficiency) and as a physical fact (for nothing is so economically expressive as silence).

---

a theory which I have not dared to extend beyond the frontiers of farce: "The anarchist and the polygamist, close-prisoned and chained in ordinary life, enjoy their release in comedy. . . . As for the polygamist . . . comedy provides him with an atmosphere in which . . . husbands are recognized as ridiculous and wives as a nuisance, where Captain Macheath and Don Juan and Célimare find a world that exactly suits them." One cannot but enjoy the contrast in mentality between the "other-directed" modernists of *The Nation* or *Better Homes and Gardens* and Professor Murray, last of the great Victorian gentlemen-scholars, when we find the latter saying: "Comedy . . . must . . . not be spoilt by any tiresome temperance or prudential considerations of the morrow."

In one of Noel Coward's short farces, a man knocks his mother-in-law out with, if I remember rightly, a straight left to the jaw.[6] As the only form of literature or theatre in which such an incident could occur, farce may reasonably claim to be the most direct of all the forms. Such are the aggressions which are rampant in human beings all day and, as we are increasingly aware, all night. In a sense, Coward's trifle is more realistic than all the realisms. For that— "crudely expressed," as the encyclopedias will have it—is what life is like.

But the most direct form is still not in all ways direct. Since, as we have seen, the wishes expressed in farce often appear there in disguised forms, there is still the duality in these fantasies, as in others, of manifest and latent content, of mask and face. Failure to render either the directness or the duality (with its *in*directness) is usually very marked in modern stage productions. When a character knocks out his mother-in-law, he is acting out[7] the fantasies of millions, yet a bad actor is able to suggest that he is acting out precisely nothing—he didn't mean to hurt the old lady and the play is just a "romp," destined to elicit from newspaper reviewers epithets like "delicious" and "cute."

There are two wrong ways of playing the indirectness of farce: the amateur way and the professional way. The amateur's failure is more or less total. He lacks the art to create a mask of actuality (normality, gravity, sophistication) and, as for the life beneath, he hasn't an inkling how to get at it or, perhaps even, that it is there to be got at. He concludes that, since farce is very energetic, he should bound about, and that, since it is very funny, he should be facetious; and so his furious efforts end in vacuity.

The professional is wiser. He knows he has no such weapon in his armory as funniness. He knows that being funny is a

---

[6] What I am remembering (and, I believe, rightly) is one particular performance. The published script of *Fumed Oak* testifies only to a light slap on the cheek, followed by a moment in which the audience thinks the mother-in-law has fallen unconscious. In not quite daring to deliver a real knock-out to the lady, Mr. Coward might be said to have been a . . . coward.

[7] "Acting out" is another psychoanalytic term of considerable pertinency in this field. Unconscious conflicts find release and relief in the famous physical exertions of farcical fantasy (our encyclopedist's "horseplay and bodily assault"). Freud quotes the proverb: *"Was man nicht im Kopfe hat, muss man in den Beinen haben."*

result, and that what God gave him is fantasy; and he uses this fantasy to create a mask. Professional productions of farce tend to be plausible, even elegant, but it is the habit of the professional to neglect the face beneath the mask. Though smooth, his work is hollow. There have been productions of *The Importance of Being Earnest* in which the manner of an upper class was very accurately rendered in voice and gesture but in which one had no feeling of the inordinate aggression of Wilde against Victorian civilization, if not against all civilization.

Not all professional productions take this "naturalistic line" with a farce. On the contrary, more of them nowadays overlook the naturalistic mask entirely and try to give direct expression to the author's fantasy. In this case, the work of the designer and the director, as well as the actor, is concentrated on announcing: This is fantasy, this is artifice, this is unreal. Everyone wears fantastic costumes and gesticulates in a curious manner that the director calls "stylized." The decor seems to be by Toulouse-Lautrec and probably is by Mr. Cecil Beaton or Mr. Oliver Messel.

There are two things wrong with such a procedure. This *kind* of fantasy is far too superficial and sophisticated for true farce; and, in any case, it is not an advantage to dispense with the façade, because the dynamic of farce proper derives from the interplay between the mask (of actuality) and the real face (of primitive instinct). Even an amateur who could impart a sense of primitive life would fail to communicate farce if he could compose no mask, while the professional who creates the most elaborate "style" is giving us scarcely anything if primitive energy is lacking.

It is, of course, only the professional that one has the right to complain of, and even he might plead that he cannot by himself counteract a trend of the times, this trend being the decline of farce. Compared with the five-course banquet that was served on the Paris boulevards half a century ago—1850 to 1920 was the heyday of modern farce—the fey pleasantries of Roussin and Husson are mere hors d'oeuvres.

But need productions of Labiche and Feydeau have fallen off quite so much as they have? I am not thinking of productions in which a director's intention was not carried out or even of productions that failed to have any sort of appeal. I have in mind shows which could not fail to amuse people who came to the theatre without special preparation or expectation but which did not realize the full potentiality of the script because they deviated too widely from the original conception. Two such productions that many Americans have seen and of which many photographs have been published[8] are Gaston Baty's staging of *An Italian Straw Hat* and Jean Meyer's of *A Trip Abroad*. Both were exquisite; and, by that token, neither was Labiche. Consider the visual side alone. For scenery, bright colors were painted on obviously two-dimensional materials, and, just as objects were reduced to pictures by losing a dimension, clothes were reduced to operetta costumes by bright contrasting colors, heavy stripes, checks, and evident flimsiness of texture.

Now look at a drawing of *An Italian Straw Hat* made shortly after the first production.[9] The clothes are clothes— a little drab, perhaps, as is proper to the period and the milieu, yet, with their high collars, their bulgy trousers, their bulbous bodices, full of drama. Here the associations would not be operetta, period charm, "stylization," but realistic plays, immediacy, forthrightness. The caricature is not delicious but manly, not cute but cutting. We are not far from Daumier, and distinctly close to Cruikshank and Dickens. Such is the world of Labiche. One can only get at it by fighting one's way through a jungle of misinterpretation that has had nearly a century to grow.

With Feydeau, though he has been dead less than forty years, there is already a similar tale to tell. Produced in England or America, his plays seem like bad Oscar Wilde or Brandon Thomas turned scabrous. Even the superbly acted Barrault production of *Keep an Eye on Amélie!* in Paris was weakened by the work of a designer who tended to substitute *chichi* decoration for robustness.[10] Recent book illustrations of either Labiche or Feydeau can be relied on to give the latter-day, effete notion of them—and of farce.

In making a certain claim for farce I have stressed that it has more in common with melodrama and even tragedy than

---

[8] In, for example, the Appleton-Century-Crofts edition of *Un Chapeau de paille d'Italie* and the Parisian compilation *Masques: Théâtre 1944-46*.

[9] And reproduced in Lucien Dubech's *Histoire générale illustrée du théâtre,* Volume V, p. 119.

[10] A sketch of his, reproduced in Barrault's *Reflections on the Theatre,* opposite p. 140, will satisfy anyone on this point. Its demonstrative delicacy suggests a Bonwit Teller store window rather than the milieu of an Amélie or the mental world of a Feydeau.

with naturalistic drama. In doing so I have understressed the differences, for most of them are obvious. They amount to the fact that tragedy presents a nobler, more profound image of man. Struck with the thought of man's weakness, Pascal, a tragic mind if there ever was one, called him a reed, a thinking reed. Farce confronts the cruder kinds of man's strength, all of which he misuses. Man, says farce, may or may not be one of the more intelligent animals; he is certainly an animal, and not one of the least violent; and one of the chief uses to which he puts his intelligence, such as it is, is to think aggression when he is not committing it. (Mona Lisa's civilized smile might mean that she was plotting murder, but is more likely to signify that she was imagining murders she would never plot.)

The people who act out his fantasies for the farceur—his characters—are what are commonly stigmatized as "not individuals but types": human nature in the abstract, in the mass, in the rough, in the raw, in anything but fine personal flower. Our encyclopedist remarks that they are stupid, which is an understatement. They are monuments to stupidity, disturbing yet, surely, deliberate reminders that God lavished stupidity on the human race with a recklessly prodigal hand. They put us in mind of our own stupidities. They even teach us (if we are not too stupid to learn) what stupidity is. For one thing, it is being absent in mind: the *distrait,* as Bergson showed, is a comic archetype . . .

Like Hitler, who acted out farcical fantasies, farce characters pass beyond stupidity into craziness, and the farceur must have the gift of some lunatics (such as paranoiacs) to build a large, intricate, and self-consistent structure of "improbabilities." *Charley's Aunt* is a loosely organized example. Any Feydeau play is an instance of the tightest and most complex organization possible, and, as a result, Feydeau has been praised by the few who appreciate such things for his superlative craftsmanship. In this department, a Labiche or a Feydeau is not excelled even by a Shakespeare, and it is fair enough to distinguish them from Shakespeare as "merely" craftsmen, and to assert that the art of farce is "all technique," provided we also see that such craftsmanship and technique arise from a certain mentality and communicate a particular vision (if not exactly a view) of life. When we praise the famous three- and five-act structures of Labiche and Feydeau, what are we praising? At the least, the efficiency with which the playwrights take a piece of life and box it up; at the most, their invention of new kinds of boxes and the virtuosity which they lavish upon packing paper, string, hammer, and nails. Dramatic critics—whose argot can also be "all technique"—speak of the "well-made play" or the closed type of structure (as against the open), which is a good beginning if we then observe that the result is a closed *mental* system, a world of its own, lit by its own lurid and unnatural sun. There is something frightening about such worlds because there is something maniacal about them. Danger is omnipresent. One touch, we feel, and we shall be sent spinning in space.[11] The farceur's structure of scenes presents points for comparison with systems of delusion.

An example of a feature that has nearly always been considered a merely technical, literary, or theatrical fact is the swift tempo of farce. Men of the theatre encourage actors in farce to "get a move on" for the sake of slick showmanship, that is, to avoid boring the audience. In my passing comments on Chaplin, I have suggested that the speeding up of movements has a psychological and moral—or rather, immoral—effect, namely, that of making actions seem abstract and automatic when in real life they would be concrete and subject to free will. This effect being of the essence, rapidity is not merely a technical asset, it is a psychological necessity. No wonder "slow" productions are dull! No wonder expert critics of the genre, like Sarcey, describe the *verve* of farce as *endiablé!* The devil is in farce rhythm. Although the great farceurs drive with a very firm rein, they are trick artists and like to give the impression of being behind a runaway horse. This being one of the farcical "facts of life," one sees what a *trouvaille* was the plot of *An Italian Straw Hat*. Later, the chase was to be the pride and glory of the Keystone Cops. . . .

It is not my purpose, however, to provide a catalogue of devices and effects, but only, by showing how farce functions, to prove that it deserves a more positive definition and could, with the aid of a little psychology, be given one.

ERIC BENTLEY

[11] Did Sarcey sense this when he compared one farce to a *feu d'artifice* and another to *feu roulant?*

A Trip Abroad

(*Le Voyage de Monsieur Perrichon*)

by

Eugène Labiche and Édouard Martin

English version by R. H. Ward

Copyright © 1958 by R. H. Ward.

CHARACTERS

Perrichon
Major Mathieu
Majorin
Armand Desroches
Daniel Savary
Joseph, *Major Mathieu's servant*
Jean, *Perrichon's servant*
Madame Perrichon
Henriette, *her daughter*
A Hotelkeeper
A Guide
A Railway Official
Porters
Tourists

A Trip Abroad

ACT ONE

SCENE 1

A railway station: the Gare de Lyon at Paris. At the back, a barrier leading to the waiting rooms. Below it on the right, a booking office window; on the left, some benches. Further down stage on the right, a refreshment stall; on the left, a bookstall. MAJORIN *is walking up and down impatiently.*

MAJORIN. Where on earth has Perrichon got to? I've waited a whole hour. And this certainly is the day he leaves for Switzerland with his wife and daughter. [*Bitterly.*] A coach-builder, and going to Switzerland! A coachbuilder with an income of forty thousand francs! A coachbuilder who has a coach! What a century to be living in. And here am I earning two thousand four hundred francs. I'm a hard worker, I'm clever, I never desert my desk. . . . Well, today I have asked for time off, said I was on sentry duty with the National Guard. I positively must see Perrichon before he leaves. I want to ask him to advance my quarter's salary—six hundred francs. And he'll put on his superior air, and feel frightfully important. A coachbuilder! Why, it's pitiable. . . . And still he doesn't come. Anyone would think he was doing it on purpose. (*To a* PORTER *who is going by with some* PASSENGERS.) Monsieur, what time does the through train for Lyons start?
Porter [*brusquely*]. Ask that fellow over there. [*The* PORTER *goes off.*]
Majorin. Thanks *very* much. [*To the* RAILWAY OFFICIAL *indicated, who is standing near the booking office.*] Monsieur, what time does the through train for Lyons start?
Official [*brusquely*]. I couldn't say. Try the timetable. [*Points to one, off left.*]
Majorin. Thanks *so* much. [*Aside.*] Wonderfully polite, these officials. If ever you come into my office, my friend. . . . Well, let's look at the timetable.

MAJORIN *goes off, left.* PERRICHON, MADAME PERRICHON, *and* HENRIETTE *come in, right.*

Perrichon. This way. Keep together, now, or we'll never

2

find each other. Where's the luggage? [*Looking off, right.*]
Ah, there it is. Now who has the umbrellas?

Henriette. I have, Papa.

Perrichon. And the handbag? And the coats?

Madame Perrichon. Here they are.

Perrichon. And my Panama hat? There! it's been left in
the cab. [*About to go.*] No, no, it hasn't, it's in my hand.
Goodness gracious, I'm hot!

Madame Perrichon. It's your own fault. You hurry us up,
you hustle us along. I don't think that's at all a nice way
of traveling.

Perrichon. It's just getting off which is difficult. Once
we're in the train. . . . Now stay where you are; I'm going
to get the tickets. [*Gives his hat to Henriette.*] Look after
my panama for me. [*At the booking-office window.*] Three
firsts to Lyons, please.

Official [*brusquely*]. It's not open yet. In a quarter of an
hour.

Perrichon. Oh, I beg your pardon. I'm not used to traveling, you see; the first time. [*Returning to his wife.*] We're
early.

Madame Perrichon. There now, I told you we'd plenty of
time. And you wouldn't even let us stop for breakfast.

Perrichon. It's much better to be early; one can look at
the station. [*To* HENRIETTE.] Well, child, are you happy?
We've started! In a few minutes, swift as William Tell's
arrow, we shall be careering toward the Alps. [*To his wife.*]
You brought the field glasses?

Madame Perrichon. Of course I did.

Henriette. I'm not reproaching you, Papa, but it's two
years since you first promised to take us on this trip.

Perrichon. My child, I had to sell the firm. A businessman
doesn't retire as easily as a young lady leaves boarding
school, you know. Besides, I was waiting until your education was finished in order to round it off by displaying to
you the magnificent spectacle of Nature.

Madame Perrichon. My, goodness, are you going on like
this all the time?

Perrichon. Eh?

Madame Perrichon. Making speeches even at the station.

Perrichon. I'm not making speeches. I'm elevating the
child's mind. [*Taking a little notebook from his pocket.*]
Wait, my dear, here's a notebook I've bought you.

Henriette. But whatever for?

Perrichon. So that you can write down what you spend on one side and remarks on the other.

Henriette. Remarks? What remarks?

Perrichon. Remarks about the journey. You shall write, and I'll dictate.

Madame Perrichon. What? Are you going to take to writing books now?

Perrichon. There's no question whatever of my writing books. But it seems to me that a gentleman may very well think thoughts, and collect them in a notebook.

Madame Perrichon. Very pretty, I'm sure.

Perrichon [*aside*]. She's always like this when she hasn't had her breakfast.

A PORTER *comes in, pushing a barrow piled with luggage.*

Porter. Here's your luggage, monsieur. Will you check it, please?

Perrichon. Certainly, certainly. But first I must count it; it's always much the best thing to know how many of us there are. One, two, three, four, five, six, my wife seven, my daughter eight, and myself nine. There are nine of us.

Porter [*familiarly*]. Off we go, then.

Perrichon [*running towards the back*]. Hurry, hurry!

Porter. No, not that way, this way. [*Points left.*]

Perrichon. Oh, of course, of course. [*To the ladies.*] Wait for me here. We mustn't lose one another. [PERRICHON *goes out, running after the* PORTER.]

Henriette. Poor Papa! He does take so much trouble.

Madame Perrichon. If you ask me, he's taken leave of his senses.

DANIEL *comes in, followed by a* PORTER *with his trunk.*

Daniel. I don't know where I'm going to yet, so wait a moment. [*Seeing* HENRIETTE.] It's she! So I was right. [*Raises his hat to* HENRIETTE, *who bows discreetly in return.*]

Madame Perrichon. Who is that gentleman?

Henriette. A young man who asked me to dance with him last week, at the ball at the Town Hall.

Madame Perrichon [*pleased and interested*]. Oh, did he, really?

Daniel. Madame! Mademoiselle! What a happy coincidence. Are you taking a train?

Madame Perrichon. Yes, monsieur.

Daniel. Doubtless you're going to Marseilles?

Madame Perrichon. No, monsieur.

Daniel. To Nice, perhaps?

Madame Perrichon. No, monsieur.

Daniel. Forgive me, madame. I thought perhaps—if I could be of some service . . . ?

Porter. Monsieur, you've only just time to get your baggage checked.

Daniel. So I have! Come on. [*Aside.*] I wish I could have found out where they're going before I took my ticket. [*Raising his hat.*] Madame! Mademoiselle! [*Aside.*] But they are going somewhere, that's the main thing.

DANIEL *goes out, left.*

Madame Perrichon. What a very nice young man!

ARMAND *comes in, carrying a handbag.*

Armand [*speaking to someone off stage*]. Take my luggage to the luggage office. I'll join you there. [*Seeing* HENRIETTE.] It's she! [*They greet each other.*]

Madame Perrichon. Who is that gentleman?

Henriette. Another young man who asked me to dance with him last week at the ball at the Town Hall.

Madame Perrichon. Well, fancy! Have they all arranged to meet here, or what? But it doesn't matter, since he asked you to dance. [*Bowing.*] Monsieur!

Armand. Madame! Mademoiselle! What a happy coincidence. Are you taking a train?

Madame Perrichon. Yes, monsieur.

Armand. Doubtless you're going to Marseilles?

Madame Perrichon. No, monsieur.

Armand. To Nice, perhaps?

Madame Perrichon [*aside*]. Just like the other one. [*Aloud.*] No, monsieur.

Armand. Forgive me, madame. I thought perhaps—if I could be of some service . . . ?

Madame Perrichon. But, after all, they do both dance at the same Town Hall.

Armand [*aside*]. I'm no further forward. I'll go and check my baggage. But I shall come back! [*Raising his hat.*] Madame! Mademoiselle! [ARMAND *goes out, left.*]

Madame Perrichon. What a very nice young man! But what can your father be doing? I declare my feet ache like I don't know what.

MAJORIN *comes in, left.*

Majorin. I was wrong, it seems; the train doesn't go for an hour.

Henriette. Why, there's Monsieur Majorin.

Majorin [*aside*]. Ah, there they are.

Madame Perrichon. Why aren't you at your office?

Majorin. I asked for time off, dear lady. I couldn't let you leave without making my adieus to you.

Madame Perrichon. What, you came specially for that? How very nice of you.

Majorin. But I don't see Perrichon anywhere.

Henriette. Papa is busy with the luggage.

PERRICHON *comes in, running.*

Perrichon [*to someone off stage*]. Get the tickets first? Yes, yes, of course.

Majorin. There he is. Good morning, my dear friend.

Perrichon [*still in a great hurry*]. Oh, it's you. Good of you to come. Excuse me, I have to take my tickets. [PER-RICHON *hurries toward the right.*]

Majorin [*aside*]. What manners!

Perrichon [*to the* OFFICIAL *by the booking office*]. Mon-sieur, they won't check my luggage till I've taken my tickets.

Official [*brusquely*]. It's not open yet. Wait.

Perrichon. "Wait"? And over there they say, "Hurry up!" [*Mops his brow.*] I declare I'm all of a sweat.

Madame Perrichon. And I declare my feet hurt like I don't know what.

Perrichon. Well, then, sit down. There are some seats over there. How stupid you are to stand there like a couple of sentries.

Madame Perrichon. But you told us yourself—"Stay there." Oh, there's no pleasing you. You're impossible!

Perrichon. Come, come, Caroline.

Madame Perrichon. You and your trip abroad! I've had quite enough of it already.

Perrichon. It's easy to see you've had no breakfast. Come, now, go and sit down.

Madame Perrichon. Very well; but hurry! [MADAME PER-RICHON *and* HENRIETTE *go and sit up stage.*]

Majorin [*aside*]. Such a charming family.

Perrichon. It's always the way when she hasn't had her

breakfast. Well, my dear Majorin, it was very kind of you
to come.

Majorin. I wanted to speak to you on a little matter.

Perrichon [*not attending*]. And what about the luggage,
left on a slab out there? I'm not at all happy about it.
[*Aloud.*] Well, my dear Majorin, it was very kind of you
to come. [*Aside.*] Suppose I go over and see?

Majorin. I wanted to ask you a little favor.

Perrichon. Me?

Majorin. I've had to move house. So if you'd be good
enough to advance me a quarter's salary? Six hundred francs?

Perrichon. What, here? Now?

Majorin. I think I've always scrupulously repaid any
money you've lent me.

Perrichon. It's not that——

Majorin. Excuse me, but I insist that I have. However,
on the eighth of next month my steamer dividends are due.
I've a dozen shares, and if you don't trust me, I'll leave the
bonds with you as a guarantee.

Perrichon. Oh, don't be so silly.

Majorin. I beg your pardon?

Perrichon. But why the dickens ask me for it just as I'm
leaving? I've brought only the right amount for my expenses
abroad.

Majorin. Oh, of course, if it isn't convenient, we won't
say any more about it. I'll go to a moneylender, who'll take
five per cent per annum off me; but that won't kill me, I
assure you.

Perrichon [*taking out his pocketbook*]. Now, come, there's
no need to get annoyed. See, here's the six hundred francs.
But don't tell my wife.

Majorin [*taking the money*]. I understand, of course. She's
always so *careful* about money.

Perrichon. What's that?

Majorin. I say, she's so *economical.*

Perrichon. Ah, but one should be, my dear friend, one
should be.

Majorin. All right, all right, I owe you six hundred francs;
I know. Good-by! [*Aside.*] What a fuss about a mere six
hundred francs! And he's going to Switzerland—a coachbuilder! [MAJORIN *goes out, right.*]

Perrichon. Goes off, and doesn't even say thank you! But
there, I know he's really very fond of me. [*Sees that the
booking office window is now open.*] Goodness gracious,

they're selling tickets! [*Dashes to the booking office and jostles a number of people already lined up for tickets.*]

A Tourist. Look where you're going, monsieur!

Official. Take your turn, you!—along there.

Perrichon [*to himself*]. And what about the luggage? And my wife? [*He joins the queue.*]

Major Mathieu *comes in, followed by his servant,* Joseph, *who carries his bag.*

Mathieu. Now, you understand me quite clearly?

Joseph. Quite, *mon commandant.*

Mathieu. If she wants to know where I am and when I'm coming back, you're to say that you know nothing whatever about it. I don't wish ever to hear of her again.

Joseph. Quite, *mon commandant.*

Mathieu. You will tell Anita that all is over between us, absolutely over.

Joseph. Quite, *mon commandant.* That is, absolutely.

Perrichon. I've got my tickets. Now for my luggage. What a business this getting off to Lyons is! [Perrichon *goes out, running.*]

Mathieu. So that's clearly understood?

Joseph. Quite. But—excuse me saying so, *mon commandant*—but it's altogether useless your going, you know.

Mathieu. Useless? Why?

Joseph. Because, as soon as you return, *mon commandant,* you'll only fall in love with Mademoiselle Anita all over again.

Mathieu. Oh, I shall, shall I?

Joseph. So that it would really be better not to leave her at all; since you always find these little reconciliations rather expensive, *mon commandant.*

Mathieu. Ah, but this time I mean it. Anita has shown herself unworthy of my affection and of all my past kindness to her.

Joseph. Indeed, she's the ruin of you, *mon commandant.* Another bailiff turned up this morning.

Mathieu. When I come back, I shall settle all my affairs. Good-by.

Joseph. Good-by, *mon commandant.*

Mathieu [*going toward the booking office, but returning*]. By the way, you will write to me *poste restante* at Geneva. You can—let me know how you are.

Joseph [*flattered*]. That's very kind, *mon commandant.*

Mathieu. And then, you can tell me if anyone has—been at all upset by my departure, if—anyone has shed any tears over it.

Joseph. Such as who, *mon commandant?*

Mathieu. Dammit, she—Anita.

Joseph [*warningly*]. There'll be a little reconciliation, you know, *mon commandant.*

Mathieu. Never!

Joseph. And that'll be the eighth time. I don't like to see a fine man like yourself so bothered by creditors.

Mathieu. Come, that'll do. Give me my bag, and write to me at Geneva tomorrow—or this evening. Good day to you.

Joseph. A safe journey to you, *mon commandant.* [*Aside.*] He'll be back within a week. Oh, these women!—to say nothing of these men. [JOSEPH *goes.*]

MATHIEU *takes his ticket at the booking office, and goes through into the waiting room.* MADAME PERRICHON *and* HENRIETTE *get up from the seat.*

Madame Perrichon. You get so tired sitting down.

PERRICHON *comes in, running. He is followed by his* PORTER, *pushing an empty barrow.*

Perrichon. At last it's all done. I've got the tickets. I've been checked.

Madame Perrichon. And about time, too.

Porter. You won't forget the porter, monsieur?

Perrichon. Oh, yes. Wait a moment. [*Consults with his wife and daughter.*] How much ought I to give him? Fifty centimes?

Madame Perrichon. Seventy-five.

Henriette. A franc.

Perrichon. Very well, a franc. [*Giving it to the* PORTER.] Here you are, my man.

Porter. Many thanks, monsieur. [*The* PORTER *goes.*]

Madame Perrichon. Can we go through now?

Perrichon. In a minute. Henriette, take your notebook and write.

Madame Perrichon. Have you begun already?

Perrichon [*dictating*]. Expenditure: cab, two francs; railway fares, a hundred and seventy-two francs and five centimes; porter, one franc.

Henriette. There it is, then.

Perrichon. Wait, wait! A remark.

Madame Perrichon [*aside*]. He's utterly impossible.

Perrichon [*dictating*]. Farewell, France, queen of all the nations— But where's my Panama hat? I've left it in the baggage office! [*Going.*]

Madame Perrichon. No, no, it's here.

Perrichon. So it is. [*Dictating.*] Farewell, France, queen of all the nations——

A bell rings. PASSENGERS *hurry by.*

Madame Perrichon. There's the bell. You'll make us miss the train.

Perrichon. Very well, we must finish it later.

The OFFICIAL *stops them at the barrier to examine their tickets.* PERRICHON *accuses his wife of having them, and of losing them. Finally,* HENRIETTE *finds them in one of his pockets. They go through into the waiting room.* DANIEL, *who has just taken his ticket, collides with* ARMAND, *who is about to take his.*

Armand. Look where you're going.

Daniel. Look where you're going yourself.

Armand. Why, Daniel! [*He now has his ticket, and turns.*]

Daniel. Armand!

Armand. You're going away?

Daniel. This very minute. And you?

Armand. Yes, so am I.

Daniel. That's delightful. We'll travel together. I've some first-class cigars. But where are you going to?

Armand. I've no idea, so far.

Daniel. That's odd. I haven't either. I've taken a ticket as far as Lyons.

Armand. Really? So have I. As a matter of fact, I'm following a perfectly charming girl.

Daniel. Fancy that! So am I.

Armand. A coachbuilder's daughter.

Daniel. Not Perrichon's?

Armand. Yes, Perrichon's.

Daniel. It's the same one.

Armand. But I love her, my dear Daniel.

Daniel. I love her quite as much as you do, my dear Armand.

Armand. I intend to marry her.

Daniel. And I intend to ask her to marry me—which comes to much the same thing.

Armand. But we can't both marry her.

Daniel. No, in France that's not allowed.

Armand. What are we going to do?

Daniel. It's quite simple. Since we're pretty well on the running board of the train already, let's continue our journey together. Let's try to please her, let's do our best to make her love us, you in your way, I in mine.

Armand [*bursting out laughing*]. A competition, eh? A chivalrous combat?

Daniel. A friendly contest, all according to the rules. If you win, I'll give way. If I carry the day, you won't bear me any grudge. Agreed?

Armand. Agreed it is.

Daniel [*holding out his hand*]. A handshake before the battle.

Armand. And another after it. [*They shake hands solemnly.*]

PERRICHON *runs in, shouting over his shoulder.*

Perrichon. I tell you there's plenty of time.

Daniel. Why, look—our father-in-law.

Perrichon [*at the bookstall*]. I want a book for my wife and daughter, a book with nothing in it about love, or money, or politics, or marriage, or death.

Daniel [*aside*]. I suggest *Robinson Crusoe.*

Woman at the Bookstall [*offering a book*]. I've the very thing you want, monsieur.

Perrichon [*reading*]. *The Banks of the River Saône.* Two francs. [*Paying.*] You swear to me that there's nothing frivolous in it? [*A bell rings.*] The dickens! Good day, madame. [PERRICHON *goes out, running.*]

Armand. Let's follow him.

Daniel. Let's. All the same, I shouldn't at all mind knowing where we're going.

A number of PASSENGERS *are seen to be running towards the barrier. Confusion.*

SCENE 2

A small hotel on the Montanvert, near the Grand Glacier. At the back, right, the entrance door; left, a window with a view of snow-covered mountains. On the left, a door, the fireplace with an old-fashioned high mantel, and a table. On

the right, another door, and another table with the visitors'
book upon it. ARMAND *and* DANIEL *are taking their lunch*
at the table, left. A GUIDE *is standing by. The* PROPRIETOR
is waiting on ARMAND *and* DANIEL.

PROPRIETOR. Will you be requiring anything further, messieurs?

Daniel. Coffee—presently.

Armand. Give the guide something to eat. Then we'll leave
for the Grand Glacier.

Proprietor [*to the* GUIDE]. Come along, then. [*The* PRO-
PRIETOR *and the* GUIDE *go out, right.*]

Daniel. Well, my dear Armand?

Armand. Well, my dear Daniel?

Daniel. We've opened the campaign; we've launched the
attack.

Armand. Our first move was to install ourselves in the
same compartment as the Perrichon family. By that time
Papa had already put on his skullcap.

Daniel. We bombarded them with thoughtful attentions,
with kindly services.

Armand. You lent your newspaper to Monsieur Perrichon,
who promptly fell asleep over it. But first he offered you
The Banks of the River Saône in exchange—such a nice picture book.

Daniel. And you, all the way from Dijon, held on to a
blind of which the mechanism had gone wrong. That must
have been distinctly tiring.

Armand. It was, but Mama absolutely stuffed me with
chocolate drops.

Daniel. Greedy fellow, you made a positive meal of them.

Armand. At Lyons we stopped the night at the same hotel.

Daniel. And Papa, meeting us there, cried, "Ah, what a
happy coincidence!"

Armand. At Geneva the same thing happened—entirely by
chance.

Daniel. At Chamonix it happened again, and again the old
gentleman exclaimed, "Ah, what a happy coincidence!"

Armand. Yesterday evening you learned that the family
proposed to visit the Grand Glacier, and came to my room
to tell me—before daybreak; a thing that only a perfect
gentleman would do.

Daniel. I merely follow the rules of fair play. Have some
omelette?

Armand. No, thank you. Speaking of fair play, I ought to tell you, my dear friend, that between Chalon and Lyons Mademoiselle Perrichon looked at me three times.

Daniel. She looked at me four times.

Armand. The deuce! That's bad.

Daniel. It'll be much worse if the time comes when she doesn't look at us at all. At present I think she prefers us both. Things may go on like that for some time. Luckily, we're both gentlemen of leisure.

Armand. That reminds me, how on earth have you contrived to get away from Paris when you're the manager of a steamer company?

Daniel. Seine Tugs, Limited: joint stock two millions. Well, it's quite simple. I asked myself to give myself a little holiday, and had no difficulty in granting my request. My staff is excellent; the steamers go under their own steam; and, provided I'm back in Paris by the eighth of next month, when the dividends fall due . . . But what about you? For a banker, it seems to me that you get about a good deal.

Armand. Oh, the bank doesn't keep me very busy. When I sank my capital in it, I stipulated that I must be a free agent. Really, I'm a banker——

Daniel. Merely for the love of the thing?

Armand. Like you, however, I must be back in Paris about the eighth of next month.

Daniel. So we've time to engage in a war of attrition.

Armand. Like the best of friends. As a matter of fact, I did for a moment think of surrendering in your favor; but I'm sincerely in love with Henriette.

Daniel. That's odd. I too thought of sacrificing myself— no, seriously. At Chalon I really wanted to back out. But when I look at her——

Armand. She's so pretty!

Daniel. So sweet!

Armand. So blonde!

Daniel. There are hardly any blondes left. And such eyes!

Armand. How we both adore those eyes!

Daniel. So I stayed.

Armand. I don't blame you for a moment.

Daniel. Then that's all right. Really, my dear Armand, it's a pleasure to have you for an enemy.

Armand [*as they shake hands*]. My dear Daniel! But where can Perrichon have got to? Do you think he's changed his itinerary? What if we were to lose them?

Daniel. The old boy's most unreliable, certainly. The day before yesterday, off we went to Ferney, where we thought we were sure to find him——

Armand. And all the time he was at Lausanne.

Daniel. It's a very queer way of traveling. [ARMAND *gets up.*] Where are you going?

Armand. I feel restless. I must see if I can find the ladies.

Daniel. But what about your coffee?

Armand. I'll go without. Good-by! [ARMAND *hurries out at the back.*]

Daniel. What an excellent fellow! Such heart, such fire! But all the same he doesn't in the least know how to live. Going off without his coffee! [*Calling.*] Hullo, there!

The PROPRIETOR *appears.*

Proprietor. Monsieur?

Daniel. My coffee. [*The* PROPRIETOR *goes.* DANIEL *lights a cigar.*] Yesterday I tried to persuade our father-in-law to smoke, but it was nothing like a success, I fear——

The PROPRIETOR *brings the coffee.*

Proprietor. Your coffee, monsieur.

Daniel [*taking a seat in front of the fire and behind the table, then resting one leg on* ARMAND'S *chair*]. Just bring up that chair, will you? That's right. [*He has indicated a third chair, on which he now rests his other leg.*] Many thanks. Poor Armand, dashing along the road in the blazing sun, while I stretch out in perfect comfort. And as to which of us will win the race, it's a question of the hare and the tortoise: "Running won't help; you must choose the right moment to start."

Proprietor [*bringing him the visitors' book*]. Will Monsieur kindly write something in the visitors' book?

Daniel. I? I never write after meals; and very seldom before. But let's see what dainty and ingenious thoughts the other visitors have had. [*Turning the pages.*] "Never have I blown my nose at such an altitude. Signed, A Traveler with a Cold." And such beautiful handwriting. "How inspiring it is to contemplate the beauties of Nature surrounded by one's wife and niece. Signed, Malaquais, retired." I've always wondered how it is that the French, so witty at home, can be so dull abroad.

Shouts and uproar off stage.

Daniel. Gracious goodness, what in the world is that?

PERRICHON *comes in, supported by* MADAME PERRICHON *and the* GUIDE, *and followed by* ARMAND *and* HENRIETTE.

Armand. Quickly! Water, smelling salts, vinegar!

Daniel. What has happened?

Henriette. Oh, monsieur, my father was very nearly killed——

Daniel. Good heavens!

Perrichon [*by now sitting down*]. My wife? My daughter? Ah, I'm beginning to feel better.

Henriette [*giving him a glass of sugar and water*]. Drink this, dear Papa. It will do you good.

Perrichon. Thank you, my child. What an upset! [*Drinks.*]

Madame Perrichon. It was all your own fault. The idea!— riding a horse, and you the father of a family. And with spurs on, too.

Perrichon. The spurs had nothing whatever to do with it. The animal shied.

Madame Perrichon. You spurred it without meaning to, so of course it did.

Henriette. And if Monsieur Armand hadn't come up just at that moment, poor Papa would have gone head first over a precipice.

Madame Perrichon. He was over it already. I saw him, rolling just like a ball. We both screamed——

Henriette. And Monsieur dashed to the rescue——

Madame Perrichon. Such courage, such coolness! But for you, my husband—my poor, dear husband—— [*She bursts into tears.*]

Armand. The danger's quite over. Don't distress yourself.

Madame Perrichon [*still crying*]. No, no, there's nothing like a good cry. [*To her husband.*] That'll teach you to wear spurs! [*Weeping more than ever.*] You don't love your family, that's what it is.

Henriette [*to* ARMAND]. Please allow me to add my thanks to Mama's. I shall never forget this day as long as I live. As long as I live!

Armand. Oh, mademoiselle——

Perrichon [*aside*]. And now it's my turn, I suppose. [*Aloud.*] Monsieur Armand—no, let me call you Armand.

Armand. But of course.

Perrichon. Armand, give me your hand. I'm no good at making speeches, but while this heart beats there will always be a place in it for you. [*Shaking his hand.*] More I cannot say.

Madame Perrichon. Thank you, Monsieur Armand!

Henriette. Oh, thank you, Monsieur Armand!

Armand. Please, Mademoiselle Henriette——

Daniel [*aside*]. I begin to think I was wrong to wait for my coffee.

Madame Perrichon [*to the* PROPRIETOR]. Send the horse back. We shall return in a carriage.

Perrichon [*getting up*]. But I assure you, my dear, I'm a very good horseman—— [*Shouting.*] Ow!

Everyone. What's the matter?

Perrichon. Nothing, nothing. Just my back. Yes, you can—er—send the horse away.

Madame Perrichon. Come and lie down for a little. Au revoir, Monsieur Armand.

Henriette. Au revoir, Monsieur Armand!

Perrichon [*shaking* ARMAND's *hand vigorously*]. We shall meet again soon, Armand. [*Shouting.*] Ow! [*Looks reproachfully at* ARMAND. PERRICHON *goes off, left, followed by* MADAME PERRICHON *and* HENRIETTE.]

Armand. Well, what do you think of that, my dear Daniel?

Daniel. It can't be helped. It's just luck. You followed her father, you hung about on precipices— It wasn't in the rules.

Armand. It certainly was a lucky chance.

Daniel. Papa calls you Armand, Mama weeps, and the girl lets fly sententious phrases from the latest novelette. It's the end of me, that's quite clear. There's nothing left for me to do but give in.

Armand. Oh, come, you're joking.

Daniel. I'm joking so little that this very evening I'm leaving for Paris.

Armand. What?

Daniel. Where, later on, you will doubtless rejoin your old friend, who now wishes you the best of luck.

Armand. You're going? Oh, thank you!

Daniel. That certainly sounds very heartfelt.

Armand. Forgive me. I withdraw it—considering the sacrifice you're making on my behalf.

Daniel. I? Please understand I'm making no sacrifice whatever. I'm retiring from the contest because it seems to me that

I now have no chance of success. But if, even now, the slightest hope were to offer, I should certainly stay.

Armand. You would?

Daniel. Is that so surprising? Now that I have no hope of her, I love Henriette more than ever.

Armand. I can fully understand that; so I won't ask you to do me the favor I was about to——

Daniel. What favor?

Armand. No, no, nothing.

Daniel. But please tell me.

Armand. I was only wondering—since you are leaving— whether I could ask you to see Monsieur Perrichon and give him some hint of my feelings, my hopes——

Daniel. Really!

Armand. Well, I can't very well do it myself. It would look as if I were claiming a reward for the service I've just done him.

Daniel. So you're suggesting I should ask for her hand on your behalf. It's somewhat unusual, you know.

Armand. You refuse?

Daniel. On the contrary, I accept.

Armand. My dear friend!

Daniel. Admit that I'm an excellent kind of rival to have— one who does the job for you! [PERRICHON's *voice is heard, off stage.*] There's her father now. Go away and smoke a cigar; then come back later.

Armand. I really don't know how to thank you.

Daniel. Don't worry. I'll do my best to play on his sense of obligation toward you.

ARMAND *goes out, back.* PERRICHON *comes in, speaking over his shoulder.*

Perrichon. But of course he saved my life! Of course he did. And while this heart beats . . . I've told him, haven't I?

Daniel. Well, Monsieur Perrichon, do you feel better now?

Perrichon. Yes, yes, I'm quite recovered. I took a drop of rum and water, and in a quarter of an hour I expect to be kicking up my heels on the Grand Glacier. But what's become of your friend?

Daniel. He went out a moment ago.

Perrichon. And a very nice fellow he is, too. The ladies have taken a fancy to him, you know.

Daniel. Ah, but wait till they know him better. A heart of gold! Good-natured, devoted, and so modest!

Perrichon. H'm, that's somewhat unusual these days.

Daniel. And he's a banker, too. Just think of that—a banker.

Perrichon. Is he really, now?

Daniel. A partner in the firm of Turneps, Desroches, and Company. When you come to think of it, it's rather distinguished to have been got out of a hole by a banker. For, after all, he did save your life, didn't he? But for him, you know——

Perrichon. Of course, of course. Very nice of him.

Daniel [*astonished*]. Very *nice?*

Perrichon [*deliberately misunderstanding*]. Surely you're not trying to make light of his meritoriousness?

Daniel. To make light of it? I?

Perrichon. My gratitude and obligation will cease only in the grave. Yes, yes, while this heart shall beat . . . But, quite between ourselves, the service he's done me isn't as great as my wife and daughter like to make out.

Daniel. Eh?

Perrichon. No, indeed. It's rather gone to their heads. Women, you know!—they're like that.

Daniel. Still, when Armand caught hold of you, you *were* rolling just like a——

Perrichon. I was rolling. True. But with marvelous presence of mind. I had already seen a little fir sapling ahead, and I fully intended to grab hold of it. In fact, I almost had it when your friend arrived.

Daniel [*aside*]. We shall hear in a minute that he did it all himself.

Perrichon. Not that I doubt for a moment that he meant well. I hope to see something more of him, and to repeat my thanks. I'll even go so far as to invite him to the house this winter.

Daniel [*aside*]. Doubtless for a nice cup of tea.

Perrichon. It appears it isn't the first time an accident has happened at that spot. The proprietor of the hotel has been telling me that last year a Russian—a prince, as a matter of fact, and a first-class horseman—and, whatever my wife may say, you know, my spurs had nothing at all to do with it—er —he rolled into the same—er—hole.

Daniel. Just fancy!

Perrichon. His guide helped him out, you see. And this Russian gave him a hundred francs for his trouble.

Daniel. Pretty high pay!

Perrichon. That's what I think. Not that it isn't worth it, of course.

Daniel. But not a sou more, all the same. [*Aside.*] Oh, I certainly shan't go.

Perrichon [*looking out at the back*]. Where the dickens has that guide got to? [*Rings the bell by the fireplace.*]

Daniel. The ladies are ready, then?

Perrichon. No, they won't be coming—rather naturally, perhaps. But I count on you, of course.

Daniel. And on Armand?

Perrichon. If Monsieur Desroches wishes to accompany us, I shan't refuse.

Daniel [*aside*]. Monsieur Desroches! In a minute he'll positively hate him.

The PROPRIETOR *comes in, right.*

Proprietor. Monsieur?

Perrichon. What about this guide?

Proprietor. He is at the door now. And here are your climbing boots, monsieur.

Perrichon. Eh? Oh, yes, it appears people slip into the holes —the crevasses out there; and since I don't wish to be under any obligation to anyone——

Proprietor [*handing him the visitor's book*]. Monsieur will be kind enough to write something in the visitors' book?

Perrichon. Certainly, certainly. But I shouldn't want to write anything commonplace, you understand. What is required is a thought, a beautiful thought. [*Handing back the book.*] I'll think about a thought while I'm putting on my boots. [*To* DANIEL.] I'll be with you in a moment. [PERRICHON *goes, right, with the* PROPRIETOR.]

Daniel. This coachbuilder is a whole treasure trove of ingratitude. Well, treasure trove belongs to him who finds it: see Article 716 of the Civil Code.

ARMAND *comes in at the back.*

Armand. Well?

Daniel [*aside*]. Poor fellow!

Armand. Have you seen him?

Daniel. I have.

Armand. And did you speak to him?

Daniel. I did.

Armand. Then you asked him . . . ?

Daniel. No, I didn't.

Armand. Oh? Why?

Daniel. My dear Armand, we undertook to be frank with each other. Well, I'm not leaving after all. I'm going on with the contest.

Armand [*surprised*]. Oh? Well, that's another matter. And may one ask the reason for your change of plans?

Daniel. I've one very cogent reason: I think I shall win.

Armand. You will?

Daniel. Yes. I propose to take a different road from yours; and get there more quickly.

Armand. Well, you're perfectly within your rights, of course.

Daniel. But the contest will be none the less fair and friendly?

Armand. Naturally.

Daniel. You don't sound very sure.

Armand. Forgive me. [*Holds out his hand.*] I promise you it will.

Daniel. Good.

PERRICHON returns.

Perrichon. I'm ready. I've got my climbing boots on. Oh, Monsieur Armand——

Armand. I hope you're quite recovered from your fall?

Perrichon. Quite recovered. We'll say no more about that little affair. It's forgotten.

Daniel [*aside.*] Forgotten! He's surpassing himself.

Perrichon. We're just leaving for the Grand Glacier. Are you coming?

Armand. I'm a little tired. You'll forgive me if I stay?

Perrichon. With pleasure! Don't think of putting yourself out. [*The* PROPRIETOR *comes in.*] Ah, give me the visitor's book, if you please.

Daniel [*aside*]. He's thought his beautiful thought.

Perrichon [*finishing writing*]. There! [*Reads impressively.*] "How small is Man when observed from the heighth of the Grand Glacier!"

Daniel. By Jove, that's good. [*Gets up and goes to the table to look at the book.*]

Armand [*aside*]. Flatterer!

Perrichon [*modestly*]. It's not perhaps the sort of thought that anybody might have.

Daniel [*aside*]. Nor the spelling either. I thought he said "heighth"—H-E-I-G-H-T-H.

Perrichon [*to the* PROPRIETOR, *pointing to the visitors' book*]. Take great care! The ink's still wet.

Proprietor. The guide is waiting with the alpenstocks, monsieur.

Perrichon. Come, then!

Daniel. Come! [PERRICHON *and* DANIEL *go, followed by the* PROPRIETOR.]

Armand. How strange that Daniel should change his mind like that. But the ladies are still here, and it can't be long before they come down; then *I* shall see *them, and* speak to them. [*Sits by the fireplace and takes up a newspaper.*] I'll wait for them here.

Proprietor [*off stage*]. This way, monsieur.

MAJOR MATHIEU *comes in, followed by the* PROPRIETOR.

Mathieu. I'm only stopping for a moment. I shall be leaving at once for the Grand Glacier. [*Sits at the table on which the visitors' book lies open.*] Be good enough to bring me some punch.

Proprietor. At once, monsieur. [*He goes.*]

Mathieu. The visitors' book, eh? Let's see. [*Reads.*] "How small is Man when observed from the—er—heighth of the Grand Glacier!" H'm. Signed, "Perrichon." Somebody ought to take spelling lessons.

Proprietor [*returning with the punch*]. Here you are, monsieur.

Mathieu [*writing in the visitors' book*]. There wasn't, I suppose, among the people who arrived here this morning, a gentleman of the name of Armand Desroches?

Armand. What's that? I am Armand Desroches, monsieur.

Mathieu [*rising*]. You, monsieur? Excuse me. [*To the* PROPRIETOR.] Please leave us. [*The* PROPRIETOR *goes out.*] Have I in fact the honor of addressing Monsieur Armand Desroches, of the firm of Turneps, Desroches, and Company?

Armand. You have, monsieur.

Mathieu. I am Major Mathieu. [*Sits, left, and sips his drink.*]

Armand. Delighted, monsieur. But I don't believe I've the pleasure of your acquaintance.

Mathieu. No? Then allow me to tell you that you're dunning me to blazes for a bill of exchange.

Armand. A bill of exchange?

Mathieu. Which I was imprudent enough to put into circulation. What's more, you've even taken out a warrant for my arrest.

Armand. That's possible, monsieur, but it's not I, but the bank, which acts in these matters.

Mathieu. I bear you not the slightest ill will, monsieur, nor your firm either. I wished merely to make it plain that I didn't leave Paris in order to evade arrest.

Armand. I shouldn't have dreamed for a moment that you had.

Mathieu. On the contrary, as soon as I get back to Paris, in a fortnight or less, I shall inform you of the fact; and I shall then be greatly obliged if you'll have me committed to the Clichy debtors' prison as soon as possible.

Armand. But—surely you must be joking.

Mathieu. Not in the very least, monsieur. I ask it as a favor.

Armand. I'm afraid I don't understand.

Mathieu [*getting up*]. Damned if I don't find it a shade embarrassing to explain. Forgive me—you're a bachelor?

Armand. I am.

Mathieu. Ah, well, then, I confess to you the more easily. I suffer from a certain weakness, monsieur. I'm in love.

Armand. You?

Mathieu. Ridiculous at my age, what?

Armand. I didn't mean——

Mathieu. Pray don't mind me. I'm insanely preoccupied with a young person named Anita; but she's the ruin of me; and she snaps her fingers at me. I spend my life buying her presents. I made up my mind to leave her; I did leave her; I traveled eight hundred kilometers; I've reached the Grand Glacier—and I can't be at all sure that I shan't return this evening to Paris. It's stronger than I am, monsieur. You understand, when one's fifty love is like the rheumatics: nothing cures it.

Armand [*laughing*]. I assure you these confidences weren't necessary in order that I should call off the pursuit. I'll write to Paris at once.

Mathieu [*eagerly*]. But not at all! Don't think of writing. I insist on being imprisoned; it may be a way of curing me after all. It's one I haven't tried.

Armand. All the same, I——

Mathieu. Excuse me, but the law is on my side.

Armand. Very well, monsieur, if you really wish it.

Mathieu. I do indeed. I insist. As soon as I am back in Paris I shall send you my card, and I beg you to take proceedings at once. I never go out before ten in the morning. [*Bowing.*] Monsieur, I'm happy to have made your acquaintance.

Armand [*bowing*]. The honor is mine, monsieur. [MATHIEU *goes out at the back.*] Well, imagine that! A distinctly original kind of man. [MADAME PERRICHON *comes in, left.*] Ah, Madame Perrichon!

Madame Perrichon. What, you're all alone, monsieur? I thought you'd be going with the other gentlemen.

Armand. I've already visited these parts once, last year; so I asked Monsieur Perrichon's permission to remain and put myself at your service.

Madame Perrichon. Oh, monsieur! [*Aside.*] He's certainly a real gentleman. [*Aloud.*] Do you like Switzerland?

Armand. Oh, well, one has to go somewhere, you know.

Madame Perrichon. I shouldn't like to live in this country at all. There are far too many precipices and mountains. My family comes from very low-lying country.

Armand. I see.

Madame Perrichon. Beauce, not far from Étampes.

Armand [*aside*]. Surely we must have a branch at Étampes? It would be a contact. Ah, yes! [*Aloud.*] I suppose you don't happen to know Monsieur Pingley at Étampes?

Madame Perrichon. Pingley? Why, he's my cousin! Do you know him, then?

Armand. Intimately. [*Aside.*] Never set eyes on him in my life.

Madame Perrichon. Such a charming man.

Armand. Isn't he?

Madame Perrichon. But I always think it's so very sad about his affliction.

Armand. Indeed it is. So very sad.

Madame Perrichon. Stone deaf at forty-seven.

Armand [*aside*]. Oh, so he's deaf, our branch manager? That explains why he never answers our letters.

Madame Perrichon. Well, now, isn't that strange?—that a friend of Pingley's should have saved my husband's life. It's a very small world, I always say.

Armand. Though, as *I* always say, we sometimes attribute

to its smallness coincidences that have nothing to do with it.

Madame Perrichon. Yes, indeed, we do sometimes attribute to its small—— [*Aside.*] What *is* he talking about?

Armand. For instance, Madame, our meeting in the train, then at Lyons, Geneva, Chamonix, and here. Would you say all that was due to the smallness——

Madame Perrichon. It's true that, when one's traveling, one does find——

Armand. Whatever one looks for carefully enough.

Madame Perrichon. What do you say?

Armand. Madame, I cannot go on blaming the smallness of the world any longer. I owe you the truth, you and your daughter.

Madame Perrichon. My daughter?

Armand. I wonder if you'll be able to forgive me? The first moment I saw her I was deeply touched, I was altogether overwhelmed. I learned that you were leaving for Switzerland—and I left for Switzerland too.

Madame Perrichon. Then—you were following us?

Armand. Step by step. I couldn't help it. I love her.

Madame Perrichon. Monsieur!

Armand. Oh, please don't alarm yourself. I love her with all possible respect, with all the discretion one owes to a young lady whom one wishes to make one's wife.

Madame Perrichon [*losing her head: aside*]. Heavens, he's asking for her hand! And Perrichon isn't here. [*Aloud.*] Of course, monsieur, I'm delighted—that is, you flatter us, monsieur. I mean, your manners, your education, Pingley, the service you've done us—— But Monsieur Perrichon is out—that is, he's on the Grand Glacier, you know. As soon as he comes back, though, I—we——

HENRIETTE comes in.

Henriette. Mama? Oh, you're talking to Monsieur Armand——

Madame Perrichon [*by now altogether upset*]. Yes, yes, we were talking—that's to say—yes! we were talking about Pingley. Just think. Monsieur knows Pingley. Don't you, monsieur?

Armand. Oh, indeed I know Pingley.

Henriette. Well, isn't that nice!

Madame Perrichon [*to* HENRIETTE]. Just look at your hair, child! And your dress; and your collar's crumpled . . . [*Whispers.*] For goodness' sake stand up straight!

Henriette. But whatever's the matter, Mama?

Shouts and tumult outside.

Madame Perrichon. Goodness gracious!
Henriette. Gracious goodness!
Armand. What on earth is that noise?

DANIEL *comes in, supported by the* PROPRIETOR *and the*
GUIDE. PERRICHON *follows.*

Perrichon [*greatly excited*]. Quickly! Water, smelling salts,
vinegar! [*Makes* DANIEL *sit down.*]

Everyone. But what's the matter? What happened?

Perrichon. A perfectly dreadful affair! Give him something
to drink, fan his temples, loosen his collar!

Daniel. Thank you, thank you. I feel better now.

Armand. But what happened?

Daniel. If it hadn't been for Monsieur Perrichon's
bravery——

Perrichon [*excitedly*]. No, no, *you* mustn't tell them! It
was terrible—terrible. There we were on the Grand Glacier.
Mont Blanc, serene and majestic, gazed down upon us——

Daniel [*aside*]. Here comes the big speech.

Madame Perrichon. Hurry up, do!

Henriette. Yes, Papa, do!

Perrichon. Give me time, child. For the last five minutes
we'd been following, deep in thought, a steep track which
wound its way between crevasses—cracks or holes in the ice,
you know. I was leading——

Madame Perrichon. That was extremely foolish.

Perrichon. When suddenly I heard behind me the noise of
a landslide. I turned. Monsieur was just disappearing into one
of the two bottomless abysses—abysses the very sight of
which would send shivers down——

Madame Perrichon [*impatiently*]. For heaven's sake!

Perrichon. Instantly, with no thought but that dictated by
my natural bravery, I—father of a family and all—I dashed
to the rescue.

Madame Perrichon. Goodness gracious!

Henriette. Gracious goodness!

Perrichon. On the very lip of the chasm, I held out to him
my alpenstock. He clung to it. I pulled. He pulled. We both
pulled. And, after a terrific struggle, I snatched him from
the aching void—er—the hungry void—and restored him to
the light of day. [*Mops his brow.*]

Henriette. Oh, Papa!

Madame Perrichon. Oh, my beloved Perrichon!

Perrichon [*embracing them both*]. Yes, my dears, it was a very beautiful moment in my life.

Armand [*to* DANIEL]. How do you feel?

Daniel [*under his breath*]. As right as rain—don't you worry! [*Rises.*] Monsieur Perrichon, you have today restored a son to his mother——

Perrichon [*majestically*]. I have indeed.

Daniel. A brother to his sister——

Perrichon. And a man to his fellow men.

Daniel. Words are powerless to express gratitude for such a service.

Perrichon. They are indeed.

Daniel. Only the heart, you understand—the heart——

Perrichon. Monsieur Daniel! No, no, let me call you Daniel.

Daniel. But of course. [*Aside.*] Everything comes to him who waits.

Perrichon [*with emotion*]. Daniel, my child, give me your hand. [*Holding* DANIEL's *hand.*] I owe to you the noblest feelings of my life. But for me, you would be nothing but a shapeless and repellent mass buried beneath the snows. You owe me everything, everything! [*Nobly.*] I shall never forget it!

Daniel. I shan't either.

Perrichon [*wiping his eyes: to* ARMAND]. Ah, young man, you cannot know what a joy it is to save the life of a fellow creature.

Henriette. But, Papa, Monsieur knows very well; only a little while ago, he——

Perrichon. Eh? Oh, yes, yes, of course. [*To the* PROPRIE-TOR.] Bring me the visitors' book.

Madame Perrichon. Now what do you want that for?

Perrichon. Before I leave this place I wish to commemorate this event in a—remark.

Proprietor [*bringing the book*]. Here it is, monsieur.

Perrichon. Many thanks. But—who has written *this?*

Everyone. What? Written what?

Perrichon [*reading*]. "I wish to draw Monsieur Perrichon's attention to the fact that the word 'height' does not contain three 'h's.' To say that it does is to commit an orthographical error. I suggest that the gentleman would be expressing himself more *characteristically* were he to *drop an 'h.'* Signed The Major."

Everyone. ? ? ! !

Henriette. It hasn't three "h's," you know, Papa.

Perrichon. Of course I know. Very well. I shall make answer to this gentleman in kind. [*Writes.*] "The Major is a—a vulgar blockhead. Signed Perrichon."

The GUIDE *comes in.*

Guide. The carriage is waiting.

Perrichon. Come, we must hurry. [*To* DANIEL *and* ARMAND.] There will be room for you gentlemen, if you care to join us. [DANIEL *and* ARMAND *bow their acceptance.*]

Madame Perrichon [*calling her husband*]. Perrichon, help me on with my cloak. [*Whispers.*] I've just been asked for Henriette's hand in marriage.

Perrichon. Have you, now? So have I.

Madame Perrichon. It's Monsieur Armand.

Perrichon. Oh, no, it's Daniel—my dear friend Daniel.

Madame Perrichon. But it seems to me the other one is——

Perrichon. We'll talk about that later.

Henriette [*at the window*]. Oh, it's pouring with rain.

Perrichon. Confound it, so it is. [*To the* PROPRIETOR.] How many seats are there in your carriage?

Proprietor. Four inside and one on the box.

Perrichon. Ah, then that's just right.

Armand. Please don't put yourself out on my account.

Perrichon. Daniel will ride inside with us.

Henriette. But what about Monsieur Armand?

Perrichon. Eh? There are only four places; he'll go on the box.

Henriette. In rain like this?

Madame Perrichon. The man who saved your life?

Perrichon. I'll lend him my waterproof. Come along, now. We must be off.

Daniel [*aside*]. I thought I should get back into the lead.

ACT TWO

SCENE I

The salon of the PERRICHONS' *apartment in Paris. At the back, a fireplace; up left, the entrance door; up right, the door to another room. On the left, the dining room. Center, a pedestal table. To the right of the table, a settee.* JEAN *is dusting the furniture.*

JEAN. A quarter to twelve. Today Monsieur Perrichon comes back from abroad with Madame and Mademoiselle. I had a letter from him yesterday. [*Reads.*] "Grenoble, July the fifth. We shall arrive on Wednesday, July the seventh, at noon. You will clean down the apartment and rehang the curtains." Well, I've done that. "You will tell Marguerite to be ready with dinner. She is to serve a stew, and the meat it is made with is not to be too fat. To follow, since it is a long time since we have tasted deep-sea fish, she is to buy a nice fresh brill. But if brill is too dear, then she is to substitute for it stewed veal." Monsieur should be here at any time now. Everything's ready—the newspapers, the letters, the cards that have been left while they were away. Oh, that reminds me, early this morning a gentleman called whom I don't know; said he was a major; said he'd call again. [*A bell rings.*] There's Monsieur Perrichon now. I know his ring. [JEAN *goes to the entrance door and opens to* PERRICHON, MADAME PERRICHON *and* HENRIETTE.]

Perrichon. It's us, Jean.

Jean. Monsieur! Madame! Mademoiselle! [*Takes various handbags, parcels, etc., from them.*]

Perrichon. Ah, how nice it is to be back in one's own home, to see one's own furniture—and sit on it. [*Sits on the settee.*]

Madame Perrichon [*sitting, left*]. We ought to have been home a week ago.

Perrichon. But we couldn't pass through Grenoble without calling on the Darinels, and they persuaded us to stay. [*To* JEAN.] Has anything come for me while I've been away?

Jean. I've put everything on the table, monsieur.

Perrichon [*looking through the cards*]. What a lot of visitors! [*Reads.*] "Armand Desroches."

Henriette. Ah!

Perrichon. "Daniel Savary"—such a nice young man. "Armand Desroches." "Daniel Savary." A delightful young man. "Armand Desroches."

Jean. Those two gentlemen have called every day to see when you were coming back.

Madame Perrichon. You ought to go and call on them.

Perrichon. Certainly I shall go and call on him—on that nice Daniel.

Henriette. And Monsieur Armand?

Perrichon. I'll call on him too—later on. [*Rises.*]

Henriette [*to* JEAN]. Help me carry these parcels to my room.

Jean. Yes, mademoiselle. [*Looking at* PERRICHON.] Monsieur has got fatter. Anyone can see you've had a good trip, monsieur.

Perrichon. Yes, splendid, splendid. Oh, of course—you don't know. I saved a man's life.

Jean [*incredulous*]. You did, monsieur? You don't say! [JEAN *goes out with* HENRIETTE, *right.*]

Perrichon. "You don't say," indeed! The fellow's a fool.

Madame Perrichon. Now that we're back, I hope you're going to make up your mind. We can't keep those two young men waiting any longer for an answer. A couple of suitors in the house at once is too much of a good thing.

Perrichon. I'm still of the same opinion: I prefer Daniel.

Madame Perrichon. But why?

Perrichon. I don't know, I'm sure. He's more—well, I like him.

Madame Perrichon. But the other one saved your life.

Perrichon. He saved my life!—always the same old story.

Madame Perrichon. But what have you against him? He comes of a good family, he has an excellent position.

Perrichon. Dash it, I've nothing against him. Nothing at all.

Madame Perrichon. Well, really, that's the last straw.

Perrichon. But it seems to me he's just a little bit—affected.

Madame Perrichon. Affected? He is?

Perrichon. Yes, affected. That is, he affects a slightly protective and patronizing air with me. Yes indeed. He always seems to be rather pleased with himself because of the little service he did me.

Madame Perrichon. But he never even mentions it.

Perrichon. Oh, I know he doesn't *mention* it. I tell you it's the tone he adopts with me. "But for me—" You see? It becomes very irritating after a time. Whereas the other one——

Madame Perrichon. The other one is always saying, "But for you—" And that flatters your vanity; therefore you like him better.

Perrichon. Vanity? I? Though, after all, I have perhaps the right to a certain——

Madame Perrichon [*impatiently*]. Oh!

Perrichon. Yes, yes, my dear, I have. The man who has risked his life to save a fellow creature . . . But, there! I prefer to keep a modest silence; which is always a sign of true courage.

Madame Perrichon. All that doesn't alter the fact that Monsieur Armand is——

Perrichon. Henriette doesn't love Monsieur Armand. She couldn't possibly love him.

Madame Perrichon. What do you know about it?

Perrichon. Confound it, I just know she doesn't.

Madame Perrichon. Well, there's one way of finding out: ask her. And we will choose whichever she chooses.

Perrichon. Very well. But don't you influence her, now.

Madame Perrichon. Here she comes. [HENRIETTE *comes in*]. Henriette, my child, your father and I want to speak to you very seriously.

Henriette. To me, Mama?

Perrichon. Yes.

Madame Perrichon. You're old enough now to get married, my dear, and two young men are in fact asking for you. Both of them seem to us quite suitable, but we don't want to go against your wishes, so we've decided to leave you absolutely free to choose.

Henriette. But——

Perrichon. Absolutely free.

Madame Perrichon. One of these young men is Monsieur Armand Desroches.

Henriette. Ah!

Perrichon [*quickly*]. Now don't influence her!

Madame Perrichon. The other is Monsieur Daniel Savary.

Perrichon [*promptly*]. A charming young fellow—distinguished, intelligent—who, I won't deny it, has all my sympathy.

Madame Perrichon. But it's you who're influencing——

Perrichon. Not at all. I'm merely stating a fact. [*To* HENRIETTE.] So now that you're fully informed as to the situation, make your own choice.

Henriette. Well, but it's really rather embarrassing—and I'm quite ready to accept whichever you wish——

Perrichon. No, no, make your own choice—absolutely freely.

Madame Perrichon. Well, child?

Henriette. Then, if you insist on my choosing, I choose Monsieur Armand.

Madame Perrichon. There!

Perrichon. Armand? But why not Daniel?

Henriette. But, Papa, Monsieur Armand saved your life.

Perrichon. What, again? Upon my word, I'm sick of this.

Madame Perrichon. So, you see, there's no reason to hesitate further.

Perrichon. Pardon me, my dear, a father may not set aside his proper responsibilities. I shall think it over. I shall make certain necessary inquiries.

Madame Perrichon [*aside to* PERRICHON]. Monsieur Perrichon, you have broken faith with me.

Perrichon. Really, Caroline!

JEAN *comes in.*

Jean [*speaking to someone off stage*]. Come in. They're just back.

MAJORIN *comes in.*

Perrichon. Well, well, it's Majorin.

Majorin [*bowing*]. Madame! Mademoiselle! I heard you were due back today, so I got time off—said I was on duty with the National Guard.

Perrichon. My dear friend, how very good of you. You'll have dinner with us? There's brill.

Majorin. Well, then, if I may——

Jean [*aside to* PERRICHON]. It's stewed veal. [JEAN *goes.*]

Perrichon. Oh. [*To* MAJORIN.] Well, well, we'll say no more about it, eh? Another day.

Majorin [*aside*]. What, now he's withdrawing his invitation, is he? As if I cared about his dinner. [*Takes* PERRICHON *aside, while the ladies sit on the settee.*] I came to have a word with you about the six hundred francs you lent me the day you went abroad.

Perrichon. You've brought them back?

Majorin. No. I don't get my steamer dividend until tomorrow; but precisely at noon tomorrow——

Perrichon. Oh, there's no hurry, of course.

Majorin. Excuse me, but there is. I'm anxious to pay off the debt.

Perrichon. Oh, of course, you don't know—I brought you a souvenir.

Majorin [*sitting by the table*]. A souvenir? For me?

Perrichon [*also sitting*]. On my way through Geneva, I

bought three watches, one for Jean, one for our cook, Marguerite, and one for you—a repeater.

Majorin [*aside*]. So he puts me after the servants. [*Aloud.*] Well?

Perrichon. Before we went through the French customs, I hid them in my cravat.

Majorin. But why?

Perrichon. Because I didn't want to pay the duty, of course. Well, they asked me, "Have you anything to declare?" and I said, "No." I went to move on, and dash me if your blessed watch didn't start to strike—ting, ting, ting!

Majorin. Dear, dear!

Perrichon. So I was caught. They confiscated the lot.

Majorin. What!

Perrichon. Oh, there was a fearful scene. I called the customs officer a beastly money-grubber. He informed me that I should hear from him further. I regret the incident deeply; it was a delightful little watch.

Majorin [*dryly*]. Naturally, I thank you none the less. [*Aside.*] As if he couldn't have paid the duty. It's positively sordid.

JEAN *announces* ARMAND, *who comes in.*

Jean. Monsieur Armand Desroches.

Henriette [*getting up from her needlework*]. Ah!

Madame Perrichon [*going to* ARMAND]. Welcome, monsieur! We were expecting to see you.

Armand [*bowing*]. Madame! Monsieur Perrichon!

Perrichon. Delighted, delighted. [*Aside.*] Still that protective tone.

Madame Perrichon [*to her husband*]. Introduce him to Majorin.

Perrichon. Naturally. [*Aloud.*] Majorin, I wish to present Monsieur Armand Desroches, a traveling acquaintance.

Henriette [*eagerly*]. He saved Papa's life.

Perrichon [*aside*]. What, again?

Majorin. Dear me, did you actually run into some *danger* or other?

Perrichon. Oh, no, no, it was nothing at all.

Armand. It simply isn't worth talking about.

Perrichon [*aside*]. There he goes!

JEAN *announces* DANIEL, *who comes in.*

Jean. Monsieur Daniel Savary.

Perrichon [*very forthcoming*]. Ah, there he is, our dear friend Daniel! [*He nearly knocks over the table in his haste to welcome* DANIEL.]

Daniel [*bowing*]. Mesdames! Good day, Armand!

Perrichon [*taking his hand*]. Come and let me present you to Majorin. Majorin, allow me to present one of my best, one of my very best friends, Monsieur Daniel Savary.

Majorin. Savary? Of the steamer company?

Daniel [*bowing*]. At your service.

Perrichon. Aha! If it weren't for me, he wouldn't be able to pay you your dividend tomorrow.

Majorin. Oh, why?

Perrichon. Why? Quite simply because I saved his life, my dear fellow.

Majorin. You did? [*Aside.*] Apparently they spent their time saving one another's lives.

Perrichon. We were on the Grand Glacier. Mont Blanc gazed down upon us, serene and majestic.

Daniel [*aside*]. The big speech all over again.

Perrichon. We were following, deep in thought, a steep path——

Henriette [*who has opened one of the newspapers*]. Oh, look! Papa's in the newspaper.

Perrichon. What? I'm in the newspaper?

Henriette. Read it. There. [*Gives him the paper.*]

Perrichon [*reading*]. "It is reported from Chamonix——"

Everyone [*drawing closer*] ? ? ?

Perrichon. "An incident which might have had deplorable consequences has recently occurred on the Grand Glacier. Monsieur Daniel S—— took a false step and disappeared into one of the crevasses so much dreaded by tourists. An eyewitness of this misfortune, Monsieur Perrichon, if he will permit us to give his name"—as if I shouldn't—"Monsieur Perrichon, the well-known Paris businessman and father of a family, obedient only to his courageous impulses and without thought of the danger to his own life, dashed into the yawning gulf." True enough. "After almost unheard-of efforts, he was fortunate enough to extricate his companion. The happiness of this outcome was only surpassed by the modesty of Monsieur Perrichon, who evaded the excited and heartfelt congratulations of the crowd. Right-thinking people in all countries will, we feel sure, agree with us in considering it our duty to draw public attention to so remarkable a feat."

Everyone. Goodness gracious! Gracious goodness!

Daniel [*aside*]. At a cost of three francs a line.

Perrichon [*slowly rereading*]. "Right-thinking people in all countries will, we feel sure, agree with us in considering it our duty to draw public attention to so remarkable a feat." [*To* DANIEL, *much moved.*] My dear friend, my dear boy, embrace me.

Daniel [*over* PERRICHON's *shoulder as they embrace*]. Most certainly I've regained the lead.

Perrichon [*indicating the newspaper*]. Nobody could call me a radical, but I say without hesitation that the popular press has much to be said for it. [*Puts the paper in his pocket: aside.*] I must get ten copies.

Madame Perrichon. How would it be, my dear, if we sent the newspaper an account of Monsieur Armand's noble action?

Henriette. Yes, yes, the two would just match nicely.

Perrichon. Oh, that's quite unnecessary. I can hardly allow my personality to *monopolize* the newspapers.

JEAN *comes in with a document in his hand.*

Jean. Monsieur?

Perrichon. What is it?

Jean. The concierge has just given me this summons for you.

Madame Perrichon. A summons?

Perrichon. Have no fear! I don't owe anybody anything. On the contrary, there are those who owe me . . .

Majorin [*aside*]. That's meant for me, I suppose.

Perrichon [*looking at the summons*]. An order to appear before the magistrates on a charge of insulting a public servant in the execution of his duties.

Everyone. Gracious goodness! Goodness gracious!

Perrichon [*reading*]. "In consideration of the official report tendered to the customs authorities of France by Sergeant Machut"——

Armand. But what can this mean?

Perrichon. A customs official who confiscated three watches from me. I became rather heated. I called him a money-grubber and—er—scum of the earth, I think it was.

Majorin. Oh, but that's very serious. *Very* serious indeed.

Perrichon [*uneasily*]. In what way "serious"?

Majorin. Why, it's a grave offense. *Very* grave. Not only did you insult a public servant in the execution of his duties;

you were attempting to swindle the State at the same time:
you were smuggling.

Perrichon and *Madame Perrichon.* Well?

Majorin. Imprisonment.

Everyone. Imprisonment? Imprisonment!

Majorin. Anything from fifteen days to three months.

Perrichon. Me? After fifty years of irreproachable behavior,
to languish, disgraced, in a prison cell? Never! Never!

Majorin [*aside*]. That will teach him to try and evade
the payment of customs dues.

Perrichon. Oh, my friends, I'm ruined, ruined for ever.

Madame Perrichon. Come, come, pull yourself together.

Henriette. Papa!

Daniel. Courage!

Armand. Wait a moment. I think I may be able to get you
out of this.

Perrichon. You can? Oh, my friend, my dear friend!

Armand. I have an intimate friend who is a high-grade
official in the administration of the customs. I'll go and see
him. It may be possible to persuade the customs officer to
withdraw the complaint.

Majorin. Oh, that would be difficult, I think. *Very* difficult.

Armand. But why? A moment of ill temper——

Perrichon. For which I'm heartily sorry.

Armand. Give me the summons. I've a very good hope of
success. Meanwhile, please don't distress yourself, my dear
Monsieur Perrichon.

Perrichon [*much moved, taking his hand*]. Ah, Daniel—I
mean, Armand—you must allow me to embrace you. [*Does
so.*]

Henriette [*aside*]. Hurrah!

Armand [*to* DANIEL]. I rather think I may be coming up
into the lead.

Daniel. It seems you may, damn it. [*Aside.*] I thought he
was simply a rival; he's nothing more nor less than a Saint
Bernard dog.

Majorin. I'll come with you. [*Joins* ARMAND.]

Perrichon. You're leaving us?

Majorin. Yes. [*Grandly.*] I'm dining in town. [ARMAND *and*
MAJORIN *go out.*]

Madame Perrichon. Well, what do you think of Monsieur
Armand now?

Perrichon. He's an angel, a perfect angel.

Madame Perrichon. Yet you hesitate to let him marry your daughter.

Perrichon. No. No, I don't hesitate any longer.

Madame Perrichon. At last! You're yourself again, I see. Well, now it only remains for you to tell Monsieur Daniel.

Perrichon. Oh, poor fellow—must I?

Madame Perrichon. Unless you mean to leave it till he gets his invitation to the wedding.

Perrichon. Oh, no, no.

Madame Perrichon. Then I'll leave you with him. [*Bows to* DANIEL.] Monsieur! [MADAME PERRICHON *goes out, followed by* HENRIETTE.]

Daniel [*aside*]. It's evident that my stock is going down. But perhaps I can still—— [*Goes and sits on settee.*]

Perrichon [*aside*]. Poor young man! But, there, it hurts me more than it hurts him. [*Aloud.*] My dear Daniel, my very dear Daniel, I've something rather painful to say to you.

Daniel [*aside*]. Now for it. [*They sit side by side.*]

Perrichon. You've done me the honor of asking to marry my daughter. I looked most favorably on this project, but circumstances—that is, events—seem to indicate—— Your friend, Monsieur Armand, has done me so many services.

Daniel. I understand, of course.

Perrichon. Because it's no use denying that the fellow did save my life.

Daniel. But what about the little fir sapling you were just —grabbing hold of?

Perrichon. Yes, of course, there was the little fir sapling. But—well, it was a very little one. It might have broken. And I *hadn't* quite got hold of it.

Daniel. I see, I see.

Perrichon. And that isn't all. At this very moment that excellent young man is in process of rescuing me from a dungeon. So I shall owe him the honor of—the honor of——

Daniel. Monsieur Perrichon, the sentiments which motivate your action are too noble for me to seek to undermine them.

Perrichon. Truly? Then you don't hold it against me?

Daniel. I can think only of your personal courage, of your personal devotion to me.

Perrichon [*shaking his hand*]. Ah, Daniel. [*Aside.*] It's quite extraordinary how much I like this young man.

Daniel. But before we part——

Perrichon [*rising*]. Part? You're leaving me? But why?

Daniel. I can't continue to pay visits which would be embarrassing to your daughter and painful to me.

Perrichon. Oh, come—the only man whose life I ever saved?

Daniel. Ah, but your image will always be in my thoughts. Indeed, I've had an idea: to perpetuate on canvas, as it is already perpetuated in my heart, the heroic scene on the Grand Glacier.

Perrichon. A painting? [*Aside.*] He wants to put me in a painting.

Daniel. I've already approached one of our most famous artists, one whose work will go down to posterity.

Perrichon. Posterity! Oh, my dear Daniel! [*Aside.*] It's quite extraordinary how much I like this young man.

Daniel. I shall insist upon an absolute likeness.

Perrichon. Oh, so shall I.

Daniel. But I fear it will be necessary for you to give the artist five or six sittings.

Perrichon. Oh, my dear friend, fifteen, twenty, thirty. I shan't be in the least bored. We will pose together.

Daniel. I too? Oh, no.

Perrichon. But why not?

Daniel. Because—well, this is what we have decided upon. Nothing will be seen on the canvas but Mont Blanc——

Perrichon. Oh? And what about me?

Daniel. Mont Blanc—and you.

Perrichon. Yes, that's right—me and Mont Blanc—serene and majestic. But where will you be?

Daniel. In the hole; at the very bottom. Nothing will be seen of me but my two hands clasped in supplication.

Perrichon. What a wonderful picture it will make!

Daniel. We'll put it in a public gallery.

Perrichon. At Versailles?

Daniel. No, no, the Louvre, naturally. But first it will be shown in the annual exhibition. And the following notice will appear in the catalogue——

Perrichon. Ah, no! No publicity. No advertisement. We'll simply reprint the article from the newspaper: "It is reported from Chamonix," *et cetera.*

Daniel. Wouldn't that be a little—uninformative?

Perrichon. Yes; but we can always amplify it. [*Effusively.*] Ah, Daniel, my friend, my own boy!

Daniel. Farewell, Monsieur Perrichon. We shall never meet again.

Perrichon. No, no, this marriage is utterly impossible. And nothing's really decided yet, you know. . . .

Daniel. But surely?

Perrichon. Stay. I insist.

Daniel [*aside*]. Fancy that now!

JEAN *announces* MAJOR MATHIEU, *who enters a moment later.*

Jean. Monsieur *le commandant* Mathieu.

Perrichon. Who on earth?

Mathieu. Pardon me, gentlemen, I hope I'm not inconveniencing you?

Perrichon. Not at all, not at all.

Mathieu [*to* DANIEL]. Have I the honor of addressing Monsieur Perrichon?

Perrichon. I am Monsieur Perrichon.

Mathieu. Ah! Monsieur, I have been looking for you for a fortnight. There are a great many Perrichons in Paris, and I have already called on a dozen or so. But I am of a very determined character.

Perrichon [*pointing to a chair by the table*]. You have something to say to me? [*Sits on the settee.*]

Mathieu [*sitting*]. Of that I can't yet be sure. Allow me, first of all, to ask you a question. Did you, a month ago, visit the Grand Glacier?

Perrichon. I did indeed, monsieur; and I'm proud to say so.

Mathieu. Then doubtless it was you who wrote in the visitors' book, "The Major is a vulgar blockhead"?

Perrichon. What? Then you're——

Mathieu. Yes, monsieur, I am.

Perrichon. I'm delighted to meet you. [*They exchange numerous little bows.*]

Daniel [*aside*]. I have the impression it's clouding over.

Mathieu. Monsieur, I am not a quarrelsome man, and I am not a habitual duelist, but I dislike the idea of such remarks remaining against my name in the visitors' books of hotels.

Perrichon. But you in the first instance wrote a remark which was distinctly—outspoken.

Mathieu. I? I merely stated that there are not three "h's" in the word "height"; that this was an orthographical error; and that one "h" should be dropped. Allow me to refer you to the dictionary.

Perrichon. But, monsieur, you have no call to correct what you consider to be my spelling mistakes. You should mind your own business, monsieur! [*They rise.*]

Mathieu. Excuse me. I regard the French tongue as a well-loved countrywoman of mine, a lady of good family, elegant, though a trifle—difficult; as you must realize as well as anyone.

Perrichon. I don't think I—er—know this lady you speak of.

Mathieu. That, I fear, is too true, monsieur. And, further, when I meet this lady in foreign parts, I do not permit people to dishonor her, monsieur. It is a matter of chivalry.

Perrichon. Then do you presume to teach me a lesson, monsieur?

Mathieu. Far be it from me to presume any such thing, monsieur.

Perrichon. Then all is well, monsieur. [*Aside.*] He's climbing down.

Mathieu. But, without wishing to teach you a lesson, monsieur, I do quite civilly ask you for an explanation.

Perrichon [*aside*]. It's my belief he isn't a major at all.

Mathieu. There appear to be two points at issue: either you persist in——

Perrichon. I dislike these arguments, monsieur. Perhaps you think to intimidate me? I have given proofs of my courage, please understand, and I am prepared to make them known to you.

Mathieu. In what way?

Perrichon. At the next annual art exhibition.

Mathieu. Forgive me, but I shall hardly be able to wait so long. I will come briefly to the point. Do you withdraw your insulting remarks—yes or no?

Perrichon. I withdraw nothing whatsoever.

Mathieu. Take care, monsieur.

Daniel. Monsieur Perrichon!

Perrichon. Nothing whatsoever. [*Aside.*] He hasn't even got a mustache.

Mathieu. Very well, then, Monsieur Perrichon, I shall do myself the honor of waiting upon you at midday tomorrow, with my seconds, in the woods at Malmaison.

Daniel. Monsieur, a word——

Mathieu. We shall expect you at the ranger's lodge.

Daniel. But, monsieur——

Mathieu. A thousand pardons, monsieur, but I have an important appointment at a furniture shop, where I have to choose certain furnishing materials. At noon tomorrow. [*Bowing.*] Messieurs, allow me to take my leave. [MATHIEU *goes out.*]

Daniel. Goodness me, you're a very stern man, Monsieur Perrichon. And with a major, too!

Perrichon. He? A major? Nonsense! Do you suppose real majors pass their time correcting other people's spelling mistakes?

Daniel. Even so, we'd better get some information—[*rings bell*]—and find out whom we're dealing with.

JEAN *enters.*

Perrichon. Why did you let in that man who's just let himself out?

Jean. He'd already been this morning, monsieur. I forgot to give you his card.

Daniel. His card, eh?

Perrichon. Give it me. [*Reads.*] "Mathieu, major in the Second Zouaves, retired."

Daniel. A Zouave!

Perrichon. Goodness gracious!

Jean. Gracious goodness!

Perrichon. That will do. You may go. [JEAN *goes.*]

Daniel. Well, now we're in a nice hole!—that is, I mean——

Perrichon. I couldn't help it if I was too outspoken. Such a polite man!—I took him for a lawyer with a commission in the National Guard.

Daniel. But what are we going to do?

Perrichon. We must think. Ah!

Daniel. Yes?

Perrichon. Oh, nothing. There's nothing to be done. I've insulted him, and I must fight him. Good-by!

Daniel. Where are you going?

Perrichon. To put my affairs in order, of course. You understand?

Daniel. But——

Perrichon. Daniel, when the hour of danger strikes, you will not see me blench. [PERRICHON *goes out.*]

Daniel. But, good heavens, it's impossible! I can't conceivably allow Monsieur Perrichon to fight a duel with a Zouave! All the same, he's a brave fellow, my father-in-law. I know him, he won't yield an inch. And, on his side, the major, too. . . . And all for a spelling mistake. [*Thinking hard.*] Now, if I were to warn the authorities? But no—

Yet, after all, why not? No one will know. And in any case,
I've no choice. [*Takes paper and ink from a table near the
door, and sits at the pedestal table.*] A note to the Prefect
of Police. [*Writes.*] "Monsieur le Préfet, I have the honor
to"—— [*Talking as he writes.*] "A police patrol can pass at
the psychological moment—all quite by chance—and everyone's good name will be safe." [*Folds and seals the letter,
and puts back the paper and ink.*] Now the thing is to get it
delivered at once. Jean should be somewhere about. Jean!
[DANIEL *goes out, calling.*]

PERRICHON *comes in with a letter in his hand.*

Perrichon [*reading*]. "Monsieur le Préfet, I consider it my
duty to inform you that two idiotic persons intend to fight
a duel tomorrow at a quarter before noon." I've put a quarter
before so that they'll be punctual. Sometimes a quarter of
an hour is—too long to wait. "At a quarter before noon in
the Malmaison woods. The meeting place is the gate by the
ranger's lodge. It is part of your high calling to guard citizens'
lives. One of the duelists is a well-established businessman,
father of a family, ever an upholder of law and order, who
rejoices in a high reputation among those who know him. I
have the honor to be, my dear Monsieur le Préfet," etc.,
etc. If that major thinks he can scare me! Now the address.
[*Writes.*] "Very urgent. Important official communication."
That ought to get there all right. Now where is Jean?

DANIEL *comes in, his letter in his hand.*

Daniel. I can't find that wretched Jean anywhere. [*Sees
PERRICHON.*] Oh! [*Hides letter behind his back.*]
Perrichon. Daniel! [*Hides his letter likewise.*]
Daniel. Well, Monsieur Perrichon?
Perrichon. I am, as you see, as calm as a statue. [MADAME
PERRICHON *and* HENRIETTE *come in.*] My wife! Sh!
Madame Perrichon. My dear, Henriette's music master has
sent us tickets for a concert tomorrow, at midday.
Perrichon [*aside*]. Midday!
Henriette. It's his benefit. You must come too.
Perrichon. Impossible. Tomorrow I'm busy all day.
Madame Perrichon. Nonsense, you've nothing at all to do
tomorrow.
Perrichon. Oh, yes, I have. Business. Very important. Ask
Daniel.
Daniel. Very, very important.

Madame Perrichon. How serious you both look. [*To her husband.*] You're as white as a sheet. Anyone would think you were afraid of something.

Perrichon. Afraid? Me? You wait till you see me, weapon in hand——

Daniel [*aside*]. That's done it!

Madame Perrichon. Weapon in hand?

Perrichon. Bother! It slipped out.

Henriette [*running to him*]. A duel! Oh, Papa!

Perrichon. Well, yes, my child, I didn't mean to tell you— it slipped out—but your Papa is going to fight a duel.

Madame Perrichon. But who with?

Perrichon. A major in the Second Zouaves.

Madame Perrichon and *Henriette* [*terrified*]. Oh! Heavens above!

Perrichon. Tomorrow at noon, at the ranger's lodge in the Malmaison woods.

Madame Perrichon. But you must be mad. You're a civilian.

Perrichon. Madame Perrichon, I disapprove of dueling, but there are circumstances in which a person owes it to his honor to fight. [*Aside.*] Where on earth is Jean?

Madame Perrichon [*aside*]. No, no, it's impossible. I shan't allow it. [*Goes to the table at the back and writes.*] "Monsieur le Préfet . . ."

JEAN *comes in.*

Jean. Dinner is served.

Perrichon [*going to* JEAN, *in a low voice*]. Take this letter to the address you see on it. And be quick about it. [*Moves away hastily.*]

Daniel [*to* JEAN, *in a low voice*]. Take this letter to the address you see on it. And be quick about it. [*Moves away hastily.*]

Madame Perrichon [*to* JEAN, *in a low voice*]. Take this letter to the address you see on it. And be quick about it.

Perrichon. Come! Dinner!

Henriette [*aside*]. I must warn Monsieur Armand. [HENRIETTE *goes out, right.*]

Madame Perrichon [*to* JEAN, *as she goes out.*] Sh!

Daniel [*ditto*]. Sh!

Perrichon [*ditto*]. Sh!

PERRICHON, MADAME PERRICHON *and* DANIEL *have now gone out.*

Jean. What the dickens is all the mystery about? [*Reads the addresses in turn.*] "Monsieur le Préfet." "Monsieur le Préfet." "Monsieur le Préfet." Hurray! Three birds with one—errand.

SCENE 2

A garden. A bench, chairs, and a garden table. On the right, a summerhouse.

DANIEL *comes in, left.*

DANIEL. Ten o'clock, and the meeting isn't till noon. [*Goes to the summerhouse and gives a signal.*] Pst! Pst!

PERRICHON *puts his head round the door of the summerhouse.*

Perrichon. Ah, it's you. Don't make a sound. I'll be with you in a moment. [*Disappears.*]

Daniel. Poor Monsieur Perrichon! He must have had a pretty bad night. But, thank goodness, the duel won't take place.

PERRICHON *comes in, wearing a heavy cloak.*

Perrichon. Here I am. I was waiting for you.

Daniel. How do you feel?

Perrichon. Cool as a cucumber.

Daniel. I have some swords in the carriage.

Perrichon [*half-opening his cloak*]. And I've some here.

Daniel. Two sets, then!

Perrichon. One might get broken. I don't want to find myself at a disadvantage.

Daniel [*aside*]. Brave as a lion. [*Aloud.*] The cab's at the door, so if you'd like to——

Perrichon. Wait a minute. What's the time?

Daniel. Ten o'clock.

Perrichon. I don't want to get there before midday—or after either. [*Aside.*] That would ruin everything.

Daniel. Quite right; one should be just on time. [*Aside.*] Otherwise everything would be ruined.

Perrichon. You see, to arrive early would look like bravado; and to arrive late would look like—reluctance. Besides, I'm expecting Majorin. I sent him an urgent message yesterday evening.

Daniel. And here he is.

MAJORIN *comes in.*

MAJORIN. I had your note. I asked for time off. Well, what's it all about?

Perrichon. Majorin, I'm fighting a duel in two hours' time.

Majorin. You are? Bless my soul! What with?

Perrichon [*opening his cloak*]. These.

Majorin. Swords!

Perrichon. And I'm counting on you to be my second.

Majorin. On me? Excuse me, but that's quite impossible.

Perrichon. But why's that?

Majorin. I've got to get back to the office. I shall lose my job if I don't.

Perrichon. But you've asked for time off.

Majorin. But not for being a second in a duel. Seconds get run in, you know.

Perrichon. Yet it seems to me, Monsieur Majorin, that I've done you a number of favors in the past. Do you now refuse to assist me in a matter of life and death?

Majorin [*aside*]. Now he's reproaching me with his miserable six hundred francs.

Perrichon. However, if you don't wish to compromise yourself, if you're afraid——

Majorin. I'm not in the least afraid. [*Bitterly.*] Besides, you leave me no choice: you've bound me in the bonds of obligation and gratitude. [*Between his teeth.*] Damn gratitude!

Daniel [*aside*]. This gratitude crops up all over the place, it seems to me.

Majorin. I ask only one thing: to be back by two o'clock, to collect my dividend. I shall reimburse you at once, and then we shall be quits.

Daniel. It's time we went. [*To* PERRICHON.] If you want to say good-by to Madame Perrichon and your daughter——

Perrichon. No, no. I wish to avoid a scene. There would be tears and I don't know what-all. They'd hang on to my very coat tails to prevent me going. So come! [*Singing is heard off stage.*] My daughter!

HENRIETTE *comes in, singing, a watering can in her hand.*

Henriette. Tra-la-la! Tra-la-la! Oh, it's you, Papa dear.

Perrichon. Yes, it's me. We were just leaving, these gentlemen and I—you see? I—er—I must. [*Embraces her with great feeling.*] Good-by!

Henriette [*calmly*]. Good-by, Papa. [*Aside.*] There's nothing whatever to worry about. Mama has warned the Prefect of Police, and I've warned Monsieur Armand. [*Starts to water the flowers.*]

Perrichon [*wiping his eyes, and thinking she is still beside him*]. Don't cry, my child. But if you never see me again, always remember your dear old—— Well, dash me, she's watering the flowers!

Majorin [*aside*]. It's disgusting; but he does it quite well.

MADAME PERRICHON *comes in, some flowers in her hand.*

Madame Perrichon. May I cut some dahlias, my dear?

Perrichon. My wife!

Madame Perrichon. I'm gathering a bunch for my vases.

Perrichon. Gather them all! At such a moment, how can I refuse you anything? Caroline, I'm just going.

Madame Perrichon [*calmly*]. Oh, yes?

Perrichon. Yes, I'm going—er—I'm going away with these two gentlemen.

Madame Perrichon. Well, try not to be late for dinner.

Perrichon and *Majorin.* What's that?

Perrichon [*aside*]. So calm? Can it be that my wife doesn't care for me?

Majorin [*aside*]. All the Perrichons are entirely heartless.

Daniel. It's time—if you want to be there by midday.

Perrichon [*firmly*]. Midday precisely.

Madame Perrichon [*equally firmly*]. You haven't a moment to lose.

Henriette. Yes, do hurry up, Papa.

Perrichon. Er—of course.

Majorin [*aside*]. They're actually packing him off. Delightful family!

Perrichon. Come, Caroline! My child! Good-by, good-by!

ARMAND *comes in at the back.*

Armand. Wait, Monsieur Perrichon! The duel will not take place.

Everyone. Goodness gracious! Gracious goodness!

Henriette [*aside*]. I knew I could rely on Monsieur Armand.

Madame Perrichon [*to* ARMAND]. But please explain.

Armand. Perfectly simple: I've just put Major Mathieu in prison.

Everyone. In prison?

Daniel [*aside*]. My rival certainly doesn't let the grass grow under his feet.

Armand. Yes, it's been arranged for a month or more between the major and myself; and there didn't seem a better opportunity of carrying out his request—[*to* PERRICHON]— and ridding you of him at the same time.

Henriette. You've saved us!

Madame Perrichon. Oh, monsieur, how shall we ever thank you?

Perrichon [*aside*]. Bother! That's not what I wanted at all, just when I'd arranged everything so nicely. At a quarter before midday we'd have taken him by surprise.

Madame Perrichon. Well, aren't you going to say thank you?

Perrichon. Who to?

Madame Perrichon. Why, Monsieur Armand, of course.

Perrichon. Ah, yes. [*To* ARMAND.] Thanks very much.

Majorin [*aside*]. Anyone would think it choked him. [*Aloud.*] Well, I'm going to draw my dividend. Do you think the office will be open yet?

Daniel. I'm sure it will. I've a cab here, I'll drive you. Monsieur Perrichon, we shall meet again soon. You've your reply to give me.

Madame Perrichon [*to* ARMAND]. Don't go yet. Perrichon has promised to give his decision today. This is a good moment; ask him now.

Armand. Do you really think so? I rather doubt——

Henriette. Courage, Monsieur Armand!

Armand. Well, if *you* say so——

Majorin. Good-by, Perrichon.

Daniel [*bowing*]. Madame! Mademoiselle! [MADAME PERRICHON *and* HENRIETTE *go out, right.* MAJORIN *and* DANIEL *go out at the back, left.*]

Perrichon [*aside*]. It's most annoying. *Most* annoying. I spent half the night writing to all my friends to say I was fighting a duel. Now I shall look a fool.

Armand [*aside*]. He *ought* to be in a good mood. Well, here goes. [*Aloud.*] My dear Monsieur Perrichon——

Perrichon. Well, what?

Armand. I can't tell you how happy I am to have been able to bring this unfortunate affair to a happy conclusion.

Perrichon [*aside*]. There he is with his protective air. [*Aloud.*] For my part, monsieur, I regret that you've deprived me of the pleasure of teaching that spelling master a lesson.

Armand. What? Surely you realize that your adversary is——

Perrichon. A retired major of the Second Zouaves. Well, what of it? I respect the army, as a whole, but I am perfectly prepared to face it. [*Proudly takes a defensive stance.*]

JEAN *comes in.*

Jean. Monsieur *le commandant* Mathieu.
Perrichon. What!
Armand. It can't be.
Perrichon. You told me he was in prison.

MATHIEU *comes in.*

Mathieu. So I was, but I've come out again. Ah, Monsieur Armand, I've just paid the total value of the bill I owe you, together with the costs.
Armand. Many thanks, monsieur. I hope you bear me no malice? You seemed so eager to go to prison, though, that——
Mathieu. I like prison very much—but not on a day when I have a duel to fight. [*To* PERRICHON.] I apologize, monsieur, for keeping you waiting. I am at your service.
Jean [*aside*]. Heaven preserve all civilians!
Perrichon. I believe, monsieur, that you will do me the justice of believing that the circumstance which has—intervened is none of my making.
Armand. Indeed, yes, Monsieur Perrichon was at this very moment telling me how much he regretted not being able to meet you.
Mathieu [*to* PERRICHON]. I've never doubted, monsieur, that you were a loyal adversary.
Perrichon [*haughtily*]. I certainly hope not, monsieur.
Jean [*aside*]. He stands his ground well—for a civilian.
Mathieu. My seconds are outside. Let us go.
Perrichon. Let us go!
Mathieu [*looking at his watch*]. It's now midday.
Perrichon [*aside*]. Midday already?
Mathieu. But we shall be there by two o'clock.
Perrichon [*aside*]. By two? They'll have gone.
Armand. What's the matter?
Perrichon. I—er—gentlemen, it has always seemed to me that there is a certain nobility in the honest admission of one's errors——
Mathieu and *Jean.* What!
Armand. What's this?
Perrichon. Jean, you may go.
Armand. Perhaps I should go, too?

Perrichon. No, no, I wish this to be said before witnesses.

Armand. But——

Mathieu. Please be so good as to stay, Monsieur Armand.

Perrichon [*to* MATHIEU]. Monsieur, I consider you a military man of noteworthy courage, and—well, I like military men. I realize that I have done you a wrong, and I ask you to believe that—— [*Aside.*] Dash it all, in front of my own servant! [*Aloud.*] I ask you to believe that it was neither my intention— [*Makes a sign to* JEAN *to go, but* JEAN *appears not to understand.*] Very well, I'll give him the sack this evening. [*To* MATHIEU.] —nor my wish to give offense to a man whom I hold in high esteem.

Jean [*aside*]. Blow me, he's backing out.

Mathieu. Come, come, monsieur, these are excuses.

Armand [*quickly*]. Regrets, monsieur, regrets.

Perrichon. Now don't add fuel to the flames. Let the major speak.

Mathieu. Are they regrets or excuses?

Perrichon. Well— [*Blandly.*] —shall we say six of one and half a dozen of the other?

Mathieu. Monsieur, you wrote, in full, in the visitors' book at the Montanvert, "The major is a——"

Perrichon [*quickly*]. I withdraw the words. They *are* withdrawn.

Mathieu. They're withdrawn *here*, yes; but *there* they remain as large as life, in the middle of the page, for every tourist to see.

Perrichon. True. I should have to go back there and erase them, shouldn't I?

Mathieu. I hardly dared to ask so much of you, but since you yourself make the offer—

Perrichon. I?

Mathieu. —I accept.

Perrichon. Excuse me, but——

Mathieu. Oh, I wouldn't ask you to set out today. No, no. Tomorrow.

Perrichon and *Armand.* But how on earth——

Mathieu. By the first train. You will erase, in person, freely and fully, the two unfortunate lines you wrote so hastily. I shall be greatly obliged.

Perrichon. You mean—I'm going back to Switzerland?

Mathieu. Formerly the Montanvert, which is in Savoy, was in Switzerland; now Savoy has been ceded to France, it is in France.

Perrichon. France, queen of all the nations!

Jean. Well, if it's in France now, it's not so far away as it was; that's something.

Mathieu [*with irony*]. It only remains for me to commend your conciliatory sentiments.

Perrichon [*with dignity*]. I dislike bloodshed.

Mathieu [*laughing*]. I am entirely satisfied, monsieur. [*To* ARMAND.] Monsieur Desroches, there are certain other bills of mine in circulation. If any of them happens to come into your hands, I'm always at your—disposal. [*Bows.*] Gentlemen, allow me to take my leave.

Perrichon [*bowing*]. Monsieur! [MATHIEU *goes out.*]

Jean [*sadly to* PERRICHON]. Well, there, monsieur, it's all over, your little upset.

Perrichon [*furious*]. You! Take a week's wages! Go and pack your traps, monster!

Jean [*astonished*]. What have I done? [JEAN *goes out, right.*]

Perrichon [*aside*]. There's no getting away from it, I've backed out—I, whose portrait will be seen by everybody in one of the public galleries. But whose fault was it? This Armand person's, of course!

Armand [*aside*]. Poor man, I hardly know what to say to him.

Perrichon [*aside*]. Dash it, why doesn't he go away? I suppose he's still got some favor or other he wants to do me. Damn his favors!

Armand. Monsieur Perrichon?

Perrichon. Well, what is it?

Armand. When I left you yesterday, I went at once to see my friend who works in the customs administration. I spoke to him about your little difficulty.

Perrichon [*curtly*]. You're too kind.

Armand. It's all settled. They won't proceed with the summons.

Perrichon. Oh?

Armand. But you'll have to send a few words of apology to the customs officer in question, naturally.

Perrichon [*exploding*]. Excuses, eh? More excuses! And what business is it of yours, I'd like to know?

Armand. But surely——

Perrichon. It's becoming a habit with you, this sticking your nose into my affairs at every turn.

Armand. But——

Perrichon. Yes, at every turn, monsieur. Who asked you to have the major arrested? But for you, we should all have been there at midday.

Armand. But there was nothing to stop you being there at two.

Perrichon. That's not the same thing at all.

Armand. But why not?

Perrichon. Why not? Because—— But, no, I shan't tell you why not. [*In a rage.*] I've had enough of your favors, monsieur, quite enough! In future, if I—get into a hole, kindly leave me there. I prefer to give the guide a hundred francs—because that is the appropriate payment, you know, so there's no need to give yourself airs. I'll thank you, what's more, not to alter the times of my duels; and to allow me to go to prison if I choose to.

Armand. But, my dear Monsieur Perrichon——

Perrichon. I don't like people who intrude, do you understand? It's indiscreet, to say the least. And you're a—a positive invasion!

Armand. But please allow me to——

Perrichon. No, no! Nobody shall rule my life for me, nobody! No more of your favors! Not another one! [PERRICHON *goes into the summerhouse.*]

Armand. I simply don't understand a thing. You could knock me down with a feather.

HENRIETTE *comes in, right.*

Henriette. Ah, Monsieur Armand!

Armand. Mademoiselle Henriette!

Henriette. Have you had your little talk with Papa?

Armand. Yes, I have.

Henriette. Well?

Armand. He's given me the fullest possible proof that he can't stand the sight of me.

Henriette. What are you saying? That's impossible.

Armand. He even went so far as to reproach me with saving his life on the Grand Glacier. I fully expected him to offer me a hundred francs tip.

Henriette. A hundred francs?

Armand. He assures me that's the proper sum.

Henriette. But that's dreadful. It's sheer ingratitude.

Armand. It's clear that my presence is offensive to him. Nothing remains, mademoiselle, but to bid you good-by.

Henriette. Oh, no, no! You must stay.

Armand. But what's the good? It's Daniel he wants you to marry.

Henriette. Monsieur Daniel? But I don't want to marry *him*.

Armand [*joyfully*]. You don't?

Henriette [*regaining her self-possession*]. That is, my mother doesn't want me to. She doesn't share Papa's feelings; she's grateful to you; she likes you. Just now she said to me: "Monsieur Armand is a good man, and a man of heart; I'd give him the thing I hold dearest in the world."

Armand. But the thing she holds dearest—that's you!

Henriette [*naively*]. I suppose it is.

Armand. Oh, mademoiselle, thank you, thank you!

Henriette. But it's Mama you should thank.

Armand. And you, mademoiselle? May I hope that you share her kind feelings for me?

Henriette [*embarrassed*]. I, monsieur?

Armand. Oh, tell me, please tell me!

Henriette [*dropping her gaze*]. Monsieur, a well-brought-up young lady always thinks the same as her Mama. [HENRIETTE *runs out*.]

Armand. She loves me—she said so! Oh, what happiness!

DANIEL *comes in.*

Daniel. Good day, Armand!

Armand. Oh, it's you. [*Aside.*] Poor fellow!

Daniel. Armand, the test of our manhood is upon us. Monsieur Perrichon is thinking things over and in ten minutes we shall know his answer. My poor friend!

Armand. What do you mean?

Daniel. In the campaign that we've been conducting, you've piled tactical error upon tactical error, I fear.

Armand. *I* have?

Daniel. Armand, I'm very fond of you, you know, and I want to give you some advice which will stand you in good stead—another time. You have one cardinal weakness, Armand.

Armand. And what may that be, Daniel?

Daniel. You're too fond of doing people favors and services. It's a most unhappy passion.

Armand [*laughing*]. Oh, come now!

Daniel. Oh, believe me! I've lived longer than you, and am perhaps rather more a man of the world. Before you do a man a service, make quite sure he isn't a fool.

Armand. But why?

Daniel. Because a fool can't bear for very long the crushing burden of being under an obligation. Indeed, there are even some intelligent persons so finely constituted that——

Armand [*laughing.*] Very well, let's have your paradox.

Daniel. I'll give you an example: Monsieur Perrichon.

PERRICHON *puts his head out of the summerhouse.*

Perrichon. He must mean me!

Daniel. You'll allow that he's hardly the most intelligent of men? [PERRICHON *withdraws.*] Well, Monsieur Perrichon has quite simply got his knife into you.

Armand. I'm afraid that's true.

Daniel. Yet you saved his life. Perhaps you think this suggests to his mind great personal devotion on your part? No. It suggests to him three things: First, that he can't ride a horse. Second, that he was mistaken to wear spurs against his wife's advice. Third, that he fell off in public and made an ass of himself.

Armand. Well, yes, but——

Daniel. Then, to make matters worse, you showed him as plain as two and two make four that you thought nothing whatever of his courage; you put a stop to a duel—which wasn't going to take place anyway.

Armand. Wasn't—— How's that?

Daniel. I had taken certain precautions. I do people little services myself sometimes.

Armand. There you are, you see!

Daniel. Ah, yes, but I do them by stealth. When I involve myself with the misfortunes of my fellows, I do it with soft shoes on and without a light—like a man going into a powder magazine. Thus I conclude——

Armand. That one must never oblige anyone?

Daniel. Oh, not at all. But one must act under cover of darkness, and choose one's victim with care. I conclude, then, that the aforesaid Perrichon hates the sight of you. Your presence humiliates him. He's under an obligation to you, and therefore your inferior. You quite overwhelm the poor creature.

Armand. But it's such base ingratitude.

Daniel. Ingratitude is a kind of pride. Some philosopher or other once called it the independence of the soul. Now, Monsieur Perrichon is the most independent coachbuilder in all France. I realized that at once. So I took a course directly opposed to yours.

Armand. And that was?

Daniel. I allowed myself to tumble—on purpose, of course —into a convenient little crevasse. Oh, it wasn't at all a dangerous one.

Armand. On purpose, eh?

Daniel. You understand? Give a coachbuilder the chance of saving the life of his fellow creature, without the slightest danger to himself—it's a master stroke. Since that day I've been the joy of his life, the triumph of his humanity, his greatest victory. The moment he sees me he's wreathed in smiles, he positively swells with pride, peacock's feathers sprout all over his waistcoat. I've got him as tight as vanity grips mankind. When he cools off, I breathe upon him, and he comes back to life—that is, I get his name in the newspapers for him; which only costs three francs a line.

Armand. Oh, so that was your doing?

Daniel. It was. Tomorrow I shall have him painted in oils —hobnobbing with Mont Blanc. And naturally I've commissioned a very small Mont Blanc and an immense Perrichon. So, my friend, remember this—and for goodness' sake keep the secret: *human beings don't become attached to us by reason of the services we do them, but by reason of those they do us.*

Armand. That's true for men, perhaps. But what about women?

Daniel. Ah, women, now!

Armand. Women understand gratitude; they know what it is to preserve in their deepest hearts the memory of benefits received.

Daniel. That's certainly a very impressively turned phrase, Armand.

Armand. And luckily Madame Perrichon doesn't share her husband's sentiments.

Daniel. Well, perhaps Mama is on your side. But on mine I have Papa's vanity: I'm safely tucked up in my crevasse on the top of the Montanvert.

PERRICHON *comes out of the summerhouse.* MADAME PER-RICHON *and* HENRIETTE *enter at the same time.*

Perrichon [*very gravely*]. Gentlemen, I am happy to find you together. You have both honored me by wishing to marry my daughter. Now you shall hear what I have decided.

Armand [*aside*]. Here we go!

Perrichon [*smiling upon* DANIEL]. Monsieur Daniel—my dear friend——

Armand [*aside*]. I'm done for.

Daniel. Oh, Monsieur Perrichon!

Perrichon [*coldly*]. A piece of advice—which may stand you in good stead another time: Don't talk so loud when you're standing near a door.

Daniel. Eh? What's that?

Perrichon. Yes. And many thanks for the lesson you've given me. [*To* ARMAND.] Monsieur Armand, you haven't lived as long as your friend; you calculate less; you please me more. I give you my daughter.

Armand. Oh, thank you.

Perrichon. Notice that I make no attempt to reinstate myself in your opinion. I desire to remain under my obligation to you—[*looking at* DANIEL]—because it's only fools who don't know how to bear the crushing burden of gratitude. [PERRICHON *goes stage-right, and* MADAME PERRICHON *directs* HENRIETTE *to* ARMAND'S *side. He gives her his arm.*]

Daniel [*aside*]. So there's for you, my boy.

Armand [*aside*]. Poor old Daniel!

Daniel [*to* ARMAND]. Well, I'm beaten. But now, as ever, let's shake hands?

Armand. With all my heart.

Daniel [*going to* PERRICHON, *shaking his head*]. Oh! Monsieur Perrichon, fancy eavesdropping like that!

Perrichon. But, good heavens, a father has a right to get all the information he can. [*Taking him aside.*] Tell me, did you really fall in on purpose?

Daniel. Fall in?

Perrichon. Into that—hole?

Daniel. Well, yes. But I won't tell anyone.

Perrichon. Don't—please. [*They shake hands.*]

MAJORIN *comes in.*

Majorin. Monsieur Perrichon, I drew my dividend at three o'clock, and I kept this gentleman's cab in order to bring you the six hundred francs the sooner. Here they are.

Perrichon. But there was no hurry, you know.

Majorin. Excuse me, there was, considerable hurry. Now we're quits, absolutely quits, I'm relieved to say.

Perrichon [*aside*]. To think I used to be like that about obligations.

Majorin [*handing* DANIEL *a card*]. Here is the number of your cab, and that's what's owing.

Perrichon. Monsieur Armand, we shall be at home to-morrow evening. Will you give us the pleasure of your company for a nice cup of tea?

Armand [*to* PERRICHON]. Tomorrow? You're forgetting your promise to the major.

Perrichon. Oh, dear me, yes. [*Aloud.*] My dears, tomorrow morning we're going back to the Grand Glacier.

Henriette. Goodness gracious!

Madame Perrichon. Gracious goodness, we've only just got back. Why?

Perrichon. Why? How can you ask? Couldn't you guess that I should want to revisit the place where Armand saved my life?

Madame Perrichon. All the same——

Perrichon. Enough! This second trip abroad is exacted by the major—I mean, by a major obligation.

Célimare

(*Célimare le bien-aimé*)

by

EUGÈNE LABICHE and DELACOUR

English version by Lynn and Theodore Hoffman

Lyrics by Eric Bentley

Copyright © 1958 by Lynn Hoffmann, Theodore Hoffman, and Eric Bentley.

CHARACTERS

PITOIS, *Célimare's butler*

ADELINE, *his maid*

CÉLIMARE, *a well-to-do bachelor of 47 years, about to be married*

COLOMBOT, *his father-in-law to be*

VERNOUILLET, *an old friend; a widower*

BOCARDON, *a newer old friend*

MADAME COLOMBOT, *Célimare's mother-in-law to be*

EMMA, *Célimare's fiancée, a young girl*

TWO DECORATOR'S ASSISTANTS

THE PLACE—PARIS.

THE TIME—1863.

LYRICS

Act One

Act Two

Act Three

Célimare

ACT ONE

CÉLIMARE's *parlor, an elegant, octagonal-shaped room of which we see half. The main entrance is upstage center. The two walls which slant in from it have windows. Downstage left, a fireplace and mantelpiece. Upstage left, a door. Upstage right, a door. Downstage right, a door leading to the linen closet. Sofa, armchairs, expensive furnishings. Upstage right, a desk, in which there is a little coffer. A table next to the mantelpiece. Clocks, candelabra, vases, etc. Two* DECORATOR'S ASSISTANTS *have just finished hanging some drapes.* ADELINE *is helping them.*

PITOIS [*entering upstage*]. Still hanging those curtains? Come on, we haven't got all day!

Adeline. We'll be through in a minute.

Pitois. The master wants the room clear by nine o'clock.

Adeline. But the wedding isn't till eleven.

Pitois. It doesn't matter. He says he doesn't want any workmen hanging around the apartment after he leaves for the marriage bureau.

Adeline. Don't tell anybody, but if you ask me he's getting a bit old for marriage.

Pitois. He's forty-seven. Well, I did my duty and gave him my considered opinion. He told me to clear out. It's his business.

Adeline. The fiancée is only eighteen. That's taking a chance!

Pitois. It doesn't mean a thing. I married a woman five years older than me, but it didn't help a bit.

Adeline. Oh, Monsieur Pitois, you don't mean . . .

Pitois. Exactly. You didn't know?

Adeline. Well, I'm just here since this morning.

Pitois. Oh, I see. Well, anyhow, if he gets into trouble it serves him right. He's had them in all shapes and sizes. He was a real playboy in his day. They used to call him "The Playboy of Lombard Street!"—when he was a young druggist.

Adeline. He used to be a druggist?

Pitois. Yes. What a brilliant career that man had in front of him! [*The bell rings.*] That's him. He wants his hair curled. I've been curling his hair for twelve years. And when I spot a white hair—snap! [*The bell rings insistently.*] Coming, sir! Coming, sir! [*Goes out upstage right.*]

Adeline [*to the* DECORATORS]. Pull back the curtains. It's prettier.

COLOMBOT *enters upstage center.*

Colombot. Don't bother. It's just me.

Adeline [*aside*]. The father-in-law.

Colombot [*to Adeline*]. Oh, my daughter's new chambermaid. The one my wife hired yesterday.

Adeline [*curtseying*]. Yes, sir.

Colombot. Where is Célimare, my future son-in-law?

Adeline. He's having his hair curled.

Colombot. Well, well, getting his hair curled! The rascal said it was natural.

Adeline. I'll go tell him——

Colombot. They'll be bringing over the trousseau and the wedding presents this morning. You're to put everything in the linen closet.

Adeline. Yes, sir.

A Decorator [*to Adeline*]. We're all though, mademoiselle.

Adeline [*going upstage*]. There are still some little curtains that go in the bedroom. [*Taking the curtains from a chair.*] Come along. I'll carry them.

Colombot [*to Adeline*]. I'm coming with you. I want to see if everything's all set. [*He motions to the decorators to go out left and follows them.*]

PITOIS *enters upstage right and goes to the fireplace.*

Pitois [*speaking to someone off stage*]. Yes, sir, I will. [*To himself.*] One crazy thing after another! Now I'm supposed to light a fire in the parlor.

Adeline. Well, if he tells you to, do it. You're not paying the fuel bills. [*Goes off left with the curtains.*]

Pitois [*lighting the fire*]. A fire! In the middle of August! On his wedding day!

CÉLIMARE *enters with his hair in curlpapers, wearing a dressing gown; a white towel is pinned over his shoulders.*

Célimare. How's the fire coming?

Pitois. I'm blowing on it.

Célimare. Well, hurry up.

Pitois. Do you feel cold, sir?

Célimare. Horribly. Open the window and finish my hair!
[*Sits down in a chair in front of the table.*]

Pitois [*going over left to open the window; aside*]. Now
he wants the window opened! Crazy! Crazy! [*Aloud.*] Where
do you want the ringlets, sir? [*Stands behind* CÉLIMARE *and
works on his hair.*]

Célimare. All over, all over! And it's got to look perfectly
natural.

Pitois [*combing out the curls*]. I don't know—a man who's
getting married and wants a fire in the middle of August.

Célimare. Have you anything else to say?

Pitois. I've done my duty, sir. I gave you my considered
opinion.

Célimare. Just because you've been unlucky with your
wife, you think the same thing has to happen to everyone
else. Anyhow, it's only a question of feeling bad for a while
after you find it out.

Pitois. Oh, I was expecting it. Pulcheria had been sticking
brilliantine on her hair for weeks and dousing her handker-
chiefs with eau de cologne. And when a chambermaid starts
using brilliantine——

Célimare [*referring to his hair*]. A bad sign! Puff it out!
Puff it out! Well, what did you do to your wife, send her
packing?

Pitois. Oh, no, sir! Why, she was making five hundred
francs a year, all going into the bank.

Célimare. Yes, I can understand. But what about your
rival—did you throw him out the window?

Pitois. Oh, no, sir! First of all, it's against the law, and,
anyhow, he was stronger than me.

Célimare. Ah! So he was a big devil, eh?

Pitois. A superb specimen—just like you, sir.

Célimare. Puff it out! Puff it out!

Pitois. Not that it brought him any happiness.

Célimare. Is he dead?

Pitois. No, sir, he's a doorman. [*Taking off the towel.*]
You're all set, sir. [CÉLIMARE *gets up and goes over to the
chair on the right.*]

Célimare. Fine! Put another log on the fire.

Pitois [*putting on a log; aside*]. In the middle of August!
Crazy, crazy! [*Goes out left.* CÉLIMARE *goes to the desk upstage right and takes out an elegant little coffer.*]

Célimare. This is my little box of collector's items—letters
from the ladies. I won't deceive you. I have loved the ladies.

[*Graciously.*] Oh, I still love them, and I shall always love them. But now that I'm getting married it's not very wise to leave these charming memories around the house. I've had the fire made and now I must consummate the sacrifice. After all, they say that fire purifies. [*Takes a pack of letters from the coffer, places them on the table, and sits down.*] Ah, Ninette's letters! She's my latest. Such wild, tempestuous handwriting—just like her character! [*Rising.*] All the same, she does have some delightful aspects. For one thing, she's got a husband. I've always preferred married women. If you pick out a married woman, with a household, then you've got somewhere to go. Besides that, it's so convenient and respectable. It's so difficult these days to find a respectable woman for a mistress. To say nothing of the money you save—a few bouquets of flowers, a box of candy now and then, that's all you need. Of course, there is the other side of the picture —the husband! A horrible bore who decides you're his best friend, tells you all his business, asks you for advice, and sends you on errands. Nevertheless, my system is to cultivate the husband. Now take Ninette's husband, Bocardon—he's in the dye business—we're thick as thieves. But that's not a very deep kind of relationship, thank goodness. You can break it off in a matter of minutes. Just the same, he's a nice fellow, Bocardon, very convenient to have around. After all, he's been delivering our letters for us—in his hat. Ninette and I cooked up a little system. Whenever Bocardon would say to me "Oh, by the way, my wife wants to know what you think about Northern Railways?" it meant: "My wife has written you a letter—look under the left side of my hatband." I look, and there it is! [*Shows a letter.*] There's a good housewife for you—saves money on postage stamps! The poor people! How they're going to miss me! I made all the decisions in that house. I was their family adviser, and poured my heart into the job! Well, let's burn these souvenirs. It breaks my heart, but it can't be helped. [*Throws the letters into the fire.*] Adieu, Ninette! Adieu, Bocardon! [*Takes another bunch from the coffer.*] On to the next!

COLOMBOT *enters from the bedroom, left.*

Colombot [*to someone offstage*]. It's all very nice, very well done!

Célimare [*quickly puts back the letters and shuts the coffer. Aside*]. Oh, my father-in-law!

Colombot. Good morning, Célimare.

Célimare. Monsieur Colombot! What brings you here so early?

Colombot. I wanted to take a last look around your place. [*Goes over to the fireplace.*] Goodness, a fire—in the middle of August!

Célimare. Yes, it's quite chilly this morning.

Colombot [*looking at the window*]. Then why have you got the window open?

Célimare. The chimney smokes.

Colombot [*noticing the coffer*]. What a pretty box! [*He is about to pick it up.*]

Célimare [*preventing him*]. Look out, it's very fragile!

Colombot. Ah, a surprise for my daughter.

Célimare. Exactly.

Colombot. Let's put it in with the other presents.

Célimare. Of course, of course, but later. [*Aside.*] When it's empty.

Colombot. Célimare, I hope you'll really love and cherish my daughter.

Célimare. Don't worry about that, sir.

Colombot. It occurs to me that you may be a bit too old for her.

Célimare. Old? I'm only forty-seven.

Colombot. First of all, let me warn you that Emma is still very much a child.

Célimare. So am I.

Colombot. You should have seen her packing her dollies yesterday. She's bringing them with her, you know.

Célimare. Oh, fine, fine! [*Confidentially.*] But if I may say so, I shall do my best to make her forget about them.

Colombot. Just what do you mean by that?

Célimare. Come on, now! [*Nudging him in the stomach.*] Eh? Eh? Papa Colombot! [*Laughing.*]

Colombot. Don't laugh so hard. You'll get crowsfeet!

Célimare [*aside*]. Really, he's too boring.

Colombot. Look here, I like to be frank. I won't hide the fact that when I first met you I didn't like your looks at all. No, sir, not at all!

Célimare. Oh!

Colombot. And neither did my wife!

Célimare. Whatever changed your mind?

Colombot. The lawyer. When he told me you had an income of forty thousand a year.

Célimare [*annoyed*]. You're so kind.

Colombot. You're not angry, are you?

Célimare. Whatever do you mean? Just the opposite!

Colombot. We said to ourselves, "Célimare isn't young. He isn't handsome. But youth and beauty pass away, whereas forty thousand a year—if it's handled properly—that lasts! I do like to be frank, you see.

Célimare. Yes, I can see. It's lucky your daughter doesn't share your sentiments.

Colombot. Well, I must admit she does find you passable, though I can't understand how!

Célimare [*annoyed*]. What's so strange about it? Lots of women have found me "passable."

Colombot [*incredulous*]. You? Don't make me laugh! With a pot like that?

Célimare. See here——

Colombot [*going upstage*]. Well, I've got to go now. You'd better finish dressing. See you later.

Célimare. Good day.

Colombot. Don't be late. Eleven o'clock sharp!

Célimare. Don't worry! [COLOMBOT *goes out.*]

Célimare [*alone*]. He says he likes to be frank. Well, I say he likes to be nasty. He talks as if I were a dried-up old lecher. That's a laugh. I had half a mind to show him what's inside this little box. [*He opens it and takes out some letters.*] The letters of Madame Vernouillet. Poor Héloïse! [*Holding up the letters.*] Here lies a grand passion that lasted five whole years! She was a very striking girl from Bordeaux, married to a dreary old man. She had only one fault, but a frightful one. Coming from Bordeaux, she naturally adored mushrooms and thought she could tell them from toadstools, poor thing. So every Sunday morning we'd leave Paris, with her husband and a little basket, and we'd go to the woods at Meudon to collect our deadly meal. She'd cry out, "Oh, there's an esculent boletus! There's an orange-agaric!" and she'd cram them all into that little basket. Vernouillet would follow behind, a long way behind—it was delightful. In the evening, I'd stay for dinner. Needless to say, I never touched that frightful fricassee seasoned with oil and garlic. I'm no less courageous than the next man, but I just don't like to eat rat poison. I'd take a bit of cold beef instead, and how right I was! One night at eleven o'clock, she said to me, "See you tomorrow," and by midnight I was a widower. [*Catching himself.*] I mean, Vernouillet was a widower. This sad event changed my whole way of life. I just didn't know what to

do with my evenings. That was when I started seeing the
Bocardons—to make me forget. Poor Héloïse! She wrote such
delightful letters. [*Taking a letter and reading tenderly.*]
"My dearest one, don't bring a melon today; my husband has
just sent me one from the country." She thought of everything, that girl. [*Reads from another letter.*] "My dearest
one, tomorrow is my husband's birthday. Don't forget to bring
him some flowers when you come." And I'd arrive the next
day with my little bouquet and my birthday card—just like a
schoolboy. I really spoiled that man. I treated him just like
a rajah. I ran his errands in the morning, played dominoes
with him at night, and every afternoon at four o'clock I'd
stop in at his office. One day he had a terrific backache, and—
I confess it—I gave him a massage. At least *she* was grateful
for all these little attentions. One heartfelt glance was enough
to repay me for all my sacrifices. Oh, well, no use getting
sentimental. Into the fire with all of them.

PITOIS *enters.*

Pitois. Monsieur Vernouillet.

Célimare [*aside*]. The husband! [*Puts the letters back in
the coffer and quickly locks it, slipping the key into his
pocket.*]

Veruouillet [*entering upstage center*]. Are you alone?

Célimare [*offering him a seat*]. Yes. [*Sits down.*]

Vernouillet [*places his hat on a chair and sits near Célimare; sighs*]. Ahh!

Célimare [*also sighs*]. Ahhh! [*They clasp hands.*]

Vernouillet. Well, after all, there's nothing we can do about
it.

Célimare [*dropping his air of gaiety and trying to look
sad*]. No, heaven knows, nothing at all. [*Aside.*] He's going
to keep me from dressing.

Vernouillet. Célimare, you never drop into the office any
more. Everyday I wait for you till four-fifteen. I say to
myself, "He'll be here any minute." But you never come.

Célimare. Forgive me. I'm so busy lately.

Vernouillet. Célimare, it's only too clear; you don't like me
any more.

Célimare [*taking his hand*]. Oh, my dear friend, how can
you say such a thing?

Vernouillet. What have I done?

Célimare. Nothing, but I'm about to get married. I've got
a lot to do.

Vernouillet. I used to see you every day and now I hardly ever see you, even from a distance.

Célimare. Why, I came to see you just last week.

Vernouillet. You only stayed five minutes.

Célimare. Well, I was in a hurry.

Vernouillet. You used to spend every evening at our house, playing dominoes with me.

Célimare [*aside*]. If he thinks that's going to go on!

Vernouillet. It's true that when I lost my wife I was very depressed. But I said to myself, "At least I still have Célimare."

Célimare [*taking his hand again*]. Oh, my friend, my friend! [*Aside.*] What a bore!

Vernouillet. When you said you were getting married, I thought, "Wonderful, now I'll have some place to go."

Célimare. Ohh!

Vernouillet. "Célimare used to visit me. Now I'll visit him." But I see now it was all a dream. You don't like me anymore.

Célimare. See here, Vernouillet, let's not be childish.

Vernouillet [*getting up*]. And, finally, you slighted me, cruelly slighted me.

Célimare [*getting up too*]. Me?

Vernouillet. You didn't even invite me to your wedding.

Célimare. I thought about it, but you're still in mourning.

Vernouillet. True enough, but one doesn't go on mourning forever. After all, it's been six months.

Célimare. Six months already?

Vernouillet. My God, yes—how time flies!

Célimare. But, my dear friend, now that I know, of course you must come. You're invited! Don't let me down.

Vernouillet [*relenting*]. You mean it? Well, in that case I'll show you I'm no ingrate. [*Searches among some papers he takes out of his pocket.*]

Célimare [*aside*]. And my mother-in-law made me promise not to invite anyone else! There's room for only sixteen at the table, and we've already got eighteen coming. Oh well, one more won't hurt. [*Smiles.*]

Vernouillet [*unfolding a sheet of paper*]. I thought of you this morning.

Célimare. What have you got there?

Vernouillet. Oh, just a little poem I amused myself scribbling for you.

Célimare. You mean you went to the trouble? Oh, how kind you are.

Vernouillet. It goes to a tune my poor wife used to sing. [*Sighs.*] Ahh!

Célimare [*taking his hand and also sighing*]. Ahhh!

Vernouillet. Well, after all, there's nothing we can do about it. [*They sing to the tune of Fiorella's couplets, "Pourquoi l'on aime."*]

POEM

Vernouillet.

I

Best friend thou art that man had ever
    And now as a husband thou'lt beat them all!
My Célimare, I'll leave thee never
    But stand at thy side though the heavens fall
For I ne'er can repay thee, such deeds of friendship are
        thine!
How shall I ever do for thy wife what thou hast done
        for mine?
Célimare [*refrain*]. Pray do not try to do for my wife
    what I have done for thine!

2

Though I may be the best friend ever
    And now as a husband may beat them all
I do not urge that you leave me never
    Or stand at my side when the heavens fall
You need never repay me, though deeds of friendship
    were mine—
Pray do not try to do for my wife what I have done
    for thine!
Vernouillet [*refrain*]. Oh, but I have to do for thy wife
    what thou hast done for mine!

Vernouillet. Héloïse could really sing that, especially the end. [*Sighs.*] Ahh!

Célimare [*taking his hand and sighing*]. Ahhh!

Vernouillet. Well, after all, there's nothing we can do about it. I'll go home and get dressed. Then I'll come back to pick you up. [*Moving upstage.*]

Célimare. Eleven o'clock sharp!

Vernouillet. Don't worry! [*Exit singing.* CÉLIMARE *accompanies him to the door, also singing.*]

Vernouillet [*Exiting*]. Well, after all . . .

Célimare. It's very funny, but since he's become a widower I find him an intolerable bore. Once I'm married, I'm not going to see much of *him*.

BOCARDON *enters upstage center, white tie and tails.*

Bocardon. It's just me, my dear friend. I'll only stay a minute.

Célimare [*aside*]. Bocardon! My Number Two.

Bocardon. I came to warn you. You're in hot water—up to your neck. Luckily I managed to straighten things out.

Célimare. What in the world . . . ?

Bocardon. Oh, nothing much. You just forgot to invite us to your wedding.

Célimare. I can explain everything. My mother-in-law——

Bocardon. I straightened it out. Ninette was furious. She said, "I'll get even! He'll see! Just wait. His footstool!" You know that pretty footstool she was embroidering for you? She wasn't going to finish it! But I fixed everything. You'll see how subtle I am. I told her that you'd asked me to hand on the invitation but that I'd clean forgotten to do it.

Célimare. What?

Bocardon. So don't worry! We'll be there. Together.

Célimare [*aside*]. The devil! That makes twenty-one, and the table will hold only sixteen.

Bocardon. That calmed her down a little. Just the same, she's been very irritable the past few days. Come to think of it, the day you announced your marriage she was in a vile temper. Why, you'd have thought she was annoyed about it.

Célimare. Why should she be annoyed about it?

Bocardon. That's just what I said to her. "What's the difference? Célimare is getting married. So much the better. You can make friends with his wife." I'm very anxious for our wives to get together.

Célimare [*coldly*]. Oh, yes, of course. [*Aside.*] We'll see about that!

Bocardon. Just between ourselves, I think I know why she's so irritable.

Célimare. Why?

Bocardon. Can't you guess?

Célimare. No.

Bocardon. It's because of you.

Célimare [*frightened*]. Because of me? Bocardon, I swear——

Bocardon. I think she wanted to make a match between you and her cousin Élodie.

Célimare [*relieved*]. Oh, you think that's it?

Bocardon. I'm no fool. Just as I told her the other day, "Élodie isn't Célimare's type at all."

Célimare. Oh, not at all.

Bocardon. "In the first place," I said, "she squints." Well, Ninette flew into a rage and called me an idiot. Just shows that I guessed the truth.

Célimare. How well you understand women!

Bocardon. Especially my wife. I can always guess what she's up to. Well, then she said the wedding wasn't over yet, and that it might never take place——

Célimare. What?

Bocardon. Just nonsense. The sort of thing women say when they're mad. She was furious at everyone. As a result, the new cook—the one you got for us—

Célimare. What about her?

Bocardon. She's leaving. There was a little scene this morning. You'd better get us a new one. We also wanted to ask you about the wallpaper in the dining room.

Célimare. Oh, my dear friend, please . . .

Bocardon. Not today, naturally. Get yourself married first, and then hurry back to us. We miss you. We don't know what to do with ourselves any more.

Célimare [*aside*]. Another one who thinks things are going to be the same.

Bocardon. Even Minotaur—our Newfoundland, you know —he's pining away for you.

Célimare. Poor brute!

Bocardon. Whenever he'd see you he'd get up on his hind legs—like this—to get a lump of sugar. You really treated him royally.

Célimare. Yes, we were great friends.

Bocardon. Even before you'd come in the door, he'd get up—like this. He could smell you coming. Man must have a very nice scent, you know.

Célimare. Oh, I think it's just that dogs have a highly developed olfactory sense.

Bocardon. Anyhow, dear friend, our evenings seem terribly long without those nice games of bezique we used to play every night.

Célimare. That's right, you're a bezique fan.

Bocardon. I do enjoy it.

Célimare. Some people prefer dominoes.

Bocardon. Not me. Well, I guess I'll be going. Have to buy some gloves. These are worn out. See you soon. [*Starts off, upstage.*]

Célimare. Good-by.

Bocardon [*pausing at the door and coming back*]. Oh, I forgot, my wife wants to know what you think about Northern Railways.

Célimare [*taken aback*]. Oh, Lord! [*Aside.*] A letter! [*Aloud, trying to take* BOCARDON'S *hat.*] Here, take your hat off!

Bocardon [*resisting*]. No, no! I've got to go. Have to buy some gloves.

Célimare. You've lots of time. You can pick them up on the way to the marriage bureau. Come on, give me your hat. I insist. [*Takes it.*]

Bocardon [*aside*]. How thoughtful! What a friend!

Célimare. You haven't said a word about my new furniture.

Bocardon. So I haven't. New furniture! It's charming. [*Goes around the room examining it.*]

Célimare [*aside, searching the hat*]. Under the band, on the left. [*Pulling out a note.*] Here it is. Whatever can she want now? [*To* BOCARDON.] What do you think of the clock?

Bocardon [*looking at the clock on the mantelpiece*]. Where did you find it?

Célimare. In your hat. [*Catching himself.*] I mean at Montbro's.

Bocardon. Very nice.

Célimare [*aside, reading*]. "Sir, your conduct is beneath my mention, but if you are a man of honor you will return my letters before noon today." [*Out loud.*] Her letters! Good Heavens, I just burned them!

Madame Colombot [*heard offstage*]. I must speak to him immediately!

Célimare. My mother-in-law! Here already!

Madame Colombot [*entering upstage center*]. Ah, there you are!

Célimare. What's the matter? Is something wrong?

Madame Colombot. I left my daughter at the hairdresser's and rushed here to demand an explanation from you!

Célimare. From me?

Madame Colombot [*looking at* BOCARDON]. It is imperative that I speak to you—alone!

Célimare. Go right ahead. The gentleman is a friend.

Bocardon. A *close* friend!

Madame Colombot. Very well. Sir, only a few minutes ago I received an anonymous letter——

Célimare [*astonished*]. An anonymous letter?

Bocardon. Unsigned?

Madame Colombot. I haven't shown it to my husband. I leaped into a cab. In another hour it would have been too late to break things off.

Célimare. But what does it say?

Madame Colombot. Monsieur Célimare, your fortune, your brilliant fortune, has already caused us to overlook many things—your age for one. Were it not for your income of forty thousand——

Célimare. I know all about it! Your husband has been kind enough to tell me all that. But what about the letter?

Madame Colombot. It contains a monstrous revelation. You have a previous attachment, sir!

Célimare. Oh, look here!

Madame Colombot. A woman with whom you spend all your evenings!

Célimare [*aside*]. Eeh! [*Pointing to* Bocardon.] Remember, we're not alone!

Bocardon. If I may interrupt—it's completely false!

Madame Colombot. Your proof?

Bocardon. He spends his evenings with me.

Célimare. Yes, playing bezique.

Bocardon. For two sous a point. I got up to fifteen hundred the other day. Oh, I do enjoy it.

Madame Colombot. Just the same, it says in this letter——

Célimare [*getting a glimpse of the letter. Aside*]. Good Heavens! Madame Bocardon's handwriting.

Bocardon. Let's see it.

Célimare [*stepping between* Bocardon *and* Madame Colombot]. No, don't bother!

Bocardon. Why not?

Célimare. One should hold anonymous letters in contempt, and not do them the honor of reading them.

Madame Colombot [*holding out the letter*]. Just the same, my son——

Célimare. Throw it away! I'd rather confess all. Yes, mother, there has been a woman in my life. You don't think I've lived this long and not . . . ? Yes, every evening for five years——

Madame Colombot. For five years!

Bocardon. Every evening? Let me repeat——

Célimare. But I can put your fears at rest. For the past six months it's been over. A tragic and premature death stole her from my affection—and her husband's esteem.

Bocardon [*aside*]. A husband! Wait till I tell Ninette about this! She'll be so amused.

Madame Colombot. And this woman, may one ask who . . . ?

Célimare. Impossible to name her while her husband is still alive.

Bocardon. He wouldn't like it.

Madame Colombot. How do I know you're not making all this up?

Célimare. Oh, mother!

Madame Colombot. Swear to me as a man of honor!

Célimare. Oh, I give you my word!

Madame Colombot. Paul, I believe you! [*She tears the letter in half and tosses it on the floor. One half falls by* CÉLIMARE, *the other by* BOCARDON.]

Célimare [*aside*]. Saved! [*Quickly snatches up the half of the letter that lies at his feet.*] The letter! [*Crumples it up and throws it in the fire.*]

Bocardon [*aside*]. He's gotten out of it. Now, there's only the husband . . .

Madame Colombot. This will be our secret. I won't breathe a word about it to either my husband or my daughter.

Célimare. How kind of you. And I assure you that in the future——

Madame Colombot. Oh, I'm not worried about that. Your age is guarantee enough.

Célimare [*aside*]. My age? They certainly think I'm doddering.

Madame Colombot. I must rejoin my daughter now. I'll be back in a little while with the trousseau.

Célimare [*bows and accompanies her to the door*]. Madame. Oh, by the way, we've having three more guests.

Madame Colombot. What? Twenty-one places to set?

Célimare. One's an old friend I forgot about. Then there's Monsieur Bocardon and his wife.

Bocardon. He forgot about us, too. The day I got married I forgot to invite the judge, but he showed up all the same.

Madame Colombot [*nodding to* BOCARDON]. The honor is mine.

Bocardon [*bowing*]. Oh, no, madame; it's mine.

Madame Colombot [*to* CÉLIMARE, *in a low voice*]. Where am I going to put them all?

Célimare [*in a low voice, at the door*]. Just set an extra little table. It will all work out. [*She goes out.*] Good-by, mother.

Bocardon [*he has moved downstage and picked up the other half of the letter*]. Oh, how I detest anonymous letters! [*Notices the handwriting.*] Great Heavens! Ninette's hand-writing!

Célimare [*seeing him, aside*]. Oof! I only burned half of it!

Bocardon [*goes over to him*]. See here, sir, this is my wife's handwriting.

Célimare. No, no, of course it isn't! Don't be silly!

Bocardon. I'd know it anywhere.

Célimare. I assure you, you're mistaken.

Bocardon. That married woman with whom you spend all your evenings—I see it all now. That story you told your mother-in-law doesn't fool me a bit. Sir, you owe me an explanation!

VERNOUILLET *enters, upstage center, in white tie and tails.*

Vernouillet. Here I am.

Célimare [*in a low voice, to* BOCARDON]. Shhh! Someone's here.

Bocardon. Get rid of him! I want to talk to you.

Vernouillet [*stepping between them*]. I put on my tails, and wrote another verse. Would you like me to sing it?

Célimare. Not just now, thank you.

Vernouillet. It's in memory of my wife, whom we both loved so well.

Bocardon [*pricking up his ears*]. What?

Vernouillet [*to* BOCARDON]. Yes, he spent every evening with us for five years.

Bocardon. Five years? Well, well!

Célimare [*to* VERNOUILLET]. Why bring that up? I'm sure it's of no interest at all.

Bocardon [*to* VERNOUILLET]. And your wife?

Vernouillet. We had the misfortune to lose her.

Bocardon [*joyfully*]. Oh, good!

Vernouillet. A tragic and premature death.

Bocardon [*bursting out laughing*]. Hee, hee, hee! So it's you, is it?

Vernouillet. Me? What?

Bocardon. Hee, hee, hee! [*Aside.*] I'd rather it was him than me!

Vernouillet [*in a low voice, to* CÉLIMARE]. What's that man laughing for? Here I am, telling him about my misfortunes, and——

Célimare [*in a low voice*]. Ignore it. It's just a tic, a nervous reaction.

Vernouillet [*moving away, haughtily*]. Then he ought to see a doctor!

Bocardon [*in a low voice, to* CÉLIMARE]. My friend, forgive me for being suspicious.

Célimare. Bocardon, you have wounded me.

Bocardon. How could I help it? It was my wife's fault, sending that letter! Stooping to such a low device to get you to marry her cousin!

Célimare. You must forgive her.

Bocardon. I should say not! We'll have a little chat about it this evening. I've never struck a woman before, but——

Célimare. Oh, Bocardon! Please!

Bocardon. I'm not making any promises.

Vernouillet [*has moved over to the mantelpiece. Looking at the clock*]. It's eleven o'clock. Shouldn't we be leaving?

Célimare. Eleven o'clock! Excuse me while I change my clothes. [*Aside.*] Dear me! I never introduced them. [*Aloud.*] My very good friend, Monsieur Vernouillet. My very good friend, Monsieur Bocardon.

Vernouillet and *Bocardon* [*bowing to each other*]. Monsieur.

Célimare [*aside, going to the door, right*]. What good fellows they are! [*Goes out.*]

Bocardon [*gazing at* VERNOUILLET, *aside*]. He's just the type you'd expect. [*Aloud.*] What a delightful person Célimare is!

Vernouillet [*aside*]. Well, well, his tic is gone. [*Aloud.*] Utterly charming.

Bocardon. You must feel great affection for him.

Vernouillet. Oh, yes, he's my best friend.

Bocardon. Naturally. [*Bursts into laughter.*] Hee, hee, hee!

Vernouillet [*watching him laugh, aside*]. There it goes again. [*Aloud.*] Do you suffer much?

Bocardon [*astonished*]. Me? No. [*Coyly.*] He came to see you for five years, did he? Every evening?

Vernouillet. Every evening. He never missed a day. We always played our little game of dominoes.

Bocardon [*aside*]. He played a game with you all right! That's really rich!

Vernouillet. But since my poor Héloïse died six months ago he has neglected me somewhat.

Bocardon. I should think so.

Vernouillet. What?

Bocardon. Nothing.

Vernouillet. I don't know what he does evenings now.

Bocardon [*aside, with a subtle air*]. Well, I do.

Vernouillet. My wife held him in the greatest esteem. She embroidered him one thing after another—a night cap, slippers . . .

Bocardon [*aside*]. Good God, slippers! That's really rich! [*Bursts out laughing.*] Hee, hee, hee!

Vernouillet [*aside*]. There goes that tic again. [*Aloud.*] Haven't you ever consulted anyone?

Bocardon [*surprised*]. Consulted anyone? What for?

Vernouillet. Oh, never mind. [*Aside.*] It's gone. [*Aloud.*] He was so kind as to dine with us every Wednesday. [*Correcting himself.*] No, every Monday.

Bocardon. I was about to say that Wednesday . . . [*aside*] . . . is our night. [*Aloud.*] And your wife would make him nice little puddings?

Vernouillet. Oh, yes.

Bocardon. And buttered new potatoes?

Vernouillet. Well, you seem to know all his preferences.

Bocardon. Oh, yes. [*Aside.*] It all hangs together. A plot for Molière!

Vernouillet. And since he has a well-stocked cellar——

Bocardon. How true!

Vernouillet. He always brought something special to drink with dessert. He has a certain brand of kirsch——

Bocardon. I know it very well.

Vernouillet. Oh, you've had it, too?

Bocardon. Every Wednesday. Sheer nectar!

Vernouillet. Absolutely! Well, delighted to have made your acquaintance, my dear sir. [*Each offers his hand.*]

Bocardon. Oh, the pleasure's been mine. [*They are shaking hands when* CÉLIMARE *appears in the doorway, dressed for the wedding.*]

Célimare [*aside*]. Well, well, they're fraternizing!

Bocardon [*in a low voice, to* CÉLIMARE, *gesturing toward* VERNOUILLET]. I've just had a little chat with him. He's been telling me a thing or two!

Célimare [*frightened*]. You're all wrong, believe me! You're just imagining things.

Bocardon. It's no use arguing. I know everything! You sly dog!

Célimare [*aside*]. Well, if he hasn't figured it out by now——

PITOIS *enters left through the door leading to the linen closet.*

Pitois [*terrified, in a low voice*]. Sir, sir!

Célimare. What's the matter?

Pitois. Madame Bocardon is in there, in your study. She got in through the linen closet.

Célimare [*aside*]. Oh, Good lord!

Pitois [*in a low voice*]. She wanted to know if you'd left a package for her.

Célimare [*aside*]. Her letters!

Pitois. I told her you hadn't, and she flew into a terrible rage. She wants to talk to you. Shall I let her in?

Célimare [*quickly*]. God, no!

Pitois [*pointing to the door, which has opened a crack*]. There she is!

Célimare. Heavens! [*He leaps for the door, pulls it shut, locks it, and puts the key in his pocket.*]

Bocardon and *Vernouillet.* What's the matter?

Célimare. Oh, nothing. [*A violent knocking is heard on the door.*]

Vernouillet. Someone's knocking.

Célimare [*leaning against the door*]. It's the decorators! What an unbearable racket! Let's go! Let's go!

Bocardon [*going toward the door*]. Wait! I know how to handle them! [*Yelling through the door.*] Hey you! Stop that racket till after we've gone! [*The noise stops.*]

Célimare [*aside*]. She recognized his voice.

Vernouillet. I can't hear a sound.

Bocardon [*triumphantly*]. Oh, well, I know how to talk to the lower classes!

Pitois [*aside*]. I'm getting out. He makes me sick. [*Leaves.*]

Bocardon [*to* CÉLIMARE]. Well, shall we go?

Célimare. Just a minute. I've got to put on my gloves. [*Aside.*] Better give her time to get out through the linen closet.

COLOMBOT *enters, followed by his wife.*

Colombot. Well, son, do we have to come and get you?
The carriages are downstairs.

Célimare. We were on our way.

Madame Colombot [*holding up a key*]. I've just had a
peek in the linen closet.

Célimare [*terrified*]. What?

Madame Colombot. I put the trousseau in there and locked
it up. I was afraid that the decorators——

Célimare [*aside*]. Fine! Now she can't get out!

Madame Colombot [*taking* CÉLIMARE's *arm*]. Come on,
come on! Give me your arm!

Célimare [*aside*]. How am I going to get her out? [*Aloud.*]
Excuse me, I have to arrange one more thing, in there.
[*Points to his dressing room.*]

Madame Colombot [*dragging him out*]. We don't have
time. We're late already. Come on, come on!

Colombot [*showing the door to* BOCARDON *and* VERNOUIL-
LET]. Gentlemen. [*Seeing the coffer on the table.*] Oh, the
pretty box! The surprise! [*Shakes it.*] Something's in there.
[*Giving it to* ADELINE, *who enters.*] We'll come for the
wedding presents this evening. Put this with them. [*To*
BOCARDON *and* VERNOUILLET.] Gentlemen, let me show you
the way. [*Goes out.*]

Bocardon [*to* VERNOUILLET]. Please, sir.

Vernouillet [*to* BOCARDON]. After you.

Bocardon. No, you were first.

Vernouillet. True enough. [*Goes out.* BOCARDON *follows
him.*]

ACT TWO

CÉLIMARE's *dining room. A door upstage center, doors on
each side. A table set for four to the right, a sideboard to
the left. As the curtain rises,* PITOIS *has just finished setting
the table.*

Pitois. Four places—papa and mama are coming for lunch.
In-laws! Very tiresome for newlyweds—they always have so
many little things to say. [*Hearing* CÉLIMARE *and* EMMA,
who enter left, arm in arm]. Monsieur and madame. I'm off.
[*Tiptoes off right.*]

Célimare [*to the audience, with his arm around* EMMA].
It's so nice to have a woman all to yourself. It's not at all
like . . . [*To* EMMA.] You look so sad, Emma.

Emma [*lowering her eyes*]. Oh, no, sir.

Célimare. Are you unhappy?

Emma. Oh, no, sir.

Célimare [*aside*]. She's frightened, poor little dove. [*Kisses her passionately.*]

Emma. Please, sir, don't do that.

Célimare. Nobody's looking.

Emma. That makes no difference, sir.

Célimare. "Sir?" What a horrible word. It's so cold, so formal. It makes me feel like a guest.

Emma. But what do you want me to call you then?

Célimare. Paul! Call me Paul. After all, I call you Emma.

Emma. Oh, I'd never dare.

Célimare. It doesn't bother your father to call your mother "Séraphine." Why, just the other day he said to her, "Séraphine, you make me sick!" To which she replied, "Don't talk rot!" There's a marriage for you—a real marriage! There's nothing formal about that one! Emma, couldn't you be a bit informal with me?

Emma [*intensely*]. Oh, not right now. Later. We don't know each other well enough yet.

Célimare. Oh, really now! [*Laughs.*]

Emma. What is there to laugh about?

Célimare. Nothing. [*Starts to embrace her.* EMMA *flees, stage right.*] [*Passionately.*] Oh, my dearest, if only you knew how good, how gentle I am with women.

Emma. What do you mean "with women"? Do you mean to say you have loved other women, sir?

Célimare [*aside*]. Oh, Lord! [*Aloud.*] Never, never!

Emma. Are you telling me the truth?

Célimare. Ask your father. He knows all about me.

Emma. Oh, believe me, if you have been untrue to me I will never forgive you as long as I live.

Célimare. What a crazy idea! Now let's be reasonable. You've never bestowed your affections before, have you?

Emma. No.

Célimare. Well, what makes you think I'm any more capable of such a thing than you are?

Emma. As a matter of fact——

Célimare. You're just jealous.

Emma. Oh, dear! I don't really know. But when I think that you may have loved some other woman, actually taken her in your arms . . .

Célimare. Oh, see here, do you think people go around

taking other people in their arms just like that? In real society the only person a man makes love to is his wife, his dear little wife. [*Kisses her.*]

PITOIS *enters.*

Pitois. Sir! [*Sees them.*] Oh!

Célimare. What? What is it?

Pitois. Sir, it's the old people.

Célimare. The old people?

Pitois. Yes. Madame's papa and mama.

Emma. Your butler is certainly polite!

Célimare [*to* PITOIS]. Idiot!

Pitois. Their carriage just pulled up.

Emma. I'll go meet them. [*Goes out quickly upstage center.*]

Célimare [*to* PITOIS]. Come here, and keep your voice down. When I got home yesterday, I was worried about how you managed to let out that person who was visiting me. [*Waves toward the door right.*]

Pitois [*in a loud voice*]. Madame Bocardon?

Célimare. Not so loud!

Pitois. Well, she certainly gave me a scare! When I got back—I'd been visiting my wife, who'd just cashed her pay check—I heard a noise in the linen closet. I was just about to pick up the fire tongs when a woman's voice called out: "Open the door!"

Célimare. You didn't have the key.

Pitois. No. She was locked in from both sides. So I picked the lock.

Célimare [*clasping his hand*]. Many thanks.

Pitois [*flattered, shaking* CÉLIMARE's *hand*]. Oh, sir.

Célimare [*taking back his hand*]. If you please! Go on.

Pitois. The poor thing was dying of hunger—seeing that it was nine o'clock at night.

Célimare. Good Lord! Ten hours in the linen closet!

Pitois. So I offered her some left-over cabbage soup, but before I knew it she'd rushed off.

Célimare [*aside*]. Luckily, Bocardon didn't suspect a thing. I saw that he was kept occupied all day, fetching ladies and taking them home. [*Aloud, taking out his purse.*] Pitois, I'm very pleased with you. Here are twenty francs——

Pitois [*thinking it is meant for him*]. Oh, sir!

Célimare. After dinner you're to take it and buy a bouquet of white roses for my wife.

Pitois [*disappointed*]. Oh, it's just for a bouquet, that money?

Célimare. Yes.

Pitois [*bitterly, aside*]. Rich people! They're all alike! [*Busies himself at the sideboard.* COLOMBOT *is heard offstage, talking.*]

Célimare [*going to the door*]. Ah, Father! Mother!

COLOMBOT, MADAME COLOMBOT, *and* EMMA *enter.*

Colombot. Shake hands, my son.

Madame Colombot. Paul, let me kiss you. [*They kiss.*]

Pitois [*Going over to the table*]. Lunch is served. [*During the scene, he goes in and out, serving the meal.*]

Emma [*going over to the table with* MADAME COLOMBOT]. Let's sit down. [*To* CÉLIMARE.] Are you coming, sir?

Colombot [*to* CÉLIMARE, *in a low voice*]. "Sir?"

Célimare [*in a low voice*]. It doesn't mean anything. She's just shy. [*They go to their places.*]

Colombot [*sitting down*]. Well, here we are. [*Raising his glass.*] If I had any sense I'd stick to tea.

Célimare. You certainly were in good form yesterday. Mother, your dinner was superb.

Emma. It was awfully crowded.

Célimare. I know at least one person sitting next to you who didn't complain. [*Tries to flick her with his napkin under the table.*]

Madame Colombot [*laughing*]. Oh, very nice!

Colombot [*laughing*]. A man of wit!

Madame Colombot. It was all your husband's fault. He invited three extra people.

Colombot. Oh, yes. Monsieur Bocardon! I liked him. He was very jolly.

Madame Colombot. And so amiable. But why didn't his wife come?

Célimare [*embarrassed*]. She was detained by circumstances beyond her control.

Emma. I've heard she's delightful.

Célimare [*forgetting himself*]. Very! What a woman!

All. What?

Célimare. I mean: what a nice woman!

Colombot. Well, to tell the truth, I didn't much like that other friend of yours—the old man.

Célimare. Vernouillet?

Madame Colombot. He seemed very grouchy.

Colombot. Why in the world did he sing that silly song warning us not to eat mushrooms?

Madame Colombot [*sharply*]. If he was trying to criticize my dinner——

Célimare. Oh, mother, how can you think such a thing?

Colombot. Do you see him very often?

Célimare. Oh, never, never.

PITOIS *enters.*

Pitois. Monsieur Vernouillet. [*He goes out.*]

Célimare [*aside*]. What in heaven's name could he want?

Vernouillet [*enters. Places his hat on a chair upstage left*]. Don't get up. Well, well, you're already having lunch. [*Bowing.*] Ladies, gentlemen. [COLOMBOT, MADAME COLOMBOT, *and* EMMA *nod coldly.* CÉLIMARE *starts to get up, but* MADAME COLOMBOT *holds him back.*]

Colombot [*to the women, in a low voice*]. That's right. Let's not be too cordial.

Célimare [*aside*]. Poor old man. He wants to be invited to eat. [*Aloud.*] Please sit down.

Vernouillet [*taking a chair, stage left, and sitting down*]. Thank you kindly. [*Long pause, during which everyone eats, ignoring* VERNOUILLET.]

Célimare [*to* VERNOUILLET]. And how are you feeling today?

Vernouillet. Very well, thank you.

Colombot [*to Célimare*]. Please pass the radishes, my son.

Madame Colombot [*coldly*]. There aren't any more. [*Long pause.*]

Célimare [*aside*]. I don't dare invite him. [*Aloud.*] And how are you feeling today?

Vernouillet. Very well, thank you. You never used to eat before one o'clock.

Madame Colombot [*coldly*]. Things have changed around here.

Célimare. Yes, they've changed, because . . . [*Pause.*] And how are you feeling today?

Vernouillet. Very well, thank you. I said to myself this morning, "Such a glorious day," because it was such a glorious day, you know.

Célimare. A perfect day for a walk!

Vernouillet. So I decided I'd come and see how you are . . .

[*Pause.*] How you are. [*Another pause.*] Well, now that I see you're enjoying perfect health, I'll take my leave. [*Gets up and goes to get his hat.*]

Célimare. Good-by.

Vernouillet [*bowing*]. Ladies, gentlemen. Don't get up. [*Aside, bitterly.*] Not even a glass of water. [*Goes out upstage center. Everyone continues to eat.*]

Colombot. At last! I thought he'd never go.

Madame Colombot. I hope he's not going to make a habit of dropping in on you like that.

Célimare. Of course not! He's an old friend—of my family. He just wanted to see how I was—and now he has. He's satisfied. He won't come back.

BOCARDON *enters.*

Bocardon [*announcing himself*]. Here I am, Bocardon! Just to let you know who I am. [*Puts his hat on a chair.*] Ladies, gentlemen.

Colombot [*aside*]. Now there's a fellow I really like.

Madame Colombot [*aside*]. Always so cheerful. [*Aloud.*] Have you dined yet?

Bocardon. Just finished, thanks. [*To* CÉLIMARE.] I want to talk to you.

Célimare [*rising*]. Me? What for?

Bocardon. She's gone!

Célimare. Who's gone?

Bocardon. The cook. There was another scene this morning, and what do you know? She's gone.

Célimare. What do you expect me to do about it?

Bocardon. I've got two in mind—one from Picardy, one from Burgundy. You'll have to look them over.

Célimare [*getting annoyed*]. But, my dear friend, I don't have the time. It was different before.

Bocardon. What do you mean, "before"?

Célimare. I mean I'm married.

Bocardon. Well, so am I! [*To* EMMA.] Madame, I warn you that I shall borrow your husband very often. We don't do a thing without him.

Emma. My husband will always be glad to be of service.

Bocardon [*coming over to* CÉLIMARE]. Good. You've got permission. Go get your hat.

Célimare. No, I'm not in the mood. I'm not going out today.

Bocardon. Well, shall I send the cooks over?

Célimare. I'm afraid that I don't know much about cooks. [*Aside.*] Isn't he ever going to let me alone?

Bocardon. Doesn't know much about cooks! [*To the others.*] He used to hire all of ours for us. [*They all rise from the table.* PITOIS *enters.*]

Pitois. May I clear the table?

Emma. Yes. [*During the following action, he clears the table, puts some things away in the sideboard, and goes out with the tray.*]

Madame Colombot. If you'll forgive me, my son, you aren't very nice to your friends.

Bocardon. Don't be hard on him. It's his nerves. Oh, I know what else I wanted to ask about. The wallpaper for the dining room. What do you think, a marble or wood pattern?

Célimare. I think—whatever you think.

Bocardon [*astonished, aside*]. What's got into him? [*Looking at the wallpaper.*] Hmm, this is pretty nice. How much is it a roll?

Célimare. Three francs seventy-five.

Bocardon. Just about what I'm prepared to pay. May I bring my wife around to see it?

Célimare [*quickly*]. There's no need——

Bocardon. What do you mean, "There's no need"?

Madame Colombot. We should be only too happy to meet Madame Bocardon.

Célimare [*aside*]. Fine! Now she's going to ask her over!

Emma. And we shall be delighted to repay her call.

Bocardon. To tell the truth, that's what I was hoping for.

Célimare [*aside*]. Yes, but don't count on it!

Bocardon. Célimare was just saying yesterday, "I do want our wives to get together."

Célimare. Pardon me, but it was you who said that.

Bocardon. Me? Oh, well, it's the same thing.

Célimare. The same thing? Not at all!

Bocardon. Why not?

Célimare. For pity's sake, you're putting words into my mouth.

Bocardon. You know what? I don't think you've ever felt any love for my wife.

Célimare. Oh, look here!

Bocardon. She told me so herself.

Madame Colombot. You do my son a great injustice. This very morning he was telling us how sorry he was not to see Madame Bocardon at the wedding.

Colombot. She wasn't home at six o'clock when we sent the carriage.

Célimare [*aside*]. Eeh!

Pitois [*aside*]. I know why.

Bocardon. Excuse me, but she was at home.

Célimare [*astonished*]. What?

Bocardon. Having an attack of neuralgia.

Pitois [*aside*]. What a woman!

Emma. Poor lady!

Bocardon. But she did go to the church.

Célimare. She did? Did you see her?

Bocardon. No. She saw me!

Pitois [*forgetting himself, bursts out laughing, and drops a plate*]. Ha! Ha! Ha!

Célimare [*turns abruptly and goes over to him*]. What's the matter?

Pitois. I dropped a plate.

Célimare. Very well. You may go now.

Pitois [*taking away the tray, aside*]. Husbands! And to think I was once like that! [*Goes out.*]

Bocardon. My friends, I must leave you. I've got lots of things to do. [*Taking out a slip of paper.*] Here's my list. [*Reading.*] "Go see Célimare." Done. "Ask him about the cook." Done. "Ask him about the wallpaper." Done.

Célimare [*aside*]. How fascinating!

Bocardon [*reading*]. "Ask him about the pump." Oh, do you know the pump in my house on Trevise Street?

Célimare. Well?

Bocardon. It doesn't work. You'd better have a look at it.

Célimare. Why don't you hire me by the year and be done with it?

Bocardon [*laughing*]. Ha, ha, ha! [*To the others.*] It's just not his good day. [*Reading.*] "Go to the concert hall."

Célimare [*going upstage and sitting down. Impatiently*]. I'm going to sit down.

Bocardon. I ought to tell you about the marvelous concert they're giving at three o'clock this afternoon. Patti is singing. Alboni is singing. Everybody's singing.

Emma. It sounds delightful.

Bocardon. That gives me an idea. Why don't you all come too? I'll introduce you to my wife.

Célimare [*still seated*]. Wonderful!

Emma. I'd love it!

Madame Colombot. What a good idea!

Colombot. Excellent!

Célimare [*aside*]. Merciful heavens! Can't he stop throwing his wife at us?

Emma [*to* CÉLIMARE]. It's all settled then, isn't it, dear?

Célimare. It's just that——

Colombot. What?

Célimare. I'm terribly sensitive. Music just shatters me.

Bocardon. Well, what did you go to the opera with us every Monday for? Ha!

Célimare [*furious*]. Oh, go to the devil! Ha!

Bocardon [*laughing*]. It's just not his good day. Wait! Ladies, I have an even better idea.

Célimare. What? [*Aside.*] He makes me shudder.

Bocardon. Instead of meeting you at the opera house, I'll just pop my wife in a carriage and bring her here.

Emma. Bravo!

Madame Colombot. How delightful!

Célimare. Delightful! [*Aside.*] I could throw him out the window.

Bocardon. That way she'll be able to meet the ladies and look at the wallpaper at the same time.

Célimare. Yes, that will make it a perfect party. [*Aside.*] She won't get in, if I have to demolish the staircase.

Bocardon [*taking his list again and reading*]. "Renew my insurance." [*Aloud.*] That concerns you. [*Reading.*] "Go see Léon." [*Aloud.*] He's a cousin of my wife's. [*Reading.*] "Ask him what he thinks about Northern Railways."

Célimare [*aside*]. My goodness, already?

Bocardon. That's done, too. I stayed longer than I meant to. Oh, he's a nice fellow—not very bright, but nice enough —but I just couldn't get away. He wouldn't give me back my hat.

Célimare [*aside*]. I bet he's carrying a reply. If only . . . [*Goes very quietly over to the chair upstage right on which* BOCARDON's *hat lies.*]

Colombot [*to* BOCARDON]. Do you go in much for Northern Railways?

Bocardon. No, I don't. It's my wife. She's very keen on it. [*Looks at his list, while* CÉLIMARE *picks up the hat, extracts a note from the hatband, and reads it.*]

Célimare [*aside*]. There. A penciled note from Léon. [*Turns*

to hide it from the others and reads it.] "Tuileries at five
o'clock." [*Aside.*] I have it! [*Takes a pencil from his pocket
and writes on the note.*] The concert is at three o'clock. Put
a three in place of the five. I know her. She'll take the
Tuileries. [*Puts the note back in the hat.*]

    Bocardon. And, finally, the barber. Useful thing, a list. I
couldn't carry all that in my head.

    Célimare. You're carrying enough on your head as it is.

    Bocardon. What?

    Célimare. Oh, nothing.

PITOIS *enters.*

    Pitois. Monsieur Vernouillet.

    Colombot and *Madame Colombot.* This is too much!

    Célimare. And now, Tweedledee.

VERNOUILLET *enters upstage and puts down his hat.*

    Vernouillet [*dryly*]. Don't trouble yourselves, ladies. I
won't stay long. I only want to have a little chat with Monsieur Célimare. [*He exchanges bows with* BOCARDON, *who has
moved a bit upstage.*]

    Emma [*in a low voice, to* CÉLIMARE]. Send him away.

    Colombot [*in a low voice, to* CÉLIMARE]. Get rid of him!

    Célimare [*in a low voice*]. Don't worry, I'll take care of
him. [*Aside.*] Then I'll take care of the other one.

    Madame Colombot [*taking* EMMA *upstage with her*]. Come,
Emma, we shall just have time to get ready for the concert.

    Bocardon [*has come downstage*]. I'd better leave now, but
we'll be here at two-thirty.

    Célimare. Fine. [*Giving him his hat.*] Don't forget your
hat. [*Aside.*] Very important. [BOCARDON *goes out upstage
center,* EMMA *and* MADAME COLOMBOT *go out left.*]

    Célimare [*aside*]. All right, let's get tough. It's time he
learned that he's been coming around a little too often.
[*Aloud.*] My dear Vernouillet, I have something I must say.

    Vernouillet [*dryly*]. So have I. That's why I came.

    Célimare. Vernouillet, there is no need to assure you of my
affection. I think I have given you ample proof of it already.

    Vernouillet [*coldly*]. Oh, yes. In former days.

    Célimare. It always gives me great pleasure to see you, but
you must understand that my situation is changed. I'm married.

    Vernouillet. What of it?

    Célimare. It's true that my wife likes you very much, but, to be honest, she has no notion of society, she dislikes making new acquaintances, and, well, a husband has to give in to these little things. But, don't worry, I'll come and see you.

Vernouillet. I understand. You're giving me the brush-off.

Célimare. Vernouillet, how could you use such a word?

Vernouillet. Actually, I should have expected it, after what happened at the wedding yesterday.

Célimare. What happened?

Vernouillet. You put me way down at the end of the table with the children.

Célimare [*quickly*]. But you love children!

Vernouillet. I love them—in between meals!

Célimare. Anyhow, it wasn't my fault. My mother-in-law arranged the seating.

Vernouillet. At dessert, when I sang my song, everyone kept talking, and you didn't even call for silence. You were talking yourself.

Célimare. Me? On the contrary——

Vernouillet [*with authority*]. I tell you, you were talking!

Célimare [*aside*]. Pretty hard to please, that brute. That's what comes of spoiling them.

Vernouillet [*bitterly*]. And when you were having dinner just now you didn't even offer me a glass of water.

Célimare. We were nearly finished.

Vernouillet. I beg to differ. You were only on the radishes.

Célimare. Are you sure?

Vernouillet. Absolutely! I left, wounded to the core.

Célimare. Vernouillet, look here.

Vernouillet. And do you know where I had dinner?

Célimare. No.

Vernouillet. I had a twenty-five-sou meal, around the corner.

Célimare. Really? They say it's not bad there.

Vernouillet. A choice of two main courses, a measly glass of wine, and stewed prunes! They gave me a beefsteak cut out of a rubber tire.

Célimare. Well, so long as your teeth are good——

Vernouillet. While I was trying to get through it, a few ideas occurred to me——

Célimare. About the state of butcher shops in France?

Vernouillet. I said to myself, "When my wife was still alive, Célimare showered me with attentions. Now that she's gone he ignores me. Why is that?"

Célimare [*aside*]. To the devil with him and his ideas!

Vernouillet. "So," I said to myself, "if he ignores me now it can't be me he was interested in, and if it wasn't me it must have been my wife."

Célimare. Vernouillet! How can you? How can you? [*Aside.*] What a time to start getting jealous!

Vernouillet. And as I began to recall various little circumstances about our friendship, a horrible suspicion entered my mind.

Célimare. Look here! Don't jump to conclusions!

Vernouillet. If I thought it was true——

Célimare. But it isn't!

Vernouillet. I have already chosen my weapon.

Célimare. A duel?

Vernouillet. No. It's against my principles. Dueling is a barbarous custom. But I shall wait for you in the evening, at the corner of your street, with a pistol!

Célimare [*terrified*]. Murder?

Vernouillet. Oh, I shall be acquitted. They always acquit you for jealousy.

Célimare. You're out of your mind, Vernouillet! You! My friend, my dear old friend! [*Aside.*] I must butter him up.

Vernouillet. There are only two possibilities. Either you were interested in me, or in my wife! I can't see it any other way.

Célimare. But it was you, and you alone!

Vernouillet. Then why are you neglecting me?

Célimare. Neglecting you? Why, I'd cut off my right hand for you. See here! Ask me to do something—anything!

Vernouillet. Words, words! Today you have given me final proof of how little you care.

Célimare. What do you mean?

Vernouillet [*bitterly*]. Today's my birthday.

Célimare [*aside*]. So that's it! [*Aloud, trying to take his hand.*] My dear friend, come here.

Vernouillet [*pushing him away*]. Where was your bouquet this morning?

Célimare [*aside*]. Oh, Lord!

Vernouillet. It's the first time you've forgotten it in five years.

Célimare. Forgotten it? What do you mean? I've ordered it. It's on its way.

PITOIS *enters, carrying a bouquet.* CÉLIMARE *goes over to him.*

Célimare. See? Here it is.

Vernouillet [*moved*]. Can it be true? Célimare!

Célimare [*taking the bouquet and offering it to* VER-NOUILLET]. Dearest friend, allow me . . .

Pitois [*aside*]. He's giving it to the old man.

Vernouillet [*taking the bouquet and falling into* CÉLIMARE'S *arms*]. Oh, my friend, my dear friend! White roses! How unjust I have been! But all the same, when I think back and remember that you never left my wife's side . . .

Célimare [*aside*]. Here we go again!

Vernouillet. There was one day in particular—— [*Suddenly clutching at the small of his back.*] Ohh!

Célimare. What is it?

Vernouillet [*in great pain*]. It's my kidney trouble.

Célimare. Oh, you poor fellow! Let me help you. [*Rubs his back.*] See? Just like old times, just like old times.

Pitois [*aside*]. He's giving him a rubdown.

Vernouillet [*letting* CÉLIMARE *massage him*]. Oh, that helps a lot!

Célimare [*aside, rubbing him*]. Condemned to an eternity of back-rubbing!

EMMA, COLOMBOT, and MADAME COLOMBOT *enter and reel back in astonishment.*

All. Look!

Colombot. What in the world is he doing?

Madame Colombot. He's rubbing that man's back.

Vernouillet [*to* CÉLIMARE]. Thanks, that's much better. [*Seeing* EMMA, *shows her the bouquet.*] Look, madame, at this beautiful bouquet. Your husband gave it to me.

Emma, Colombot, Madame Colombot. What?

Célimare [*embarrassed*]. Yes. You know, just a little bouquet.

Vernouillet. You see, today's my birthday.

Célimare [*embarrassed*]. Oh, it's really only his saint's day. Saint Vernouillet.

Vernouillet. But you never gave me such a magnificent bouquet before.

Emma. It isn't the first one?

Vernouillet. He gives me one every year, on my birthday. [*Goes upstage, to* PITOIS.] Here, my boy, put it in water. [PITOIS *takes it and goes out.*]

Emma [*in a low voice, to her mother*]. What can it all mean?

Colombot [*in a low voice*]. If that's the way he intends to get rid of him . . .

Vernouillet [*coming downstage to them. To* CÉLIMARE]. You gave me a surprise. Now I shall give you one. I had myself photographed. [*Takes some small mounted portraits of himself out of his pocket.*] And I didn't forget the ladies. There's one for each of you.

Madame Colombot [*coldly*]. You're too kind.

Vernouillet [*offering a photograph to* COLOMBOT]. Here. Wait a minute—I want to autograph it, personally.

Célimare. Please do. All of them. You can do it in my study. [*Shows him to the door, right.*]

Vernouillet [*going out right*]. Don't bother! I know my way around here. [*Enters the study.*]

Madame Colombot. And what is the meaning of this, my son?

Colombot. I thought you were going to get rid of him.

Emma. And instead you give him a bouquet.

Célimare. For his birthday!

Madame Colombot. Worse yet, you go and rub his back for him—for his birthday!

Colombot. Do you owe him money?

Célimare. Me? [*Aside.*] What an idea! [*Aloud.*] It's more than that. He once did me a great favor—the sort of favor that can never be forgotten.

Madame Colombot [*quickly*]. What?

Colombot. What?

Emma. What?

Célimare. Wait, I'll tell you! [*Aside.*] I've got to think. [*Aloud.*] It all happened one evening; no, one day. It was very hot. I'd been taking a few swimming lessons. Suddenly my foot caught in some nets on the bottom.

All. Good heavens!

Célimare. I pulled and I pulled but I couldn't get free. I began to realize the seriousness of my situation. "I'm too young to die!" I yelled. [*Correcting himself.*] I mean I thought. Naturally, one can't yell for help under water.

Colombot [*naïvely*]. How true.

Célimare. There I was, when a man—why should I hesitate to name him?—Vernouillet, the intrepid Vernouillet, threw himself into the waves.

Emma. What?

Célimare. Even though he had just had dinner—a significant detail—in he plunged! He swam over to me and shook my hand, saying to me, "Courage, Célimare, do not give up hope!"

Colombot. Underwater?

Célimare. His look seemed to say to me, "Courage, Célimare!" Then, with a strength which you would not think he possessed, he cut the net.

Madame Colombot. With what?

Célimare. With a knife. [*Catching himself.*] With his finger-nails! With his teeth! At such moments one can't be choosy. Well, in short, he grabbed me by the arm and brought me to the surface, while the crowd cheered wildly.

Madame Colombot. How breathtaking!

Colombot. Magnificent!

Emma. What a brave man!

Colombot. He must be a very accomplished diver.

Célimare. Oh, he can stay twenty-two minutes underwater without food or drink.

Colombot. Hmm. That reminds me. While I was fishing near the Pont-Neuf eight days ago my watch fell into the water. He might be able to dive in and get it back.

Célimare. Oh, he can do anything. And this is the man you begrudged my giving a miserable bunch of flowers to on his birthday.

Madame Colombot. But how could we have known?

Célimare. The man you wish to banish from my home. No! Accuse me! Blame me! There is one quality I lack—the courage to be ungrateful.

Colombot [*deeply moved*]. Good, good, my son.

Madame Colombot. Heavens! If only we had known. Why didn't you tell us before?

Célimare. Vernouillet hates to have people talk about it. It upsets him—he possesses the humility of the true underwater diver.

Colombot. Enough said. We will not breathe a word of it to him.

PITOIS *enters.*

Pitois [*to* CÉLIMARE]. Sir!

Célimare. What?

Pitois. Some cooks want to speak to you.

Emma. The ones Monsieur Bocardon spoke of.

Célimare. Lord, won't these two leeches ever let me alone?

Colombot. Leeches?

Célimare. Yes! I know what I'm saying. [*To* Pitois.] Tell them I'm not at home.

Madame Colombot. But your friend asked you to see them. How can you refuse?

Emma. It would be most unkind.

Célimare. It would? Well, I'll go. [*Aside.*] I'll see if I can't give them some bad advice. [*Goes out.*]

Madame Colombot [*to* Emma]. Your husband certainly isn't very obliging.

Emma [*seeing* Vernouillet *return*]. Oh, Monsieur Vernouillet!

Colombot [*aside*]. Brave heart!

Vernouillet [*holding the photographs in his hand*]. Dear ladies, allow me. They're a bit messy but the pen wasn't any good.

Madame Colombot [*graciously*]. All we care about is your picture.

Emma. I shall paste it in the front of my album.

Vernouillet [*to* Emma]. Here's the dedication to you. [*Reading.*] "To the one who is destined to make Célimare forever happy."

Colombot [*aside*]. Not bad.

Vernouillet. That's prose, you know.

Emma [*smiling*]. So I gather.

Vernouillet [*to* Madame Colombot]. Now here's some poetry. [*Reading.*] "To you in whom all virtues do transpire . . ." [*Stops.*]

Colombot. Well?

Vernouillet. I finished only one line. I'm waiting for the next to come. Don't worry, I'll find it.

Madame Colombot [*kindly*]. You mustn't tire yourself.

Vernouillet [*giving a photograph to* Colombot]. Here's yours.

Colombot [*reading*]. "To the father of the angel and the husband of the Graces."

Vernouillet [*to* Emma]. The angel, that's you, and the Graces is madame. [*Points to* Madame Colombot.]

Madame Colombot [*flattered*]. How gallant!

Colombot [*looking at the picture*]. It's a very good likeness. You ought to have had it taken in a bathing suit.

Emma. Oh, papa!

Madame Colombot. Very true.

Vernouillet [*astonished*]. But what for?

Colombot. As a diver.

Vernouillet [*astonished*]. As a diver?

Madame Colombot. We know everything!

Colombot [*going over to him*]. Do you think you could find a watch at the bottom of the Seine?

Madame Colombot. That shouldn't be any more difficult than bringing up a man.

Vernouillet. Well, a man is a bit bigger, generally speaking——

Emma. How ever can you go so long without breathing?

Vernouillet. Breathing? Why, I breathe whenever I want to. [*Inhales.*]

Colombot. But you can't when you're diving underwater.

Vernouillet. When I'm diving underwater?

Colombot. Like the time you fished up Célimare.

Madame Colombot. When he was drowning.

Vernouillet. But I don't even know how to swim!

All. What? [*All move forward slightly.*]

Emma [*in a low voice*]. How very strange.

Madame Colombot. But I don't understand.

Colombot [*aside*]. He doesn't want anyone to know. He possesses the humility of the true underwater diver.

Vernouillet [*has seated himself left. Aside*]. "To you in whom all virtues do transpire." [*Counts the measure on his fingers.*]

CÉLIMARE *enters upstage back.*

Célimare [*shouting to someone offstage*]. Not another one! Get along with you!

Madame Colombot and *Colombot.* What's the matter?

Célimare. The cooks! We differed on the question of how many bottles of wine a week they'd get. They wanted eight.

Madame Colombot. Too many.

Célimare. Sheer alcoholism! I offered them three.

Colombot [*to* CÉLIMARE, *pointing to* VERNOUILLET]. See here, he says he can't even swim.

Célimare. Who does?

Colombot. Him.

Célimare [*changing the subject*]. Do you know how much eight bottles a week would amount to per year? Four hundred and sixteen!

Colombot. But——

Célimare. It's disgusting! [*Walks away from him. The noise of a carriage is heard.*]

Madame Colombot [*going upstage*]. A carriage!

Emma [*going upstage*]. It must be Monsieur Bocardon and his wife.

Célimare [*aside*]. I only hope she's looked in the hat.

Madame Colombot. I'm not ready yet. I'll go get my wrap. [*Starts off.*]

Emma. And my bracelets!

Madame Colombot. Where are they?

Emma. With the wedding presents.

Madame Colombot. Please ask Madame Bocardon to wait. I'll be right back. [*Goes out right.*]

Célimare [*aside*]. They're taking a long time to get up the stairs. That means there's a woman.

PITOIS *enters.* BOCARDON *follows him.*

Pitois. Monsieur Bocardon.

Célimare [*relieved, aside*]. He's alone.

Emma [*to* BOCARDON]. But where's your wife?

Bocardon. I'm terribly chagrined. We were just about to leave, my wife and I; in fact my wife had just handed me my hat when—bang!—her neuralgia came back.

Colombot. Oh, poor lady.

Emma. How unfortunate!

Célimare. And we were going to have such a gay old time. [*Aside.*] She took the Tuileries.

Bocardon. I offered to stay and keep her company, but she refused.

Célimare. Naturally.

Bocardon. What?

Célimare. Nothing.

Emma. It's really a shame. Isn't she going to do something about it?

Bocardon. Yes. I'm determined to take her to a doctor. [*To* CÉLIMARE.] What about tomorrow?

Célimare. What? [*Aside.*] Now he's dragging me into consultations.

Bocardon. Here are our tickets. It's a very good box.

Vernouillet [*to himself*]. I have a second line, but it's got four feet too many.

MADAME COLOMBOT *enters, with her hat on, carrying the little coffer.*

Madame Colombot [*to* EMMA]. My dear child, your bracelets have disappeared! I've searched high and low, and all I can find is this box.

Célimare [*aside, recognizing it*]. Oh, good God! [*Aloud.*] Where did you find that?

Madame Colombot. With the wedding presents.

Colombot. I put it there. It's a surprise.

Emma [*shaking it*]. Oh, there's something in it.

Célimare [*aside*]. Héloïse's letters.

Emma. Well, where's the key?

Célimare. I don't know. [*Searching his pockets.*] I had it yesterday. [*Aside.*] It's gone. I'm saved!

Pitois [*coming forward and giving the key to* EMMA]. Here it is. [*To* CÉLIMARE.] I found it in your vest pocket this morning.

Célimare [*in a low voice, giving* PITOIS *a jab*]. Idiot! Numbskull!

Pitois. What's the matter?

Célimare [*aside*]. Right in front of Vernouillet!

Emma [*opening the coffer*]. Letters!

Célimare [*aside*]. Horrors!

Emma. It's a woman's handwriting. [*Turning one over.*] They're signed.

Célimare [*in a low voice, quickly*]. Hush! Not in front of him. [*Pointing to* VERNOUILLET.]

All. Why?

Célimare [*in a low voice*]. He's the husband! Hush! He's the husband!

Colombot and *Madame Colombot.* What?

Emma. Sir, how could you?

Bocardon [*in a low voice to* EMMA]. Didn't you know? I did.

Vernouillet [*rising, paper in hand*]. I have it!

Emma [*very upset*]. Monsieur Vernouillet, I must speak to you. I must tell you something about your *closest* friend——

Célimare [*in a low voice*]. Emma!

Madame Colombot [*same way*]. Don't you dare . . .

Emma [*going quickly over to* VERNOUILLET]. Monsieur Vernouillet . . .

Vernouillet. Speak, lovely lady.

Emma [*aside*]. I can't. Poor man! [*Aloud.*] My husband, your very good friend——

Vernouillet. How well I know it!

Emma. It would give him great pleasure if you would come to the concert with us. There's an extra place.

All. What?

Bocardon [*aside*]. Inviting him to come. What a sweet little thing!

Vernouillet. I assure you, I would be only too glad, but, in my position—it's too soon. Next month, maybe.

Célimare. See? He really can't come. Let's go.

Emma [*in a low voice, to* CÉLIMARE]. In that case, sir, neither can you!

Célimare [*in a loud voice*]. Why not?

Emma [*in a low voice, ironically*]. It's too soon.

Célimare [*in a low voice*]. My dear, if you please——

Emma [*to* VERNOUILLET]. In that case, Monsieur Célimare will stay behind and keep you company.

Célimare. Me?

Vernouillet. Oh, he's too good. I could never allow it.

Emma [*with determination*]. My husband knows his duty. He will stay.

Célimare [*in a low voice*]. But——

Emma [*in a low voice, earnestly*]. Sir, the only thing you lack is the courage to be ungrateful! I forbid you to accompany me. [*She goes upstage with* COLOMBOT *and* MADAME COLOMBOT.]

Célimare [*aside, downstage*]. Fine! We're quarreling already!

Vernouillet [*to* CÉLIMARE]. If you like, we could play a little game of dominoes. Just like in the old days.

Bocardon. Play a little game?

Vernouillet [*going off left*]. I'll get the table.

Emma [*upstage*]. Are you coming, Monsieur Bocardon?

Bocardon [*hesitating*]. It's just that . . . Italian singers . . . [*Aside.*] A game! [*Aloud.*] My wife is still suffering. Perhaps I shouldn't go either. I'll get the table! [*Goes off left.*]

Célimare [*going upstage, to* EMMA]. Emma, look here!

Emma. Please let me alone!

Madame Colombot. Oh, my son . . .

Bocardon and Vernouillet [*entering*]. Here's the table. [*They place it in the middle of the stage.*]

PITOIS *comes in carrying coats and wraps.*

Célimare [*coming back downstage, aside*]. Good lord, am I going to have to drag that two-wheeled donkey cart after me all my life?

EMMA, MADAME COLOMBOT *and* COLOMBOT *get ready to leave.*

Pitois *stays upstage left.* Vernouillet *and* Bocardon *set up the table.* Célimare *goes upstage to* Emma, *as if he might get out of the game of dominoes.*

To the tune of the rondo "Après avoir pris à droite," the three gamesters sing.

ROUNDELAY

Bocardon.	Célimare is wed.
Vernouillet.	Precisely!
	And I rather like his wife.
Bocardon.	Things are really going nicely.
Vernouillet.	We'll play dominoes for life.
Célimare.	Things were really going nicely
	And I rather like my wife.
	That's not what I want precisely—
	Playing dominoes for life.
Emma.	Were you acting really nicely
	When you wooed another's wife?
	No! My sentence is precisely:
	You'll play dominoes for life.
Bocardon.	Any man who's married nicely
	And who rather likes his wife
	What is his ideal precisely?
Vernouillet.	Playing dominoes for life.
Célimare.	I don't find it goes so nicely
	Playing dominoes for life
	And the reason is precisely
	That I rather like my wife.

Vernouillet [*taking him by the arm*]. Let's start.
Bocardon [*forcing him to sit down*]. Here's your place.
Célimare [*sitting down*]. Hurrah! [*Aside.*] Sentenced to three solid hours of dominoes. [Vernouillet *arranges the dominoes.*] I shall sulk the whole time!

Emma, Colombot, *and* Madame Colombot *go out upstage center.* Célimare *tries to get up and follow, but* Bocardon *and* Vernouillet *force him to stay in his chair. The music continues until the curtain falls.*

ACT THREE

The elegant sitting room of a country house. Three French doors, with blinds, open upstage center onto a garden. There

*are doors upstage and downstage in both the left and right
walls. A sewing table left with chairs and footstools; armchairs etc. stage right. Potted plants in the left and right
upstage corners.* COLOMBOT *and* MADAME COLOMBOT *enter left.*

COLOMBOT. Well, I really ate a good lunch!

Madame Colombot. You ate like a pig!

Colombot. And how! It's the country air. What a good idea
of Célimare's—to rent this house!

Madame Colombot. It certainly didn't take long. In five
minutes the whole thing was settled.

Colombot. A couple of hours later we were off—with two
moving vans.

Madame Colombot. And here we are, comfortably settled
at Auteuil for the past eight days.

Colombot. Right in the middle of a honeymoon. They're
cooing like doves. Reminds me of the time when we——

Madame Colombot. Hush now! Really!

Colombot. All right. Where's the newspaper?

Madame Colombot [*taking it from the table*]. The *Gazette*?
Here it is.

Colombot. Not even opened yet. Célimare is so in love that
he doesn't even have time to unwrap his newspaper. It reminds me of the time when we were first married and I sat
one night reading that same newspaper. You got so sore you
threw it in the fire, and then we——

Madame Colombot. Will you be quiet! I don't know what's
got into you today.

Colombot [*laughing*]. It's the country air.

EMMA *enters from the garden, carrying a bunch of flowers.*

Emma. Look at these lovely flowers, Mama! I found them
right in our garden

Madame Colombot [*taking the bouquet*]. How pretty!
Where is your husband?

Emma. He's finishing his coffee, near the fishpond. I just
left him.

Colombot. Then we won't have long to wait for him. [*Seeing* CÉLIMARE, *who enters from the garden.*] Here he is.

Célimare [*carrying his cup of coffee*]. What happened,
darling? Why did you leave me?

Emma. Well, you were taking so long to finish your coffee.

Célimare [*amorously*]. I was taking so long because I was
looking at you.

Colombot [*aside*]. Amazing how much life there is in the old boy!

Célimare. I swallow a mouthful—like this—then I take a look at you—like this—and it doesn't taste so sweet any more.

Emma. Don't be silly, you!

Célimare [*aside*]. She's a lot less formal now!

Colombot [*in a low voice to his wife*]. What turtledoves! It reminds me——

Madame Colombot [*irritated*]. Monsieur Colombot, that is quite enough of that!

Emma. What are we going to do today?

Célimare. Well, let's see. What about a game of cards?

Colombot. Oh, no! Let's take a walk.

Célimare. Then I propose that we take our walk in a boat.

Emma. Oh, good! A boat ride!

Célimare. We'll take two. One for papa and mama Colombot, and the other——

Madame Colombot. Why two?

Célimare. Just like Venice. Everyone has his own gondola. And you can go first.

Colombot. Oh, no! It will be much nicer if we're all together. We'll go down the Seine to Saint-Cloud.

Emma. That sounds lovely.

Célimare. Agreed! We hoist anchor at two o'clock. [*Taking a piece of bread out of his pocket.*] Oh, look, Father! A bit of bread for your goldfish.

Colombot. I've got my pockets full already, but, never mind, we'll give them a feast.

Célimare. Are you making a study of goldfish?

Colombot. They're very interesting creatures. They know me by sight.

Emma. They do?

Colombot [*speaking to the ladies*]. They come up when they see me and give me the sweetest looks. When I've got them tamed we'll catch them in a net and eat them all up.

Emma. Oh, Papa!

Madame Colombot. Are goldfish edible?

Colombot. Why not? You eat shrimp, don't you? [*To his wife.*] Come along with me. Come along and gaze into their sweet little eyes.

Madame Colombot [*giving him her arm, coyly*]. Well, each to his own sport. [*They go out into the garden.*]

Célimare. Thank God they're gone. At last we can be alone.

Emma [*sitting down*]. It seems to me you manage that a great deal.

Célimare. I like this house better every day. A charming garden, a rockery, and a maze. Wouldn't you like a little stroll in the maze?

Emma. No!

Célimare. You don't know yet, but I'm thinking of adding something to our garden.

Emma. Adding what?

Célimare. Oh, a little something. An aviary. I've consulted an architect.

Emma. Whatever are you going to do with an aviary?

Célimare. It's just a piece of whimsy—a superstition, you might say. I'm going to fill it with turtledoves.

Emma [*rising*]. What a silly idea!

Célimare [*following her*]. Your father has his goldfish. Why shouldn't I have my doves? Each age has its little vice.

Emma. I think you're going mad.

Célimare [*taking her arm*]. I have good reason to. I'm so happy here. Far from the noise and the crowds——

Emma [*smiling*]. Far from Monsieur Vernouillet, you mean.

Célimare [*half in reproach*]. Oh, Emma, you naughty girl! You promised never to mention that again.

Emma. I did?

Célimare. Yes! You forgave me. You forgave me last Monday.

Emma [*lowering her eyes*]. I may have forgiven you but I shall always hold it against you. Such conduct——

Célimare. In the first place, I hadn't met you yet. And anyhow I was young. I was swept off my feet. But it was my only mistake, my only crime, I should say.

Emma. But can I really believe you, sir?

Célimare. I've already sworn to it on the photograph of your mother. Do you want me to start over again?

Emma. There's no need.

Célimare. Anyway, you can be sure that a young man who's been burned once isn't likely to try it again.

Emma. I can well believe it. You know, I had the funniest dream last night.

Célimare. About me?

Emma. Not exactly. I dreamed that Monsieur Vernouillet turned up here with a box of dominoes in his hand.

Célimare. Indeed! I should be very surprised if he did.

Emma. Why?

Célimare. I'll tell you what I wrote him before we left. "Dear Friend: I had a violent attack of fever last night."

Emma. Liar!

Célimare. "My doctor has ordered me to get a change of air, so I am leaving for the country. I beg you to come and visit me as soon as you can."

Emma. Then he must be on his way!

Célimare. No. [*Laughing.*] I forgot to include my address.

Emma [*laughing*]. What?

Célimare. And since our doorman in Paris doesn't know it either, he can go fish for it!

Emma. And your other friend, Monsieur Bocardon?

Célimare. He got the same little bulletin.

Emma. Oh! Why?

Célimare. I've always treated them as equals.

PITOIS *enters.*

Pitois. Sir, you have a visitor.

Emma. A visitor?

Célimare. Some country neighbor, I suppose. I'm not at home.

Pitois [*in a low voice, to* CÉLIMARE]. Sir, it's your rheumatism. Number One.

Célimare. Vernouillet!

Emma. Monsieur Vernouillet!

Célimare. But, see here! It's impossible!

Pitois [*seeing* VERNOUILLET, *who comes in*]. Well, see for yourself.

Vernouillet [*carrying a suitcase and a small bag, running to* CÉLIMARE *and embracing him*]. Oh, my friend, my friend!

Célimare. Good old Vernouillet! [*Aside.*] Where the devil did he come from?

Vernouillet. But you shouldn't be up. That's very foolish. And how did you ever catch such a terrible fever?

Célimare. Oh, you know! I wasn't thinking of anything in particular when all of a sudden—[*Shivering.*]—Brrr!

Vernouillet. You're flushed. It's the crisis! You've got to go to bed.

Célimare. If you don't mind——

Emma [*mocking him*]. My dear, would you like me to turn the sheets down?

Célimare [*aside*]. She's teasing me. [*Aloud.*] I feel much better now, thank you; quite all right.

Vernouillet. Lucky I got here. I shall keep a constant watch over you, since madame obviously knows nothing about these things. I'll sleep by your bed.

Célimare [*jumps*]. Oh, no you won't!

Vernouillet [*energetically*]. I've got a little medical kit in my suitcase—emetics, milk of magnesia, arnica, court plaster. We'll give you the full treatment.

Célimare. Oh, indeed we shall!

Vernouillet. In the meantime I'll make you a little herb tea with honey, lettuce, and an apple cut in quarters.

Célimare. Why in quarters?

Vernouillet. It was my wife's favorite prescription. [*Sighs.*] Poor Héloïse.

Célimare [*trying to silence him*]. Shh, shh, shh.

Vernouillet. What's the matter? Are you in pain?

Célimare. No!

Vernouillet. I'm sure you must hold it against me for not coming sooner.

Célimare. Me? Oh, you misjudge me!

Vernouillet. But it wasn't my fault. Your letter said, "Come and visit me as soon as you can," but you forgot to include your address.

Célimare. How could I?

Emma. How thoughtless!

Vernouillet. For eight days I searched for you. Then an inspiration came to me, straight from the heart. I remembered that you subscribe to the *Gazette.*

Célimare. Well?

Vernouillet. I said to myself, "He must be having it sent to the country." So I went directly to the newspaper office. They wouldn't give me your address without a letter from you. I explained to them that I couldn't very well get a letter from you unless I had your address. So they slammed the window in my face.

Célimare [*aside*]. What an excellent newspaper! I must renew my subscription.

Vernouillet. I refused to be intimidated. I demanded to see the editor-in-chief on an important matter. He saw me. I explained what I wanted and he sent me to the managing editor, who sent me to the man in charge of out-of-town circulation, who sent me to the man in charge of suburban distribution. It took four hours. Finally I got your address—44 Fontaine Street, Auteuil. And here I am. Your subscription runs out in October.

Célimare [*shaking his hand*]. Thanks for the information. [*Aside.*] The subscription is canceled!

Vernouillet. Friendship is the mother of invention! Perseverance wins the crown!

COLOMBOT *is heard offstage.*

Colombot. Do come in, Monsieur Bocardon.

BOCARDON *appears at the door, wearing a gray hat.* COLOMBOT *and* MADAME COLOMBOT *enter behind him.*

Bocardon [*shouting offstage*]. Down, Minotaur! Down! Sit down! Sit down! Lie down! Lie down!

Emma. Monsieur Bocardon!

Célimare [*aside*]. Marvelous! We're all together again.

Bocardon [*seeing* VERNOUILLET]. Monsieur Vernouillet!

Madame Colombot. What a pleasant surprise!

Bocardon [*to* CÉLIMARE]. Well, if you aren't an absolute scatterbrain! You write, "Come and visit me," and you don't even give me your address!

Vernouillet. Same with me.

Célimare. Then how did you find it out?

Bocardon. By a miracle! Are you lucky! My wife wanted us to take a house for the summer, so I was walking through Auteuil this morning, looking to see which ones were vacant. Suddenly, at 44, my dog Minotaur got up on his hind legs—like this. I called him, but he refused to budge, and he kept giving me the strangest look—like this. So I said to myself, "Célimare must live here." Sure enough. I rang and recognized Pitois. Minotaur had smelled you out!

Célimare. Fantastic!

Madame Colombot. What a display of instinct!

Bocardon [*to* CÉLIMARE]. That dog really loves you!

Célimare [*aside*]. I'll give him a good kick if I get him alone.

Bocardon. Since I've found you, I might as well spend the day here.

Vernouillet [*aside*]. They'll tire him out.

Bocardon. I should go to Léon's and get some advice, but I'll go tomorrow.

Célimare. Don't let me hold you up, my friend.

Bocardon. No, it's just about Northern Railways. There's no hurry.

Célimare [*aside*]. The service was better in my time. As a postman, he's gone to pot.

GLENDALE COLLEGE LIBRARY

PITOIS *enters.*

Pitois. Sir, the architect is here about the aviary.

Célimare. Fine! I'll be right out.

Vernouillet. Where's my room?

Colombot [*pointing to the door right*]. In here. I'll show you.

Madame Colombot. We want you to be as comfortable as possible. [MADAME COLOMBOT *and* COLOMBOT *show* VERNOUILLET *to his room.* CÉLIMARE *goes out upstage center.*]

Bocardon [*to* EMMA]. I've just seen the most adorable house for rent—right next door. I'm waiting for Célimare so he can arrange to get it for us.

Emma [*seated right, working at some embroidery*]. Why, then, we'll be neighbors!

Bocardon [*standing behind a chair*]. Next-door neighbors. My wife can come over evenings. You two can chat while we have our little game of bezique.

Emma. How delightful it all sounds.

Bocardon. I don't mean to boast, but I can tell you'll like Ninette. She's homeloving—just like you! [*Confidentially.*] She knits.

Emma. Really?

Bocardon. The only thing I can say against her is that she's a bit timid. We never see anyone, except Léon. And that's only because I insist on it. She can't stand him.

Emma. Well, then why do you continue to see him?

Bocardon. Oh, he's a relative! The first time I bring Ninette to see you, I know she'll be trembling with fright. That's the way she is.

Emma. But it's I who should pay the first call. I've owed it to her for some time.

Bocardon. Well, if I may speak frankly, I think you ought to go see her as soon as possible.

Emma. Why?

Bocardon. Oh, for various reasons. I didn't want to say anything, but it's as plain as the nose on your face. Every time I mention Célimare to her she changes the subject to Léon, whom she can't stand. My theory is that she's a bit annoyed at your not coming to see her.

Emma [*rising*]. Oh, in that case I'll go see her today.

Bocardon. Good! This is the day she receives callers.

Emma. We were going to take a boat ride, but that can wait until tomorrow.

PITOIS *enters.*

Pitois. Sir, it's your dog.

Bocardon. Minotaur? You mean my Newfoundland?

Pitois. He's in the vestibule, chewing up a lady's gray coat.

Emma. Mama's coat!

Bocardon. Why don't you stop him?

Pitois. Because he snarled at me, sir.

Bocardon. Wait a minute! I'll tie him up somewhere. [*Goes out upstage with* PITOIS, *shouting.*] Minotaur! Minotaur!

Emma [*alone*]. Mama will love that—her new coat!

CÉLIMARE *enters.*

Célimare. I've ordered the aviary. Fifteen feet by nine. Fifteen feet of turtledoves!

Emma. My dear sir, I have some good news for you. We're going to have a couple of new neighbors.

Célimare. Really? Who?

Emma. Can't you guess? Monsieur and Madame Bocardon.

Célimare. What? Where?

Emma. Right here! They're going to rent the house right next door.

Célimare [*aside*]. He's made of glue!

Emma. It's our turn to pay them a visit.

Célimare. Oh, there's no rush about that!

Emma. But there is. I promised to go today.

Célimare. Today?

Emma. We'll take the carriage. It's only for an hour. Go get ready.

Célimare. Darling, I hate to refuse you anything, but certain reasons—reasons of a personal nature—prohibit our making this visit.

Emma. You don't seem to realize that you're going to hurt the feelings of your old friends. You're going to hurt that sweet, simple, timid Madame Bocardon.

Célimare. Her timid? Timid like a wolf!

Emma. Well, I must say, my dear, Monsieur Bocardon wasn't exaggerating when he said you didn't like his wife.

Célimare. I'll admit it, I don't. And to tell the truth, I'm not very eager for you to make her acquaintance.

Emma. Why?

Célimare. Why? Why? Because . . .

Emma. Because what?

Célimare. Because Madame Bocardon is not the kind of person you ought to see. That's why.

Emma. Why shouldn't I? She's a quiet, home-loving woman.

Célimare [*between his teeth*]. That's what her husband thinks!

Emma. Excuse me?

Célimare. I mean, I mean that Madame Bocardon is rather fast.

Emma. I don't understand.

Célimare. She has affairs!

Emma. What?

Célimare. You mustn't breathe a word—with Léon, my successor—[*Catching himself.*]—her cousin!

Emma. No! I can't believe it!

Célimare. I can tell you one thing. They're in correspondence.

Emma. I'm sure it's a malicious rumor.

Célimare. So you don't believe me? Where's the hat? [*Seeing* BOCARDON's *hat on a chair by the door.*] There it is! Good! [*To* EMMA.] What would you say if I waved my hand and suddenly produced a letter from the timid Madame Bocardon to her cousin?

Emma. You've found such a letter?

Célimare. Please be so kind as to fetch that imperturbable gray hat over there. [*Pointing.*]

Emma [*going over to get the hat*]. But I don't understand.

Célimare. Now look under the hatband. [*Stopping her.*] Wait! I should first tell you that Ninette, that Madame Ninette Bocardon, has no confidence in the postal services, which is why she prefers to slide her little communiqués, free of charge, under her husband's hatband.

Emma [*suspiciously*]. How do you know all this?

Célimare [*embarrassed*]. How? Oh, it was Léon! That chatterbox, Léon! He told me. Now go on and look.

Emma [*running her fingers under the hatband*]. I can't find anything!

Célimare. I can't believe it. [*Aside.*] He did mention Northern Railways. [*Aloud.*] The left side, the left!

Emma. Oh, yes, a note. [*Takes it out.*]

Célimare. Go on! Read it! [*Watches her open the note.*] Well?

Emma. I simply have to know——

Célimare [*quickly*]. Don't read the postscript. [*Aside.*] They're usually pretty spicy.

Emma [*reading*]. "My darling Célimare——"

Célimare [*leaping up*]. What?

Emma [*reading*]. "How silly of you to be jealous. You know I love you."

Célimare. Good God! It's last year's hat! A letter we missed!

Emma. How could you, sir? How horrible! How low!

Célimare. I can explain everything.

Emma [*weeping*]. Go away. I never want to speak to you again. I hate you!

Célimare [*taking the hat*]. You cheapskate! Why couldn't you buy a new one? [*Crushes the hat and throws it on the table.*]

Emma. One day Monsieur Vernouillet, the next Monsieur Bocardon. Have you pressed all your friends into service, sir?

Célimare. Why, what an idea!

Emma. You'd better give me a list of all these gentlemen, so I know where I stand.

Célimare. There are no more! I swear there aren't.

Emma. I suppose she's very pretty, this Madame Bocardon?

Célimare. Heavens, no! Nose like a trumpet—big lips—chin like a bucket—eyes——

Emma. Well, why ever . . . ?

Célimare. I was young—swept off my feet——

Emma. After eight days of marriage!

Célimare. But you don't understand! It's his last year's hat! Look! Think a minute! I haven't left your side. I haven't been out once. [*Taking the letter from her.*] And look at the paper! It's yellow, faded. [*Noticing the date.*] Look! December 7, 1862. She dated it! [*Kisses the paper.*] Oh, thank you, thank you!

Emma [*shocked*]. What are you doing, sir?

Célimare. I'm kissing the date! [VERNOUILLET *appears at the door, right.*] Are you convinced now?

Emma. Yes, but that doesn't alter the fact that you were Madame Bocardon's lover!

Vernouillet [*entering*]. Well, well! Poor fellow.

Célimare [*seeing* VERNOUILLET—*to* EMMA]. Hush!

Vernouillet. Please forgive me. I overheard without meaning to.

Célimare [*aside*]. Now won't the news spread! They'll be putting it in the papers next!

Vernouillet [*laughing*]. Poor Monsieur Bocardon! But you can't say he doesn't look the part.

Célimare. Vernouillet, believe me, you have no right to laugh at him! You above all!

Vernouillet. Why me above all? [BOCARDON *is heard yelling at his dog.*]

Célimare. Shhh! The husband! [CÉLIMARE *goes over and poses by the table, next to* EMMA, *who has just sat down and resumed work on her embroidery.*]

BOCARDON *enters upstage center.*

Bocardon. I've just tied up Minotaur. He wouldn't go with me because he smelled you. That dog really loves you!

Emma [*aside*]. I can't bear the sight of these men another minute.

Bocardon. Speaking of Minotaur, that reminds me of a very funny story. [*To* EMMA.] One evening I was just coming back from taking him for a walk—I take him for a walk every evening—and I happened to go into my wife's bedroom. Suddenly Minotaur sprang at the door of the wardrobe and began scratching and barking at it. I thought to myself, "It's either a rat or a thief!" and threw open the door. It was Célimare!

Célimare [*aside*]. I wish he'd go to hell with his story!

Vernouillet [*aside*]. Very awkward, him telling a story like that.

Bocardon. My wife had made him hide there to see if Minotaur would smell him out. [*Gaily.*] And, sure enough, he did!

Emma [*with distaste*]. Oh, how amusing!

Bocardon. Isn't that the funniest story!

Vernouillet [*to* BOCARDON, *in a low voice*]. Please keep quiet, sir!

Bocardon [*astonished*]. Why?

Vernouillet [*to* EMMA, *trying to distract her*]. Well, my wife had a parrot even more remarkable than his dog. Célimare loved to teach it things.

Célimare [*aside*]. Great! Here we go with the parrot!

Vernouillet. His cage was in the vestibule, and whenever he'd hear me coming in he'd shout, "Here comes the master! Here comes the master!"

Emma [*with distaste*]. How convenient!

Bocardon [*aside*]. Telling that story in front of the wife! What an idiot!

Vernouillet. Do you get it? I never had to be announced.

Bocardon [*to* Vernouillet, *in a low voice*]. Please keep quiet, sir!

Vernouillet [*astonished*]. Why?

Célimare. Have you seen the new production at the Opera?

Bocardon. No. I haven't been there since that bet of ours.

Célimare [*aside*]. Fine! The bet! Just my luck!

Emma. What bet?

Célimare. It's not worth talking about.

Bocardon. Well, madame, I'd just received a genuine Arabian burnoose from Algiers——

Célimare. And he bet that he could run up the Champs Élysées with two pots of mustard on his nose.

Bocardon. Not at all! I bet that I would sit in the orchestra of the opera wearing the burnoose.

Célimare. Oh, that was another bet.

Bocardon. I went up to the box office saying, "Mamamuth . . . karamba——"

Célimare [*trying to change the topic*]. And when he got to the Arch of Triumph, that superb monument to the glory of France——

Bocardon. If you please——

Célimare [*moving upstage*]. Shall we take a walk in the garden?

Bocardon. To cut it short—he lost!

Célimare. All right, I lost! Now, let's go look at the goldfish!

Bocardon. And since we weren't betting for nothing, he had to take Ninette to visit her aunt at Chalon-sur-Saône—way out in the country! He was furious!

Emma [*aside*]. This is unbearable!

Vernouillet [*to* Célimare]. He's a boor, an utter boor!

Bocardon [*noticing the footstool on which* Emma's *feet are resting*]. Oh, that's familiar!

Emma. What is?

Bocardon. That footstool. It's Ninette's handiwork. [Emma *gets up and kicks it violently.*] Hey!

Emma. I can't stand it any longer.

Bocardon [*to* Célimare]. What's got into her?

Célimare [*quickly, in a low voice*]. A cramp! And Vernouillet's been upsetting her.

Bocardon [*aside*]. I don't wonder.

Célimare. Get him out of here.

Bocardon [*aloud*]. Papa Vernouillet, let's have a little game of billiards.

Vernouillet. Thanks a lot, but billiards——

Célimare [*in a low voice, to* VERNOUILLET]. Go play with him! He's upsetting my wife.

Vernouillet [*aside*]. I don't wonder.

Célimare. Get him out of here!

Vernouillet. All right, let's go! But no playing for money.

Célimare. Just for honor.

Vernouillet [*smiling*]. Yes! For honor.

Bocardon [*smiling*]. Yes! For honor! [*They go out, right.*]

Emma. At last! They're gone.

Célimare. Yes, they did get a bit—tiresome.

Emma. Tiresome? You mean gruesome! With all their stories! I had to go through a whole hour of your little exploits.

Célimare. Emma, see here!

Emma. It's intolerable. The least you could do is spare me the sight of your—of these gentlemen.

Célimare. But I don't want them around any more than you do.

Emma. Well, get rid of them!

Célimare. How?

Emma. That's your business. All I know is that I don't want to see any more of them! If they stay, I go!

Célimare. But——

Emma. Them or me—choose! [*She leaves, left.*]

Célimare. Choose? Heaven knows I choose my wife, but what can I do? If I throw Vernouillet out, his suspicions are sure to come back, and he's got those grand ideas about using pistols. And I really can't blame the fellow. [*Smiling.*] After all, he was very hospitable to me for five years.

PITOIS *enters.*

Pitois. Sir!

Célimare. What?

Pitois. The dog chewed the rope in two and is now tearing up the bushes.

Célimare. What do you want me to do about it?

Pitois. That's how you pay for your wild oats. You get saddled with dogs you don't even have the right to kick out. It's divine retribution.

Célimare. Will you take your moralizing and get out of here!

Pitois. Since he's privileged to tear up the garden—let him tear up the garden!

COLOMBOT *enters, left.*

Colombot. My son, I must talk to you.

Célimare [*to* PITOIS]. Get out! [PITOIS *leaves.*] What's the matter, father?

Colombot. Sir, I have just seen my daughter, and she has told me everything. It's disgusting! Having a past is bad enough, but having two of them! Why, you seem to have made a profession of it.

Célimare. Excuse me, father, but my past has nothing to do with my wife.

Colombot. Maybe so, but there's no reason to drag it into your home life! All those revolting stories about dogs and parrots! Outrageous!

Célimare. What can I do?

Colombot. I'm just warning you that the ladies are packing their bags.

Célimare. My wife, too?

Colombot [*in a wheedling voice*]. I trust you'll permit my daughter to take along the jewelry she received as a present.

Célimare. Oh, all of it! Anything, so long as she stays!

Colombot. How can she take them with her if she stays?

Célimare. But I don't want her to leave!

Colombot. She has sent you an ultimatum: If within the next ten minutes you haven't got rid of those two . . .

Célimare. Go ahead! Say it!

Colombot [*proudly*]. No, sir, I shall not utter that word. Your two pensioners, then we shall leave!

Célimare. But how? What can I tell them?

Colombot. Tell them the truth!

Célimare. Oh, sure! While we're having dinner! With dessert! You're crazy, father!

Colombot. I don't give a hoot about those two people. If you don't want to tell them, I will.

Célimare [*quickly*]. No!

Colombot. Just as you like. But you have no right to make my daughter suffer for your sins, and as soon as our bags are packed we're leaving!

BOCARDON *and* VERNOUILLET *enter as the last words are spoken.*

Vernouillet. Bags?

Bocardon. Who's leaving?

Célimare [*in a low voice, to* COLOMBOT]. Wait, I've got it! [*Aloud.*] My friends, I'm terribly sorry but we shall have to part.

Vernouillet. Part?

Bocardon. Oh, never!

Célimare [*clasping their hands*]. Oh, thank you, thank you for those kind words. But I've just seen my doctor. He discovered that there was something wrong with my respiratory tract.

Vernouillet and Bocardon. Your lungs?

Célimare. Not exactly. Just a small bronchial adhesion. He's ordered me to spend a few months beneath the blue skies of Italy—in Venice!

Colombot [*aside*]. Very clever!

Vernouillet. Oh, my poor friend!

Bocardon. What a blow!

Vernouillet. But I'm worried. Who's going to take care of you?

Célimare. My wife.

Vernouillet. What does she know about it? Look! I happen to be free now. It's my vacation. I'll go along with you.

Colombot. What?

Célimare [*aside*]. He's like a vise!

Bocardon. I've got a great idea! Ninette's been hounding me for ages to visit Italy. So, instead of renting a house in the country, we'll come with you!

Célimare [*aside*]. I give up. They're unshakeable! [*Moves upstage, dejected.*]

Colombot [*determinedly*]. Now see here! Things have gone quite far enough! Since Célimare doesn't have the courage to confess his sins, I'll do it for him!

All. What?

Célimare [*comes quickly over to* COLOMBOT *and interrupts*]. No! Let me tell them!

All. What?

Célimare [*aside*]. I've got them now. [*Aloud, to* VERNOUILLET *and* BOCARDON.] My friends, I shall indeed confess all. This trip I've been telling you about isn't just a trip. It's a flight—an escape!

All. What?

Célimare. I am ruined! Bankrupt! Hunted down! My credit has run out——

Colombot. What's that?

Célimare [*in a low voice, to* COLOMBOT]. Shut up! You don't understand anything! [*To the others.*] To put it bluntly, I owe nine hundred seventy-four thousand francs, not counting legal fees!

Bocardon and *Vernouillet* [*staggering back*]. Heavens!

Célimare. Don't worry! I shall not ask you to make it up!

Vernouillet [*clasping his hand*]. Oh, my poor friend!

Bocardon [*taking his other hand*]. My brave friend!

Célimare. Thank you, thank you, for those kind words. But I shall recoup my losses. I have wind of a fantastic deal —a way of making zinc out of clay. It's a deep secret. Don't breathe a word!

Bocardon. Oh . . .

Vernouillet. Don't worry.

Célimare. And here is where I need every proof of your friendship.

Vernouillet [*taking hold of his hand*]. Never doubt me!

Bocardon [*taking hold of the other hand*]. I am yours till the death!

Célimare. Thank you, thank you for these kind words. I need one hundred thousand francs! [BOCARDON *and* VERNOUILLET *begin to gently disengage their hands. Noticing this, aside.*] Here we go! [*Aloud.*] I might have raised the money from countless other sources, but you would never have forgiven me.

Bocardon and *Vernouillet* [*feebly*]. Oh, no . . .

Célimare [*aside*]. Their grip on me is loosening. [*Aloud.*] So I have divided the sum equally between you—fifty thousand francs each. That's to avoid jealousy.

Vernouillet [*embarrassed*]. Naturally, an old friend like you . . . [*Takes his hand away.*]

Bocardon [*in the same tone*]. Who is plunged into misfortune . . . Our duty is clear. [*Takes his hand away and moves upstage.*]

Célimare. Curse it all!

Colombot [*in a low voice, to* CÉLIMARE]. You'll see! They'll give you the money.

Célimare [*in a low voice*]. If they do, I'll treasure them for life. [*Aloud.*] At any rate, I'm in no hurry. Just so long as I get the money by five o'clock. [*Takes out his watch.*] It's three now.

Vernouillet [*taking out his watch*]. Two thirty! You're fast.

Bocardon [*taking out his watch*]. I've got a quarter past.

Colombot [*taking out his watch*]. Ten after three!

Célimare. Well, it doesn't matter.

Vernouillet [*sharply*]. What do you mean, "It doesn't matter"? Do you think your watch is the only one that keeps correct time?

Bocardon [*sharply*]. Always has to have it his way! It becomes very boring at times!

Colombot [*astonished*]. What's got into them?

Célimare [*aside*]. Notice that I'm not saying a word.

Vernouillet. This gentleman appears to be extremely fond of imposing his views on other people.

Bocardon. He likes to play the high and mighty. Well, I maintain that it is two-fifteen.

Vernouillet [*to* CÉLIMARE]. Why don't you come out with it and say that my watch is a piece of junk?

Bocardon [*bursting out*]. A piece of junk? My mother's watch?

Vernouillet. Now he's insulting our mothers.

Célimare [*aside*]. Notice that I'm not saying a word!

Vernouillet [*going upstage toward the door*]. Sir, I do not take offense easily, but there are certain things . . .

Bocardon [*also going upstage*]. . . . which a man of honor . . .

Vernouillet. . . . cannot tolerate . . .

Bocardon. . . . without relinquishing his self-esteem.

Vernouillet. And if this is a subtle way of telling us that our presence is unwelcome . . .

Bocardon [*to* VERNOUILLET, *bursting out*]. Why he's as good as shown us the door!

Vernouillet [*pompously*]. The door!

Bocardon. Sir, let us leave. [*They step toward the door.*]

Célimare [*aside*]. Notice that . . .

Vernouillet [*at the door*]. I had hardly foreseen that our relationship would be terminated in such a painful manner.

Bocardon [*also at the door*]. Nor I, I confess. Come, let's go. I've suffered quite enough as it is.

Vernouillet. Ah, Friendship! [*Both leave upstage center as* EMMA *and* MADAME COLOMBOT *enter left.* CÉLIMARE *and* COLOMBOT *break into a dance.*]

Madame Colombot. What are they dancing for?

Emma. Have they gone?

Célimare. For good!

Madame Colombot. But how did you manage it? Such warm friends!

Célimare. I treated them to a cold shower.

Emma and *Madame Colombot.* Cold shower?

Célimare. It's all very simple. I asked them to lend me money!

Colombot. The blight of true friendship!

Emma. Is that all?

Célimare. There is one cardinal principle of friendship. You may ask anything of a friend, take anything from a friend—[*Aside.*]—even his wife—[*Aloud.*] but you must never touch his purse!

PITOIS *enters.*

Pitois. Sir, the dog's run off with your raincoat.

Madame Colombot. Mercy, run after it!

Emma. Goodness, no! They might come back.

Célimare. Anyway, why should I get angry if they do take something of mine? It makes things even.

Pitois [*aside*]. Honestly, he makes me blush!

Célimare. And if ever I'm attracted to a married woman again . . .

Emma. What was that, sir?

Célimare [*catching himself*]. I mean if ever I should have a son—— [*Watching* EMMA, *who lowers her eyes.*] What a good idea!

Colombot and *Madame Colombot.* Tsk, tsk, tsk!

Célimare. When he makes his entrance into the world, I shall say to him: [*Pretending that he is holding a baby in his arms and patting it.*] "Young man, keep away from married women! If you happen to sow a few wild oats, I won't scold you, but hands off married women! At least until they're widows!"

He sings to the tune of "Duetto du Notaire." EMMA *echoes his words, and all join in the chorus, even* BOCARDON *and* VERNOUILLET, *who return for the purpose.*

CRADLE SONG

I

A man should not
  Woo married women
A man should not
  Love ladies who are wed
Their husbands hot-
  -ly will do him in:

So take, my son, a single girl instead.
(And if your heart excited
To someone's wife is plighted
Wait, wait, my son, at least until she's widowèd.)
[*Rocking the imaginary child in his arms.*]
Wait, wait! Wait, wait!
Don't look pale, little male,
    But keep off married women.
    If you find she is wed
    Take a single girl instead.

Chorus

Ev'ry pale little male
    Should keep off married women
    For their men will do him in
Even though they land in jail.
    If you should find that she is wed
    Just take a single girl instead.

2

A man should not
    Live just for money
For he was not
    Created cold as ice
We need a spot
    Of friendship, sonny,
    Although like other things it has its price.
(Dear audience, we'll miss you,
In friendship's name we kiss you.
    Although, of course, like other things it has its price.)
[*Pretending to pass the hat round.*]
You agree? You agree?
[*Again addressing the "baby."*]
Ev'ry day let us pray
    Not to live just for money.
    We are not cold as ice
    Although all things have their price.

Chorus

Ev'ry day let us pray
    Not to live just for money
    You'll have friends, little sonny,
They will help you on your way
    For men are not as cold as ice.
    However, all things have their price.

Let's Get a Divorce!

by

VICTORIEN SARDOU and ÉMILE DE NAJAC

English version by Angela and Robert Goldsby

Copyright © 1958 by Angela and Robert Goldsby.

CHARACTERS

HENRI DES PRUNELLES, *a rich property owner, aged 40 to 45 years*

ADHÉMAR DE GRATIGNAN, *a government forester, aged 25 to 30 years*

CLAVIGNAC, *40 to 45 years*

BAFOURDIN

POLICE OFFICER

BASTIEN, *a manservant*

JOSEPH, *the headwaiter*

CYPRIENNE, *wife of* DES PRUNELLES, *25 years*

MADAME DE BRIONNE, *a young widow*

MADAME DE VALFONTAINE

MADEMOISELLE DE LUSIGNAN, *an old maid*

JOSÉPHA, *a lady's maid*

TWO WAITERS, A CARETAKER, TWO POLICEMEN, AND A MESSENGER

PLACE—REIMS.
TIME—1880.

Let's Get a Divorce!

ACT ONE

*The scene is a very elegant little winter garden, half draw-
ing room, half conservatory. The entire right side, looking
toward the garden, is frosted glass and decorated with climbing plants. A door gives into the garden down right, and
upstage of this there is a window with a practical green lattice
blind. At the beginning of the act, the blind is raised, as are
all the other blinds along this right wall. Down left is the
door to* CYPRIENNE'S *room. Upstage of her door is a mantelpiece; beyond this is the door to the dining room. At the rear,
through a large archway, can be seen the vestibule, which
leads to the main entrance of the house, offstage left, and to*
DES PRUNELLES' *study, offstage right. A richly carved stair-
way leads to the second floor. Everywhere there are pictures,
cut glass vases, knickknacks, figurines, Chinese lanterns, etc.
The furniture is elegant, and of every sort. There are plants,
flowers, palm trees, basins, etc. Left of center is an oval table.
To the left of this is an armchair. A wing chair is between
the table and the armchair. Behind the table is a large sofa.
At the right of the table is another wing chair and a little
farther right a "pouf." Under the table is a seat without a back.
Stage right is a large armchair against the wall. In front of
the window is a work table. On the center table are pen, inkwell, a blotting case, a summoning bell, and piles of books
relating to divorce. The books are well worn, noted, and some
of them open. On a little table by the window is a coffee cup
and liquor service. On the work table is a sewing basket. On
the mantel are a clock and a coffee cup. As the curtain rises,*
JOSÉPHA *is discovered leaning over the table, reading one of
the books on divorce.* BASTIEN *enters through the arch, followed by a* MESSENGER *who is carrying a package of books,
wrapped and tied, to which is attached a note.*

BASTIEN. Mademoiselle Josépha?

Josépha [without moving]. Hmmm?

Bastien. It's the messenger from the bookstore with a
package of books for Madame.

Josépha. Put them on the table.

*Bastien [taking the package of books from the messenger
and putting them on the center table].* Is that all?

Josépha. Wait! [*Taking the note from the package, opening it, and reading.*] The Question of Divorce, About Divorce, Divorce, On Divorce, In Behalf of Divorce. No. That's fine.

Bastien [*to the messenger*]. That's fine.

Exit MESSENGER. BASTIEN *leans against the armchair and gazes ardently at* JOSÉPHA.

Josépha [*untying the books*]. What are you doing, busy one?

Bastien. I am worshipping you, Josépha . . . from afar.

Josépha. I know that; you would do better to clear away the coffee things. Here it is three o'clock, and it's her day to receive.

Bastien [*crossing upstage*]. Where have they scattered their cups this time?

Josépha. Hers is there on the mantel and his is here on the little table.

Bastien [*crossing to the little table*]. I see . . . Hmmm! Not even close enough to toast. [*He pours himself a drink.*]

Josépha [*not looking up*]. If he should ever catch you drinking his good liqueur . . .

Bastien [*pointing to* DES PRUNELLES' *study*]. There's no danger of that. He's in his study, snoring away, or making his billiard balls and napkin rings . . . I ask you! One of the richest men in Reims. [*He drinks and crosses to* JOSÉPHA.] You're the one who'll get caught, sticking your nose into her books.

Josépha. Ha! Monsieur's in his room, so Madame's in her room.

Bastien. Is she snoring too?

Josépha. Very likely. She's bored enough.

Bastien. I believe it, with a husband who's always doodling with his locks, fussing with his clocks, and tinkering with his chimes . . . What a way to live! [*He puts his glass on the little table.*]

Josépha [*still reading*]. What can you expect of marriage?

Bastien [*crossing to her*]. Oh, Josépha, we'd be different. If you would only marry me there'd be no time for snoring, we'd be so busy toasting!

Josépha. Oh, yes, the first six months.

Bastien. A year, Josépha. One year guaranteed.

Josépha [*turning to him*]. And then?

Bastien. Then?

Josépha. Well?

Bastien. Oh, well. Really! After that?

Josépha [*rising*]. That's it. There's the vice of wedlock. The whole ridiculous system is too long. We ought to marry for a year, eighteen months, two years at the most, and then all switch partners.

Bastien. Now, Josépha, that's the ideal. You ask too much.

Josépha. It's coming, and soon. First we'll get the divorce law passed. Here, listen to this: [*Reading.*] "The thing that deters many people from entering into marriage is the impossibility, once one is in it, of getting out of it."

Bastien. That's putting it bluntly.

Josépha. And correctly. So, until the divorce law is passed, my fine friend, please don't talk to me of marriage. I want to see an out.

Bastien. All right. We won't talk of marriage, Josépha. We'll talk of love—free love! Now that's the in and the out right together. [*He tries to embrace her.*]

Josépha [*struggling to get free*]. You . . . you let go, or you'll be sorry!

Bastien. Everybody's doing it; it's the latest thing.

Josépha. Shh! Someone's at the window.

Bastien [*lowering his voice but not moving*]. His cousin?

Josépha. Monsieur Adhémar? No! He wouldn't risk it at this time of day. [*She turns to the window, where the face of the* CARETAKER *has appeared.*] Oh, heavens! It's just the caretaker.

Caretaker [*outside*]. Monsieur Bastien!

Bastien [*opening window*]. Hey, you! What are you doing there instead of coming to the door?

Caretaker [*putting his head in the window*]. It's locked, Monsieur Bastien.

Bastien. The garden door?

Caretaker. Yes.

Bastien [*going to door and trying to open it*]. He's right. It's locked.

Josépha. Monsieur must have done it.

Bastien [*whispering*]. He must guess his cousin comes in this way.

Josépha. Keep quiet, you fool! [*To the caretaker.*] Well, what do you want?

Bastien. Yes, what do you want?

Caretaker [*handing in the newspapers*]. I brought the Paris papers.

Josépha. It's about time. Madame has been waiting for them. She's asked for them three times.

Bastien. So has Monsieur.

Josépha [*to Caretaker*]. A fine mess, thanks to you.

Bastien [*closing window on him*]. Back to your roost.

Josépha [*unfolding newspaper without tearing the band*]. Now what do you suppose interests them so much? [*She crosses and sits in the armchair.*]

Bastien. Some scandal——

Josépha. Keep your eyes open!

Bastien [*kneeling on chair and leaning over her*]. I certainly will . . . for the scandal. Turn the page.

Josépha. Hold on! The Stock Market first. The florin . . . up four per cent.

Bastien. How nice. Now the races.

Josépha. You and your races. [*Looking at the first page.*] Ah!

Bastien. What?

Josépha. Here it is.

Bastien. What?

Josépha. This must be why they're so eager for the news. [*Reading.*] "If, as is believed, the Chamber of Deputies discusses the report of the Commission on Divorce today, the ensuing debate promises to be extremely lively and interesting."

Bastien. I bet.

Josépha. Will you be quiet! [*Reading.*] "According to reliable sources, the vote——"

Des Prunelles [*offstage*]. Bastien!

Bastien [*crossing upstage*]. Watch out—it's him!

Josépha [*rising and gathering papers together*]. Oh. That's just like him.

Bastien [*getting coffee cup*]. Hide them! Hide them! We'll read them later.

Josépha. Good. [*She hides the papers behind her.*]

DES PRUNELLES *enters from his study.*

Des Prunelles. Bastien.

Bastien. Monsieur?

Des Prunelles. Haven't the Paris papers come yet?

Bastien [*getting the other cup*]. No, monsieur.

Des Prunelles. It's three-thirty.

Bastien. I'll check with the caretaker, if Monsieur so desires.

Des Prunelles. Yes, do that. [*Exit* BASTIEN *into dining room, carrying cups. To* JOSÉPHA, *brusquely.*] What are you doing?

Josépha [*by the mantel, pretending to be very occupied*]. The clock has stopped, monsieur, and I was trying——

Des Prunelles. Don't touch it. That's my concern. You know very well I don't want anyone touching my clocks.

Josépha. It's the same with bells. I haven't heard any of them all morning, not one bell.

Des Prunelles. Yes, yes, I know. They aren't working. Don't touch them!

Josépha. I just thought Monsieur should know——

Des Prunelles. Well, I do know. They're my bells. [*Exit* JOSÉPHA *into the dining room. Door bell.*] Ah! Visitors already for the little wife.

Bastien [*entering with card on a tray*]. It's for you, monsieur.

Des Prunelles. What about the papers?

Bastien. They haven't arrived as yet, monsieur.

Des Prunelles [*reading card*]. Clavignac! Show him in.

Exit BASTIEN. Enter CLAVIGNAC.

Des Prunelles. Well! So you're back in Reims.

Clavignac [*cheerfully*]. That's right. I'm back in Reims.

Des Prunelles [*shaking hands*]. Everyone thinks you're dead. Where the devil have you been?

Clavignac. In Spain.

Des Prunelles. In Spain?

Clavignac. A pleasure trip.

Des Prunelles. Lucky man! You're free—free as a bachelor.

Clavignac [*taking the chair from under the table and sitting*]. Only separated.

Des Prunelles [*sitting on pouf*]. It's the same thing——

Clavignac. Oh, not at all. My wife still dreams up ways to madden me. By the way, I trust your wife is well?

Des Prunelles. My God, yes. But how does Madame Clavignac drive you mad?

Clavignac. As you know, I'm giving her alimony. That in itself is unfair. The situation I surprised her in made it apparent that she could handle her own affairs. But that was the verdict, so I said nothing, and I paid, and I'm still paying. But my wife finds this allowance too niggardly, and so, to increase it, she has devised an abominable trick. The moment I settle down, no matter where, riverside, seaside, or mountainside, she arrives flaunting some idiotic male or other, and a flood of scandal follows, a torrent. People smile at me knowingly; the local newspapers ring with her prowess; the lawsuit is once again revived. This drives me mad. I beg her to leave me alone. "Oh, I'd be only too happy," she replies, "but who will pay my transportation, my hotel, my dressmaker, etc." Then the bill—ten, twelve thousand francs. . . . I pay up. She flies off . . . and the game has been played.

Des Prunelles. You mean she followed you to Spain?

Clavignac. Ah, no. This time the game was mine. I let it be known I was going to spend the winter in Algeria. And at this moment she is descending upon Africa. . . . That's my revenge.

Des Prunelles. Then you'll stay here?

Clavignac. Twenty-four hours.

Des Prunelles. No longer?

Clavignac. Just time enough to collect my rents and take some papers to my lawyer.

Des Prunelles. Another lawsuit?

Clavignac. No. But the divorce law will be voted in, and I intend to waste no time in deepening the abyss between Madame and me. Once divorced, she can play whatever game she likes. If she wants, I'll play with her.

Des Prunelles. Then you think divorce will be voted in?

Clavignac. I certainly hope so.

Des Prunelles. Ah, if we only knew! . . . You'll dine with me?

Clavignac. No, it's you who'll dine with me.

Des Prunelles. Indeed?

Clavignac. This morning at the Club, we got together a party for dinner tonight—a bachelor party like the good old days. It's all on me. We plan to have some lovely ladies. That thought doesn't fill you with terror, does it?

Des Prunelles. Oh dear! Lovely ladies . . . at a time like this?

Clavignac. Bah! They'll make you young again. Seven-thirty tonight at Dagneau's. Agreed?

Des Prunelles. No, I really can't.

Clavignac. Come, now.

Des Prunelles. Word of honor.

Clavignac. You're not going to try and make me swallow that nonsense, are you?

Des Prunelles. But I just can't do it, really!

Clavignac. Don't go too far, you know, or I'll send you my seconds.

Des Prunelles. That's fine. Exactly what I want.

Clavignac. What? A duel?

Des Prunelles. I'm reaching that point.

Clavignac. You?

Des Prunelles. Me!

Clavignac [*lowering his voice*]. And for your——?

Des Prunelles. Naturally!

Clavignac. Oh, ho! In that case, let's be serious, and tell me all. There's certainly no one better qualified to understand such a problem than I.

Des Prunelles [*putting his hands on* CLAVIGNAC's *shoulders and seating him on the pouf*]. Ah, my good old friend, in our marrying, the two of us have done——

Clavignac. A remarkably silly thing. I agree.

Des Prunelles [*sitting*]. But you, you deserved your fate.

Clavignac. Thank you.

Des Prunelles. You married a flirt, who was continually bombarded by billets-doux sent by slingshot over the convent wall, and who returned their fire.

Clavignac. And you never warned me before I married?

Des Prunelles. Play fair. You never asked.

Clavignac. That's true.

Des Prunelles. Whereas I, I married a modest young thing, well brought up . . . You should know; you've been a guest in their house. A little lively, perhaps——

Clavignac. I'll say! She used to box the ears of all her servants.

Des Prunelles. You never told me that.

Clavignac. Play fair. You never asked.

Des Prunelles. In any case, everything promised happiness, and after a rather tempestuous youth I felt I had earned my tranquillity.

Clavignac. And instead of a haven?

Des Prunelles. Ah, my good friend, it's the open sea in a raging storm!

Clavignac. Stirred up by?

Des Prunelles. Does one ever know? It's just the incompatibility of wills. Madame wants to go out; monsieur wants to stay in. One is stifling where the other freezes. One gets up when the other goes to bed. In brief, they agree on only one thing—the need to avoid each other. My marriage is like

Florian's fable of the Rabbit and the Duck. Imagine *them* married! It's idiotic, but what can you do?

Clavignac. My case exactly.

Des Prunelles. The comedy is heightened by the entrance of a fop, bedecked with the most tantalizing cravats, and gifted by nature with that fine aroma of silliness which women so drunkenly inhale. "Ah! How beautiful he is! How empty-headed he is! He shall be everything to me and I shall be everything to him." And, to top it off, this insipid beauty is my cousin.

Clavignac. Adhémar?

Des Prunelles [*rising*]. The glorious Adhémar—government bird-watcher supreme! He arrives on the scene booted up to here, jangling his spurs, snapping his whip . . . What chance have I against a musketeer?

Clavignac. The fable changes: "Leda and the Swan."

Des Prunelles. Oh, no. Not yet.

Clavignac [*rising*]. Hmmmm . . .

Des Prunelles. No. There are still two reassuring signs.

Clavignac. Namely?

Des Prunelles. First, Madame des Prunelles always acts like a sulky bulldog in my presence. The first day she smiles at me, my fate is sealed.

Clavignac. I see.

Des Prunelles. And secondly, she's very preoccupied with divorce! Proof that she's still struggling. When she stops struggling, she *won't* be bothered with divorce.

Clavignac. She's talked to you about it?

Des Prunelles. No, but this literature! Look. Lawbooks. [*He points to the books and picks one of them up.*] Volume VI, "On Divorce"—all of them: divorce, divorce, and divorce. Footnoted, annotated, underlined, and every page dogeared.

Clavignac. My poor man, defend yourself!

Des Prunelles. To the last bullet. . . . Only I'm sick—oh, I'm so sick, my poor friend. Catastrophe is all around me. I feel it, I smell it. . . . One moment of forgetfulness and I'm lost.

Clavignac. If that's the way it is, you'd better go slow.

Des Prunelles. I plan to strike an unexpected and brilliant blow—today.

Clavignac. Today?

Des Prunelles. Within the hour. I have declared that the visits of this creature were odious to me, and that I would only tolerate him, like any other relative, on official "at home" days: otherwise I would throw him out the window. This lead to that familiar scene with all its wifely clichés, "That's all that was needed, monsieur, for you to insult your wife . . ."

Clavignac. ". . . with your slanderous suspicions . . ."

Des Prunelles. ". . . it would serve you right . . ."

Together. ". . . if I justified them."

Des Prunelles. I held firm! Now I only see Adhémar on visiting days. But the minute my back is turned, he rushes in through the garden. You see, the scoundrel has rented a room right opposite my house. [*He crosses to window, and points off right.*]

Clavignac [*following him*]. And so?

Des Prunelles. And so, thanks to my mechanical talents, all last night I worked on a little trap in which he will be caught this afternoon. He will get angry. I will tweak his ears. He will provoke me. We shall fight a duel.

Clavignac. And he will kill you.

Des Prunelles. Then I shall find peace.

Clavignac. How does this mousetrap work?

Des Prunelles. Oh, it's childish. Imagine, a little piece of coiled spring—— Ssshhh! Here she is.

Clavignac. Your wife?

CYPRIENNE *appears in the vestibule, followed by* JOSÉPHA, *to whom she gives an order. She is evidently in a sour mood.*

Des Prunelles. Oh, my God!

Clavignac. What?

Des Prunelles. Isn't she smiling?

Clavignac. I should say not.

Des Prunelles. No?

Clavignac. Damn it, no!

Des Prunelles [*brightening*]. Ah, my friend, thank God! You reassure me. [*Exit* JOSÉPHA; CYPRIENNE *crosses down.*]

Clavignac [*bowing to* CYPRIENNE]. Dear madame.

Cyprienne. Monsieur Clavignac . . . How kind of you.

Clavignac. In passing through Reims, I wanted above all to pay my respects to you.

Cyprienne. I won't ask you for news of Madame Clavignac——

Clavignac. Wonderful!

Cyprienne. Still separated?

Clavignac. Still!

Cyprienne. How nice—for both of you. [*She crosses the stage.*]

Des Prunelles [*whispering*]. You see . . .

Clavignac. She's biting.

Des Prunelles. That's nothing, just wait.

BAFOURDIN *is shown in by* BASTIEN.

Bastien. Monsieur Bafourdin.

Bafourdin [*wise and solemn*]. Dear madame.

Cyprienne. Good afternoon, Monsieur Bafourdin. I hope you are well?

Bafourdin. Very well, thank you.

Des Prunelles [*shaking his hands*]. My dear monsieur. [*Presenting* CLAVIGNAC.] My friend, Monsieur Clavignac. [*To* CLAVIGNAC.] Monsieur Bafourdin, tax collector.

Clavignac. Charmed!

MADAME DE BRIONNE *is shown in by* BASTIEN.

Madame de Brionne [*to* BASTIEN]. Don't announce me. I'm at home.

Cyprienne [*taking her hand*]. You look wonderful.

Madame de Brionne. Yes, darling! [*They cross to* DES PRUNELLES, *who takes her hand*.] Hello, hello, hello, dear neighbor. [*Crosses in front of him to* BAFOURDIN.] Good afternoon, Monsieur Bafourdin. [*Crosses in front of him to* CLAVIGNAC.] Heavens, you've come back to life!

During the following conversation between MADAME DE BRIONNE *and* CLAVIGNAC, BAFOURDIN *sits on the couch,* DES PRUNELLES *places the stool under the table and then takes the books to the little table near the window. At the same time* CYPRIENNE *takes the pamphlets and puts them on the mantelpiece.* JOSÉPHA *enters from dining room with a tea service on a tray, places it on the table, and pulls the armchair up to the table. Exit* JOSÉPHA.

Clavignac. One would return from anywhere to see you, my dear . . . and still the widow?

Madame de Brionne. Still. And you?

Clavignac. Not yet.

Madame de Brionne. What a pity! We two might have united in our solitude.

Clavignac [*eagerly*]. I don't need to be a widower for that.

Madame de Brionne [*laughing*]. Ah, ah, ah! It's a husband I want.

Cyprienne [*calling her while preparing the tea*]. Estelle!

Madame de Brionne [*crossing to her*]. My dear?

Clavignac [*to* DES PRUNELLES]. How is it that such a lovely woman never remarried?

Des Prunelles. It's not desire that's stopping her; it's money.

ADHÉMAR *is shown in by* BASTIEN.

Bastien [*announcing*]. Monsieur Adhémar de Gratignan. [CYPRIENNE *starts at the sound of his name.*]

Des Prunelles [*low voice, to* CLAVIGNAC]. Here's the peacock!

Adhémar [*crosses directly to* CYPRIENNE, *taking her hand*]. My dear cousin, how have you been— [*With affection.*] — since last Monday?

Cyprienne [*smiling*]. Thank you, not badly.

Des Prunelles [*in a whisper to* CLAVIGNAC]. Charlatan! He sees her every day. [ADHÉMAR *bows to* DES PRUNELLES, *who pretends not to see him.* CLAVIGNAC *goes up stage to talk with* MADAME DE BRIONNE. BAFOURDIN *stands with a cup of tea that* CYPRIENNE *has given him.*]

Bafourdin [*to* ADHÉMAR]. So you are going to leave us, Monsieur de Gratignan?

Adhémar [*to himself, annoyed*]. Oh, perfect! [CYPRIENNE *stops pouring tea and turns to him quickly;* DES PRUNELLES, *who was crossing up stage with* CLAVIGNAC, *stops and listens.*]

Cyprienne. Leave us? [*To* ADHÉMAR.] Are you going somewhere?

Adhémar [*quickly*]. No. Forgive me, but that's incorrect.

Bafourdin. Just this morning I read in *The Independent Quarterly* that you had been named assistant inspector of the Arachon forests.

Cyprienne [*bothered by her husband's presence*]. And we knew nothing about it?

Adhémar. Precisely. I was just going to tell you the position had been offered me; I refused it.

Des Prunelles. You refused a promotion?

Adhémar. Anything to stay in the bosom of my family. [*Crosses to mantelpiece and puts his hat on it.*]

Des Prunelles [*whispers to* CLAVIGNAC]. That does it. We will fight.

Madame de Brionne [*at the back, looking at figure on wall*]. Monsieur des Prunelles?

Des Prunelles. Madame? [*He crosses up to her.*]

Madame de Brionne. This dragon is Ming Dynasty, isn't it?

Des Prunelles. No, Japanese. [*They talk.* BAFOURDIN *sits down on the couch.* CYPRIENNE *crosses to* ADHÉMAR *with a cup of tea for him, which she stirs tenderly.*]

Cyprienne. All this for me? You mustn't make this sacrifice, my darling. You must take this position.

Adhémar [*in a half voice, taking the tea*]. And leave you, Cyprienne? Rather, death! [*He drinks his tea.*]

Cyprienne [*whispering*]. I must talk with you—very soon.

Adhémar. In my room?

Cyprienne [*flustered*]. Your room? Never! Some other time . . . I won't say.

Adhémar. Why not?

Cyprienne. Shhh! People are looking at us. [*Aloud.*] Monsieur de Clavignac, would you care for some tea? [CLAVIGNAC *and* DES PRUNELLES *cross down right.* MADAME DE BRIONNE *leafs through a copy of* La Vie Parisienne *up stage.*]

Adhémar [*alone stage left, drinking his tea. Aside*]. Accept the position! I already have. I'm not such a fool. But tomorrow I leave, and I'd like to complete some unfinished business.

Bastien [*announcing*]. Mademoiselle de Lusignan.

She appears.

Clavignac. Still a spinster?

Des Prunelles. More so every day!

Cyprienne. How kind of you to come, mademoiselle. [CYPRIENNE *shows her to a chair near the table, then turns to talk to* BAFOURDIN.]

Mademoiselle de Lusignan. Isn't Monsieur de Gratignan here?

Adhémar. Pardon!

Mademoiselle de Lusignan [*going to him as she talks*]. I thought so . . . I've seen you earlier today. You were running past my window. I called good day to you, but you didn't hear me. You were running so fast— [*to* DES PRUNELLES] —that I said to myself: "Well, surely he's going to his cousin's house." [*She sits in the wing chair at the right of the table.*]

Clavignac [*whispering to* DES PRUNELLES]. Lovely!

Cyprienne [*quickly, in order to change the conversation*]. Won't we have the pleasure of seeing Madame Bafourdin?

Bafourdin. A slight indisposition has compelled her to stay in bed.

Madame de Brionne [*crossing down and sitting on pouf*]. In bed? Oh, that reminds me, isn't it today that notorious divorce bill is being discussed?

Adhémar. It certainly is.

Des Prunelles [*to* CLAVIGNAC]. Listen to this! [*He sits at the extreme right.* CLAVIGNAC *sits between him and* MADAME DE BRIONNE.]

Cyprienne [*serving tea to* MADEMOISELLE DE LUSIGNAN]. Yes . . . today's the day our deputies will finally deign to attend to it.

Mademoiselle de Lusignan. You think it could possibly pass?

Cyprienne. So many deputies have a personal interest in it.

Bafourdin. The whole country is behind it.

Cyprienne. Undoubtedly!

Adhémar. To a man!

Cyprienne and Madame de Brionne. And to a woman!

Clavignac [*to* MADAME DE BRIONNE, *who is still looking at* La Vie Parisienne]. What can it do for you? You're a widow.

Madame de Brionne [*laughing*]. Goodness! It'll put more husbands into circulation. I'll have more of a choice.

Bastien [*announcing*]. Madame de Valfontaine.

MADAME DE VALFONTAINE *enters.* DES PRUNELLES *and* CLAVIGNAC *rise and bow to her, then take their seats.*

Cyprienne [*crossing up to greet her, and bringing her into the scene*]. Ah! I'm certain that Clarissa is for it, too.

Madame de Valfontaine [*shaking* CYPRIENNE'S *hand, waving to* ADHÉMAR, *and crossing to* MADAME DE BRIONNE]. For what?

Cyprienne. For divorce.

Madame de Valfontaine. It's frightful. [*She shakes hands with* ADHÉMAR.]

All [*surprised*]. Oh?

Clavignac [*to* DES PRUNELLES]. Well!

Des Prunelles. She does just as well without it.

Clavignac. You don't say!

Cyprienne [*offering her a chair*]. What, my charmer, you're against it?

Madame de Valfontaine [*sitting, while* CYPRIENNE *pours her tea*]. Oh really, it's the height of abomination, your divorce! Married for life, one resigns oneself, one makes concessions. With the hope of divorce, one would make the worst of everything in order to break it up. It will be the end of marriage.

Mademoiselle de Lusignan. So much the better.

All. Oh, Mademoiselle!

CYPRIENNE *brings some tea to* MADAME DE VALFONTAINE, *and* ADHÉMAR *takes advantage of her move by taking* CYPRIENNE's *hand behind the armchair.*

Mademoiselle de Lusignan [*noticing the byplay*]. We might then be spared the horrors it parades before our very eyes.

ADHÉMAR *and* CYPRIENNE *separate quickly.* CYPRIENNE *crosses to upstage of the sofa, puts her elbows on the back of the sofa between* BAFOURDIN *and* MADEMOISELLE DE LU-SIGNAN, *and listens.*

Madame de Valfontaine [*to* ADHÉMAR, *in a whisper*]. Don't be so obvious!

Bafourdin [*rising in place*]. I beg madam's pardon, but I believe that, far from discouraging marriage, divorce will encourage it: it offers the possibility of escape. [*He sits down.*]

Clavignac. Ye gods! Marriage is an impasse: divorce opens an exit.

Mademoiselle de Lusignan. Who wouldn't avoid a dead end?

Bafourdin. Who wouldn't prefer a busy intersection?

Madame de Valfontaine. Intersection! What a way to put it! So marriage will only be a busy intersection. It's indecent.

All. Indecent?

Adhémar. It's agreeable. [*He takes his cup and puts it on the table.*]

Clavignac. And useful! No more sterile unions.

Bafourdin. Increase the population.

Madame de Valfontaine. The less said about that the better.

Mademoiselle de Lusignan [*spitefully*]. And Monsieur des Prunelles, who sits in his corner, saying nothing?

Everyone turns and looks at DES PRUNELLES.

Des Prunelles. In theory, I'm against divorce.

All [*surprised*]. Oh?

Des Prunelles. In practice, I am for it.

Clavignac, Adhémar, Bafourdin. Just like everyone else.

Adhémar. As for me, do you know what I find so admirable about divorce?

All. Tell us. Do tell!

Adhémar. It prevents murder! At present a luckless young gentleman cannot forget himself with an unhappy young wife without everyone crying to the husband, "Kill them!" *

Madame de Brionne [without thinking]. Oh, no one ever says that.

Adhémar. No one ever says, "Kill him, kill her, kill them"?

Madame de Brionne [laughing]. Excuse me, I wasn't thinking.

Adhémar. So the tyrant executes the couple. Bang! Bang! Now, that's barbaric. It's not in keeping with the times. And why this massacre? Because the husband has no other way of dealing with an embarrassing situation. Let's give him divorce!

Clavignac. Then you would have nothing more to fear.

Adhémar. That's right, I'd have nothing—he'd have nothing more to fear.

Clavignac. And the husband has only to pitch his wife into your arms to be revenged.

Adhémar. That's right. That is to say . . .

Clavignac. Oh yes! That's so right!

Des Prunelles [aside]. What an idiot!

ADHÉMAR *crosses to* MADAME DE VALFONTAINE.

Cyprienne [crossing to CLAVIGNAC*].* Revenge? Pardon me, but you said revenge. And revenge for what, if you please?

Des Prunelles [rising and speaking to CYPRIENNE *over the head of* CLAVIGNAC*].* For the crime, madame, for the crime the wife committed!

Cyprienne. The crime?

Des Prunelles. The indiscretion, if that word seems adequate to you.

Cyprienne. Indiscretion? But, with divorce, monsieur, there will be no indiscretions: divorce will excuse them.

Clavignac [embarrassed at being caught between them, rises and crosses away]. Well, uh, that's one side of the question . . .

Des Prunelles [following CYPRIENNE *as she crosses down].* And what about the husband's honor, madame?

Cyprienne [to DES PRUNELLES, *over the head of* MADAME DE BRIONNE*].* Ah, monsieur, divorce restores his honor to

---

* "An adulteress is not Woman. She is not even a woman. She is a beast. She is Cain's mate. Kill her!"—DUMAS *fils.*

him, unblemished and as good as new. What has he to complain of?

Adhémar [*supporting her*]. Right!

MADAME DE BRIONNE *rises discreetly and crosses up to*
CLAVIGNAC.

Cyprienne [*taking center stage*]. Oh, certainly I understand
that a virtuous woman, bound in endless wedlock, must curb
the raptures of her heart and quell her passions. She must
say to the one she loves— [*talking to* ADHÉMAR.] —"No! I
will not yield! For if we were discovered, there would be
scandal, dishonor, and perhaps death." But with divorce—
[*gaily to her husband.*] —she can say, "That's how it is,
monsieur, I've deceived you. Let's get a divorce, that's all
there is to it, we'll say no more about it." Now isn't that
honest? Isn't that frank? Isn't that virtuous? What more
could anyone want?

Des Prunelles [*crossing to her*]. That's fine—and as a result, no more scruples, no more hesitations. How truly moral!

Cyprienne. Oh, come now, monsieur. It's so obvious that
the high morality of divorce is precisely in this willingness
to excuse the indiscretion.

Des Prunelles [*exasperated*]. Which it encourages one to
commit!

Clavignac and Madame de Brionne. Calm down! Take it
easy!

Everyone rises. MADAME DE BRIONNE, MADAME DE VALFON-
TAINE, MADEMOISELLE DE LUSIGNAN *cross up stage.* CYP-
RIENNE *goes up to bid them farewell.* BAFOURDIN *goes to get
his hat.* CLAVIGNAC *tries to calm* DES PRUNELLES.

Adhémar [*aside*]. Perfect! If that's all that's stopping
her . . . she is mine. She's mine! [*Aloud.*] And to think
that while we're here talking about this divorce law, it may
already have been voted in.

Madame de Valfontaine. Or voted out.

Bafourdin [*behind the couch*]. In either case, we won't
know the result until later in the evening.

Adhémar. Oh, no. [*Looking at his watch.*] We can know
in one hour.

All. An hour?

Adhémar [*taking a piece of paper from writing case on
center table and writing*]. Certainly; I have a friend in the

newspaper business. I'll wire him at Chalons to send word as soon as the news is out.

The Four Women. Oh, hurry, hurry, please!

Adhémar. I will send the telegram. [*He gets his cane and hat.*]

Cyprienne [*accompanying him*]. And let us know the result.

Adhémar. Immediately! [*Exit.*]

Mademoiselle de Lusignan [*crossing to* BAFOURDIN]. And is Madame Bafourdin against divorce?

Bafourdin [*drily*]. Yes, mademoiselle. She's against the single life.

Mademoiselle de Lusignan [*aside*]. How insolent!

Mademoiselle de Valfontaine [*to* CYPRIENNE]. Good-by, my pet.

Cyprienne. Good-by.

Bafourdin [*taking his leave*]. Ladies . . . [*Exit* BAFOURDIN *with* MADAME DE VALFONTAINE.]

Mademoiselle de Lusignan [*coming back to* MADAME DE BRIONNE]. Aren't you leaving, my dear?

Madame de Brionne. After you, my dear.

Mademoiselle de Lusignan. How modest of you to dread the compliments I plan to give you after you've gone.

Madame de Brionne [*laughing*]. Compliments? It's the opposite I dread. [*Crossing upstage.*] Would you accept a lift in my carriage?

Mademoiselle de Lusignan. With pleasure. [*Aside.*] Little fool!

Madame de Brionne [*going to* CYPRIENNE]. You lose, my lamb. Now she'll gossip about you.

Cyprienne. Let her gossip!

Madame de Brionne [*laughing*]. You can depend on it. [*She waves to* DES PRUNELLES *and* CLAVIGNAC, *and exits with* MADEMOISELLE DE LUSIGNAN.]

JOSÉPHA *enters with a tray and starts to collect the cups.*

Cyprienne [*coming down right, to* CLAVIGNAC]. Won't you stay to dinner?

Clavignac. I'm terribly sorry, but I'm dining with friends this evening.

Cyprienne. Some other time, perhaps. [BASTIEN *enters, bringing* DES PRUNELLES' *hat and overcoat.*] Bastien! Have the horses ready. I'm going out.

Bastien. Yes, madame.

Des Prunelles [*to* CLAVIGNAC]. Are you coming with me?

Clavignac. Where to?

Des Prunelles. To the Club.

Clavignac. Gladly.

Cyprienne. Well, if I don't see you again . . . Pleasant journey! [*She offers her hand to* CLAVIGNAC.]

Clavignac [*taking it*]. Thank you, thank you. [*Exit* CYPRIENNE *into her room.*]

Des Prunelles [*making sure she's gone. Then brusquely*]. You know what's happening?

Clavignac. Not at all!

Des Prunelles [*in a low voice*]. I said I was going to the Club—I'm not. She said she was going out—she's not. Adhémar is waiting across the street for the signal. She will give the signal, and he will come—right into my little mouse-trap. [*He adjusts a button on the garden door.*] Let's wait in my study.

Clavignac [*getting his hat*]. And to think that in every household——

Des Prunelles. Sshhhh! She'll hear us. [*Loudly.*] Have a cigar.

Clavignac. For the road.

Des Prunelles. Come, let's go.

Clavignac. We're off!

Music. They cross up stage and pretend to exit left. DES PRUNELLES *catches* CLAVIGNAC *and the two tiptoe into the study. The door closes softly. As it closes,* CYPRIENNE *enters with great precaution, looks about, crosses up to vestibule, and having assured herself that they have gone, crosses to the window and lets down the blind.*

Cyprienne. The signal! [*She crosses slowly downstage.*] I have been thinking for a long time about this problem of how to be a dutiful wife and have a lover. And I have finally solved it. It was hard, but I did it. I will break off with Adhémar until the divorce bill is passed. So much for my duties. . . . Here he comes.

Adhémar [*entering stealthily*]. Are you alone?

Cyprienne. Alone—he's at the Club. Quickly!

Adhémar [*starting toward her*]. Oh Cyprienne! [*The door closes behind him. Immediately an electric bell goes off and continues through the rest of the scene.* ADHÉMAR *stops, astonished.*] Huh!

Cyprienne. That ringing?

Adhémar. What is it?

Cyprienne [*terrified*]. I don't know!

Adhémar. A telegram?

Cyprienne. It's horrible. Make it stop!

Adhémar [*bewildered*]. I was going to ask you to stop it.

Cyprienne [*running to the door*]. It's the door! Can't you see it's the door!

Adhémar [*more bewildered*]. The door?

Cyprienne. Oh! Oh! [*She crosses behind the sofa.*]

Adhémar [*trying to open the door*]. Curse it! The door's stuck.

Cyprienne. It's locked!

Josépha [*entering from* CYPRIENNE'S *room*]. Did you ring, madame?

Cyprienne [*beside herself*]. No, not me—it's my husband! [*Another bell adds to the tumult.* CYPRIENNE *crosses down right.*] A trap—it's a trap! We're lost! Run!!

Adhémar [*frantic*]. But where?

Cyprienne and Josépha [*pointing to the hall*]. There!

Adhémar [*running in circles*]. Where's there? Where?

Cyprienne and Josépha. The hall!

ADHÉMAR *dashes toward the hall. At the same time* DES PRUNELLES *throws open his study door and cuts off his escape.*

Cyprienne. Too late!

ADHÉMAR *backs toward the garden door, terrified.* DES PRUNELLES *follows him with a menacing air.* ADHÉMAR *bolts to stage left.* DES PRUNELLES *goes to the door and shuts off the bell.*

Adhémar. Trapped!

Des Prunelles [*to* JOSÉPHA]. Leave us.

Josépha [*under her breath*]. Have a good time, madame! [*Exit* JOSÉPHA *into* CYPRIENNE'S *room.* CYPRIENNE *and* ADHÉMAR *stand rooted to the spot.*]

Des Prunelles [*to* ADHÉMAR]. You and I shall talk later; I was under the impression that you were about to leave.

Adhémar [*stupefied*]. Yes, I think so . . . I believe I was . . . but . . . which way?

Des Prunelles [*opening the garden door*]. This way.

Adhémar [*hesitatingly crossing toward door*]. No music?

Des Prunelles. No music.

Adhémar [*bowing*]. A thousand pardons. [*Exit* ADHÉMAR, *in a rush.*]

Des Prunelles [*closing the door sharply*]. Good-by for now.

Cyprienne [*behind the armchair at left*]. It's come, the crisis! The crisis is here!

Des Prunelles [*motioning his wife to sit down*]. And now, madame, let us talk, if you would be so kind. You are perhaps asking yourself how I learned that you continued to see Adhémar against my wishes?

Cyprienne [*seated*]. Not at all.

Des Prunelles. No? Well, then, I'm going to tell you. [*Sits.*] Last night I was at the Club. Adhémar came in. I heard some laughter and a few slightly improper remarks. The reason for the hilarity was rather frivolous—a thread of wool was hanging from his suit like a tail. Adhémar was removing the object in question when he spotted me. He bit his lip, threw the thread to the ground, and said, very loudly and very affectedly, "Anyone can see I have just been dining with my sister." I said nothing, but I didn't lose sight of that string of wool on the carpet. When no one was looking I pocketed it—and here it is! [Cyprienne *reacts*.] Yes. Chinese red! [*He rises and crosses to the sewing basket.*] I returned home, I went straight to this basket, and I picked up this ball of yarn. [*He does so.*] I compare— [*He crosses to her, holding the two objects in front of him.*] —and the similarity has too much eloquence for me to prolong the effect by useless comment.

Cyprienne [*coldly*]. And so?

Des Prunelles. And so . . . Since Adhémar was obviously here, please tell me why you have been receiving him in secret? What could possibly inspire and justify such neglect of your duty to me? As a husband I'm not hard to get along with. I'm not surly, vulgar, stingy, or quarrelsome. I have given you the easiest and most pleasant life possible. I never get angry. I have simple tastes. I lead a regular life; as a matter of fact I married for that. My figure may not be of classic proportions, but I have a certain air of distinction. I'm not particularly passionate, but from time to time I have admirable bursts of tenderness. . . . In sum, madame, without flattering myself, I presume I make you as happy as a woman can be!

Cyprienne [*to herself, with a bitter laugh*]. Hah! Hah!

Des Prunelles. You disagree?

Cyprienne. I thought you'd say that. How magnanimous! "As happy as a woman can be." But how should I know?

You tell me so, but how happy *can* a woman be? Where could I have learned that? When? How? With whom?

Des Prunelles. But——

Cyprienne. When you discuss me with your friends, you say, "What a first-rate woman!" You size me up, and you have a comparison in mind. But where are my terms of comparison? How can I proclaim that *you* take the cake?

Des Prunelles. I——

Cyprienne. No, it's extraordinary, this male smugness. Oh, you have certainly arranged things well for yourselves, you men! It's delightful, this society you've created—delightful for you! You're young. You paw the ground. You jump for joy. The mama says, "Have fun, my child, it's proper at your age." The papa says, "Sow a few wild oats, my boy, it's good for you." So you skip and dance from blonde to brunette to redhead! Then, when you've had enough of it, when your back is broken and you're foundering, spent, and there's nothing left—it's "Whew, time to get married!" They fling into your arms some poor trembling girl, completely naïve, continuously sheltered, who knows nothing of life except that it's hidden from her, and nothing of love except what she can guess. You say to this child, as you clasp her weakly in your exhausted arms, "Aren't you thrilled to have found such a dashing swain as I? No one could love a woman more than I love you. No one kisses more passionately than I kiss you." And the poor girl, who finds the embrace a little slack, sighs to herself, "What! Is he serious? There's nothing better? I had thought . . . How funny. Ah, well . . ." The lazy one is convinced by him; the indifferent one puts up with him; but the woman, the real woman, like me, says to herself, "What a joke! There must be something better. I'm not carried away. I'm not lifted to the heights of madness, to crime. People poison and kill for *this?* Romeo risked breaking his back for such feeble embraces? The game isn't worth the candle. There must be more!" And this same woman, my dear sir, searches, examines, studies, inquires, and after thorough investigation and exhaustive research, she is able to put it bluntly: "Come, come! [*She hits him on the shoulder.*] You are a humbug. And I have been robbed!"

Des Prunelles [*rising*]. Madame!

Cyprienne. I've been robbed, that's all there is to it, I've been robbed! What's worse, that's how it's supposed to be. It's the same everywhere. Marriage! What is it for you disabled veterans? For us it's the beginning of the campaign! [*She sits on the pouf.*] All through school, my dreams were of a marriage that would bring me all the giddiness of passion, a husband who was both hero and lover. I saw you as young, handsome, slim, elegant, at times tender, at times threatening; both submissive and tyrannical; either groveling at my feet— [*She rises.*] —or leaping on me like a tiger and bruising my palpitating flesh with terrifying embraces! Those were my dreams. And in their place, there's nothing, absolutely nothing! Just a dreary solitude, a swamp, a pool of flat and stagnant water. . . . Just the regular tic-toc of the domestic cuckoo clock, the monotonous bubbling of the family stew. No spice, no tang. Nothing to sharpen the taste, to tempt the tongue, to stimulate the appetite. I appeal to your hand-me-down heart that can only stomach soft food, I cry out to it, "I'm young and healthy! For God's sake, I beg of you, a few bonbons, some champagne, just one hot pepper!" And you answer, "A little more mush, if you please, some turnips, and a soft-boiled egg. [*She throws herself into the armchair.*]

Des Prunelles. I really don't know what to do with you. I've done my utmost——

Cyprienne. Ohhh, fine! Ohhhh, Mama!

Des Prunelles. You can't really expect me to disguise myself as a one-eyed pirate and leap into your bed through the window.

Cyprienne. Of course not. Such performances were only given for your mistresses, when you were young. You even *over*-acted then.

Des Prunelles. I?

Cyprienne. As proved by a certain closet in which Monsieur Bafourdin accidentally locked you. It was in his wife's bedroom. You almost suffocated.

Des Prunelles. How did you——

Cyprienne. Or that time you seduced Madame Brignois, disguised as a dressmaker.

Des Prunelles. That was long ago.

Cyprienne [*rising*]. There was passion, romance, adventure—a real Don Juan!

Des Prunelles [*modestly*]. Oh, for heaven's sake——

Cyprienne. But I know nothing of these things except by hearsay.

Des Prunelles. I'm glad to know that.

Cyprienne. Thanks to this cursèd society. When we're girls you shut us in; when we're women you shut us out; and when we're old and gray, you shut us up.

Des Prunelles. And what would you like it to do, this wretched society?

Cyprienne [*crossing to him*]. What would I like? Instead of imprisoning girls, let them do as they please, like the boys. When they've lived a little, they'll be able to retire into marriage like you, and you'll have a virtuous and faithful wife. Her overwhelming curiosity will have been satisfied.

Des Prunelles. Where on earth did you pick up such lovely ideas?

Cyprienne. From thinking, monsieur, and from reading. [*Goes to the table.*] Read the latest book by——

Des Prunelles. Do you really think there is a man mad enough to marry a girl under such conditions?

Cyprienne. There are plenty of girls mad enough to marry men under such conditions.

Des Prunelles. But, damn it all, between men and women there's a huge abyss.

Cyprienne. Agreed. It's called marriage.

Des Prunelles. Now wait a minute!

Cyprienne. You wait a minute! You want routine, I want progress. We shall never understand each other . . . so let's get back to the question.

Des Prunelles. Good! The question is Adhémar.

Cyprienne. Adhémar!

Des Prunelles. Your intentions toward Adhémar?

Cyprienne. I was about to dash all his hopes when you made your ridiculous appearance.

Des Prunelles. Then I regret it.

Cyprienne. You wouldn't be a husband if you didn't do silly things.

Des Prunelles. You were saying, madame . . .

Cyprienne. Monsieur, I will be frank.

Des Prunelles. Please do!

Cyprienne. If I were not a virtuous woman, this afternoon's incident would be enough to make your situation hopeless.

Des Prunelles. !

Cyprienne. But I am a virtuous woman—unfortunately. From childhood on, a host of false ideas and absurd prejudices was instilled into me. I am unable to rid myself of them. Among these superstitions is the vow of fidelity which

I made before the mayor. I am weak enough to attach some importance to it. Absurd or not, I made the vow. I will keep it.

Des Prunelles. That's good.

Cyprienne. No matter what it costs me.

Des Prunelles. That doesn't matter—just keep it.

Cyprienne. Only I warn you, in all fairness, that this fidelity has only a temporary and transitory character.

Des Prunelles. Huh?

Cyprienne. Once divorce is voted in . . . don't try to keep this Cinderella from the ball.

Des Prunelles. Ah!

Cyprienne. Don't be so silly as to think I won't avail myself of the law. Divorce excuses everything——

Des Prunelles. Yes, I know the theory.

Cyprienne. Consider yourself warned.

Des Prunelles. We'll see about that. But until that time, no more Adhémar.

Cyprienne. From now till the emancipation! I agree.

Des Prunelles. Or I will cut off his ears before the emancipation.

Cyprienne. That's well said.

Des Prunelles. It'll be well done.

Cyprienne. Have we exhausted the subject?

Des Prunelles. Entirely.

Cyprienne. Then if you don't mind I will bow out of the discussion. [*She crosses toward her door.*]

Des Prunelles [*crossing toward study*]. If it pleases you.

Cyprienne [*at her door*]. It does.

Des Prunelles [*at his door, bowing*]. Madame!

Cyprienne [*at her door, bowing*]. Monsieur!

Exeunt both, slamming the doors violently. As soon as the doors have slammed shut, Adhémar *opens the garden door and sticks his head in with great precaution. He next half-enters, but keeps hold of the door for fear that the bell will start ringing. At this moment* Josépha *enters from the hall and crosses toward* Cyprienne's *room.*

Adhémar [*in a loud whisper*]. Josépha.

Josépha. Oh!

Adhémar. Ssshhh.

Josépha. But the bell, the door!

Adhémar. It only rings when it's closed. I've got hold of it. Where's your mistress?

Josépha. In her room.

Adhémar. Tell her to come.

Josépha. But——

Adhémar. Quickly! It's urgent. Get going, idiot! [*Exit* JOSÉPHA.]

Adhémar [*alone*]. Well, crafty husband, I can play with wires too. I just wired my friend Dumoulin, and dictated a reply to him, telling him it was for a good practical joke. Some practical joke, ha! [*He makes a gesture, lets go of the door, and just catches it in time.*] Just in time! He wired back, and here is his telegram. This ends it. Now she can no longer hide behind her scruples. She'll be mine, mine! [*He lets go of the door again and barely catches it.*] God, what a nuisance!

CYPRIENNE *appears in her door, afraid of being surprised by her husband.*

Cyprienne. You?

Adhémar. Me.

Cyprienne. Again?

Adhémar. Forever.

Cyprienne. The bell!

Adhémar [*showing his foot which is keeping the door from closing*]. No, my foot.

Cyprienne [*indicating the study door*]. My husband! Come to me later.

Adhémar. Never!

Cyprienne. What?

Adhémar. You will come to me.

Cyprienne. To you?

Adhémar. Oh, my angel, didn't you say that, with divorce, there could be no indiscretion?

Cyprienne. Yes.

Adhémar. That, once the law was passed, no virtuous woman need hesitate to betray her husband?

Cyprienne. Yes! A dream.

Adhémar. A reality.

Cyprienne. What!

Adhémar. It's done.

Cyprienne. A law?

Adhémar. Passed.

Cyprienne. Ah!

Adhémar. See for yourself.

He holds the telegram, and, in order to shorten the distance between them, holds the door with his cane and stretches out his arm toward her.

Cyprienne [*frightened*]. The door!

Adhémar. No, the cane! I'm about to split. Take it!

Cyprienne [*crossing to him and seizing the telegram*]. "Divorce law passed. Enormous majority.—Dumoulin." Free! [*They hear* DES PRUNELLES' *voice. Music.*] Go! [*She drops the telegram on the table and runs to her door.*]

Adhémar [*about to leave*]. My place. I'll be waiting.

Cyprienne [*about to leave*]. So soon?

Adhémar. Right now!

Cyprienne. Why?

Adhémar. Divorce——

Cyprienne. But——

Adhémar. Excuses everything!

Cyprienne. Well . . .

Adhémar. We'll celebrate!

Cyprienne. Yes! [*She runs off.*]

Adhémar [*radiant, rushes out*]. Ah!!

The door closes, and the bell starts ringing.

Des Prunelles [*rushing into the room, followed by* CLAVIGNAC]. Betrayed! He was here!

Clavignac [*bewildered*]. That ringing?

Des Prunelles [*stopping the bell. Music ceases*]. His death knell!

Clavignac. Henri!

Des Prunelles [*beside himself*]. I'll kill him!

Clavignac. Calm down!

Des Prunelles [*sitting at the table and ringing for the Servants*]. Jump in a carriage and take my challenge to that scoundrel. [*He writes furiously.*] "Wretch! One of us is one too many: and it's you!"

Clavignac. I beg your pardon.

Des Prunelles. "It's you!" Where's the ink? I'm so angry I can't see. Ink! Ink! [*As he stabs about with the pen, he spears the telegram.*] A telegram? "To Adhémar." [BASTIEN *and* JOSÉPHA *enter.* DES PRUNELLES *rises and crosses to the right reading the telegram to himself. He looks at the garden door with a sardonic laugh.*] Ah! ha! you impostor! What a cheap trick! [*He leaps at* JOSÉPHA *with a loud cry.*]

Clavignac and the Servants [*terrified*]. Huh!

Des Prunelles [*pointing at* CYPRIENNE'S *door*]. Is she—?

Josépha [*quaking*]. Madame is dressing to go out.

Des Prunelles [*to himself*]. Woof! Just in time. She was going to him. [*To* JOSÉPHA.] Get out of here. [JOSÉPHA *races off;* BASTIEN *starts after her. To* BASTIEN.] Don't you move! [BASTIEN *stops short.* DES PRUNELLES *crosses to the table and stares out front.*]

Clavignac [*stupefied*]. It's a fit!

Des Prunelles [*hand on forehead in an "inspired" pose. He tears up the challenge, and writes another letter without sitting*]. A better way! "My dear cousin, would you be so kind as to come and have a chat with me? I have a friendly proposal to make to you." [*He folds the letter and puts it in an envelope.*]

Clavignac [*with concern*]. A cold shower might help.

Des Prunelles [*handing him the telegram*]. Here, read this. [*Giving* BASTIEN *the letter.*] Bastien! Take this to Monsieur Adhémar. Hurry!

Clavignac [*reaching for his hat*]. The divorce bill has passed. I'm off to tell my lawyer.

Des Prunelles. And the whole town!

Clavignac. The whole town. You can be sure of that! [*He runs off.*]

Des Prunelles [*coldly, lighting a cigarette, and looking at* CYPRIENNE'S *door*]. Now for a cigarette—and some fast playing.

ACT TWO

The scene is the same. There are some new flowers. The position of the center table has been changed so that it is now perpendicular to the footlights. To the left of the table is the couch, which faces front at a raked angle. At the left of the sofa is the little work table with a wing chair behind it. The armchair which had been on the left is now on the right. The stool is under the table. On the table are pen and ink, stamps, and several pamphlets. The pouf is in front of the window. The rest is the same as in Act One. The blind is raised. JOSÉPHA *enters from down left. She places* CYPRIENNE'S *coat on the chair and then brushes off* CYPRIENNE'S *hat.*

JOSÉPHA [*to* BASTIEN, *who enters from the vestibule carry-*

ing newspapers on a tray]. Well, slowpoke, have you done everything?

Bastien. Yes, my angel.

Josépha. The carriage is ready?

Bastien. What carriage?

Josépha. The one Madame is waiting for.

Bastien. I wouldn't know. I've been on an errand. I'll find out as soon as I've seen Monsieur.

Josépha. Well, for heaven's sake, hurry! [*Exit* JOSÉPHA *down left.*]

Bastien. There he is!

DES PRUNELLES *enters from his study.*

Bastien [*behind the table*]. Here are Monsieur's newspapers. [BASTIEN *puts the papers on the table.*]

Des Prunelles. Have you been to Monsieur Adhémar's already?

Bastien. I just came back, monsieur.

Des Prunelles. You saw him?

Bastien. Yes, monsieur. I had no sooner rung the bell than he opened the door with a big smile and cried out, "At last, my little darling." Then he saw me and stopped smiling.

Des Prunelles. You gave him my letter?

Bastien. Which he read, monsieur, twice.

Des Prunelles. Did he give you any reply?

Bastien. He said, "Tell Monsieur I will most certainly be there." He was still annoyed about the way he greeted me.

Des Prunelles. That's enough! You may go. [*He picks up the newspaper.*]

Josépha [*to* BASTIEN *as she enters*]. Madame is getting impatient for that carriage.

Bastien. I'm off!

Des Prunelles [*calmly, crossing down right*]. Don't bother! Tell Madame the carriage is not ready.

Josépha. Huh?

Des Prunelles. I told the coachman not to harness the horses.

Josépha [*stupefied*]. I beg your pardon, monsieur?

Des Prunelles. The horses are sick!

Josépha. They are?

Des Prunelles. Yes. [*To* BASTIEN.] You, what are you waiting for? [*Exit* BASTIEN *through vestibule.*]

Josépha [*to herself as she backs away to the left*]. Things will be topsy-turvy here, and very soon!

Des Prunelles. What are you saying?

Josépha. Nothing, monsieur. I was only saying, "Oh, those poor sick horses." [*To herself.*] It's every man for himself. [*Exit* JOSÉPHA *down left.*]

Des Prunelles [*alone*]. Just in time. He was expecting her. I was right about that false telegram. How pleasant it will be, my dear cousin, to catch you in another trap, your own! "My little darling"? What gives him the right to talk that way? [*He opens paper and sits in armchair to the right of table.*]

Cyprienne [*offstage left, exasperated*]. Oh, he did?

Josépha [*offstage*]. Yes, madame.

Des Prunelles. This is it.

Cyprienne [*offstage*]. He actually dared to—— [*Breaking into a strident laugh and approaching the door.*] Oh well, if he wants to play games . . .

Des Prunelles [*pretending to laugh*]. This is really it!

Cyprienne [*entering and throwing her hat on the chair*]. Ah! There you are, monsieur! [*Crossing to him.*] Was it you who forbade *my* coachman to harness *my* carriage?

Des Prunelles [*quietly, closing his paper and rising*]. It was I, my belovèd.

Cyprienne. Under the pretext that my horses were ill?

Des Prunelles. Just as you say, my dear.

Cyprienne. Oh!

Des Prunelles. Excuse me, my sweet. [*He puts the paper on the table and crosses to close the door that* CYPRIENNE *has left open. He then returns to her, takes her hands, and leads her to the couch. Bewildered,* CYPRIENNE *hesitates to sit down. He insists gallantly.*] Please. [CYPRIENNE *sits and watches him in a stupor.*] There. [*He sits next to her.*] From now on, we shall always talk like this, like good friends, [*He takes her hand, which she surrenders automatically.*] hand in hand, thanks to this little piece of paper. [*He pulls the telegram out of his pocket and shows it to her.*]

Cyprienne [*surprised*]. Oh!

Des Prunelles [*happily*]. Do you understand?

Cyprienne [*with a cry of joy*]. Divorce!

Des Prunelles. Blessèd divorce!

Cyprienne [*uneasily*]. But a little while ago, you talked as if——

Des Prunelles. A little while ago, sweet child, I didn't dare believe in it. But now the law has been passed.

Cyprienne. You will consent?

Des Prunelles. Yes! I should think so.

Cyprienne. And we can get a divorce?

Des Prunelles. Whenever you please.

Cyprienne [*kissing him wildly*]. Oh, you are wonderful. You're simply wonderful. I love you so much. [*She stops herself.*] Is this a joke? Is it really true? Don't fill me with false hopes. Can we get a divorce? Is it a promise?

Des Prunelles. A gentleman never goes back on his word.

Cyprienne. Oh, my sweetest darling! How happy I am! Now what do we do?

Des Prunelles. Well that, my dear cherub, is up to us. But let's talk about it later. At the moment, let's bask together in the friendliness of separation.

Cyprienne. The frankness!

Des Prunelles. The tenderness!

Cyprienne. Ah, that is so true. I have never loved you so much. [*She takes his head in her two hands and kisses him.*]

Des Prunelles [*kissing her*]. It's the only thing to do. We don't like each other any more. Why not part good friends instead of living together, like cat and dog, always fighting, and filling our lives with deceits and miseries?

Cyprienne. Oh, how miserable you made me!

Des Prunelles [*laughing*]. And how you deceived me! Well, we can laugh about it now.

Cyprienne [*gaily*]. Yes, it's really very funny! How much did you spy on me, you big tyrant? Hm? [*She pinches his chin.*]

Des Prunelles [*pinching her chin*]. Not enough.

Cyprienne [*pinching his chin*]. Oh, no? And that game with the electric bells?

Des Prunelles [*pinching her chin*]. Oh, that! My little bell found enough, didn't it?

Cyprienne [*pinching his chin*]. But the funniest thing is that I heard you last night.

Des Prunelles [*pinching her chin*]. You didn't!

Cyprienne [*pinching his chin*]. Oh yes, I did! I said to myself, "What can he be up to in the greenhouse?"

Des Prunelles [*pinching her chin*]. I was very, very quiet.

Cyprienne. But I have excellent ears. And you gave me nightmares.

Des Prunelles. Ha!

Cyprienne. I dreamed about daggers and poison. I could see you sharpening your sabers.

Des Prunelles [*laughing*]. Ha! Ha!

Cyprienne [*starting to laugh*]. Wasn't that silly?

Des Prunelles. To even the score, there was something that kept me from sleeping, too.

Cyprienne. What?

Des Prunelles. How the devil did Adhémar always know when I was out?

Cyprienne [*laughing, stopping herself*]. You won't get mad?

Des Prunelles. Of course not.

Cyprienne. Are you sure?

Des Prunelles. Why, yes. At a time like this? Come now!

Cyprienne. All right. A signal.

Des Prunelles. Wonderful! But how? Where?

Cyprienne. Here.

Des Prunelles. Here?

Cyprienne. Yes. Guess!

Des Prunelles [*pointing to the right*]. At the window?

Cyprienne. Naturally.

Des Prunelles. A big piece of paper? You wrote on it with charcoal? [*He mimes large letters in the air.*]

Cyprienne [*laughing*]. Oh! That's too complicated.

Des Prunelles. Was it a candle? [*He mimes raising and lowering candle.*]

Cyprienne [*laughing*]. Oh, you'll never guess it. I'd better tell you. The window blind!

Des Prunelles. The window blind?

Cyprienne [*running to the window and undoing the blind*]. Yes! Watch. This means: He is here. [*She lowers it half-way.*] He is going out. [*She lowers the blind all the way.*] He is gone!

Des Prunelles [*gaily*]. Ah! Charming, but dangerous. The possibility of a servant——

Cyprienne [*crossing to the table*]. No one touches that blind but Josépha and I.

Des Prunelles. So! Josépha was your little helper?

Cyprienne. I should say so!

Des Prunelles. Brave girl! I thought she was. And what about the handsome Adhémar? I use the word "handsome" to please you, but confidentially, and this is the only criticism I would allow myself, he isn't as tempting as all that, is he?

Cyprienne [*leaning on the back of the armchair*]. Ah! He's a very nice boy.

Des Prunelles. That may be, but truthfully, damn it, he's no Apollo.

Cyprienne. I'm not used to dealing with Apollos.

Des Prunelles. Er . . . quite so.

Cyprienne [*crossing behind armchair*]. And then again, one doesn't have much choice in the provinces. It takes so little to satisfy one. One is so bored.

Des Prunelles. In short, you are mad about him.

Cyprienne. Mad? Oh, no! You mustn't exaggerate.

Des Prunelles [*crossing to her*]. Can't you tell me about it now we have nothing to hide from each other?

Cyprienne. Why should I?

Des Prunelles [*taking her hand*]. Well, in the interest of our divorce it's important that we straighten out all these little questions.

Cyprienne. Right!

Des Prunelles. You said this morning, "I am a virtuous woman. I have never forgotten my duties to you." Hm? Now confess. That was just a good little joke, wasn't it?

Cyprienne. Why no!

Des Prunelles. Come now, we can be honest with each other. We've agreed to it. You can't expect me to believe you didn't put one little pin prick into our marriage contract.

Cyprienne. Not one.

Des Prunelles. Oh, come, come, my little cupid!

Cyprienne. Never! I——

Des Prunelles. Not even a little, tiny tear? A teensy, weensy tear?

Cyprienne. On my word of honor!

Des Prunelles. In all the three months it has lasted?

Cyprienne. Four months.

Des Prunelles. Four? Why I thought——

Cyprienne. Four!

Des Prunelles. All the more reason. In all those four months you only plucked daisies together?

Cyprienne. Oh, my poor darling! If you only knew how inconvenient it is. Everyone spies on you; you're never alone.

Des Prunelles. Fine! But didn't you even joggle a bit in the carriage with him?

Cyprienne. Never! And not because I wasn't asked.

Des Prunelles. And you never went to his rooms?

Cyprienne. Never, never, never. Word of honor! I was going there tonight for the first time, because of the telegram. But I had warned you about that.

Des Prunelles. But you must have been together in other places besides this.

Cyprienne. Oh, here and there. In courtyards, side streets, the museum.

Des Prunelles. And in all these places you did nothing but chat?

Cyprienne. We chatted tenderly.

Des Prunelles. Nothing more serious? Not the slightest little kiss?

Cyprienne. Oh, yes.

Des Prunelles. Ah!

Cyprienne. But that's not serious. You were talking of serious things.

Des Prunelles. Well?

Cyprienne [*laughing*]. Why do you want to hear all these little stories now?

Des Prunelles. They amuse me.

Cyprienne [*gaily, pulling the armchair closer to him*]. Oh, then listen! Here's the list: the first kiss—that was four months ago—on the shoulder, at the Mayor's Ball while putting on my cloak.

Des Prunelles. That's one.

Cyprienne. The second was this summer— [*She stops.*] —you're sure you're not angry?

Des Prunelles. Can't you see I'm not?

Cyprienne. The second was this summer, between two doors, on my bare upper arm. He even bit me.

Des Prunelles. Two.

Cyprienne. The third one was eight days ago, on my neck, while watching the little goldfish.

Des Prunelles. Go on.

Cyprienne. That's all.

Des Prunelles. Cyprienne!

Cyprienne. If there was anything else I would tell you . . . now.

Des Prunelles [*rising*]. There's something I would be most curious to see.

Cyprienne. What?

Des Prunelles. Your correspondence.

Cyprienne. His letters? You want them? They're right here.

Des Prunelles. Here? I searched everywhere. [*He crosses right and automatically puts his hand on the table as he indicates the whole room.*]

Cyprienne [*laughing*]. Ha! Ha! Ha!

Des Prunelles. What are you laughing at?

Cyprienne [*laughing*]. Your hand is right on them.

Des Prunelles [pulling out the drawers of the work table].
In here?

*She runs to the table and pushes a button, and a secret drawer
opens on the side of the table.*

Cyprienne. See!
Des Prunelles. Ah!

CYPRIENNE *takes the drawer and sits on the stool by the
center table.* DES PRUNELLES *crosses behind the table and sits
in the armchair.*

Cyprienne [taking the letters from the drawer]. They are
all in the order in which they were written.
Des Prunelles [very anxiously]. Let me see the last one?
*Cyprienne [taking a letter from the packet and keeping the
drawer on her knees].* Here it is. You can see I dated it in
pencil: "November 16, 1880."
Des Prunelles. Yesterday! That's good. [*Reading.*] "My
dearest love, this day makes it one hundred twenty-two when
added to the rest, since my great love for you I first con-
fessed." It's in verse!
Cyprienne. You think so?
Des Prunelles [continuing]. "And I'm no more advanced
in your favor than that first hour." [*He makes a satisfied
movement.*] "O Cyprienne, take pity on my suffering!"
Cyprienne. Poor boy.
Des Prunelles [wiping his brow and returning the letter].
Phew!
*Cyprienne [returning the letter to its place in the packet,
which she puts in drawer].* You see I have not betrayed you.
Des Prunelles. And, in spite of our divorce, I am glad.
[*Rummaging through drawer.*] And all these knickknacks?
Cyprienne. Souvenirs.
Des Prunelles. Flowers, ribbons, a match? [*He takes it.*]
Cyprienne [taking it from him]. Oh, that! That is in
memory of the beautiful fright you gave us fifteen days ago.
Des Prunelles. Hm?
Cyprienne. The night you came home unexpectedly. I
was here with Adhémar. I heard you open the front door;
I barely had time to turn out the lamp. We hid in the dark,
terrified. You came in, cursing the servants and groping your
way to the fireplace. You found a box of matches; you struck
one—crack! It flared up—and went out. Another—crack!
It flared up—and went out. A third—crack! This one didn't

even flare up. And there were no more. You went out cursing; Adhémar stole away; and I preserved this match as an expression of gratitude for the miserable matches matchmakers make. [*She puts the match back in the drawer.*]

Des Prunelles [*gaily*]. I had a feeling you were there. [*Searching in the drawer and pulling out a button.*] A button?

Cyprienne [*putting the drawer on the table*]. The overcoat. Ah, this is really funny! Don't you recognize it? [*She playfully raises* DES PRUNELLES' *arm so that the button is at his eye level.*]

Des Prunelles. No.

Cyprienne. This is the button you picked up from the carpet and gave to Josépha. "Here," you said, "here is a button to be sewn on my overcoat." [*She laughs.*] It was Adhémar's.

Des Prunelles [*laughing with a little effort*]. Ha! Ha! Very funny, indeed! [*Replacing the button and pulling a leaf out of the drawer.*] A vine leaf?

Cyprienne [*taking the leaf quickly*]. Ah, ha! This is a little spicier. It's a vine leaf I found one day in my hair.

Des Prunelles. Huh!

Cyprienne [*rising*]. But it's such a long story.

Des Prunelles [*restraining her*]. Tell me!

Cyprienne. Oh, it is too complicated.

Des Prunelles [*pulling her onto his knees*]. That's all right. Tell me. Please . . . I beg you!

Cyprienne. Really? All right. Do you remember last autumn we gathered grapes at our vineyard in Glisonnière?

Des Prunelles. Yes.

Cyprienne. We were getting along together, and you barely gave Adhémar a thought. Well, he was in charge of the wood-chopping in the neighboring field, and the day before we left I told him, "Tomorrow, at two, go to the pressing house. I will join you there." [*At a movement from* DES PRUNELLES *she starts to rise.*] Am I too heavy?

Des Prunelles. No, no. Go on.

Cyprienne. At two o'clock the next day I started out, and to avoid both the sun and discovery, I used the path under the covered trellis. Suddenly I saw you among the vines, going somewhere in a great hurry. Where? To the pressing room! Imagine my fear! Adhémar was there. You would bump right into him. All would be lost. Trying to stop you, I quickly called out, "Henri! Where are you going?" thinking Adhémar would hear and hide in some old wine keg. Without stopping, you called back, "I am going to the pressing room to find a certain wine keg we need." Even worse! You would search everywhere for your wine keg, only to find Adhémar inside it. And you were nearly to the door. Terrified, I screamed, "Come here first!" You stopped. "What's wrong?" "Please, please hurry. I've been stung by some horrible flying creature!" And holding my breath, I stung *myself* with my brooch just above my garter. You came running. "Let's see!" I limped behind a tree. "Where's the bite? Where is it?" "See? Right here. Now look very carefully or it will bite me again." And you searched . . . very carefully——

Des Prunelles. And of course there was no "horrible flying creature," except Adhémar.

Cyprienne. Adhémar used the time to run away, if that's what you mean.

Des Prunelles. He was a busier bee than I thought. But I wasn't too big a fool. If I remember correctly——

Cyprienne [*covering his mouth with leaf*]. Shhhh!

Des Prunelles. So this vine leaf——

Cyprienne [*putting it in his lapel*]. Is yours. Now you can't truthfully call that an infidelity.

Des Prunelles [*gaily*]. Well, well, I am untainted. But, by God, didn't I handle that well?

Cyprienne [*laughing and embracing him*]. Mmmm, yes! I should say so!

BASTIEN *enters from the vestibule, followed by* ADHÉMAR.

Bastien. Monsieur de Gratignan. [ADHÉMAR *and* BASTIEN *stop short and stare stupefied at the sight of* CYPRIENNE *in* DES PRUNELLES' *arms. Exit* BASTIEN, *hurriedly.*]

Cyprienne [*astonished*]. Adhémar!

Des Prunelles [*to* CYPRIENNE]. Yes. I wrote and asked him to come.

Adhémar [*bewildered and talking to himself as he crosses left*]. Was it to show me this?

Des Prunelles [*gaily*]. Come in, young man, come in! Don't feel you're not wanted!

Adhémar. Humph!

CYPRIENNE *rises quickly.*

Des Prunelles [*also rising and crossing to* ADHÉMAR, *jovially*]. Well, my good friend, so it's impossible to extinguish this fervor of yours? It's so wild a passion, almost a delirium?

Adhémar. Monsieur!

Des Prunelles. Cyprienne has told me all. [*Showing him the drawer.*] The match, the button, the vine leaf, the kisses on the neck, the shoulder, the arm. Heavens, but you were doing well. And what a devil! It seems you even bite.

Adhémar [*looking at* CYPRIENNE, *who smiles at him*]. You know?

Des Prunelles [*smiling at him and talking familiarly*]. In short, you can't live without my wife, and that's all there is to it? She is an absolute necessity to you?

Adhémar [*still astonished*]. But——

Des Prunelles. In that case, my dear boy, take her. [*Crossing to* CYPRIENNE.] Take her. I give her to you!

Adhémar [*stunned, down left*]. Huh!

Des Prunelles. Isn't that nice of me?

Cyprienne [*gaily*]. He doesn't understand.

Des Prunelles [*to* ADHÉMAR]. The divorce law.

Cyprienne [*to* ADHÉMAR]. We are getting a divorce.

Des Prunelles. And you two will marry. I will give the bride away.

Adhémar. Divorce?

Cyprienne. It was just voted in.

Adhémar [*forgetting*]. Ridiculous!

Cyprienne [*startled*]. What? Your telegram!

Des Prunelles. Shh. I understand. In spite of the telegram, he still can't believe his good fortune, isn't that right? You're afraid.

Adhémar. My God!

Des Prunelles. It's only natural. I was the same. I had to reassure myself; I had to rush over to the City Hall. Authentic, official. It couldn't be more certain.

Adhémar. It *is* a law?

Cyprienne. Without a doubt.

Adhémar [*to himself*]. Oh, what luck!

Des Prunelles. Of course, I said to myself: Let's put it to use. Let's put it to use at once. And after a very cordial chat with this dear child, we are agreed. It is signed, sealed, and with no hard feelings, I deliver her to you.

Adhémar [*a little worried, crosses toward him*]. Oh, monsieur! This is more than I had hoped for.

Des Prunelles. I believe you, my dear boy. A pretty little lady who will bring you four hundred thousand francs, all her own.

Adhémar [*brightening*]. Four hundred——

Des Prunelles. Four hundred. A love match that is also

good business. Why, you don't have a penny. You are very lucky!

Adhémar [*overjoyed*]. Yes! Four hundred! Ah, monsieur! [*He puts his hat on the mantel and crosses to* DES PRU-NELLES.] My benefactor!

ADHÉMAR *holds out his hand.* DES PRUNELLES *takes it and reaches out with his other hand for* CYPRIENNE. *They all join hands, forming a circle.*

Des Prunelles. Of course, my friend, of course. Now, my dear ones, let's stop being emotional and be more businesslike. [*To* ADHÉMAR.] Sit down. Let's discuss this divorce, and thoroughly examine the ways and means.

DES PRUNELLES *sits on the couch.* CYPRIENNE *sits on the stool to the right of the table.* ADHÉMAR *takes a chair and sits left in front of the work table.*

Adhémar [*seated*]. Good idea.

Des Prunelles [*seated*]. Now then.

Cyprienne [*seated and leaning on the table*]. Yes!

Des Prunelles. I know a little about the divorce law. Cyprienne knows everything about it.

Cyprienne. Everything.

Des Prunelles. So we need no outside help. The actual law is only Section IV of the civil code, slightly modified. Now, there are several ways to proceed. The first, and by far the simplest, is divorce by mutual consent. That certainly fits our case. And we have fulfilled the required conditions: two years of marriage.

Cyprienne. But that takes too long.

Adhémar. Too long?

Cyprienne [*briskly*]. Yes. Request for divorce must be renewed every three months, with written permission of those parents not deceased, requisitions for four witnesses not less than fifty years of age, and a presentation before the President of the Tribunal, which entails remittance of official records and reports, a petition for admittance, a paternal speech from the magistrates, friendly hints from the witnesses, and stubbornness from the man and wife, all neatly written down. Another official journal, a disposition for an application to a judge, decisions from the public authorities, verification, declaration of admittance, an appearance before the mayor, and at last, you are pronounced divorced . . . too late. By this time you have gone mad.

Adhémar. How long do these formalities take?

Des Prunelles [*who has picked up a lawbook from the table and opened it*]. Oh, ten months.

Adhémar [*jumping up*]. Ten months!

Des Prunelles. If nothing goes wrong.

Cyprienne. And that isn't all.

Adhémar. Huh?

Cyprienne. No. Article 297. [*To* DES PRUNELLES, *who is looking for it in the lawbook.*] At the bottom of the page. "In the case of divorce by mutual consent, neither party will be allowed to contract a new marriage until three years from the date of the divorce."

Adhémar. Three years!

Des Prunelles [*passing him the lawbook*]. All together, four years.

Cyprienne. Oh, no! Do you expect me to wait four years, with my hands tied, between a husband who isn't any longer and another who isn't yet? Oh, no! Don't expect that of me.

Des Prunelles. Never!

Cyprienne. That's just what I say.

Des Prunelles. Impossible! Therefore, we must change our thinking to divorce on definite grounds.

Adhémar [*putting his finger on a page of the lawbook*]. Adultery! You surprise the two of us "in flagrante delicto."

Cyprienne. In that case, we would never be able to marry.

Adhémar [*frightened*]. What?

Cyprienne. Article 298. [*To* ADHÉMAR, *who is looking for it in the lawbook.*] At the top of the next page. "If divorce is granted on the grounds of adultery, the culpable person shall not be allowed to marry with his or her accomplice."

Adhémar [*reading passage*]. Impossible!

Cyprienne. It is felt that they wouldn't repent their misdemeanor.

Des Prunelles. May I also point out that I am being divorced so as not to be you-know-what, and if I were divorced on *those* grounds, that's just what I would be. Which would be too ridiculous.

Adhémar and Cyprienne. That's right.

Des Prunelles. Another way!

Cyprienne. There's not much choice. We can't plead insanity, desertion, libel, or moral excesses.

Adhémar [*still reading the lawbook, pointing to an article*]. I have it! We could invoke a certain physical weakness in the husband.

Cyprienne [*quickly*]. Oh, no! It doesn't go that far.

Des Prunelles [*squeezing her hand*]. I thank you!

Cyprienne. There's nothing left but assault and battery.

Adhémar. Hitting?

Des Prunelles. That's it. We are forced to give each other a good whack on the noggin.

Cyprienne. But the only one that will count will be the one *I* get.

Des Prunelles. Absolutely.

Cyprienne. And before witnesses, in public. How jolly!

Des Prunelles. My goodness, we can stage it very prettily. We shall invite some friends for dinner. We shall argue through every course, and for dessert——

Cyprienne. That's enough. I object!

Des Prunelles. Overruled. There are many women who wouldn't mind at all.

Cyprienne [*rising*]. Of course not! In a rage!

ADHÉMAR *rises and replaces his chair.*

Des Prunelles [*rising*]. Very well, mutual consent, four years.

Cyprienne [*crying out*]. Oh, no!

Des Prunelles. Or a slap.

Adhémar [*going to* CYPRIENNE]. Oh, my dearest, for my sake, please! Face it!

Des Prunelles. Just one insignificant slap. So dainty, so delicate, delicacy itself.

Cyprienne. There's no other way. It must be.

Des Prunelles. Then you agree?

Cyprienne. I agree.

Des Prunelles. Stout fellow! This way, at least, you'll only have to wait ten months. [*He crosses between them.*] And while we are on the subject, permit me a few deeply felt words. My cooperation has been enormous, you will admit, and you wouldn't like to repay such unmatched generosity with ingratitude.

Adhémar. Oh, monsieur!

Cyprienne. Oh, my sweet!

Des Prunelles. Then I beg you, in the short ten months you have to wait, be a little more patient than you have been thus far. If you indulge in such dangerous and exciting kisses now, there won't be anything left to do with your evenings later. I might add, young man, that for your own good—and I realize a heart so overwhelmingly smitten is not selfishly inclined—but for your own good you should restrain yourself. It's a great stroke of fortune to marry twenty thousand francs when you have a salary of two thousand. Don't take any risks. Ten months—that's a long time. Who can guarantee that your ardor won't burn itself out? And then the wedding day would arrive and one of you, the bride perchance, might cry out, "Gracious me, no! I've had enough."

Adhémar. Oh!

Des Prunelles. In your situation satiety is perilous. Don't spoil your dinner by eating too much lunch.

Adhémar. I wouldn't think of it!

Des Prunelles [*to* ADHÉMAR, *with great friendliness*]. You know what I would do if I were you? Remember that post at Arachon? I would accept it immediately, and I would leave tonight. I wouldn't be seen around here for the next ten months.

Adhémar. You think so?

Des Prunelles. Ah! That would be the wisest thing. [ADHÉMAR *and* CYPRIENNE *look at each other piteously.*] Think over what I've said. It's a friendly piece of advice I give you. May it not be the last. [*With feeling, as he puts* CYPRIENNE's *arm on his*]. When you two are one, I hope you'll let me visit you from time to time. You could save a little place for me at your fireside? Hm? At your table? On Sundays?

Cyprienne [*touched*]. Of course, my darling.

Adhémar [*touched*]. Of course!

Des Prunelles. Why, my goodness, I might even be able to help you sometimes. The advice which comes from experience! [*Patting* CYPRIENNE's *hand.*] I know her so well. And then your business affairs—I could advise you in the investment of your little savings, if you have any. One can't do much on twenty-two thousand francs. [CYPRIENNE *reacts.*] Especially if you're used to spending sixty thousand francs just for food, like Cyprienne. [*She reacts.*] But with a little management and some economies on things like food, having a smaller house, and above all, buying fewer clothes—oh, me, so many sacrifices! But to sacrifice for the one you love is pure happiness. [*Taking* ADHÉMAR's *arm.*] And I will look at you both and say, "They are so happy! And I did it." That's such a sweet, sweet thought! It's silly, but I am touched. [*To* CYPRIENNE, *taking her in his arms.*] My dear, dear child! [*To* ADHÉMAR.] May I ?

Adhémar. Oh, please.

Des Prunelles [*kissing* CYPRIENNE *on the forehead*]. Madame will think of me sometimes, won't she? [*He arranges a little curl on her forehead.*]

Cyprienne [*moved*]. You are so formal.

Des Prunelles. That's as it must be. [*To* ADHÉMAR.] Just one more? [*He kisses her and returns her to* ADHÉMAR.] Thank you. Now, you must want to be alone. You'll dine here, won't you, my dear successor?

Adhémar. Oh! You're too kind.

Des Prunelles [*crossing right*]. Please! Dine here before you leave. That would please me. [*He offers his hand.*]

Adhémar [*crossing to him, above the table*]. How can I ever thank you!

Des Prunelles [*shaking his hand, with emotion*]. By making her happy. Till later, my dear children, till later. [*He opens the door of the study, turns to give* ADHÉMAR *a last clasp of hands, then goes quickly out.* ADHÉMAR *watches him in admiration.*]

Cyprienne [*to herself, at left in front of table*]. Twenty instead of sixty thousand. This no longer seems so cheerful.

Adhémar [*joyously crossing to* CYPRIENNE]. Oh, Cyprienne! We are going to be so happy!

Cyprienne. Yes, dear, of course. I'm sure you will.

Adhémar [*pacing back and forth energetically*]. Ah, to love openly! No mystery, no little plots, no dangers.

Cyprienne. Did you find it so boring! My, isn't that odd? Those are precisely the things I found so delightful.

Adhémar [*quickly, crossing up to* DES PRUNELLES' *door*]. I did, too. But I did have regrets about deceiving such a fine gentleman. Now we have security, peace.

Cyprienne. A noble peace, my dear. Oh, how peaceful!

Adhémar [*crossing back to* CYPRIENNE, *without looking at her*]. Cyprienne, do you think we will ever be able to live up to the sacrifices he has made for us?

Cyprienne. Yes, dear, of course.

Adhémar [*still not looking at her*]. And we won't betray his trust in us, will we?

Cyprienne. No, dear, of course not.

Adhémar [*crossing back to* DES PRUNELLES' *door*]. That man! What generosity—what a heart—what a soul!

Cyprienne [*calmly*]. Yes, dear, and I am a beast.

Adhémar [*looking at* CYPRIENNE]. Hm?

Cyprienne. By all that's holy! If he is so virtuous, you must admit I'm wrong to leave him for a lover.

Adhémar [*quickly*]. Don't ever say that word again, Cyprienne. Your lover is gone; I'm your lover no longer.

Cyprienne. Of course not. Now you are my husband.

Adhémar. Your intended. A husband in waiting, who now looks on you only as his fiancée, and as such, will honor and respect you.

Cyprienne. That's right, dear, you respect me. *He* respects me. I am a terribly respected woman.

Adhémar [*transported in his own thoughts*]. After all, what's ten months?

Cyprienne. Lost time!

Adhémar [*without hearing her*]. Oh, I'll be only too glad to wait.

Cyprienne. Thank you.

Adhémar [*still not listening*]. I'll leave first thing in the morning, just as he wished, to show him how far my respect goes.

Cyprienne [*ironically and calmly*]. Oh, say it once more, dear, and then I'll believe it.

Adhémar [*surprised by her tone*]. You're a little nervous, Cyprienne?

Cyprienne. Do you think so?

Adhémar. But of course, these emotions—this sudden change! [*He crosses behind table to get his hat from mantel.*] Be calm, soul of my life. My sister expects me for dinner, so I'll run over, excuse myself, and come right back.

Cyprienne. You do that, dear, and be careful you don't get too cold on the way.

Adhémar [*behind sofa*]. Oh no. I have my overcoat.

Cyprienne. Oh. Well . . .

Adhémar. And after dinner?

Cyprienne [*sarcastically*]. We might play dominoes.

Adhémar [*excitedly*]. If you'd like to.

Cyprienne. Oh, ecstasy!

Adhémar. I won't be long, my love, my life, my treasure. [*Aside, as he exits.*] Four hundred thousand francs. Treasure is really the word! [*He exits.*]

Cyprienne [*after a moment's reflection*]. Oh, dear! It's true. Now it's no longer forbidden, it doesn't have quite the same —relish!

MADAME DE BRIONNE *enters hurriedly and crosses to* CYPRIENNE. MADAME DE VALFONTAINE *follows her.* CLAVIGNAC *crosses down left.*

Madame de Brionne. Oh, my little peach, is it really true?

Madame de Valfontaine. Has it happened?

Cyprienne. What?

Madame de Brionne and Madame de Valfontaine. Divorce?

Cyprienne. Passed? Oh, yes.

Madame de Brionne. I've won! I've won!

Clavignac [*to* MADAME DE VALFONTAINE]. Now you must see.

Cyprienne. What's going on?

Clavignac. I met these two ladies on the street. Madame de Valfontaine wouldn't believe the news.

Madame de Brionne. We made a little wager.

Madame de Valfontaine. And I still don't believe I've lost.

Cyprienne. Oh, really!

Clavignac. The telegram!

Madame de Brionne. You have it?

Cyprienne. Monsieur des Prunelles has it. Wait a minute. [MADAME DE VALFONTAINE *sits on sofa,* MADAME DE BRIONNE *stands to her left, and* CLAVIGNAC *is at the extreme left.* CYPRIENNE *knocks on* DES PRUNELLES' *door.*] Henri!

Des Prunelles [*half-opening the door and with great tenderness*]. My dearest?

Cyprienne [*affectionately*]. I'm sorry to bother you, my pet. Just one word.

Des Prunelles. Dear child, I'm yours. One moment.

Madame Valfontaine [*to* MADAME DE BRIONNE]. My! They're so nice to each other!

Clavignac. There you see it—the blessèd state of divorce.

DES PRUNELLES *enters in dress suit and white tie. He takes* CYPRIENNE'S *hand in his and walks downstage with her.*

Des Prunelles. What is it, my little rabbit? [*Seeing the ladies, gaily and gracefully.*] Ah! Ladies! I beg your pardon.

Madame de Valfontaine. We've come back.

Des Prunelles [*gallant and friendly, completely different from the first act*]. Never too often! [*He shakes hands with* MADAME DE BRIONNE.]

Cyprienne. My love, these ladies would very much like to gaze on that precious telegram.

Des Prunelles. Why, of course. It never leaves me. [*He takes it out and presents it to* MADAME DE VALFONTAINE.] There.

Madame de Valfontaine [*reading*]. "Divorce voted in! Enormous majority!"

Madame de Brionne. Ah, ha! You lose, my pretty. It's all over.

Madame de Valfontaine. So it's all over. Not yet! There's the Senate.

All [laughing]. Oh!

Madame de Brionne. We needn't bother about that.

Cyprienne. The surprising thing is that the married woman is annoyed . . . and the widow rejoices.

Madame de Valfontaine. It was so pleasant the way it was. The husband went his way; the wife went hers. Who needed divorce?

Cyprienne [to MADAME DE BRIONNE]. I see. But you, Estelle, why are you so radiant?

Madame de Brionne. First, I won my wager. But, mainly, I always wanted to marry a widower because he would have exhausted all his bad temper driving his first wife to the grave. But a divorced man is even better. The first wife would have exasperated him so much that the second would be a delight.

Des Prunelles [laughing]. Ah! Very, very prettily put. So charming! [*He kisses her hand as* CYPRIENNE *looks on in amazement.*]

Madame de Brionne [taking the telegram from MADAME DE VALFONTAINE]. Excuse me. [*To* DES PRUNELLES.] Would you mind, dear?

Cyprienne. Mind what!?

Madame de Brionne. Some twenty ladies followed us here to learn if the telegram really existed. They didn't dare come in. But they are at the garden gate, and I promised to show it to them from a distance.

Des Prunelles [opening the door on the right]. Show it, dear lady, show it! We mustn't be selfish.

Madame de Brionne [turning to him]. They're all married.

Clavignac. Go and enlighten them.

Madame de Brionne. They would be even happier if they could touch it. [*To* DES PRUNELLES.] Could we make copies?

Des Prunelles. I think so.

MADAME DE BRIONNE *exits into the garden.* MADAME DE VALFONTAINE *and* CYPRIENNE *stand on the threshold to watch.*

Des Prunelles [aside to CLAVIGNAC, *whom he pulls to the left*]. Thanks, friend.

Clavignac [in a low voice]. What for?

Des Prunelles. For giving such swift wings to my decoy.

A murmur is heard outside, followed by cries of satisfaction.

Clavignac. What's that? The telegram?

Des Prunelles. Adhémar sent it. It's as false as your teeth.

Clavignac [*crying out*]. What!

Des Prunelles. Sshh, you fool!

Clavignac. You scoundrel, what do you mean, giving me this empty hope by making believe you believe it yourself.

Des Prunelles. That's the way I must play it.

Clavignac. And you couldn't take me into your confidence?

Des Prunelles. Would you have spread the news with such enthusiasm?

Clavignac. Listen! You deserve a—— But what good does all this do?

Des Prunelles. I will regain my wife, that's all.

Clavignac. Pooh! And Adhémar?

Des Prunelles. Ha! I've already ruined his ammunition. And I am going to crown them both with a fool's cap.

Clavignac. How?

Des Prunelles. I get a divorce. And I unite them.

Clavignac. Well?

Des Prunelles. Heaven help me!

Clavignac. Well, and then?

Des Prunelles. And then, then, you blockhead, who can't see farther than your nose, *he* becomes the husband——

Clavignac. And you are the lover!

Des Prunelles [*seeing the women returning*]. Shh.

Madame de Brionne. Ecstatic! They were ecstatic! Here, dear monsieur, here is your talisman. [*She returns the telegram to him.*]

Des Prunelles [*kissing her hand*]. May it bring you happiness.

Madame de Brionne. Something tells me it will. [*To* CYPRIENNE.] Toodeloo, sweetheart! [*She crosses up to the vestibule.*]

Cyprienne. Till tomorrow! [*Conducting* MADAME DE VALFONTAINE *to the vestibule.*] Come, dearest, cheer up!

Madame de Valfontaine. Never! Romance is dead. [MADAME DE VALFONTAINE *and* MADAME DE BRIONNE *exeunt accompanied by* CYPRIENNE.]

Clavignac. So now you can dine with me.

Des Prunelles. I'll be there, but not with you.

Clavignac. How's that?

Des Prunelles [*hearing his wife returning*]. Sh! Be gone, and not a word.

Clavignac [*to* CYPRIENNE, *bowing*]. Madame! [CYPRIENNE *bows without speaking.* CLAVIGNAC *exits. As this is happening* BASTIEN *enters from the study with* DES PRUNELLES' *hat and coat. He puts them on the pouf.* BASTIEN *then goes out.*]

Des Prunelles [*going over to put on his hat and coat*]. And now, sweet cherub, I shall also bid you good evening.

Cyprienne [*distressed*]. What do you mean, good evening. Aren't you dining here?

Des Prunelles. Oh, no.

Cyprienne. Didn't you invite Adhémar to dinner?

Des Prunelles. With you, dear. Not with me!

Cyprienne. Oh! I had thought—— It would have been so lovely! A little engagement party with just us three.

Des Prunelles. It will be even lovelier with just you two. I would get in the boy's way.

Cyprienne [*still at the left*]. It's just the opposite. You would stir him up. Now that he's going to marry me, he's curdled . . . like an old pudding.

Des Prunelles [*crossing back to her, behind the couch*]. And also, to be frank, I'm not sorry to get a breath of air and stretch my arms now that my confinement is over.

Cyprienne. There's my whole evening spoiled. Please stay!

Des Prunelles [*crossing away*]. Really, I can't. Once more, good night. [*He holds out his hand.*]

Cyprienne [*taking his hand and holding it*]. But where are you dining?

Des Prunelles [*trying to get loose*]. At Dagneau's, in the Grand Vatel.

Cyprienne [*still holding on*]. Alone?

Des Prunelles. Probably. [*He disengages his hand.*]

Cyprienne. Ah! You're not certain?

Des Prunelles. Please!

Cyprienne. Someone's waiting for you?

Des Prunelles. No. But I might possibly find some friend . . .

Cyprienne. A woman?

Des Prunelles [*laughing*]. Ha! ha!

Cyprienne. Admit it! You're dining with a woman.

Des Prunelles [*laughing*]. I assure you I'm not.

Cyprienne. Henri! Don't lie.

Des Prunelles [*still laughing*]. But I'm not lying.

Cyprienne. You're hiding something. It's not fair. I told you everything. Now you tell me! Who is she—I beg you—tell me who she is?

Des Prunelles [*laughing*]. How can I, when I don't know myself?

Cyprienne [*going to him and rumpling his tie with her fingertips*]. Did you dress so prettily to dine alone?

Des Prunelles. Of course.

Cyprienne. You never made yourself so handsome for me.

Des Prunelles. Oh, come now!

Cyprienne [*half-annoyed and half-coaxing*]. Really, in our situation, don't you think it's rather quaint? All this secrecy about nothing? Why? [*Taking his arm in a friendly way.*] Why should it bother me now? We're nothing but good friends, aren't we? Like two comrades—two playboys!

Des Prunelles. Precisely.

Cyprienne. Well then?

Des Prunelles. Well then, why *does* it bother you?

Cyprienne. Because I want to know. It irritates me not to know.

Des Prunelles [*laughing*]. Then I'll say once more there's no such person.

Cyprienne [*letting go of his arm*]. You can't say it without laughing.

Des Prunelles. I'm laughing . . . because it's so charming, this flurry of posthumous jealousy.

Cyprienne. But it isn't jealousy. It's curiosity. It's quite normal. Name any woman . . .

Des Prunelles. Nevertheless, I cannot tell you.

Cyprienne [*quickly*]. Ah! Ha! You can't . . . You see!

Des Prunelles. Because——

Cyprienne. You're afraid to compromise her.

Des Prunelles. No, because——

Cyprienne [*without listening*]. Do I know her?

Des Prunelles. No more than I.

Cyprienne [*quickly*]. But as well! Is she one of my acquaintances?

Des Prunelles. If you——

Cyprienne. I'll wager it's one of my friends.

Des Prunelles. Oh!

Cyprienne. That's always the way! I'm almost positive that if I looked— [*Suddenly.*] —Madame de Brionne!

Des Prunelles. Estelle?

Cyprienne. Estelle! Ah! You've betrayed yourself.

Des Prunelles. Oh, no!

Cyprienne. Oh! "Estelle." Oh God, it's all so clear.

Des Prunelles. But I call her "Estelle" just as you do.

Cyprienne [*crossing away from him*]. Just as I do? Oh, do tell! *I* say, "Estelle"—very clipped—but you: "Est-e-elle!" You bleat her name. It goes on for an hour.

Des Prunelles. But——

Cyprienne. Oh! I thought as much. Hmph!

Des Prunelles. Ah!

Cyprienne. She was always slinking about my house. I've never been able to endure her, that sly busybody with her giddy affectations—that snooping, jealous, man-eating flibbertygibbet!

Des Prunelles. Oh!

Cyprienne [*leaning against table*]. Naturally you defend her! And false from head to toe! Her hair, her eyebrows, even her eyelashes, nothing's hers. Painted, polished, and varnished. And that simpering smile—I wonder how she glues that on!

Des Prunelles. Oh!

Cyprienne [*leaving the table*]. Besides, she didn't hide it very well when she told us she was hoping for divorce so as to help herself to someone else's husband. . . . A few minutes ago, right here under my nose, she was ecstatic—she was dancing with joy! You kissed her hand. That was shameful of you.

Des Prunelles. If you would let me——

Cyprienne. So! That one! Your conquest, really! I can't compliment you on it.

Des Prunelles. Now, that's not in very good taste, my little bunny rabbit. I don't rip your Adhémar apart.

Cyprienne [*crossing up left*]. Estelle! . . . I ask you . . . Estelle! Is it possible that you're idiotic enough to marry her?

Des Prunelles. I would like to point out to you——

Cyprienne [*her two hands on the back of the sofa*]. You *are* going to marry her?

Des Prunelles. I didn't say that.

Cyprienne. But you are. [*With a cry of horror.*] Oh! You're going to marry that painted clown, who will deceive you as she did her first husband, and who will deceive her third husband after you are dead, poisoned by her chemical products. [*As she talks, she moves to the right behind the table.*]

Des Prunelles. You go too far. [*He sits on the couch and puts on his gloves.*]

Cyprienne [*crossing down right*]. And that rouge pot will take my place here. She'll install herself in my house— [*She crosses to armchair.*] —sit in my furniture. She'll splatter mud on me as she rides by in my own carriages. [*Crosses to* DES PRUNELLES.] If I knew it would be like that—I'd rather not give you a divorce!

Des Prunelles. But Adhémar——

Cyprienne [*falling on the armchair*]. Oh! Adhémar!—To be left for that overstuffed doll! No, no! That one! Truly, it's too much.

Des Prunelles [*standing*]. I'm not leaving you; we're leaving each other.

Cyprienne [*rising and crossing down*]. Anyone else, it wouldn't make any difference to me. But that one—oh!

Des Prunelles [*behind her*]. Well then, be happy. It isn't she.

Cyprienne [*turning quickly and seizing his lapels so she can look him straight in the face*]. So it's someone else?

Des Prunelles. I——

Cyprienne. Who?

Des Prunelles. But it doesn't make any difference to you.

Cyprienne. It doesn't make any difference . . . But this is different. Tell me who!

Des Prunelles. But——

Cyprienne. Is she young? . . . Pretty?

Des Prunelles. Since——

Cyprienne. Prettier than I?

Des Prunelles. Why should that matter?

Cyprienne [*resolutely but close to tears*]. It bothers me.

Des Prunelles. Bah!

Cyprienne. It does, it bothers me!—that you would fly off like this, so soon, to have a jolly runaround with someone else. It's ridiculous, I know, but I can't help it. It infuriates me!

Des Prunelles [*laughing*]. Ha! ha!

Cyprienne. And another thing, you're so cheerful! You look so happy. I've never seen you so happy.

Des Prunelles [*taking her hand as if to say good-by*]. But there's every reason, my little kittycat. My freedom, your contentment, our mutual good fortune. . . . I'm happy to see you happy—because, after all, you are happy, aren't you?

Cyprienne [*kneeling in the armchair, without conviction*]. Yes.

Des Prunelles. Well then?

Cyprienne [*ready to cry*]. But there's a big fat fly in my milk!

Des Prunelles. What fly?

Cyprienne [*falling in his arms across the arm of the chair*]. You're not sorry to leave me.

Des Prunnelles. Oh!

Cyprienne. No! You're not being polite. You're tossing me in the corner like some old bouquet. You boor! It's humiliating; I don't want to be cast off like that!

Des Prunelles [*holding her against his breast and patting her shoulder*]. Aren't you pleased about our separation?

Cyprienne. Yes, but that doesn't stop me from having regrets. At least I have some regrets. But you, you don't have one. After all, we did have good times together.

Des Prunelles. Sometimes.

Cyprienne. Oh, many times! You see, you've forgotten. I'm the only one who still remembers.

Des Prunelles [*still holding her and kissing her forehead*]. That's not so.

Cyprienne. Have dinner with me one more time. People dine together on holidays. This is a holiday. You can have dinner with her tomorrow.

Des Prunelles [*still holding her*]. But she doesn't exist.

Cyprienne. Oh!

Des Prunelles. Do you want me to prove it?

Cyprienne. How?

Des Prunelles. Come dine with me.

Cyprienne [*joyously lifting her head*]. At Dagneau's?

Des Prunelles. Just the two of us.

Cyprienne. Alone?

Des Prunelles. Like men-about-town.

Cyprienne. The farewell banquet.

Des Prunelles. A divorce banquet—what a charming thought.

Cyprienne. Yes!

Des Prunelles. I will give you a nice little feast.

Cyprienne. Will you make me drunk?

Des Prunelles. If you wish.

Cyprienne [*laughing and jumping for joy, she gets her coat and hat*]. Ah, how amusing! What a wonderful idea. And on the spur of the moment . . . so original, so inspired!

Des Prunelles. Isn't it?

Cyprienne [*putting on her hat and coat*]. Oh, I'm so happy! This is more like it. I'm tingling all over! Hoorah! I must kiss you. [*She kisses him and crosses down right.*] And this way I'll be sure you won't dine with her. [*She ties the ribbons on her hat.*]

Des Prunelles [*quickly, pretending surprise*]. You mean you're really coming?

Cyprienne. Of course.

Des Prunelles. I only offered as a joke.

Cyprienne. Well, that's too bad; I took you at your word.

Des Prunelles. But poor Adhémar?

Cyprienne [*picking up her muff*]. Oh, Adhémar! I'll be dining with Adhémar the rest of my life.

Des Prunelles. And if he gets angry?

Cyprienne. Well, he'll be angry.

Des Prunelles. He'll make a scene.

Cyprienne. I'll tell him not to. [*With dignity.*] Besides, how could I dine with him alone, without you? What would it look like . . . in front of the servants?

Des Prunelles. The future.

Cyprienne. Who knows about that? All three of us, good. Or just you and I.

Des Prunelles. Better still.

Cyprienne [*taking his arm tightly and putting on her gloves*]. It's so enchanting . . . a wedding breakfast in reverse!

Des Prunelles. Our last *tête à tête!*

Cyprienne. Let's go! He's coming back. [*She rings the bell.*]

Des Prunelles [*going to pick up his coat and hat in the vestibule, and looking off right*]. Here he is!

Cyprienne. Adhémar?

Des Prunelles. In the courtyard.

JOSÉPHA *enters from down left.*

Cyprienne [*to* JOSÉPHA]. Josépha.

Josépha. Madame.

Cyprienne [*quickly*]. Monsieur has just come back. No, I mean Adhémar.

Des Prunelles. Yes, yes. Monsieur! That's exactly it.

Cyprienne [*agitated*]. Tell him I've been forced to go out.

Des Prunelles [*opening the garden door*]. Alone.

Cyprienne. Alone! Alone!

Josépha [*surprised*]. Ah!

Cyprienne [*crossing to* DES PRUNELLES]. Someone came to fetch me, any excuse—you've always been able to make one up. Ask him please to excuse me. . . . Ah! . . . he may dine here if he wishes.

Josépha [*stupefied*]. Yes, madame.

Cyprienne [*pushing* DES PRUNELLES *in front of her*]. Hurry up. He'll catch us. [*They run off.*]

Josépha [*watching them wide-eyed*]. Ah! Are they back together?

ADHÉMAR *comes in through the vestibule in tails, white tie, white gloves, and carrying a bouquet of white roses. He looks like a bridegroom.* BASTIEN *appears in the door of the dining room dressed as a waiter.*

Josépha [*quickly*]. Monsieur is not home.

Adhémar [*radiant, crossing to the right*]. Never mind Monsieur! Madame?

Josépha. Madame begs you to excuse her, monsieur. She had to leave.

Adhémar [*astonished*]. Leave?

Josépha. Yes, monsieur . . . Her aunt is very ill.

Adhémar [*dismayed*]. Already! [*Throwing the bouquet on the table.*] Her aunt? Well, we'll see about that. I will go to her aunt's! [*Exit* ADHÉMAR, *quickly.*]

Bastien. Dinner is served, madame.

He offers his arm to JOSÉPHA, *who picks up the bouquet from the table; and the two of them sweep into the dining room in an imitation of their masters.*

ACT THREE

The scene is an intimate private dining room at Dagneau's, a very elegant restaurant. Upstage center are two swinging doors, in back of which can be seen a service table. On either side of these doors, the walls are raked so that the playing area is triangular. Downstage left is a door which opens into a dressing room. Upstage of this door is a piano with a piano stool, and between the piano and the swinging doors is a small serving table with knives, forks, spoons, plates, and a cruet stand. There is a chair beside the serving table, with a window over it. Downstage right is a fireplace with a mantelpiece adorned by two candelabra, a decanter, and two finger bowls. Upstage of this is a folding screen with seven leaves, folded so that it is half-open. Upstage on the right wall is another door. Center stage is a round table set for two. Left of the table is a chair. Stage left is a love seat with cushions. An armchair is by the fireplace. There is an unlighted chandelier. The only light is from two candles in each of the candelabra. As the curtain rises, the maître d'hôtel, JOSEPH, opens the door at the rear for DES PRUNELLES, who enters with CYPRIENNE on his arm. Two WAITERS follow, one of whom has a lighted taper with which to light the chandelier.

JOSEPH. This cozy room will be perfect for Madame.

Des Prunelles. Yes.

Cyprienne. If only it were warmer.

Joseph. Oh! Madame, with the fire kindled, and the gas light glowing . . . [*One* WAITER *lights the fire and the other starts to light the chandelier.*]

Des Prunelles. No, no. Don't light the chandelier, just the candles.

Joseph [*to the first* WAITER]. The candelabra! [*First* WAITER *lights them; the second prepares the service at the rear table. To* DES PRUNELLES.] It's been at least two years since we've seen Monsieur. [*He helps* DES PRUNELLES *with his overcoat.*]

Des Prunelles. This is room number eight, isn't it?

Joseph. Monsieur remembers?

Des Prunelles. Yes . . . you've made a few changes, though.

Joseph. For the convenience of our guests. In back of you, an antechamber; over here, a dressing room where Madame may remove her hat and coat.

Cyprienne. When I'm a little warmer. [*She crosses to the fireplace and warms her feet.* JOSEPH *takes* DES PRUNELLES' *hat and coat into the dressing room.*]

Des Prunelles [*taking off his gloves*]. Are you expecting Monsieur Clavignac this evening?

Joseph [*returning*]. Yes, monsieur. Room eleven, party for six. Monsieur expects no one else? Just two?

Des Prunelles. Yes.

Joseph. Would it please Madame to have the table closer to the fire?

Cyprienne. Yes, and open the screen more. There's a teensy little draft in here.

Joseph. Yes, madame.

The two WAITERS *move the table in front of the fireplace, arranging one chair to the left of it and the armchair to the right. They open the screen and place it perpendicular to the right wall, upstage of table. Then they cross up and busy themselves at the service table, as the dialogue continues.*

Joseph [*handing* DES PRUNELLES *the menu*]. Monsieur will like our oysters. Marennes? Ostend?

Des Prunelles [*to* CYPRIENNE *as he sits down on the chair*]. Do you like oysters, my love?

Cyprienne [*leaning against the armchair as she warms her feet*]. I don't care for them.

Des Prunelles [*looking at menu*]. Neither do I.

Joseph [*taking out his notebook and pencil, ready to write*]. Meat broth, consommé Crécy, or Saint-Germain?

Cyprienne. Meat broth.

Joseph [*writing*]. Fish course: turbot, salmon?

Des Prunelles. After meat broth?

The two WAITERS *leave.*

Joseph. It's proper.

Cyprienne. I prefer lobster.

Des Prunelles. Yes, no fish course. We will have lobster bordelaise, later.

Joseph. Very good, monsieur. For an entrée, may I suggest a *timbale.*

Des Prunelles. No! Lamb chops, piping hot.

Joseph [*writing*]. Piping hot . . .

Des Prunelles. What's next?

Joseph. Some succulent fowl. Quail? Our quail is very good.

Des Prunelles. No. Glazed partridge.

Joseph [*writing*]. Glazed . . .

Des Prunelles. And a Russian salad . . . a real one!

Joseph. Our salad is famous.

Des Prunelles. Then the lobsters.

Joseph [*drily*]. No sherbet?

Des Prunelles. No sherbet. Unless Madame?

Cyprienne. No. Some fruit, that's all. Be sure there's a big bunch of grapes.

Des Prunelles. Is that clear?

Joseph. Very clear, monsieur. An unusual selection, monsieur, but very, very distinguished. Of course you will have demitasse?

Des Prunelles. No. We don't care for it at night.

Joseph. Will monsieur choose his wines?

Des Prunelles. The usual: iced champagne.

Joseph. Moët? Cliquot?

Des Prunelles. No! Roederer . . . and your Chambertin, if you still have it.

Joseph. Sixty-eight?

Des Prunelles. Yes.

Joseph. I'm sure there will be some for Monsieur.

Des Prunelles. Hurry things up a bit.

Joseph. Yes, monsieur. [*To the* WAITERS, *who have just entered.*] Come! Quickly. [*Exeunt* WAITERS *and* JOSEPH.]

Des Prunelles. Well now, are you warming up?

Cyprienne [*taking off her hat and coat and leaving them on the armchair*]. A little. You seem to be well known here.

Des Prunelles. I used to be.

Cyprienne. And you will be again?

Des Prunelles. Very likely.

Cyprienne. Ah! So this is where Monsieur played his little farces?

Des Prunelles. Not as many as you might think.

Cyprienne. I'm sure when those waiters saw me with you, they took me for a loose woman.

Des Prunelles. For heaven's sake, they probably just thought you were my mistress!

Cyprienne. So suddenly I'm compromised.

Des Prunelles [*laughing*]. A little.

Cyprienne [*turning to the mirror and arranging her hair*]. How curious. . . . Oh! all those names on the mirror!

Des Prunelles. Don't be fooled by them, please.

Cyprienne. What do you mean?

Des Prunelles. The owner scratched those names there with his wife's ring so that his room would have a well-used look.

Cyprienne. Oh!

Joseph [*enters with a card on a tray*]. Monsieur! There's a person outside who was told Monsieur was here, and who begs Monsieur's permission to come in. [*He passes the tray, and* DES PRUNELLES *takes the card. A* WAITER *enters carrying the soup tureen, which he places on the serving table and exits.*]

Des Prunelles [*having looked at the card, to* CYPRIENNE]. Adhémar!

Cyprienne. Oh!

Des Prunelles [*to* JOSEPH]. All right. . . . Wait! [JOSEPH *discreetly retires upstage.*] Shall I invite him in?

Cyprienne. Heavens, no.

Des Prunelles. But, my dear——

Cyprienne. No! no! no! I don't want you to!

Des Prunelles. It's very embarrassing, having invited him to eat at home.

Cyprienne [*tearing up the card*]. Let him go and eat there! What's he doing here? Why can't he let us get divorced in peace? [*She throws the pieces in the fire.*]

Des Prunelles [*rising*]. Well, as long as he doesn't know you're here, I'll send him away. Hide in there. [*He indicates the dressing room.*]

Cyprienne [*taking her hat and coat*]. That's it. Hello and good-by. . . . Hurry up! I'm hungry. [*She goes into the dressing room.*]

Des Prunelles [*to* JOSEPH]. Show him in.

Joseph [*opening the door in the rear, speaking offstage*]. If Monsieur would——

Adhémar [*entering*]. Ah! I can come in?

Exit JOSEPH.

Des Prunelles. Yes, yes, come in.

Adhémar [*he is wet. He has an umbrella*]. Please excuse me, my dear sir. I'm not intruding? [ADHÉMAR *puts his hat on the love seat.*]

Des Prunelles. Heavens, no! I'm waiting for someone. [*Offering him a chair.*] Do come in. How did you find me?

Adhémar [*putting his umbrella against the back of the chair*]. Your Club told me you were supposed to dine here with Monsieur de Clavignac.

Des Prunelles. Oh, of course. Well, what is it?

Adhémar [*sitting on the chair*]. You are looking at a very troubled man! Wasn't it agreed that we were to dine together?

Des Prunelles. Not with me! You and Cyprienne.

Adhémar. Exactly, Cyprienne and I—excuse me, your wife and I . . . I mean, no . . . my wife. Er . . . well, anyway, *our* wife.

Des Prunelles. Yes.

Adhémar. I arrive. No one! They told me you had just left.

Des Prunelles. Indeed!

Adhémar. And Cyprienne too.

Des Prunelles. She had left?

Adhémar. After you.

Des Prunelles. Where did she go?

Adhémar [looking at him piteously]. To her sick aunt's house.

Des Prunelles. Ah!

Adhémar [quickly]. You knew nothing about it, did you?

Des Prunelles. No.

Adhémar [rising]. I believe you. I've just come from the aunt's house. She couldn't be healthier! And Cyprienne was no more there than she is here.

Des Prunelles. Pardon. You're talking of Aunt ——

Adhémar. Guérin, the widow Guérin, boulevard du Temple.

Des Prunelles. Oh! She wouldn't be the one.

Adhémar. No?

Des Prunelles. Oh, no. It would be Aunt Nicole: asthmatic, eighty-three, rue de Paris, number ninety-two.

Adhémar. Damnation! That's so far. And in such weather.

Des Prunelles [crossing to the window]. Is it raining?

Adhémar [getting his hat]. Raining and snowing, and no carriages.

Des Prunelles [crossing back]. The devil!

CYPRIENNE *opens the door and listens.*

Adhémar. If I were only sure! . . . Tell me, just between us—what do you think about this aunt of hers?

Des Prunelles. Me?

Adhémar. Yes.

Des Prunelles. Er! . . . I don't know her very well.

Adhémar. It smacks slightly of a fib to me. Don't you think so?

Des Prunelles. Ye gods! You know, as for myself, I don't have any opinion about it. It no longer concerns me.

Adhémar. Yes, but as my predecessor, couldn't you enlighten me? Has she ever used this aunt of hers with you?

Des Prunelles. I couldn't say. Why?

Adhémar. So I'll know if she has a habit of indulging in these little tricks.

Cyprienne [behind the door, to herself]. Oh!

Des Prunelles. You suspect her?

Adhémar. Oh! I know how spiteful she is, that woman. I've watched her put you on the merry-go-round.

Des Prunelles. Oh ho!

Adhémar. She whirled you through a whole rainbow of tricks.

Des Prunelles. They worked with me . . . but with you?

Adhémar. Oh, with me, they won't work at all, these habits of hers.

Des Prunelles. Good boy!

Adhémar. Oh, no! I won't be as gullible as you. Not I! [*He puts on his hat with authority.*] With me, she'll have to toe the mark.

Des Prunelles [*with a wink at* CYPRIENNE]. Spoken like a jolly old sport!

Adhémar. What did you say—Aunt who?

Des Prunelles. Nicole, ninety-two, rue de Paris.

Adhémar [*sitting on the couch*]. Damnation! [*He rolls up his trousers.*] If it wasn't for the four hundred thousand . . . but there it is. [*He rises.*] Well, I'm off—a thousand pardons —have a good time! [*He crosses upstage.*]

Des Prunelles. Thank you. [*Calling him back and picking up his umbrella.*] Your umbrella.

Adhémar [*returning*]. Oh, that's right. Thank you. [*They shake hands with the umbrella.*]

Des Prunelles. Have a good trip. [*Exit* ADHÉMAR. DES PRUNELLES *closes the door after him and crosses toward the dressing room.*] I'd fix that fellow for good if he weren't playing his part in the game so well.

Cyprienne [*half-whispering*]. He's gone?

Des Prunelles [*pretending to call* ADHÉMAR *back*]. A regret? I'll call him back.

Cyprienne [*still half-voice*]. No, no, no, no, no!

Des Prunelles [*crossing back in*]. Poor boy! He's galloping off on a fool's errand.

Cyprienne. I hope he trots. It'll take longer. This little man who has the audacity to suspect me already!

Des Prunelles. Oh, it's wicked!

Cyprienne. And my "tricks," and that "that woman"! So it's a "fib"! And I "put you on a merry-go-round"! Is this any way to talk?

Des Prunelles. No.

Cyprienne. And the way he said it. [*Imitating him.*] "That won't work at all with me. Ah ha! she'll have to toe the mark with me." I'll mark *him* with my toe, I will!

Des Prunelles [*egging her on*]. By all means.

Cyprienne [*crossing to the right*]. What a way to talk! He's such a fool!

JOSEPH *and the two* WAITERS *enter through the vestibule.*

JOSEPH *carries a plate of fruit, which he places on the table at the rear. He begins serving the soup.*

Des Prunelles. Calm down. [*To the* WAITERS.] You may serve. [*To* CYPRIENNE.] Calm down and let's have dinner. [*They sit down at the table,* DES PRUNELLES *in the chair,* CYPRIENNE *in the armchair. The two* WAITERS *serve each of them with soup. Exeunt* WAITERS *and* JOSEPH, *leaving the door open.* JOSEPH *can be seen in the rear.*]

Cyprienne. The soup will be cold. Thanks to him.

Des Prunelles [*as he takes his soup*]. My goodness, little one. You must forget this idea that you can ever combine husband and lover. He's playing his role, this boy. He's clumsy, I grant you.

Cyprienne. And grumpy! . . . and annoying, and——

Des Prunelles [*interrupting her*]. But that's not his fault. That's part of being a husband. Why was I so grumpy myself this morning, and why am I in such good spirits tonight? Because this morning I was the husband, and tonight I'm not. It's his turn to growl: he's defending himself.

Cyprienne. But he threatens to be even more annoying than you.

Des Prunelles. Naturally, he's younger. He hasn't lived as much.

JOSEPH *and the two* WAITERS *re-enter.* JOSEPH *carries a bottle of champagne in a bucket, which he places to the right of* DES PRUNELLES. *The first* WAITER *carries the platter of lamb chops, which he places in the middle of the table. The second* WAITER *removes the soup bowls. Exeunt all three. This action takes place as the dialogue continues.*

Des Prunelles [*continues talking so the* WAITERS *will not understand*]. But it would be in bad taste for me to vilify the man to whom I am entrusting the continuation of my affairs. On the contrary, I find him to be a man of superior intelligence, who has all the facilities necessary to make the enterprise prosper. However, he will not be able to avoid the disadvantages of his new position. [*At this moment the door closes after the* WAITERS. *He places the champagne between them.*] In short, all husbands can be lumped together as a single type: the husband. And all lovers as the other type: the lover. The husband has all the faults: the lover has all the virtues. Everyone will agree. Actually, the husband has only one fault: being a husband. And the lover has only one accomplishment: being a lover. [CYPRIENNE *pours herself a glass of champagne.*] This is so true that the same man, at one and the same time, can be a most annoying husband to his own wife and a most agreeable lover to someone else's wife. The difference, therefore, lies not in the individual, but in the function. [*He pours himself a drink.* JOSEPH *enters with another bottle of wine lying in its basket.*]

Cyprienne. Then one shouldn't marry?

Des Prunelles. There are so many disadvantages if one doesn't!

Cyprienne. Such as?

Des Prunelles. Oh, my goodness! [*To* JOSEPH, *who is about to refill his glass.*] I'll serve myself. Please see that we're disturbed as little as possible. [*Exit* JOSEPH, *closing the door.*] Happiness is not found in extremes—a good happy average, a good regular life, there's happiness.

Cyprienne. But it has to be good, really good.

Des Prunelles [*ringing for the* WAITERS]. It always is—with a few mutual concessions.

JOSEPH *and the two* WAITERS *re-enter.* JOSEPH *has a plate in one hand and the partridge in the other. He goes to* DES PRUNELLES' *right. The first* WAITER, *with a plate, goes to between* DES PRUNELLES *and* CYPRIENNE. *The second* WAITER *carries a salad bowl, which he places on the table at the rear.*

Des Prunelles [*continuing*]. Take, for example, the very ingenious custom they once had in Switzerland. I don't know if it still exists. [*To* JOSEPH.] Put it there; I will carve.

CYPRIENNE *and* DES PRUNELLES *pass their plates to the first* WAITER, *who gives* CYPRIENNE *the plate he had in his hand, while* JOSEPH *does the same with* DES PRUNELLES. JOSEPH *removes the platter of lamb chops and replaces it with the partridge. The two* WAITERS *go out, and* JOSEPH *goes up to the serving table to prepare the salad.* DES PRUNELLES *begins carving the bird.*

Des Prunelles [*continuing*]. When a married couple wanted to get a divorce, they were locked up in a room for eight days, with one table, one chair, one plate, and one bed. And their food was passed in to them through a tiny hole in the wall.

Cyprienne [*laughing*]. Ha! ha!

Joseph [*coming down to* DES PRUNELLES *with a little pot*]. Would Monsieur like some hot pepper?

Des Prunelles. Ye gods, yes! [JOSEPH *goes back to season the salad.*] At the end of eight days, the good citizens arrived at the door—knock, knock. [*He taps on the table with his knife.*]

Joseph [*coming back quickly*]. Monsieur?

Des Prunelles. No! Not you. [*Going on.*] "Yoo, hoo, inside there, how're we doing? What about that divorce?"

Cyprienne. Absolute silence! They'd eaten each other up.

Des Prunelles. Not at all. Three out of five no longer wanted a divorce. [JOSEPH *brings the salad, puts it down, and starts to leave.* DES PRUNELLES *calls him back.*] Wait! [*He tastes the salad.*] Good! Go! [JOSEPH *goes.*]

Cyprienne [*laughing*]. Do you think they should lock us up?

Des Prunelles. Oh, I'm not talking about us. We are reasonable people, we are. We know what we're doing. That's obvious.

Cyprienne [*gaily*]. It wouldn't be too bad, if it were here.

Des Prunelles. Just like home. . . . What I have is very good.

Cyprienne. Yes, but too peppery.

Des Prunelles. Your glass. [*He pours some of the Chambertin for both.*] Of course, during those eight days we might at least get to know each other.

Cyprienne [*laughing*]. What do you mean, know each other?

Des Prunelles. Just that.

Cyprienne [*bursting with laughter*]. Oh, how silly you are! Gracious, we've been married two years.

Des Prunelles. And twenty-two days . . . the twenty-sixth of October. [*They toast.*]

Cyprienne. And we don't know each other?

Des Prunelles. Not at all.

Cyprienne. Ha!

Des Prunelles [*serving her*]. All right, admit you've never seen me in such good spirits.

Cyprienne. That's true.

Des Prunelles. You see; you don't know me. And how could you? In two years we've only had fifteen days alone together.

Cyprienne [*crying out and laughing*]. Oh! Come now!

Des Prunelles. I will prove it if you wish. [*He rings.*] Shall we place a little bet? [*To* JOSEPH, *who enters.*] Have you a pencil?

Joseph. Yes, monsieur.

Des Prunelles. Here. Now go.

JOSEPH *goes out.* DES PRUNELLES *pushes back the plates, etc. He pushes the table closer to the fireplace with* CYPRIENNE'S *help. She puts the bucket of champagne to his left.* DES PRUNELLES *takes the menu and pulls his chair closer to* CYPRIENNE'S *armchair.*

Des Prunelles. We are liquidating. We must make an inventory. [*Writing numbers on the back of the menu.*] Let's say: two years and twenty-two days of marriage. That makes seven hundred thirty plus twenty-two. A total of seven hundred fifty-two days, which gives us in hours . . . I'll give you the advantage: I'll only count twelve hours to a day.

Cyprienne. That's all?

Des Prunelles. Be fair! I never see you in the morning before lunch at noon. At night we part company between eleven and one, right? Then the average—always the average, my dear—from noon to midnight makes only twelve hours that we live together.

Cyprienne. That's true.

Des Prunelles. Then seven hundred fifty-two multiplied by twelve makes— [*Writing numbers, adding them up under his breath.*] —two, four, five, fourteen . . . nine thousand and twenty-four hours of marriage.

Cyprienne [*laughing*]. And we haven't had time to know each other . . . in nine thousand hours? [*She rises, glass in hand, and warms her feet.*]

Des Prunelles. Oh, but wait! How many of those twelve hours in one day are we alone together? Completely alone?

Cyprienne. I'd say five or six hours.

Des Prunelles. Not on your life! I'm not counting meals; there are the servants. We'll put down one hour, and I'm being generous.

Cyprienne. Good! One hour a day.

Des Prunelles [*taking a drink from time to time, becoming more animated*]. Now we must also subtract the days on which we were not truly alone. Days when we entertained or were entertained: the dinners, the plays, the visits, the trips, etc. For all this, will you grant me a deduction of at least half?

Cyprienne. Make it three-quarters.

Des Prunelles. So we are left with an average of one-quarter of an hour. This means that out of nine thousand twenty-four hours, there were one hundred and eighty-eight hours of intimacy.

Cyprienne [*surprised*]. Oh!

Des Prunelles. Here are the figures. And out of this, a good third has been spent bickering with each other, and another third not speaking to each other.

Cyprienne [*leaning on his shoulder*]. Yes, but that's part of being intimate.

Des Prunelles. I'm including it. Divide by twelve: fifteen and a fraction. The conclusion: In two years of marriage, we have had fifteen days and four hours of intimacy. I was wrong by four hours.

Cyprienne [*laughing*]. Oh, no! It's not possible.

Des Prunelles. There are the figures.

Cyprienne. Ha! ha! ha!

Des Prunelles. That amuses you?

Cyprienne [*who is beginning to get a little tipsy*]. No . . . I'm laughing at . . . at . . . Ha! ha! ha!

Des Prunelles. What?

Cyprienne [*sitting on his knees*]. Just a thought! . . . Ha! ha! ha! I would very much like to know . . . Ha! ha! ha!

Des Prunelles [*laughing*]. Well, what?

Cyprienne. How many of those hours . . .

Des Prunelles. Well?

Cyprienne [*snuggling in his lap*]. How many of them were devoted to— [*She stifles the word by collapsing with laughter on his shoulder.*] —love-making!

Des Prunelles. Oh! that's very simple. [JOSEPH *enters with a platter of lobster bordelaise. Seeing* CYPRIENNE *on* DES PRUNELLES' *lap, he tiptoes to the table, puts the platter down discreetly, and tiptoes out. They sense his presence and react to it. After he leaves,* DES PRUNELLES *goes back to his figures.*] Without exaggeration, we can establish that love had its three good hours per week.

Cyprienne [*crying out*]. Oh!

Des Prunelles. Oh, even more.

Cyprienne. Oh, no!

Des Prunelles. Oh, yes. . . . Because in the beginning——

Cyprienne [*laughing*]. Yes, but what about the end?

Des Prunelles. Exactly, it balances out. Three hours, you agree?

Cyprienne [*still on his lap, kissing him*]. Braggart! Go ahead! Put down three hours.

Des Prunelles [*adding up*]. Let's see, two years and twenty-two days make— [*Mumbling numbers very quickly.*] —fifty-two, two, three, one hundred and seven weeks at three hours per week, total: three hundred and twenty-one hours!

Cyprienne. Of love-making?

Des Prunelles. Of love-making!

Cyprienne [*drinking and laughing*]. Oh, come now! As much as that?

Des Prunelles. There are the figures. Now, three hundred and twenty-one divided by twelve gives us twenty-six and a fraction. The final result: Out of fifteen days of intimacy, twenty-six and a fraction were devoted to love-making.

Cyprienne [*laughing*]. Whee! I agree to the fraction!

Des Prunelles. Twenty-six out of fifteen. See how unjust you are?

Cyprienne [*laughing*]. Ha! ha! [*She kisses him.*] Oh, my big rooster! How funny you are!

Suddenly there is the sound of voices outside the door. The WAITERS *are struggling to prevent* ADHÉMAR *from entering.*

Waiters [*offstage*]. No, monsieur! You cannot.

Adhémar [*offstage*]. I wish to enter! I shall enter! [*The discussion continues.*]

Des Prunelles. Adhémar!

Cyprienne [*jumping up*]. Again! He's such a bore, that creature.

Des Prunelles [*rising*]. Hide! [*They push the table all the way over to the fireplace, and* DES PRUNELLES *puts the screen so that it hides her from the rest of the stage but not from the audience.*]

Cyprienne. But this time, throw him out once and for all. Get it over with.

She sits in the armchair which is now left of the table. At this moment the door opens violently, and ADHÉMAR *hurtles into the room, pushing aside the* WAITERS. *He is streaming with water; his umbrella inundates the room; his hair and mustache are in a lamentable state. During the scene that follows* CYPRIENNE *eats her lobster and washes her fingers in the finger bowl.*

Des Prunelles [*napkin in hand*]. Well, well, well! What is all this?

Adhémar [*very hoarse*]. Monsieur . . . words fail me.

Des Prunelles. Does it hurt?

Adhémar. Your conduct is unfathomable. I have just come from Aunt Nicole's house.

Des Prunelles. Oh? How is she?

Adhémar. She's dead! [*He thrusts his umbrella under his arm, drenching* DES PRUNELLES, JOSEPH, *and the two* WAITERS. *They all dry themselves with their napkins.*]

Des Prunelles. Oh!

Adhémar. Has been for three months.

Des Prunelles. Ah! I didn't know . . . a very distant aunt . . . [*He signals* JOSEPH *to leave. The three* WAITERS *retire.*]

Adhémar [*opening his umbrella and standing it up to dry stage left*]. Two and one-half miles, going and coming. And no carriage. And no Cyprienne! I raced back to your house at full speed to see if she hadn't returned, and all I found was your Josépha and your Bastien eating your dinner and swilling your best wine. They'd had much too much of your wine. When they saw me, the blackguards, they were rollicking, especially the maid. She almost had a fit. "Madame? You're still running after Madame, you jilted jackass!"

Des Prunelles. Oh!

Adhémar. "Jilted jackass!" That was a clue. I rushed over here. I questioned the woman downstairs, the one who opens the oysters. She knows me well. "Did you see Monsieur des Prunelles come in?" "Yes, monsieur." "With a lady?" "Yes." "Describe her." "Small, plump, like a little quail." [*He utters a savage cry.*] Ah! [DES PRUNELLES *jumps.*] "Jilted jackass" explains it. I've been cheated. You are dining here. Both of you! It's treason. You gave her to me. You're trampling on our agreement!

Des Prunelles. My dear successor—stop and think. If she were here, where would she be?

Adhémar. Behind that screen!

Des Prunelles. She would be in your arms. [CYPRIENNE *giggles.*]

Adhémar. Oh, a man never knows. Women are so whimsical. Perhaps by now she finds it amusing to deceive me with you.

Cyprienne [*letting out a little involuntary cry of protest*]. Oh!

Adhémar. That cry! She's here. [*He lunges at the screen.*]

Des Prunelles [*catching him by his sleeve and twirling him around*]. Excuse me, the wife of one of my friends.

Adhémar. Let me see her.

Des Prunelles. That's not done.

Adhémar. Have her say something.

Des Prunelles. Impossible. But there's another way—and this is most obliging of me.

Adhémar. What?

Des Prunelles. You are certainly familiar with Cyprienne's foot, which is so charming.

Adhémar. I certainly am!

Des Prunelles. Well, then, I hope Madame will consent to show us her foot. That should steady you. [*Crossing to the screen.*] If you consent, madame, tap on your plate.

CYPRIENNE *gives two little taps on her plate with a knife.*

Adhémar. Ah!

Des Prunelles. Don't move. Are you ready? [ADHÉMAR, *at the left, bends over to see better.* DES PRUNELLES *also leans over next to the screen.* CYPRIENNE, *on her side, is sitting in the armchair.* DES PRUNELLES *to* CYPRIENNE.] Would you be so kind as to lightly slide your slipper the length of the screen in such a way as to cause the tip of it to stick out? [CYPRIENNE *executes the order very slowly, and the point of her shoe begins to show at the edge.*] That's all. Good. Enough! [*To* ADHÉMAR.] Well? Is that her?

Adhémar [*with a gesture of desolation*]. No!

Des Prunelles and Cyprienne [*together*]. Ah! [CYPRIENNE *mimes a kick in* ADHÉMAR's *direction.*]

Adhémar [*straightening up*]. Ah, madame, I'm so confused. I beg your pardon. [*To* DES PRUNELLES *as he shakes his hand and motions toward the screen.*] My compliments.

Des Prunelles. Thank you.

Adhémar [*picking up his umbrella and closing it*]. Well, where is the wretched woman?

Des Prunelles. Ah, that's your business. Keep looking.

Adhémar. I'm dying of hunger; I think I'll get some hot soup.

Des Prunelles [*seeing him to the door*]. A good gargle with salt water would be better. You're catching a cold.

Adhémar [*getting ready to sneeze*]. It's awful, just awful. [*He sneezes.*] This situation. Now she's mine, she's less mine than she was when she wasn't mine.

Des Prunelles. It's often like that.

Adhémar [*at the door*]. You say salt water?

Des Prunelles. Boiling! Make sure it's boiling.

Adhémar. Thank you. [*He sneezes and goes out.* DES PRUNELLES *closes the door after him.*]

Des Prunelles. God bless you!

Cyprienne [*bursting out with laughter*]. What an idiot! A real idiot! He didn't even know my foot.

Des Prunelles [*gaily, coming to her*]. That's how one is cheated by these dashing swains. [*Touching her toe.*] As for me, it's the first thing I admired about you.

Cyprienne. Oh, heavens! That was too much! A man who courted me four months!

Des Prunelles [*laughing*]. There you are.

Cyprienne [*laughing and crossing left to sit on couch. She is pleasantly tipsy*]. But he's a ninny, a ninny, a ninny! [*Patting the cushion.*] Is it permissible to be such a ninny?

Des Prunelles. It would seem so.

Cyprienne. Heavens! Do you think it would be any fun to play tricks on that dunderhead?

Des Prunelles [*going to her*]. Oh . . . some day.

Cyprienne. Some day? What about now?

Des Prunelles. Hmm?

Cyprienne. It would be so simple . . . It wouldn't be worth it.

Des Prunelles. Even if our roles were really reversed, and I were courting you?

Cyprienne. What? Hmm? What do you think?

Des Prunelles. Hmm! What do *you* think? If he were the husband, and I the lover?

Cyprienne. Well . . .

Des Prunelles. Cock-a-doodle-doo.

Together [*with passion*]. Oh!

Des Prunelles [*putting his arms around her waist*]. Brought together in secret rapture.

Cyprienne [*squeezing his arm*]. Really?

Des Prunelles [*letting her go*]. Instead of the weariness that separates us.

Cyprienne. Weariness! You can't be that tired after twenty-six days!

Des Prunelles. I was thinking of you.

Cyprienne. Me? I'm only tired of Adhémar. [*She rises and goes to the piano. She sits and plays while singing.*]

> It was hardly worth the troublement
> To make this change in government . . .

Des Prunelles [*on one knee next to the couch*]. Careful, he might be next door, gargling!

Cyprienne. Well, he has his umbrella. [*She laughs.*] Ha, ha! ha! Oh, my heart! [*She leans her elbows on the keyboard.*]

Des Prunelles [*sitting on the couch*]. Why are you laughing?

Cyprienne [*without looking at him*]. No reason . . . just a thought . . . a bit of folly. Something that can't be said. [*She plays a tender waltz.*]

Des Prunelles [*after a moment of music, without looking at her*]. Then again, it wouldn't be honest.

Cyprienne [*still playing*]. It wouldn't be honest?

Des Prunelles. Because now you're no longer mine.

Cyprienne [*attracted by this thought, but still playing*]. That's true . . .

Des Prunelles. It's forbidden us.

Cyprienne [*playing with only one hand*]. Forbidden?

Des Prunelles. It's taboo.

Cyprienne [*quickly*]. Taboo? [*She stops playing.*]

Des Prunelles. It would be a transgression—a sin!

Cyprienne [*wheels on the stool to face* DES PRUNELLES. *They are still separated by the couch*]. A sin? Do you think so? Would it be a sin?

Des Prunelles. Cyprienne, don't look at me with those eyes! [*He turns away, facing front.*]

Cyprienne [*rising*]. Whew, I'm so warm! My mouth's burning up from your rascally lobsters. [*She goes up to the table at the rear and gets a bunch of grapes and crosses back to behind* DES PRUNELLES. *She eats a grape.*] Oh! how refreshing . . . So you think it would be abominable, do you?

Des Prunelles. Heavens, yes!

Cyprienne [*feeding him a grape*]. Here, my sweet. It would be wicked, very wicked. Are you sure?

Des Prunelles [*his head leaning back on the back of the sofa, looking up at her*]. Oh, Cyprienne!

Cyprienne [*another grape, looking deep into his eyes*]. Here, my lover!

Des Prunelles. To deceive that man . . . Oh!

Cyprienne [*another grape*]. Yes, my treasure. Here! [*Holding the bunch of grapes over his head.*] Don't these grapes remind you of anything?

Des Prunelles. Adam and Eve!

Cyprienne [*crossing around the sofa*]. Wretch! What about the vine leaf?

Des Prunelles. Oh, that! That was very amusing.

Cyprienne. This could be more so! [*She sinks down alongside him and slips her arm around his neck. We hear some voices coming down the corridor outside the room. Oblivious,*

Des Prunelles *and* Cyprienne *feed each other the last few grapes on the bunch.*]

Des Prunelles. Hmmmm?

Adhémar [*offstage*]. You are there, madame! I recognized your voice. But I will be revenged! Tremble! Tremble! Vengeance is near!

Des Prunelles. Vengeance?

Waiters [*offstage, pulling* ADHÉMAR *away*]. Let's go, let's go, take him away!

Adhémar. But that's my wife!

Voices. To the guardhouse with him! [*The voices fade away.*]

Des Prunelles. They've gone.

Someone knocks at the door.

Cyprienne. Someone's knocking.

Des Prunelles [*rising*]. Who's there?

Joseph [*offstage*]. Monsieur!

Cyprienne. It's the waiter.

Des Prunelles. The waiter? [*He crosses to the door.*]

Joseph [*knocking again*]. Open quickly, monsieur!

Des Prunelles [*half-opening the door*]. What?

Joseph [*half-appearing*]. A policeman is taking him to the guardhouse across the street. But they will probably come back. As a disguise, would Madame like to change clothes with me?

With a gesture of refusal, CYPRIENNE *runs to the window.*

Des Prunelles. No! [*He pushes* JOSEPH *out the door.*]

Joseph. But that's what they do in Paris!

Des Prunelles. No, no! Thank you. [*He closes the door, locks it, and goes to pour himself some champagne at the table.* CYPRIENNE *has climbed up on a chair in order to see out the window.*]

Cyprienne [*shaking with laughter*]. Look, it's true! The policeman has got him. Ha! ha! ha! He's streaming with water. . . . He looks like some old rain gutter. Ah! ha! ha! He's so ludicrous! And so ugly!

Des Prunelles [*glass in hand, crossing to her*]. Really?

Cyprienne. My God, he's so ugly! [*Jumping out of the chair, she falls into* DES PRUNELLES' *arms.*]

Des Prunelles. How nice! Champagne all over my coat.

Cyprienne. My poor big tomcat. Hold still. [*She tries to wipe him off with her handkerchief.*] There!

Des Prunelles. I'd better put it in front of the fire. [*She helps him off with his jacket. One of the sleeves turns inside out.*]

Cyprienne [*taking his coat*]. There! [*She hangs it on the armchair near the fire.*] Whew! this heat! I'm stifling! [*She undoes the top of her dress.*]

Des Prunelles. Revenge for what? What does that mean—a duel?

Cyprienne. A duel! [*She runs to him.*] I forbid you to fight, do you hear?

Des Prunelles. But——

Cyprienne [*throwing herself into his arms*]. I don't want you to fight. He might kill you!

Des Prunelles. Bah!

Cyprienne. And all for him—for that man? Oh! that man! Is it possible? I was so blind! I was out of my mind! [*She falls on the couch.*] Oh! it's all my fault! [*Then she turns suddenly on* DES PRUNELLES, *who is standing over her, grabs his arm, and pulls him down on his knees alongside her.*] On your knees, you miserable wretch, and beg my pardon!

Des Prunelles. Huh?

Cyprienne. For having thrown me into the arms of that idiot! For wanting to give him to me for a husband!

Des Prunelles. But——

Cyprienne. He's odious, do you hear? He's ridiculous, he's ugly, he's stupid, your Adhémar! I hate him, do you hear me? I only love you. Tell me you still love me. Tell me quickly!

Des Prunelles. I——

Cyprienne. And that you repent having left me like this. And that you will never leave me. Never! Never! Never!

Des Prunelles. Never, I——

Cyprienne. Enough! You repent! I've forgotten everything. I forgive you. Come to my arms. I adore you!

There are three loud knocks at the door.

A Voice. Open, in the name of the Law!

Des Prunelles [*to* CYPRIENNE]. The police!

Cyprienne [*frightened*]. Why?

Des Prunelles [*rising*]. Who knows? Outrage to the public morals . . . Scandal in a public place.

Cyprienne. Ah!

The Police Officer [*offstage*]. You refuse to open?

Cyprienne [*noticing the disorder of her appearance*]. Not yet! . . . Now, I'm ready. Here, your coat! [*She has crossed to the fireplace and throws him his coat.*]

Officer [*offstage*]. Open, or I will break down the door!

CYPRIENNE *folds the screen around her to hide.*

Des Prunelles. All right! All right! [*He unlocks the door.*]

An Officer and two POLICEMEN *enter. The two* POLICEMEN *take up their posts stage right.* JOSEPH *and the two* WAITERS *enter and stay far up left.* ADHÉMAR, *with his umbrella, crosses behind and appears between the piano and the couch.*
Some of the curious guests may be seen at the door.

Des Prunelles [*stupefied, trying to put his coat on.*] Excuse me, officer, but——

Officer [*quickly, pointing to the dinner table*]. Monsieur, you are here with a woman. Don't deny it!

Des Prunelles. Yes, officer, my wife.

Officer. Your wife! We'll see about that. [*Pointing at* ADHÉMAR.] This gentleman created such a disturbance they brought him to me. He justifies himself by claiming that you are here with his wife. *His* wife!

Des Prunelles. Adhémar! [*He bursts into laughter.*]

Everyone looks at ADHÉMAR *with pity.*

Adhémar [*aside*]. This could mean two months in prison, but I don't care. At least I broke up their orgy!

Des Prunelles. Oh, that's good! That's very good! [*Speaking to* CYPRIENNE *behind the screen.*] Did you hear? Adhémar, your husband! [*Above the screen,* CYPRIENNE's *hands appear in gestures of protestation.*] Look, my dear officer, she's convulsed at the thought. Look at those gestures!

Officer. Indecent, monsieur. . . . Like your appearance. . . . Put your sleeve the way it should be!

Des Prunelles. Let's put everything the way it should be. I am the real husband!

Officer. You add insult to outrage.

Des Prunelles. God in heaven!

Officer. No swearing! Respect the law!

Des Prunelles. But——

Officer. Silence! [DES PRUNELLES, *intimidated, finishes putting on his coat as he crosses all the way to stage right. The* OFFICER *looks at* ADHÉMAR *with friendly interest.*] Monsieur, I am going to question your wife. Perhaps it would be better for you to leave the room. This screen . . . the state she is probably in . . .

ADHÉMAR *blows his nose and wipes his eyes with his handkerchief.*

Adhémar [who is so hoarse he is scarcely audible]. No, monsieur. I will be strong. Thank you.

The OFFICER *taps on the screen with his cane.*

Officer. Madame!

Cyprienne [behind the screen]. Monsieur?

Officer. Are you presentable?

Cyprienne. Always, monsieur. *[She comes out, her hair in disorder, her dress buttoned up crooked. All react.]*

Adhémar. Ah! Faithless woman! *[He falls on the couch.* JOSEPH *puts a bottle of vinegar under his nose.* WAITERS *fold screen and place it against wall.]*

Des Prunelles [rising]. You know, it's very peculiar that a man and his wife——

Officer [crossing to him]. Be silent!

Des Prunelles [intimidated by the POLICEMEN*].* It's the end of free speech. That's what it is! *[He falls back into the chair in front of the table.]*

Officer [to CYPRIENNE*].* Madame, you realize that you have been surprised here with this individual, under conditions which leave no doubt that your relations with him are——

Cyprienne. Everyday, monsieur!

All present are revolted.

All. Oh!

Officer [to ADHÉMAR*].* Courage, monsieur, courage! *[To* CYPRIENNE.*]* So, you confess?

Cyprienne [pointing to DES PRUNELLES*].* He is my husband.

Officer [sarcastically]. Ah! You're going to pretend, too? Well, if that individual is your husband— *[Pointing to* ADHÉMAR.*]* —who is he?

Cyprienne. He's an imbecile.

Adhémar [passing the vinegar back to JOSEPH *and standing].* Oh! Cyprienne!

Cyprienne. Don't you come near me. I'll scratch your eyes out!

Officer. And you say he's not your husband?

Cyprienne. There's my husband! There! He's the one I love! *[She tries to run to* DES PRUNELLES.*]*

Officer [stopping her, and forcing her to the extreme left]. Such barefaced impudence!

Des Prunelles [rising exasperatedly]. Officer, you are blind. Anyone will tell you she's my wife. Wait: in room eleven, there are some friends of mine.

The OFFICER *turns to* JOSEPH.

Joseph. They've gone.

Des Prunelles. What luck!

Officer [*to one of the policemen*]. Have a carriage brought around for Madame, so we may proceed to the station and draw up the charges.

Joseph. There's quite a crowd in the street.

Cyprienne [*crying*]. Oh! in front of everyone!

Des Prunelles. Like common thieves! [*They rush toward each other and fall into each other's arms, center stage.*]

Officer [*beside himself*]. Separate them! At once! They've gone mad!

The POLICEMEN *grab* DES PRUNELLES. *The* OFFICER *tries to pull* CYPRIENNE *away.*

Cyprienne [*holding on for dear life*]. No! no! I'm his . . . Even unto death!

Des Prunelles. And I'm hers!

They are separated.

Cyprienne [*furious*]. Monsters! Assassins! Cutthroats! [*She collapses on the couch.*]

Des Prunelles [*upstage*]. It's so ridiculous! There are no words for it. And we're only three steps from the notary who married us. . . . I'll get him! [*He rushes out the open door.*]

Officer. Stop him!

One POLICEMAN, JOSEPH, *and the two* WAITERS *all rush out after him, crying out "Stop," "halt," etc.*

Cyprienne. Henri . . . Wait for me! [*She tries to run after him.*]

Officer [*barring her way*]. No, madame, no! You cannot follow him. [*The other* POLICEMAN *has opened the dressing room door.*] In there with you!

Adhémar [*begging*]. Oh, Cyprienne!

Cyprienne [*crossing in front of the* OFFICER]. Don't come near me!

Adhémar. Oh, Cyprienne, forgive and forget!

Cyprienne. Take that, you brute! [*She slaps his face and flounces into the dressing room.*]

Adhémar [*spinning around and falling on the couch*]. Oh!

Officer [*as the* POLICEMAN *locks the door with a key*]. That will also be on the report. Let's find the culprit.

He runs out the door, followed by the POLICEMAN *and* ADHÉMAR, *holding his cheek.* DES PRUNELLES *enters by the other door, stage right, followed by* JOSEPH, *the second* POLICEMAN, *and the two* WAITERS.

Des Prunelles. Failed . . . trapped! [*They surround him.*] I surrender. Lower your arms.

Joseph. Lock him up. [*He crosses to the dressing room door.*]

Waiters. Yes, lock him up.

Des Prunelles [*crossing in front of the* WAITERS]. Don't touch me.

Joseph. Here! in the dressing room! [*He opens the door.*]

Des Prunelles. I'm going. . . . But don't touch me! Don't touch me! [*He goes into the dressing room where* CYPRIENNE *is.*]

Joseph [*turning the key*]. There, that will calm him down. Where's the woman?

All [*looking about*]. Vanished!

Joseph. Gone! After her!

They start to rush out. The OFFICER, ADHÉMAR, *and the first* POLICEMAN *come in the other door.*

Officer and his party. The man? Where is the man?

Joseph and his party. The woman? Where's the woman?

Officer. We have the woman.

Joseph. We have the man.

Officer [*pointing to the dressing room*]. She's in there.

Joseph [*pointing to dressing room*]. He's in there.

Officer [*correcting him*]. She!

Joseph [*correcting him*]. He!

Officer. Both of them?

All [*looking at the door*]. Together?

Adhémar [*forgetting himself*]. With his wife?

All [*quickly turning to him*]. His wife?

Adhémar [*horrified*]. Caught! Escape! [*He dashes out the door, stage right.*]

Officer. Stop him! Stop the villain! [*The* POLICEMEN *and* the WAITERS *pursue* ADHÉMAR *out the door. The* OFFICER, *alone.*] His wife! Well! The one thing I'm supposed to encourage! [*He goes to the dressing room door and unlocks it.*] A thousand pardons, monsieur. It's all right, everything is all right. You've done nobly, monsieur. Love in marriage! [DES PRUNELLES *half-opens the door, sticks one hand out, and shakes hands with the* OFFICER.] My congratulations, monsieur. Keep it up! Keep it up!

DES PRUNELLES *comes out with his wife, who has put on her hat and coat.*

Des Prunelles. Allow me to present Madame des Prunelles.
Officer. Ah, madame! Ah, monsieur! Please excuse me.

All the others pile into the room, pushing ADHÉMAR *in front.*

All. Here he is. We have him.
Officer. As for this individual who makes a game of the Law——
Cyprienne. Oh, officer! Forgive him, for my sake.
Des Prunelles. The restorer of our marriage.
Officer. Only to earn my pardon by pleasing you. [*To the others.*] Let him go.
Adhémar [*to himself, aside*]. I was counting on that.

Music.

Des Prunelles [*crossing to* ADHÉMAR, *in a low voice*]. Be quiet! or I'll have you locked up for misuse of the mails. [*He waves the phony telegram under his nose.*]
Adhémar [*in a low voice*]. You knew?
Des Prunelles. Of course! Come now, my pretty boy, you were no threat.
Adhémar. Maybe I wasn't . . . but tomorrow . . . someone else!
Des Prunelles. Bah! Tomorrow. [*To* CYPRIENNE.] Why does he keep rubbing his cheek like that?
Cyprienne [*laughing as she passes in front of the* OFFICER]. That's my fault. [*She mimes a slap.*]
Des Prunelles. A slap? You slapped him? [*Making her stand between them. Severely.*] Erase it!

ADHÉMAR *flirtatiously removes his hand, waiting for the kiss.* CYPRIENNE *looks at his cheek, then kisses* DES PRUNELLES' *cheek. She takes her husband's arm and they bow politely to the* OFFICER.

Together. Monsieur!
Officer [*bowing*]. Keep it up, monsieur, keep it up!

ADHÉMAR *falls into the chair.* JOSEPH *rubs his cheek with a wet napkin.* DES PRUNELLES *and his wife cross upstage as the* POLICEMEN *and the* WAITERS *bow respectfully.*

These Cornfields

(*Les Boulingrin*)

by

GEORGES COURTELINE

English version by Eric Bentley

Copyright © 1957 by Eric Bentley.

CHARACTERS

HERRING, *an elderly caller*
FELICITY, *the maid*
MR. CORNFIELD, *the host*
MRS. CORNFIELD, *the hostess*

PLACE—NEW YORK.
TIME—*around 1900.*

These Cornfields

SCENE—*A middle-class drawing room.*

The maid, FELICITY, *brings in* HERRING.

HERRING. These Cornfields, whom I met at dinner the other day at the Joneses, and who invited me to drop in for tea from time to time, seem to be extremely charming people. I expect to take infinite satisfaction in their company.

Felicity. If the gentleman would care to sit down I'll go and tell the master and mistress.

Herring. Thank you. Oh!

Felicity. Sir?

Herring. What's your name, my dear?

Felicity. Felicity. What's yours? . . . Not to be indiscreet. Just to know who to announce.

Herring. Fair enough. Herring.

Felicity [*tickled*]. Herring?

Herring. Herring.

Felicity. I've known worse. Wait, yes, back home in Ohio, we had a neighbor called Ramsbottom.

Herring. Now run along and tell Mr. and Mrs. Cornfield I am here.

Felicity. Right away. [*False exit.*]

Herring. One moment though. Come here. There's something I want to tell you. [*Takes her by the chin.*] You're a pretty girl, you know that?

Felicity [*modestly simpering*]. Hm.

Herring. Also quite a sly one.

Felicity. Hm.

Herring. I might venture to add that I am no fool, either.

Felicity. Hm . . . Excuse me, my thoughts were wandering.

Herring. I'm sure we shall come to an understanding. You've been in service here long?

Felicity. Nearly two years.

Herring. Just the woman I've been looking for.

Felicity. You want to marry me?

Herring. It is not a question of marriage.

Felicity. Anyone can make a mistake.

Herring. Listen, Felicity, and take care to answer me quite frankly. If you lie, my little finger will tell me. If you are sincere, on the other hand, I will give you twenty-five cents.

Felicity. It's too much.

Herring. Think nothing of it.

Felicity. In that case, question me.

Herring. Between you and me, the Cornfields are pleasant people?

Felicity. I quite agree.

Herring. Simple folk, aren't they?

Felicity. The simplest in the world.

Herring. A bit on the homey side?

Felicity. More than a bit.

Herring. A loving couple, to boot?

Felicity. Loving? I get quite embarrassed! No arguments, only agreement! Two homing pigeons, two turtledoves!

Herring. I have to conclude that my instinct was right in that too. This house will be a veritable honey pot. Here are your twenty-five cents, little pet.

Felicity. The loss won't inconvenience you?

Herring. No.

Felicity. Then thank you.

Herring [*very much the grand seigneur*]. Never have I regretted a disbursement less. Hail, tranquil dwelling! Haven of peace whither I propose to repair for the evening three times a week all this winter, my feet warmed at fires which will cost me nothing but the trouble of holding my soles up to them, my whole body refreshed with cups of tea which will cost me nothing but the effort of drinking them! O pleasing perspective! Dream I have fondled so long! Vision of infinite sweetness to the soul of a poor sponger who has "fallen into the sere and yellow leaf" and asks nothing more than to fall free of charge beneath the hospitable roof of another! [*Provoked by the end of this speech,* FELICITY *has been miming the cutting of a throat, the slapping of a face with the back of the hand, and the squeezing of a nose between index finger and thumb. As* HERRING *turns in her direction, she stops.*] You see, my child, the more one sees of this life, the more one perceives its futility. What is desire? An empty word. What is pleasure? Outward show. For an aging bachelor, you may say, the life at a saloon in the Bowery is not without appeal. True. But it has its inconvenient side. In the long run it becomes burdensome, even monotonous, you get to the age when——

Felicity. Oh!

Herring. What's the matter?

Felicity. I've forgotten to turn off the cistern tap.

Herring. That'll be a fine old mess.

Felecity. I must run. I'll announce you at the same time. [*Exit* FELICITY.]

Herring [*alone*]. No brains. But plenty of spirit. The child does not displease me. Nor does the apartment, for that matter. The furniture—middle-class but comfortable. Window stripping on the windows, also round the doors. [*He bends down at the fireplace.*] The chimney snores like a night watchman and draws like a fencing master. [*Letting himself drop into an armchair.*] What springs! Herring, you little monkey, you've found your Old Folks' Home all right. This house, I repeat, will be a honey pot. Congratulations! [*A noise.*] That'll be the Cornfields.

Enter both CORNFIELDS.

Herring [*continuing*]. Mr. and Mrs. Cornfield, your humble servant.

Mr. Cornfield. Well, how are you, Mr. Herring?

Mrs. Cornfield. Very nice of you to have dropped in, Mr. Herring.

Mr. Cornfield. And just at the right time.

Herring. You don't say so.

Mrs. Cornfield. The psychological moment.

Herring. I'm so glad.

Mrs. Cornfield. Tell me, Mr. Herring——

Herring. Mrs. Cornfield?

Mr. Cornfield [*taking him by the left arm*]. Excuse me. I'm first.

Mrs. Cornfield [*pulling at his right arm*]. No, me!

Mr. Cornfield. No!

Mrs. Cornfield. Don't listen to him, Mr. Herring, my husband is talking sheer rubbish.

Herring. Rubbish?

Mrs. Cornfield. That's what I said. Rubbish.

Mr. Cornfield. I'm afraid I'll have to knock a little politeness into you. Halfwit!

Mrs. Cornfield. Clod!

Mr. Cornfield. What did you call me?

Mrs. Cornfield. I called you a clod.

Mr. Cornfield. Thunder and brim—— And you're annoying Mr. Herring. Will you please let go of him this minute?

Mrs. Cornfield. Let go of him yourself.

Mr. Cornfield. You let go of him!

Mrs. Cornfield. You!

Herring [*quartered*]. Ouch!

Mrs. Cornfield. Hear that? You're making him scream.

Herring. Pardon me, Mr. and Mrs. Cornfield, but I see you are busy. I wouldn't like to be in the way.

Mr. Cornfield. Not at all.

Mrs. Cornfield. Not in the least.

Mr. Cornfield. On the contrary.

Herring. And yet . . .

Mr. Cornfield. On the contrary, I tell you. [*Bringing forward a chair for him.*] Here!

Mrs. Cornfield [*doing likewise*]. Exactly. Take a seat.

Herring. Thank you.

Mr. Cornfield. Not that one. This one.

Herring. A thousand pardons.

Mrs. Cornfield. Not this one. That one.

Mr. Cornfield. No.

Mrs. Cornfield. Yes.

Mr. Cornfield. How long is this to continue? Is Mr. Herring to get no peace?

Herring. I'm really terribly sorry.

Mrs. Cornfield. But why?

Mr. Cornfield. Think nothing of it.

Mr. and Mrs. Cornfield. Be seated!

Mrs. Cornfield [*who has managed to push a chair under* HERRING'S *buttocks*]. There!

Mr. Cornfield [*rushing forward*]. Not that one, I tell you! [*He whips his wife's chair from under* HERRING *just as the latter is lowering himself onto it.* HERRING *falls on the floor.*]

Mrs. Cornfield [*triumphant*]. You see! Idiot! [*And she repeats the word "idiot" during the next lines.*]

Mr. Cornfield [*who is legitimately indignant*]. What? It's your fault too! Why did you have to force him onto a chair he didn't like? You'd have been in a pretty pickle if he'd smashed his face up. . . . Idiot? Idiot yourself! Monster! Why did a thing like this have to cross my path? [*To* HERRING.] You're not hurt, I hope?

Herring [*ruefully rubbing his behind*]. Nothing worth mentioning.

Mr. Cornfield. Overjoyed to hear it. Draw up to the fire.

Herring [*aside*]. I wish I hadn't come.

Mrs. Cornfield [*solicitous*]. Put this cushion under your feet.

Herring. Thank you very much.

Mr. Cornfield [*getting irritated at his wife's politeness and pushing a second cushion under the first*]. Put this one under too.

Herring. Much obliged.

Mrs. Cornfield [*who can't take a lesson in courtesy from her husband without losing a trick, slips a third cushion under the two others*]. And this one.

Herring. Actually . . .

Mr. Cornfield [*armed with a fourth cushion*]. And this!

Herring. No.

Mrs. Cornfield. This little stool!

Herring [*his knees on the level of his eyes*]. Please!

Mr. Cornfield. Oh, let us alone with your stool! [*In exasperation, he kicks the scaffolding of cushions from under* HERRING'S *feet. The structure collapses, and carries with it, naturally,* HERRING'S *chair and Herring on it.*] You're boring Mr. Herring!

Herring [*arms and legs in the air*]. Oh, not at all!

Mrs. Cornfield. It's you—you'll be the death of him.

Herring [*with authority*]. Now be quiet!

Mrs. Cornfield. I'll be quiet if I want to.

Mr. Cornfield. If you want to!

Mrs. Cornfield. If I want to.

Mr. Cornfield. God in heaven!

Mrs. Cornfield. And I *don't* want to, so there!

Mr. Cornfield. This is too much. Hussy!

Mrs. Cornfield. Good-for-nothing!

Mr. Cornfield. Slut!

Mrs. Cornfield. Cuckold! [*Pause.*]

Mr. Cornfield. What a life!

Mrs. Cornfield. Complain: go on! [*To* HERRING.] An idler and a swindler who sits home twiddling his thumbs and getting drunk on my inheritance, my poor father's hard-won savings!

Mr. Cornfield [*overflowing with joy*]. Your father . . . ! Ten years at hard labor for forging business documents!

Mrs. Cornfield. At least they didn't send him to jail for inciting a minor to debauchery like the mother of an idiot I know!

Mr. Cornfield [*to* HERRING]. You hear?

Herring. Have you noticed how unseasonably cool it has been for the past two weeks?

Mr. Cornfield [*to his wife*]. Don't force me to reveal where I found you! And fished you out with my own hands!

Mrs. Cornfield. You have your nerve. Who fished who, I'd like to know?

Mr. Cornfield. Ermyntrude!

Mrs. Cornfield [*dangerous*]. Silence! Or I'll tell all!

Mr. Cornfield [*stamping his foot*]. Ha!

Herring [*eager for conciliation*]. Don't get excited. Mrs. Cornfield is right.

Mr. Cornfield [*jumping out of his skin*]. Right?

Herring [*sweetly smiling*]. Yes.

Mr. Cornfield. Right!

Herring. But . . .

Mr. Cornfield. Right! Listen, Mr. Herring, do you want me to exterminate you?

Herring. By no means, Mr. Cornfield. Don't give it a second thought.

Mr. Cornfield. I've had to listen to plenty of nonsense in my time, but may my face sprout potatoes if I've ever heard such lunacy as this!

Herring. Oh, dear. Excuse me.

Mr. Cornfield. Right!

Herring. Would you allow me . . . ?

Mr. Cornfield. Right!

Herring. Listen to me.

Mr. Cornfield [*beside himself*]. A stick! Bring me a stick! I'm going to break this Herring's back. Patience has its limits, and this, after all, is beyond everything. What? That pest of a female, a thief and the daughter of a thief, that lards me and scorches me, turns me on the spit, roasts me on a slow fire— *she* is right! A hag that sucks my blood, gnaws at my brain, my lungs, my kidneys, my feet, my liver, my spleen, my esophagus, my pancreas, my peritoneum, my very intestines— *she* is right!

Herring. Now look——

Mrs. Cornfield. Take no notice. He's crazy.

Mr. Cornfield. Right! You say she's right because you speak in ignorance—like the old fool you are!

Herring [*quite drily*]. You're too kind.

Mr. Cornfield. If you were in my shoes, you'd soon change your opinion. Oh, how I'd like to see you in my shoes! Wouldn't *you* boil over if they stuck you on the spit with a clove of garlic under your skin and held you over the fire from the first of January till New Year's Eve?

Herring. Over the fire?

Mr. Cornfield [*continuing*]. Over the fire, yes! *Barbecued* herring! . . . Oh, I don't know what I'm saying.

Mrs. Cornfield. He should be in a padded cell.

Mr. Cornfield. Padded cell? Witch! Bane of my life! [*He grabs* HERRING *by one button of his tailcoat and shakes him like a plum tree.*] Yes, Mr. Herring, even to my food! She sticks rat poison in it and ruins my digestion! [*The button comes off.*]

Mrs. Cornfield. The gall of the man! [*She grabs* HERRING *by a second button, which comes off like the first one.*] The truth is he does things to the wine. You drink it at your peril.

Mr. Cornfield. That's a lie.

Mrs. Cornfield. A lie? We'll see about that. [*Exit* MRS. CORNFIELD.]

Mr. Cornfield. May I never see you again! May I never hear of you any more!

Herring [*aside*]. What's the matter with these people? Let us flee with all convenient speed.

Mr. Cornfield [*approaching him*]. Mr. Herring?

Herring. Mr. Cornfield?

Mr. Cornfield. I owe you an apology. I fear I let myself get carried away and failed to treat you with the respect you deserve.

Herring [*playing surprised*]. When was that? Where?

Mr. Cornfield. Just now. Here.

Herring. I don't know what you mean. On the contrary, you were irreproachable. I am touched to the heart by the excellent reception I've had here. [*Smiling and confused,* MR. CORNFIELD *warmly shakes him by the hand.*] Good-by.

Mr. Cornfield. Already?

Herring. Alas, yes. An urgent piece of business awaits me.

Mr. Cornfield. You're not serious.

Herring. I am.

Mr. Cornfield. Oh, come, you'll accept a little liquid refreshment?

Herring. I couldn't.

Mr. Cornfield. You could! How can we part without drinking to our future friendship? [*Gesture from* HERRING.] Now don't insist, or I might be hurt. [*He rings.*] I might think you harbor some little grudge against me. [*To the* MAID, *who has entered.*] Find me a bottle of champagne.

Felicity. Yes, Mr. Cornfield. [*Exit* FELICITY.]

Herring [*agreeing to surrender*]. Oh, well!

Mr. Cornfield [*delighted*]. Ah!

Herring. But I decline to be involved in your internal dissensions. They put me in a false position . . . not to speak of the buttons still remaining on my coat or the buttocks still smarting on my body.

Mr. Cornfield. It's a deal.

Herring [*extending his hand*]. Agreed?

Mr. Cornfield [*slapping him on the back*]. Agreed.

Herring. In that case, let's sit down. [*Each takes a chair, sits in it next to the other, smiles, exchanges a look in silence. Finally:*]

Mr. Cornfield [*very sprightly*]. I'm convinced, Mr. Herring, that you and I are going to be bosom friends.

Herring. Exactly my opinion, Mr. Cornfield.

Mr. Cornfield. You are most congenial to me. [*Discreet gesture from* HERRING.] I speak not merely of the outward man. It's true I appreciate the charm of your conversation—replete as it is with ingenious observations, prolific of pungent anecdotes and incisive sayings—but there's one thing I like above all: the aroma of frankness—of integrity—that emanates from your person. Shall we wager that sincerity is your principal merit?

Herring [*modest but veracious*]. I can't deny it.

Mr. Cornfield. Wonderful! We shall clinch the point at once. Give me your word to answer the question I shall now put to you without evasion, subterfuge, or equivocation.

Herring. I do.

Mr. Cornfield. Good. Tell me. On the level—man to man—do you think anything ever existed—for ignominy, horror, infamy, sheer abjection—like my wife's face?

Herring [*rising*]. Here we go again.

Mr. Cornfield. Ah? So you agree with me?

Herring. Excuse me.

Mr. Cornfield. And then: if it was only her face. But there's worse, Mr. Herring: indescribable treachery, unexampled baseness of soul. I'll give you one small example in a million. We sleep in a double bed——

Herring [*losing patience*]. What on earth——

Mr. Cornfield. Let me finish! Your turn comes later. Well now, we sleep in a double bed—her down the middle, me at one side. That annoys her. Very good. What does she do? She kicks me in the legs all night long. Like this. [*He kicks* HERRING *on the tibia.*]

Herring [*yelling*]. Ouch!

Mr. Cornfield. You see? Filthy creature! Or she pulls my hair. Like that.

Herring [*bellowing*]. Aaaah!

Mr. Cornfield. Hurts, doesn't it? And that's only a beginning. In the morning, pretending to stretch out, she hits me with the full force of both arms. She does it this way. [*He yawns noisily and at the same time, acting the part of a person stretching his limbs on awakening, strikes* HERRING *a tremendous blow.*] Do you consider that nice?

Herring. No, no! Enough of all this! I didn't come into this world to be maltreated! Never, never, shall I set foot in here again——

At this instant MRS. CORNFIELD *blows in like a whirlwind. She has a glass of wine in her hand.*

Mrs. Cornfield. Drink this.

Herring [*with a start*]. What *is* that?

Mrs. Cornfield. Drink!

Mr. Cornfield. What? *You're* still alive?

Mrs. Cornfield. You go to hell. Drink, Herring! Judge for yourself!

Mr. Cornfield. Scurvy wretch! You won't keep this up in the next world! [*Exit* MR. CORNFIELD.]

Mrs. Cornfield. Good-by and good riddance!

Herring [*aside*]. What people!

Mrs. Cornfield. Are you going to drink that or not?

Herring. Frankly, I'd just as soon not.

Mrs. Cornfield [*astonished*]. It's not dirty. It's *my* glass.

Herring. I don't deny it. But I find myself forced to withdraw.

Mrs. Cornfield. Just like that? At once?

Herring. This instant. What have I done with my hat? [*He puts his hat on. Bowing low.*] Mrs. Cornfield . . .

Mrs. Cornfield. Listen, Mr. Herring, would you like to do me a favor?

Herring. Gladly.

Mrs. Cornfield. Good. Abduct me.

Herring. I beg your pardon?

Mrs. Cornfield. I said: abduct me.

Herring [*stifling*]. For heaven's sake. That's the end. You want me to abduct you?

Mrs. Cornfield. Please!

Herring. Well, I can't.

GLENDALE COLLEGE LIBRARY

Mrs. Cornfield. Why not?

Herring. I have a girl friend. There'd be hell to pay.

Mrs. Cornfield. You refuse?

Herring. To my great regret. But, look . . .

Mrs. Cornfield. You refuse?

Herring. As I say . . .

Mrs. Cornfield. Very well. I warn you of one thing. You are about to be the cause of great misfortune.

Herring. Me?

Mrs. Cornfield. You. It's no use making faces. Before you can say President McKinley—I hope you take my meaning —there will be a corpse lying here! May the blood you have caused to flow not fall on your own head!

Herring [*his fists to his temples*]. It's maddening. What have I done to you? This gets on a man's nerves after a while!

Mrs. Cornfield. At that, one should never pull too hard at the string or—smash! I've given it all I've got for ten years. And now I've had enough, understand?

Herring. To be sure. But I don't care.

Mrs. Cornfield [*not without irony*]. Naturally not: it's no skin off your nose. You can settle the question with all the impartiality of a hog pickled in its own selfishness. Very convenient! [*Shrilly.*] You might change your tune if you were bound hand and foot and turned over to the fury of a bloodthirsty brute who treats you as a slave and beats you like a carpet! He beats me. Don't you believe that?

Herring [*cautiously beating a retreat*]. I do, I do!

Mrs. Cornfield [*advancing slowly on him*]. He not only bruises me, you understand, to the point of staving my ribs in, he pinches me, what's more, to make me scream, unhappy man! . . . and not like this— [*She pinches* HERRING.] —which would be nothing . . . no: between the bone of the index finger and the second joint of the thumb! Like this. [*She adds example to explanation with such effect that* HERRING, *trapped in a pincer movement, lets out agonized shouts.*] You see: it forms a vise.

HERRING *is yelling all five vowels when* MR. CORNFIELD *returns with a plate of soup.*

Mr. Cornfield [*to* HERRING]. Taste this.

Herring [*with a start*]. What may *this* be?

Mr. Cornfield. Rat poison. Taste! Taste it! God in heaven! It'll ruin your digestion.

Herring. I'll take your word for it.

Mrs. Cornfield [*to her husband*]. Pig! I won't be out-done!—Drink!

Herring [*threatened with the glass of wine*]. No!

Mr. Cornfield. Taste this!

Herring [*threatened with a spoonful of soup*]. Never!

Mrs. Cornfield [*still offering the wine*]. I assure you even the smell is awful!

Mr. Cornfield [*still offering the soup*]. I swear to you that this is poison!

They have laid hold of HERRING *and—both equally eager to be in the right—they force soup and wine down his throat, while the unhappy victim puts up a heroic defense by stubbornly clenching his teeth.*

Mrs. Cornfield. What a fool!

Mr. Cornfield. Funny how pigheaded he is! [*To* HERRING.] You can't win, I tell you!

Mrs. Cornfield [*to her husband*]. You'd think he was a chick the way you force the stuff down his throat!

Mr. Cornfield. What about you? Do you take him for a sponge?

Mrs. Cornfield. Cad!

Mr. Cornfield. Hag!

Mrs. Cornfield. Plague!

Mr. Cornfield. Cholera! I know: take that. [*He hurls the contents of the soup plate in his wife's direction.*]

Herring [*who, however, receives it*]. Ow!

Mr. Cornfield [*apologetic*]. Excuse me. Pure carelessness.

Mrs. Cornfield [*crazy with rage*]. Peasant! Yokel! Wait!

Herring [*streaming with red wine*]. Aaaah!

Mrs. Cornfield. Excuse me. I didn't aim straight. Now let's get it over with. [*She takes a revolver from her pocket.*] Upon your own head be it!

Mr. Cornfield [*in panic*]. Help! Save me! [*He takes refuge behind* HERRING.]

Mrs. Cornfield. You are about to die.

Herring [*to* MR. CORNFIELD, *who has made a screen of him*]. Hey, no, no! Let go of me. Enough of this!

Mr. Cornfield [*terrified out of his wits*]. Don't move—by all that's holy!

Mrs. Cornfield [*taking aim*]. Remove yourself, Herring!

Mr. Cornfield. No, no!

Mrs. Cornfield. Remove yourself. I'm firing.

Mr. Cornfield.	*Mrs. Cornfield.*	*Herring.*
Stay where you are. I'm a goner. She'd stop at nothing. Protect me, Herring, it's *my* life she's after. The hag! Help, help, help!	So that's how it is! You don't propose to remove yourself? So much the worse for you! Clear the terrain: shooting in progress!	Mr. Cornfield, for pity's sake! I don't want to die yet. Great heavens, what a ghastly idea it was of mine to come to this place!

Mr. Cornfield [*of a sudden*]. I have a notion! [*He puts the light out.*] Now take aim at me!

The stage is completely dark. So is the auditorium. From the heart of deepest darkness voices are heard howling the following speeches.

Voice of Mr. Cornfield. Ah! So you were going to murder me? Take that! [*Sound of a blow.*]

Voice of Herring. Ow!

Mrs. Cornfield. Now it's my turn. Take that!

Voice of Herring. Ow!

Nocturnal tumult. One hears the words: "Pig!" "Sow!" "Wolf!" "Louse!" and the noise of four more blows given one after the other to HERRING, *who shouts his protestations.*

Voice of Mrs. Cornfield. And now: I fire!

A shot is heard.

Voice of Herring [*in tears*]. It hit me in the leg!

Voice of Mr. Cornfield. So you're firing. Very well. I break the glassware.

Voice of Mrs. Cornfield. So you're breaking the glassware. Very well. I break the clock.

Voice of Mr. Cornfield. So you're breaking the clock. Very well. I break everything!

Sound of furniture falling and breaking.

Mrs. Cornfield. So you're breaking everything. Very well. I set fire to the place!

Screams, violent rushings to and fro.

Voice of Herring. In God's name, be careful, you're walking on my face!

Mr. Cornfield. She-camel!

Mrs. Cornfield. He-goat!
Mr. Cornfield. Daughter of a thief!
Mrs. Cornfield. Son of a . . .

HERRING *gives out sighs and groans of pain. Suddenly, through open doors at the center and on both sides, the red light of the fire. The stage is the color of blood.*

Herring [*crazed*]. The fire! Fire! Fire!

He rushes toward the center door, but FELICITY *arrives just as he gets there. Bucket of water in hand, she has come to bring help.*

Felicity. The fire? Here goes!

She hurls the contents of the bucket at random into the air. HERRING *is drenched from head to foot.*

Herring. Altogether a charming evening.

The scene is ending amid the deafening din of a house given over to lunatics, while outside the fire engine is approaching at full gallop and repeatedly sounding the two lugubrious notes of its horn. MR. CORNFIELD *suddenly appears in the doorway, clearly defined in silhouette against the bright background of Bengal flame.*

Mr. Cornfield. Don't go away, Mr. Herring, you're going to join us in a glass of champagne.

Keep an Eye on Amélie!

by

GEORGES FEYDEAU

English version by Brainerd Duffield

Copyright © 1958 by Brainerd Duffield. All inquiries concerning performing and other rights to be directed to the agents of the Feydeau Estate, Dr. Jan van Loewen Ltd., 81-83 Shaftesbury Avenue, London W.1, England.

The drawing, by the distinguished French caricaturist De Losques, shows the Amélie, Pochet, and Marcel of the first production of *Keep an Eye on Amélie!*

CHARACTERS

POCHET, *a retired policeman*
MARCEL COURBOIS, *an impoverished young man*
ÉTIENNE DE MILLEDIEU, *friend of* MARCEL
VAN PUTZEBOUM, *godfather of* MARCEL
THE PRINCE OF PALESTRIA
KOSHNADIEV, *aide to the* PRINCE
ADONIS, *a valet*
BIBICHON ⎫
BOAS ⎪
VALCREUSE ⎬ *friends of* ÉTIENNE
MOUCHEMOLLE ⎪
VALÉRY ⎭
THE MAYOR OF THE DISTRICT
THE COMMISSAIRE OF POLICE
MOUILLETU, *clerk at the Registry*
CORNETTE, *another clerk*

AMÉLIE D'AVRANCHES, *a cocotte*
IRÈNE, *Comtesse de Premilly*
CHARLOTTE, *servant at* MARCEL'S
YVONNE ⎫
PALMYRE ⎪
GABY ⎬ *friends of* AMÉLIE
GISMONDA ⎪
PAQUERETTE ⎭
VIRGINIE, AMÉLIE'S *aunt*
A LITTLE GIRL

BOYS *from florist's shop,* PHOTOGRAPHERS,
    GUESTS *at wedding, etc.*

PLACE—PARIS.
TIME—1908.

Keep an Eye on Amélie!

ACT ONE

Salon of AMÉLIE D'AVRANCHES' *apartment in Paris. Down right, a bow window. Up right, facing audience, door to vestibule. Farther upstage, extending the length of the entire wall from right to left, a glass partition through which may be seen a passageway and portions of the room beyond. Up left, facing audience, an arched double doorway leading to an adjacent salon. Down left, door to a bedroom. Upstage center, a grand piano with keyboard to stage right. On this piano, a gramophone with a large trumpet horn and a selection of disks. On the left end of the piano, a box of cigars, candlestick, and matches. Below the piano, set against the curvature, a small table with a tray of liqueurs. To the right of this table, a small chair. Farther right and downstage, a settee. Left of center and somewhat downstage, a card table with two chairs. Other furniture, potted plants, objets d'art, paintings, etc., ad libitum. Electric bell on wall at upstage right near the vestibule door.*

At the rise of the curtain, AMÉLIE *is standing by the piano, entertaining her guests with the music of the gramophone.* BIBICHON, *cigar in mouth, is seated on the sofa between* YVONNE *and* PALMYRE. PALMYRE *is perched on the arm of the sofa.* VALCREUSE, *back to audience, and* BOAS, *facing audience, are on opposite sides of the card table, playing cards. The gramophone is playing a Caruso record: "Di quella pira" from* Il Trovatore. *For the most part, the guests listen enraptured, nodding ecstatic approval. (The curtain should be lowered when the record begins to play. Curtain rises slowly on the eighth measure of recitative with the words: "Marse avvanpo.")*

YVONNE [*after an upsurge of Caruso's at about the thirteenth or fourteenth measure*]. Ah!! Incredible!
All [*entranced*]. Ah-h!!
Amélie [*with utter refinement*]. Can you believe it?
All. Ah-h-h!! [*They all listen attentively.*]
Bibichon [*at about the seventeenth measure of the aria*]. Who is this loudmouth anyway? Is it Caruso?
Amélie [*moving toward him*]. "Loudmouth"!

209

Bibichon. Well, who's doing the singing? He's got lots of talent.

Yvonne. Sssh! Be quiet!

Bibichon. What they call a "God-given" voice.

All. Sssh-sssh!

Bibichon. All right, all right.

Religious silence. The ladies are in seventh heaven. As Caruso approaches a climactic note at about the twenty-ninth or thirtieth measure, BIBICHON *joins in, singing in a forced falsetto.*

Bibichon. Ah! Ah! Ah! Ah!

All [*hissing him*]. Sssh! Oh, no! Not you! Be quiet!

Bibichon. Huh?

Palmyre. One Caruso at a time!

Yvonne. You haven't any God-given voice!

Bibichon. I was only helping him out.

Palmyre. He doesn't need any help from you.

Yvonne. We want to listen.

Bibichon. Who's stopping you? Not me.

All. Idiot! That's enough. Shut up! Quiet!

Bibichon. I was right on key too. Listen. [*Singing.*] Ah! Ah!

All [*shouting*]. Shut him up! Can't you be quiet? Sssh!

The argument flares up again and continues intermittently until the conclusion of the aria.

Bibichon [*as music ends*]. I wasn't bothering anybody. My voice has been admired by experts.

Yvonne. Shut your mouth, you idiot!

Palmyre [*clenching her fist*]. If somebody doesn't prevent me, I'll hit him.

Amélie. Go on. Hit him. Somebody ought to.

Palmyre. Caruso sings, and all we hear is Bibichon.

Bibichon. I was here in the flesh. That's better than a gramophone record.

Amélie [*nods agreement*]. Nobody has to wind you up and you never run down.

Valcreuse [*playing cards*]. Hey, Amélie. You got any brass band music?

Amélie. I've got a recitation from *Andromache* by Sarah Bernhardt.

All [*in one voice*]. No!! [AMÉLIE *shrugs.*]

Bibichon [*helping himself to a fresh cigar*]. Great invention. Think of it. A century from now we'll be able to hear the voices of people who will have been dead for years.

Palmyre [*laughing*]. A century from now you won't be hearing anything.

Bibichon [*holding match to taper in candlestick*]. Everybody in my family lives to a ripe old age. [*He uses candle to light his cigar.*]

Amélie [*seeing this*]. Oh, Bibichon, not another! No one can breathe in here as it is.

Bibichon. It's my last one today. I'm cutting down. [*He blows out the candle.*]

Amélie [*putting a new disk on the machine*]. Now, let's see who'll be first to guess this selection.

Yvonne. Quiet, everybody. We're going to try and guess.

Bibichon [*crossing left*]. I don't care for highbrow music. It all sounds the same.

AMÉLIE *starts the machine. A band plays* La Marseillaise.

All [*laughing and hooting*]. That's enough. Take it off. We've heard that one. Stop it, Amélie.

Laughing, AMÉLIE *turns off the machine.*

Bibichon. None of that revolutionary stuff. I'm a royalist, you know.

Yvonne [*with a wink*]. I never took you for a blueblood.

Bibichon. All my family are aristocrats.

Palmyre. Was your family acquainted with the Bonapartes?

Bibichon. We called once but they were out to lunch. [*He gives* PALMYRE *a playful poke and crosses down left.*]

Valcreuse [*dealing cards*]. If you're one of the nobility, why don't you hang out with your own crowd?

Boas [*chuckling*]. Yes, what are you doing here with us *hoi polloi?*

Bibichon. If I explained, you wouldn't understand. Peasants!

All laugh. ÉTIENNE's *voice is heard from bedroom left.*

Étienne [*angrily*]. Damn it! Double damn! Damn it to hell!

Yvonne [*to* AMÉLIE]. The voice of your beloved.

Amélie [*calling*]. Étienne darling! What's the matter?

Étienne [*as he enters*]. I'll show you what's the matter. [*He crosses center to* AMÉLIE. *He is collarless and in shirtsleeves, with a military jacket over his arm. He is wearing the trousers of a uniform. They are far too short for him.*]

All [gathering round]. What's happened, Étienne? What's it all about? Tell us.

Étienne. Look me over. Don't you notice anything about my appearance?

Bibichon. The face is much the same.

Étienne. It's these pants. There's only one explanation. My legs are still growing.

Amélie [embracing him]. Good. I prefer big boys.

Bibichon. She likes boys of all sizes.

Étienne. But this is serious. My legs are three inches longer than they were last year. Lucky I tried these on, or I'd have shown up on the parade ground tomorrow looking like this. [*He hoists up his pant legs and marches about.*] Neat, huh? The colonel would have gone wild with joy.

Amélie. If anyone can fix 'em, I can. Come try on the coat while you're here. [*She helps him into coat, as they start up right.*]

Étienne [with a glance at BIBICHON]. Gad, what a poisonous cigar!

Bibichon. I'll admit it's terrible. It's one of *your* cigars.

Amélie [to BIBICHON, *over her shoulder*]. I told you to stop smoking. We've got to get this place aired out. [*She rings bell for servant.*]

Étienne. Yes, open up some windows.

Bibichon. Here now, don't start that. [*Turning up coat collar.*] You know I'm susceptible to chills.

Yvonne. He's so delicate.

Bibichon. I'll catch my death, then you'll be sorry.

Palmyre. Sorry? I'd laugh my head off.

Bibichon. You girls will have to help keep me warm. [*He plumps down between the legs of* PALMYRE, *who is sitting on the sofa. At the same time, he grabs* YVONNE *and pulls her down on his lap. The girls scream.*]

Yvonne and *Palmyre [slapping at him].* Stop that! Get up! Let go!

Bibichon. I'm surrounded by beauty. [*He tickles* YVONNE's *neck.*] Here, kitty-kitty!

Yvonne. Quit it! You old tomcat!

Boas. Lay off, that's my kitten you're tickling.

Bibichon. I'll bet she's looked over the fence more than once.

YVONNE *gouges him with her elbow and breaks free.*

Yvonne [straightening her dress]. Some day you're going to fool around once too often.

Bibichon [rises and winks]. Who's fooling? What Boas doesn't know won't hurt him. You've probably got twenty boy friends on the side.

Yvonne [giggling]. You're awful!

BOAS *continues to play cards.*

Boas [amused]. Yvonne can take care of herself.

Bibichon. That's what you think. [*He pinches* YVONNE. *She jumps.*]

Enter ADONIS, *a boy of fifteen, dressed as a valet with brass buttons on his coat. He goes to* AMÉLIE, *who is finishing the readjustment of* ÉTIENNE's *uniform.*

Adonis. You rang, madame?

Amélie. Yes. Open the window. Then remove the cups and empty glasses.

ADONIS *goes center to pick up tray.*

Bibichon. Wait, boy. There's a little left. [*He drains his glass and puts it back on tray.*] All right, it's yours.

ADONIS *takes tray to a tabouret down right, then opens the window.*

Amélie. Who's ready for a bite to eat?

All rise at once except BOAS, *who is gathering up the cards. General movement toward the door up left.*

Bibichon. Come along, you optimist.

Amélie [at the doorway]. Why do you call him that?

Bibichon. Because he thinks he's got exclusive rights to this alley cat. [*He gives* YVONNE *a friendly pat. Laughter from group.*]

Boas [rising to follow them]. Not a bit funny.

All go out into the adjoining salon with the exception of ADONIS. *Finding himself alone, he takes the chartreuse bottle, pours a glassful, and gulps the contents. At this moment,* AMÉLIE *returns to the doorway.* ADONIS *is looking front, glass in hand, rubbing his belly.*

Adonis. I like it.

Amélie [swooping down on him]. How do you like this? [*She gives him a slap across the mouth.*]

Adonis. Oh!

He recoils a step, then delivers a wallop to her jaw, bringing one up from the floor. Most of the others have reappeared in the doorway up left and stand amazed. AMÉLIE *totters for an instant. Unaware of the onlookers,* ADONIS *crosses up right, as if about to exit.* ÉTIENNE *bounds after the valet, followed closely by* BOAS *and* VALCREUSE. *They collar him, and bring him back to right center.*

Étienne. Stop! You little monster!

Amélie. Étienne! He struck me! Did you see, Étienne?

All [simultaneously]. Oh! The brute! Beast! Assassin!

ADONIS *is brought forward and jostled about. He shakes his fist at* AMÉLIE.

Adonis. Serves her right, the old slut!

Amélie [aghast]. You hear what he calls me?

Adonis [muttering]. Dirty old slut, that's all she is!

All [outraged]. What impudence! Hoodlum! Barbarian!

The men shake him and pummel him. All except BIBICHON.

Amélie. Get the hottentot out of here! Get him out!

Adonis. Let me go, you cowards! Bunch of bullies! Yah!

The men bustle him off through the door up right, kicking and cuffing at him as he goes.

Amélie. Take the cannibal out of my sight, that's all I ask. *[She follows the men offstage.* BIBICHON *remains with* YVONNE *and* PALMYRE.]

Palmyre. That boy's got a savage temper. *[They smile at one another.]*

Yvonne. Cute little savage, don't you think?

Bibichon [going down right to close window]. Damned inconsiderate, opening windows. I don't know why I come to this place. *[He goes to card table and sits, crossing his legs.]*

AMÉLIE *returns with the other men, all jabbering at once.*

Amélie. A lady isn't safe in her own house any more.

Étienne. I ought to break every bone in his body.

Amélie [fanning with handkerchief]. You all saw what happened? And he called me a slut, too. *[She sits on sofa.]*

Valcreuse. Hell of a way to talk to a lady.

Étienne [striding up and down]. Why did you ever hire such a roughneck?

Amélie. Adonis came highly recommended.

Étienne. You made a serious mistake.

Amélie [*to the others*]. It'll turn out to be my fault now.
[*To* ÉTIENNE.] He had the best of references.

Étienne [*disgustedly*]. "The best of references"!

Amélie. You approved of him yourself. You said you liked
his manners.

Étienne. Who recommended the little bastard?

Amélie. People I have great confidence in.

Étienne. Who, for instance?

Amélie. Members of his own family, for instance.

Étienne. A high-toned lot *they* must be!

Amélie. Matter of fact, they are.

Étienne. He'll be lucky to get another job after the references I'm going to give him. If he isn't packed and out of
here in fifteen minutes, I'm going to personally kick him
down the stairs.

Amélie [*protesting*]. We can't turn the boy out in the
cold.

Étienne. Cold? It's the middle of summer.

Amélie. We can't send him into the streets with no bed
to sleep in.

Étienne. Why not?

Yvonne. I've got an idea. You turn him out, and I'll take
him over to my place.

Boas. Over my dead body, you'll take him to your place.

Yvonne. Who knows what dangers the boy might face on
the streets?

Boas. Nothing like the dangers of staying at your place.

Palmyre. Had your eye on him, did you, Yvonne?

Valcreuse. Can't you wait till they grow up?

Yvonne [*loftily*]. The sordid minds some people have!

The right door opens and POCHET *bustles in.*

Pochet [*ferociously*]. What's been going on here?

All. Ah, Monsieur Pochet! How are you, Monsieur Pochet?

Amélie. Papa, you are just in time to help us.

Pochet [*descending on* AMÉLIE *and* ÉTIENNE]. What have
you done? What did you do to poor Adonis?

Étienne. What did *we* do?

Pochet. I found him in tears. [*To* AMÉLIE.] He said you
slapped him in front of everybody.

Amélie. Suppose I did? He deserved it.

All. He was the one who hit Amélie. You should have

been here. He ought to be in jail. [*They cluster around*
POCHET. *He pushes them back vigorously.*]

Pochet. Stand back! Back, I say! Silence! [*To* AMÉLIE.]
Do you or do you not admit striking the first blow?

Amélie. He was drinking the liquor.

Pochet [*glaring*]. I'm not speaking of that. Did you slap
the boy first?

Amélie [*gestures evasively*]. Of course!

Pochet. Aha! In cases of this sort, the person who strikes
the first blow is guilty.

Étienne. If I may say so——

Pochet. No opinions, please! I am capable of judging affairs
of honor. Retired brigadier of the civil guard. Former provost
of my regiment.

Boas [*aside to* VALCREUSE]. That's a fancy way of saying
ex-traffic cop.

Pochet. That unfortunate lad was struck first. *He* is the
offended party.

Amélie. I'd like to know what I did wrong.

Pochet. A female should never strike a male. That's taking
unfair advantage. [*Mingled laughter and protests from all.*]

Étienne. You don't let her explain.

Pochet [*haughtily*]. Why should I?

All. Look here. You're not being fair, Pochet. Let her
speak.

Pochet [*shoving them back*]. All right. Keep moving. On
your way. Move along.

Palmyre [*aside to* YVONNE]. Once a cop, always a cop.

Yvonne. That's all he is, a broken-down flatfoot.

Pochet. A duel is out of the question, so all you can do is
offer your apology.

Étienne. What! Why should Amélie apologize to a servant?

AMÉLIE *is standing between them.* POCHET *leans forward and
prods* ÉTIENNE *with his forefinger.*

Pochet. Étienne, I'm talking to my daughter. Kindly don't
meddle. When you and she are having an argument, do I butt
in? No? Then, move along, move along.

Étienne [*turning away*]. Idiot!

Pochet. Now, Amélie, all you have to do is tell the boy
you're sorry.

Yvonne [*to* AMÉLIE]. If I were you I'd——

Pochet. Who asked you for your opinion? Shut your big
mouth.

Yvonne. I was going to say that I agree with you absolutely.

Pochet. In that case, go right on talking.

Amélie. Must I really apologize?

Étienne [*annoyed*]. You're not going to do it?

Pochet. Be quiet, sir!

Étienne. No, damn it, I won't be quiet. I count for something around here. I pay all the bills.

Pochet. Be content. That's plenty for one man to do.

Étienne [*huffily*]. I won't put up with this. [*Crossing right center to* BIBICHON.] He's going too far, don't you think?

Bibichon. I don't know. I wasn't listening.

Pochet. Then it's all settled? You'll apologize.

Amélie. Whatever you say, papa darling.

Étienne. I'm getting out of this madhouse. [*He exits up left.*]

Pochet. Good riddance. [*To* AMÉLIE.] I'll send Adonis to see you. Remember, no reproaches. Just apologize.

Amélie. Yes, papa.

Pochet. I know the lad will forgive you. [*He goes out up right. The others close in upon* AMÉLIE, *all expressing their opinions simultaneously.*]

Boas. If it were me, I wouldn't do it.

Valcreuse. He has no right to do this.

Palmyre. There's such a thing as being too dutiful.

Yvonne. After all he is her father.

Amélie. I have no choice. What else can I do?

Bibichon [*rising*]. It makes no difference to me one way or the other.

Amélie. Let me see Adonis alone. It won't take a minute.

General conversation as guests go up left and exit. There is a tapping at the door up right.

Amélie. Come in. [ADONIS *enters.*] Oh—it's you?

Adonis [*sulkily, without looking at her*]. Madame sent for me?

Amélie. I believe I did. [*Slight pause.*] You silly boy, Adonis. Are you still cross with me? Oh, you! What's the matter? I didn't slap you very hard. [*He shrugs a shoulder.*] It didn't hurt you that much.

Adonis. As if that was what mattered!

Amélie [*sitting by the piano*]. Well? What was it? How did I hurt you? Come here, you big baby! [*She pulls him onto her lap.*]

Adonis [*blubbers*]. You hurt my feelings!

Amélie. Let's kiss and make up. [ADONIS *hesitates, then buries his head on her shoulder.*] You know I *love* you! [*She kisses him. He clings to her.* ÉTIENNE *and the guests reappear in doorway left.*]

Étienne [*gasping surprise*]. Oh!

All [*echoing his astonishment*]. Oh!

Adonis [*seeing* ÉTIENNE]. Let me up! Let me go!

Amélie [*unaware she is observed*]. Now don't be so bashful. I love you, you know I do!

Pochet [*appearing in doorway right*]. Everything going all right?

Étienne [*furiously, coming left center*]. Sir, I hope you're satisfied! Here she is with the valet on her lap!

Pochet. Good, good. Peace is restored, eh?

All [*shocked by his reaction*]. What? What did he say?

Étienne. What's good about Amy kissing the valet? By heaven, he's her lover! She's been sleeping with the servants!

Adonis [*rising*]. What's the matter with him?

Amélie [*to* ÉTIENNE]. You ought to be ashamed of yourself.

Pochet. How dare you, sir! [*Striking a theatrical pose.*] That child is her brother!

All [*in a flurried reaction*]. Oh, what's this he's saying? Her brother!

AMÉLIE *and* ADONIS *take adoring positions on either side of* POCHET. *He puts his arms about them.*

Amélie and *Adonis.* Papa!

Pochet [*protectively*]. My children! We weren't going to tell them, were we? Personally I think it's all to Amy's credit. She said, "I have a little brother. I shall do my duty by him." So she took him into her house as a servant. How many of *you* would have done as much?

All [*nodding approval*]. Of course. She did right. Yes, indeed.

Pochet [*patting* ADONIS' *head*]. My brave little son! And they thought you were capable of—at your age! [*To* ÉTIENNE.] You presumed to accuse this innocent youth. I dare say you are now prepared to withdraw your vile accusations.

Étienne. Huh?

Pochet. I might even say your incestuous accusations.

Amélie [*indicating* ADONIS]. Come on . . . shake hands!

Étienne. With *him!* [*He folds his arms proudly.*]

Bibichon. Go ahead. He's practically your brother-in-law.

Étienne. He *would* be, if I were married to his sister!

Amélie [*agreeably*]. Don't be stuffy. Shake hands anyway.

Étienne [*reluctantly shaking hands*]. How are you? How've you been?

Adonis. Pretty good. How are things with yourself?

Étienne. Not bad, thanks. [*To* AMÉLIE.] Well, are you satisfied?

Doorbell rings.

Amélie. Adonis, the doorbell! [ADONIS *starts out.*]

Adonis. Yes, madame.

Amélie. Kiss me. [ADONIS *returns and does so.*] That's my darling. Now answer the door.

Adonis. Yes, madame. [*He exits up right with a hop and a skip.*]

Bibichon. Charming little scene.

Étienne. Were you expecting anyone to call?

Amélie. No, I wasn't.

Yvonne. Listen, Amélie, if you're expecting callers . . .

Palmyre. We really must run along.

Amélie. Don't go. Wait for me in there. [*Indicating the next room.*] I shan't be long. [*To* ADONIS, *who has returned.*] Well, who is it?

Adonis. Someone to see you, Amy, dear.

Étienne [*annoyed*]. "Someone to see you, Amy, dear"! [*To* AMÉLIE.] If he's a servant, let him talk like one. If he's your brother, get him out of uniform.

Amélie. Don't fuss. [*To* ADONIS.] Who is it?

Adonis [*smiling oafishly*]. I dunno.

Amélie. Why don't you know?

Adonis. She wouldn't give her name.

Amélie. It's a lady then?

Adonis. Very high-class. Not like your usual friends.

Étienne. I'd like to strangle the boy.

Adonis [*assuming the air of a femme fatale*]. She walks like this, and she's wearing a veil.

Amélie. It must be a bill collector. But I'll see her.

ADONIS *goes out. The guests exit up left.*

All [*as they go*]. We'll be waiting for you. Don't be too long now.

ÉTIENNE *and* POCHET *follow the others.*

Bibichon. I'll be talking to Yvonne.

Boas. Shut up, you.

Adonis [ushering in IRÈNE]. Step this way please, madame.

IRÈNE *enters. She is elegantly gowned. A heavy veil con-
ceals her face.*

Amélie. Won't you come in?

Irène. Am I addressing Amélie d'Avranches?

Amélie. Yes, madame, you are. [*She indicates the sofa,*
ADONIS *exits, closing the door.*]

Irène [seating herself]. Madame, I've come to see you
about a delicate matter.

Amélie. Oh, have you? Well, if there's any way I can be of
help . . .

Irène. I hope you won't think it rude of me—but you see—
it's—it's—how can I put it?

Amélie. Speak freely, madame.

Irène. It's a matter which concerns a friend of mine.

Amélie [seating herself on sofa beside IRÈNE]. A friend of
yours, you say?

Irène [examining AMÉLIE *through lorgnette].* Now that I
look at you closely . . . it seems to me . . . It's a very
curious thing, but I could almost swear I've seen your face
before.

Amélie. It is possible, madame. I go out a great deal.

Irène [hesitant]. Where have I seen you? Have you always
been . . . ?

Amélie. Perhaps you've met someone in my family. My
father is an old functionary of the republic, an ex-officer of
the grenadiers——

Irène. I must have been mistaken. It was just a fleeting
resemblance.

Amélie. No harm done. Now, what did you say you wanted
to see me about?

Irène [hastily]. Not for myself, you understand. I come
in behalf of a friend. Friendship does impose its little obligations. You'll pardon me if I don't tell you the lady's
name?

Amélie [amused]. Of course, madame, as you like.

Irène. She is a married woman, so one can't be too careful.

Amélie. Ah? Then it's her husband you want to discuss?

Irène. Oh, no, not her husband. Quite the contrary. It's her
lover I came to talk about.

Amélie. Aha?

Irène [*romantically*]. Ah, madame, if you only knew—if you could only imagine how much I love him!

Amélie [*mildly malicious*]. You mean this friend of yours?

Irène [*startled*]. What? Yes, my friend! It's her first lover, mind you, her very *first!*

Amélie [*with a sympathetic smile*]. The poor dear!

Irène. Can you realize what it is like for a married woman —her *first* lover! The anguish of it! The rapture! The remorse!

Amélie [*sighs*]. Yes, I know.

Irène. No doubt you remember your first love affair?

Amélie. I hope to tell you I do. It was with a German shepherd.

Irène [*stunned*]. You mean——

Amélie. Oh—not what you think. He was a shepherd who came from Germany.

Irène [*relieved*]. Ah! A shepherd from Germany.

Amélie. At least that's what he told me.

Irène. It must have been interesting.

Amélie [*nonchalantly*]. And I have counted a good many sheep since then.

Irène. As for my friend—my unfortunate friend—for her, it is the first transgression. The first chance she's ever had to do anything remotely wicked. If she were to lose him, it would be tragic!

Amélie. Do you love him as much as that?

Irène. Yes! Madly! Passionately!

Amélie [*smiling*]. You're very charming.

Irène [*rising in confusion*]. Madame, what have I said? It isn't myself—it's this friend of mine. She's the one who has the lover . . .

Amélie [*rising sympathetically*]. Why don't you trust me?

Irène. Can I do that?

Amélie. We owe it to each other. As women of the world, we must have the courage of our indiscretions.

Irène. True. I have nothing to be ashamed of. Yes, madame. I am the lady. I am the one. [*She sits again.*]

Amélie. It didn't take me long to figure *that* out.

Irène [*imploringly*]. Please, madame, be generous. You could take your choice of a dozen lovers. But I have only one. Take any other man in the universe. Take all of them. But not him. Let me keep *him*.

Amélie [*a trifle irked*]. Just what man are you talking about?

Irène. Say it isn't true. You're not going to marry him?

Amélie. Marry? Me? Who the devil are you talking about?

Irène [in a hushed voice]. Marcel Courbois.

Amélie. Marcel Courbois? Marry *him?* [*Laughing.*] Ah—ha, ha, ha! [*She goes up left to doorway, trying to suppress her laughter.*]

Irène [rises and follows]. What is it? Where are you going?

Amélie. You'll see. [*Calling.*] Étienne! [*She beckons.*]

Étienne [offstage]. What's the matter?

Amélie. Hey, come here! Come here for a minute! [*She crosses back to center.*]

Étienne [entering]. What's the matter, Amy?

Amélie [choking for breath]. This lady here, she thinks— she said—ah, ha, ha! [*Bends double with laughter.*]

Étienne [bowing gravely to IRÈNE]. Madame!

Amélie. She came here all excited to ask me if——

Irène [interrupting]. I came here as a favor to a friend of mine——

Amélie [to mollify her]. Yes, she came to ask a question for a friend of hers . . .

Étienne. Really? What question?

Amélie. She wants to know if I'm going to marry Marcel Courbois.

Étienne [convulsed]. Marcel!

Amélie. It seems that Marcel is the lover of—of this friend of Madame's.

Étienne. You marry Marcel? Ah, ha ha ha!

Amélie [subsiding on sofa]. Did you ever hear anything as funny as that? [*Both go into gales of laughter.*]

Irène [rather pleased]. Is it really so amusing?

Amélie and *Étienne [barely coherent].* Oh, yes . . . yes!

Irène [laughing too]. This is wonderful. You don't know how happy it makes me. [*Sits again.*]

Étienne. It does?

Irène. I am probably the happiest woman in the world.

Étienne [chuckling]. Apparently, madame, you take your friend's problem very much to heart?

Irène [floundering]. Oh, I didn't mean that I—that *I* personally was happy——

Amélie. You see, you can't fool anyone in this place.

Irène [with sudden decision]. Very well. I shan't pretend any more. I shall be brazen.

Amélie. Good idea.

Étienne [*marveling*]. Marcel Courbois? Well, well!

Irène. Yes, monsieur. He and I are devoted to one another. I haven't seen him since last Sunday. Naturally, I went to mass at an early hour . . .

Étienne. Naturally.

Irène. And as I happened to be passing his house on the way home . . .

Étienne [*helpfully*]. You stopped in for a visit?

Irène. As a married woman, I'm not free to come and go as I please. So, while he was getting dressed——

Étienne [*naïvely*]. The first time?

Irène. No, the second time.—Well, I couldn't help noticing some papers on his desk.

Étienne. You read them? Why not? It's a feminine prerogative.

Irène. I found a letter. That horrible letter! Marcel had written to his godfather announcing his marriage to a certain Amélie d'Avranches.

Amélie [*perplexed*]. That *is* horrible.

Étienne. What could he be thinking of?

Amélie. It's way beyond *me.*

Étienne [*to* IRÈNE]. Did you ask Marcel about this?

Irène [*rising again*]. No, I wouldn't dare do that. I shouldn't like him to think I would read his mail.

Amélie [*rising*]. So you decided to call on me instead?

Irène [*with determination*]. Yes.

Étienne. When I see Marcel, I'll find out about this. I'm sure he has an explanation. He is a very close friend of mine.

Irène. A close friend?

Étienne. My best friend, in fact. He tells me all his troubles. Lord knows he has a lot of them.

Irène. He tells you everything?

Étienne. His innermost thoughts.

Irène [*hopefully*]. Then you must have heard about *me?*

Étienne [*puzzled*]. About you? No, I wouldn't say that.

Irène [*distressed*]. Then he doesn't love me after all.

Étienne. Why not?

Irène. If he loved me, you'd have heard about me. He'd confide in his best friend. I know what men talk about.

Étienne. Marcel is a gentleman. If he hasn't spoken of you, it's because he is protecting your good name.

Irène. Tell him not to do that. I'd much prefer to be talked about.

Étienne. Wait. Now that I think of it, Marcel did mention a certain lady. [*Lowering voice.*] Are you, by any chance, madame la comtesse?

Irène [*radiant*]. "Madame la comtesse!" He did tell you. You see he does love me, after all! [*She relaxes on the sofa again, much relieved.*]

Amélie. "Madame la comtesse!" I knew there was something about you. Are you, by any chance, la Comtesse de Premilly?

Irène. You know me? [*She lifts her veil.*]

Amélie. You said yourself you recognized *me*.

Irène [*using her lorgnette*]. Then I was right. It's Amélie. Amélie Pochet.

Amélie. Exactly, madame. Amélie Pochet.

Irène. My former chambermaid.

Amélie [*with a deferent curtsey*]. The same.

Irène [*compassionate*]. Alas, you poor miserable child!

Étienne. You used to be her chambermaid?

Amélie. For a very brief time.

Irène [*peering through lorgnette*]. I thought I knew you, but the background, the atmosphere was different. And your hair—I remember another color.

Amélie [*airily*]. It got quite light all of a sudden. I don't know why.

Irène. "Amélie d'Avranches"—such a pretty name! You dropped the name "Pochet"?

Amélie [*wrinkling her nose*]. In my profession, a little glamor never does any harm. But tell me, madame, how are things with you? How is your husband?

Irène. He's very healthy, thank you. He had a slight cold not long ago.

Amélie. I'm so sorry to hear it.

Irène. He's completely recovered now.

Amélie. I'm so glad to hear that.

Irène [*graciously*]. Won't you sit down again?

Amélie [*dismayed*]. Oh, I couldn't. Not in the presence of madame.

Irène. But I insist.

Amélie [*sits primly*]. It's too great an honor. [*A nervous pause ensues.*] Well, this is an unexpected pleasure, isn't it?

Irène. Yes, isn't it? I'd thought today I might be meeting a woman of uncertain character—but now that I see it's you—I'm no longer uncertain.

Amélie [*uncertain herself*]. Oh? Thanks a lot, I'm sure.

Irène [*commiserating*]. You poor sweet child—whatever brought you to a life like this?

Amélie [*matter of factly*]. Ambition, I guess. I always had it in the back of my mind. I wasn't cut out to be a chambermaid.

Irène. You always gave such good service.

Étienne. Still does.

Amélie [*severely*]. Étienne!

Étienne. Beg pardon.

Irène. I remember, Amélie, you were always a coquette—and now . . .

Amélie [*nods*]. Now I'm a cocotte.

Irène. You were always fond of baubles and trinkets.

Amélie. Yes, ever since I was a baby.

Irène. And you loved perfume.

Amélie. Yes.

Irène. You were always using mine.

Amélie. With the salary you paid, I couldn't afford to buy my own.

Irène. You were always borrowing my dresses to wear to parties.

Amélie. I ironed them neatly before I put them back.

Irène. I was very fond of you until that day—the time my husband found you . . . [*A slight pause.*] Er—you recall what you were doing.

Étienne [*curiously*]. Doing what?

Irène. She was in the greenhouse one afternoon—cultivating the gardener.

Amélie [*with a glance at* ÉTIENNE]. We needn't go into that.

Irène. That was the day you left us.

Amélie. It seems a long time ago.

Irène. Things have changed for you since then.

Amélie. Yes, I've come up in the world.

Irène [*with a sigh*]. I missed you, Amélie, when you were gone.

Amélie. Madame is kind to say so.

Irène. Yes, it is difficult nowadays to find good chambermaids.

Amélie. Don't I know it? I have a time to get any decent servants at all.

The guests appear again at left door, waving good-by.

Irène. Oh, you have company? [*She lowers her veil.*]

Yvonne. It's only us. We're going now.

Amélie [*to* IRÈNE]. Will you excuse me a moment?

Irène. Certainly. [AMÉLIE *goes up left.* ÉTIENNE *follows.*]

Étienne. Are you all leaving?

Amélie. Must you go?

All. Don't disturb yourselves. It was lots of fun. We'll see you again soon.

Étienne. Don't forget, I go to Rouen tonight. I won't be back for twenty-eight days.

All. Good-by, Étienne. We'll see you then. A month from now. Good-by, Amélie.

Amélie. Excuse me for not going to the door with you. Papa, will you do the honors?

Pochet. By all means. I'll see them out. Come this way.

Led by POCHET, *the guests are seen passing from left to right behind the glass wall. They wave and blow kisses to* AMÉLIE *as they go.*

Amélie. Good-by, good-by, everyone.

Étienne. Au revoir. Come again soon. [*He returns to center.*]

Amélie [*returning to* IRÈNE]. Madame la comtesse, you don't know how pleased I am you came to call. I hope we're going to be close friends from now on.

Irène [*less enthusiastic*]. Do you?

Amélie. I've always been your devoted admirer.

Irène. You have?

Étienne. Strange, isn't it, how devoted servants become after they've ceased to work for a person?

Irène [*smiling at* ÉTIENNE]. As a close friend of Marcel's, you must be Étienne de Milledieu.

Étienne. He has spoken of me?

Irène. Often, but he never told me you had such a patriotic occupation. Where are you stationed?

Étienne. Me? At the stock exchange. I'm a broker's agent.

Irène. I didn't know they wore uniforms.

Étienne [*glancing at his costume*]. Oh, you mean this? I'm in the reserves. I have to report for twenty-eight days' special duty.

Irène. That explains it.

Pochet [*entering left*]. Well, they've gone, the no-good riff-raff. [*Seeing* IRÈNE.] Oh, I beg your pardon! [*He starts to withdraw.*]

Amélie. Wait, Papa. I want to introduce you.

Pochet. Madame.

Irène [*looking through lorgnette*]. Oh, yes, I remember him very well.

Amélie [*to* POCHET]. You remember Madame, too, don't you?—la Comtesse de Premilly.

Pochet. Ah, yes. How could I forget her?

Irène. You often came to my house to visit your daughter. You were a policeman in those days.

Pochet. Eh? I was a brigadier in the civil guard. Well, and how have you been? [*He extends his hand to* IRÈNE.]

Irène [*turning away and polishing lorgnette*]. I've been in fairly good health, thank you.

Pochet [*pauses a moment, looks at his hand, and returns it to his pocket*]. Only fair? Well, of course, you're not as young as you used to be. But then, none of us are.

Irène. I beg your pardon?

Amélie [*sharply*]. Papa!

Pochet. I don't mean that Madame looks older or anything like that. It's just that Madame has matured. She's matured a hell of a lot.

Irène [*to* AMÉLIE, *changing the subject*]. You used to have a little brother. He must have grown into quite a man by now.

Amélie. Oh, he has.

Irène. He should be very handsome, I imagine. What have you done with him?

Pochet. He's right here with us.

Irène. He was a darling child. Did he keep his good looks?

Amélie. Well, opinions vary on that subject.

Pochet. He's like me in miniature.

Amélie. Would Madame like to see him?

Irène. I'd adore to see him.

Amélie [*ringing bell*]. I wonder if he'll remember you.

Adonis [*appearing right*]. Madame rang?

Amélie. Yes, come in, Adonis.

Adonis. Yes, madame?

Amélie. Say "bonjour" to the lady.

Adonis. Bonjour.

Irène [*gazing through lorgnette*]. Is this the one? He's the same boy who let me in a little while ago.

Amélie. Of course. [*To* ADONIS.] You remember Madame?

Adonis [*grinning*]. No.

Amélie. But it's Madame la Comtesse. You used to visit her house when you were little. [ADONIS *sticks out his chin and frowns.*]

Irène. Surely you remember me, young man? Don't you remember when I gave you the beautiful gold-plated watch?

Adonis. Oh, I remember the watch. I swapped it with a chum for a squirt gun.

Amélie. You didn't.

Étienne. Why a squirt gun?

Adonis. I needed one—to squirt water on people. Can't do that with a watch.

Amélie. No, naturally you can't.

Adonis [*coming forward a step or two*]. I was sorry later. Because you can't tell time with a squirt gun.

Irène. You don't remember me at all?

Adonis [*same foolish grin*]. Nope, not at all.

Amélie. Madame finds him changed?

Irène. Oh, yes. But not for the better. Yesterday he was a mere boy. Today . . . *today* I'm not sure what he is.

Adonis [*whispers hoarsely to* POCHET]. Who is she, anyway?

Pochet [*whispers back*]. It's the Countess.

Adonis. Oh, sure! The one that fired Amy for fooling around with the gardener!

Pochet. See? You have a good memory when you want to use it.

Doorbell rings.

Amélie. Madame was saying? [*To* ADONIS, *who starts to exit.*] Where do you think you're going?

Adonis. Got to answer the door, don't I?

Amélie. Oh, yes. Go ahead. [ADONIS *exits.*]

Irène. I'm afraid, Amélie dear, that I must tear myself away. Especially since you have other visitors . . .

Adonis [*entering*]. Monsieur Marcel Courbois!

Irène [*startled*]. Marcel!

Marcel [*entering*]. Bonjour, everybody. [*Face to face with* IRÈNE.] Ah!—Darling . . . I mean, madame, what are you doing here—in a place like this?

Amélie. What's wrong with this place?

Irène. I can explain, Marcel. You see——

Étienne. He's the one that's got to explain. What's all this about you marrying Amélie?

Pochet. Marry! Nobody's going to marry Amélie. Especially Marcel. I'll never permit it.

Marcel. How did you know? I mean, I hadn't told anybody yet.

Irène. I'm afraid it's my fault.

Marcel. What do you know about this?

Irène. I read the letter you'd written.

Marcel. You did?

Étienne. By mistake, of course.

Marcel. You mean you read my correspondence?

Irène [*abjectly*]. Yes.

Marcel [*reproachfully*]. And you doubted my fidelity?

Irène. That letter would have made anyone suspicious.

Amélie. Tell us, Marcel, what exactly *did* you have in mind?

Marcel. If you must know, I'm in trouble. I'm in hot water right up to my ears. Marrying Amélie seems to be my only way out. [*He crosses to the left.*]

All. What? Marry Amélie! You don't mean it! You're not really serious!

Irène. You wouldn't—you couldn't marry a woman like that.

Marcel. Certainly not. I wouldn't marry her if she were the last woman on earth.

Amélie. This is extremely flattering, I must say.

Marcel. All I want is to *pretend* to marry her.

All. Pretend? What's this? Why should he pretend?

Irène. Why even pretend?

Marcel [*sinks to sofa*]. Because I'm up the well-known tree. I'm hanging by a straw.

Irène. What tree? What straw?

Marcel. I mean I'm flat. I haven't a sou or a centime. I'm so broke I don't know which way to turn.

Irène. Broke? But, darling, if it's only a matter of money, I can always ask my husband for some.

Marcel [*nobly*]. No, Irène. Not that. After all, I still have some pride.

Amélie. Aren't men stupid, stubborn things?

Irène. This one is.

Marcel [*rises and crosses down right*]. I've got so many debts to pay. Creditors are hounding me all the time. I keep telling them I have twelve hundred thousand francs on deposit, but that doesn't seem to impress them.

Étienne. Naturally not. Who'd believe it? But it's true.

Irène. Did you say twelve hundred thousand francs?

Amélie. Twelve hundred thousand?

Pochet. You have that much money in the bank?

Marcel [*nods*]. Deposited in my name.

Étienne. Only trouble is, he's not allowed to touch it.

Pochet. I see. He can't touch it. [*Reacts.*] Why *not?*

Étienne. He can't, that's all.

Marcel. That's what's so infuriating. One of my father's notions. A dear old fellow. But he was afraid I'd waste my money on wine, women, and music lessons.

Irène. I'm sure he misjudged you.

Marcel. When he died, he left me twelve hundred thousand francs. And that's why I'm in this mess today.

Amélie. Too bad. I certainly feel sorry for you.

Pochet [*to* AMÉLIE, *tapping his forehead*]. And I thought Adonis was the only booby around here.

Marcel. Here I am starving to death with all that money in the bank.

Amélie. But why?

All. Yes, why?

Marcel. It's all tied up in trust, that's why.

Irène. In what?

Marcel. It's held in a trust fund.

Étienne. Marcel's fortune is all his, but he can't spend a penny until he gets *legal* permission. The money's entrusted to a third party who's supposed to take care of it for him.

Amélie. Oh? Like when I give Bibichon twenty francs to bet on a horse and he hands the money to a bookie.

Étienne. That's the general idea.

Marcel. The money is held in trust by my godfather, and I won't get it until the day I get married.

Irène. I begin to understand. This marriage to Amélie?

Marcel. It's my only hope. If my godfather thinks I'm married, he'll have to give me the money.

Pochet. That's why you told him you were engaged to my daughter?

Marcel. Exactly.

Étienne. Nice trick, if you can get away with it.

Marcel. I told him Amélie d'Avranches was the charming daughter of a distinguished military hero.

Pochet. That's all true so far.

Marcel [*to* AMÉLIE]. I even enclosed your photograph.

Amélie. I'll give you another to replace it.

Marcel. That's the main reason I chose you for my bride-to-be. Yours was the only photograph I had handy.

Amélie. Much obliged, Marcel. So you sent my picture to your godfather in Holland? That's where he lives, isn't it?

Marcel. Yes, he was born in Dudelsackburg-am-Rhein, but he lives in Holland.

Étienne. I hope this scheme of yours pays off.

Marcel [*morosely*]. That's the problem. It's *not* paying off. Not working out at all!

Étienne. Didn't your godfather believe the story?

Marcel. Oh, yes. But he wasn't satisfied with getting the letter, he had to come to Paris and see for himself.

All. To Paris! No! You mean he's here now?

Marcel. He arrived at my place an hour ago. He told me: "Ach, sonny, I was so happy. Life is standing in front of you at last. Where please is she, your pyootiful innozent bride?" They talk like that in Holland.

Étienne. Didn't he send word he was arriving?

Marcel. No. He wanted to surprise me. A surprizement, he calls it.

Amélie. And I'm supposed to be the beautiful innocent bride?

Étienne. Now it's your turn to surprise him.

Pochet. Amélie'd make a first-class bride, and why not? She's never been married in her life.

Marcel. You can imagine how I felt seeing him there on my doorstep. I rushed over here as fast as I could to warn you he was coming.

All. What! Coming here? Not here?

Marcel. Certainly, coming here. My godfather has got to see my fiancée.

Étienne. This joke of yours is getting out of hand.

Marcel. Look, Étienne, we've got to go through with this. [*Turning to* AMÉLIE.] You're not going to let me down, are you? You wouldn't want me to lose twelve hundred thousand francs?

Irène. Amélie, dear, you wouldn't want him to lose that money, would you?

Amélie. What do I care? I'm not going to stay here and talk to any old coot. I'm leaving. [*She turns and starts up left.*]

Pochet [*barring her way*]. You've got to stay. It's your duty.

Marcel. Remember, twelve hundred thousand francs! I'll be able to give you a nice little present.

Amélie. I don't want your old present.

Pochet [*indignantly*]. Marcel is offering you money. Never refuse money. Remember your upbringing.

Amélie [*reconsidering*]. That's true, Papa.

Marcel. You'll help me out then? You'll pretend we're engaged?

Amélie. I'll do my best, just this once.

Marcel. You'll never regret it.

Irène. Thank you, Amélie, darling. It's for my sake too.

Marcel. Thank you too, Étienne.

Étienne. Don't thank me. What about this godfather? He's going to want to see a wedding.

Marcel. I was worried about that, but he has to leave right away for America. He won't be back for two months. "Listen, sonny," he said to me, "even if I can't be there at the zeremony, you get your money chust the same."

Étienne. In that case, there's nothing to worry about.

Amélie [*clowning*]. Marcel, will you marry me?

Marcel. With the greatest of pleasure! [*He kisses her hands.*]

Pochet [*making gesture of benediction*]. Bless you, my children.

Étienne. When will he be here?

Marcel. Any second now. Immediately, in fact. [*Doorbell rings.*] Here he is now!

Irène [*starting left*]. I think I'd better run along. I don't want to watch this family get-together.

Marcel [*to* ADONIS, *who enters right*]. Is he here? My godfather?

Adonis [*announcing majestically*]. General Koshnadiev.

All [*in amazement*]. What? Who? What did he say?

Marcel. That's not my godfather. [*He crosses to join others up left.*]

Amélie. Who did you say? Koshnadiev? Who's he?

Adonis. I dunno.

Amélie. Go and ask him. Find out what he wants.

Adonis. Yes, madame. [*He exits.*]

Irène [*embracing her*]. Darling Amélie. Au revoir.

Amélie. Madame la comtesse.

Pochet. Always at your service, madame.

Irène. Thank you, my dear Pochet.

Adonis [*re-entering*]. The General says he's come on a diplomatic mission.

Amélie. Diplomatic? How peculiar!

Étienne. You'd better see him.

Amélie. Show him in. Say I'll be with him directly.

Étienne. I'll get back to my civilian clothes.

Marcel [*embracing* IRÈNE]. Au revoir, my precious pigeon.

Amélie. I'll go with you to the door.

Irène [*to* ÉTIENNE]. Good-by, monsieur.

Étienne. Madame! [*He bows. Then, to* MARCEL.] Come along, Marcel. [MARCEL *and* ÉTIENNE *exit down left.*]

Amélie. This way, madame la comtesse. [POCHET, IRÈNE, AMÉLIE *exit up left, and are seen passing behind glass partition.*]

Adonis [*ushering in the visitor*]. Please to come in, monsieur.

KOSHNADIEV *enters, wearing a frock coat, a rosette designating a foreign order in his buttonhole. He speaks with a Slavic accent.*

Koshnadiev. Ah! Charming, charming. [*Glancing about the room.*] But where is she?

Adonis. Beg pardon, monsieur?

Koshnadiev. Where is the lady of the house?

Adonis. She'll be coming right away.

Koshnadiev. Ah, good! [ADONIS *starts toward exit.*] Tell me, lackey?

Adonis. Monsieur?

Koshnadiev. How many lovers does she have?

Adonis. Who?

Koshnadiev. The lady of the house.

Adonis. You'll have to ask her yourself.

Koshnadiev [*mutters*]. Stupid peasant!

Adonis [*aside*]. Old stewpot!

Koshnadiev. Hep! Lackey!

Adonis [*coming back*]. Monsieur?

Koshnadiev [*taking coin from pocket*]. Take this.

Adonis. Thank you, monsieur. [*Starts to exit.*]

Koshnadiev. Hep! [ADONIS *returns.*] Get it changed for me.

Adonis [*disgustedly*]. Will that be all?

Koshnadiev. Yes, that is all for now.

Adonis [*aside*]. Cossack! [*Seeing* AMÉLIE *returning.*] Here comes madame! [*He exits up right.*]

Amélie [*appearing left*]. Monsieur?

Koshnadiev [*bowing*]. General Koshnadiev. [AMÉLIE *indicates sofa. He respectfully declines, bowing again.*] General Koshnadiev, envoy extraordinary to his Imperial Highness, Prince Nicolas of Palestria. His Highness sent me to see you.

Amélie [*astounded*]. His Highness?

Koshnadiev. The Prince is madly in love with you, madame.

Amélie. With me? How could he be? His Highness doesn't know me.

Koshnadiev. I beg pardon, madame, did you not attend the reception at the opera house on the occasion of the first official visit of His Highness to Paris? Were you not sitting in the first parterre of boxes?

Amélie. Perhaps I was.

Koshnadiev. The Prince noticed you.

Amélie. Noticed *me?*

Koshnadiev. He asked the President of the Republic what was your name.

Amélie. He didn't!

Koshnadiev. But the President was unable to tell him.

Amélie. That's too bad.

Koshnadiev. Therefore, we assigned an attaché of the Palestrian embassy to discover your name and address.

Amélie. You don't say so?

Koshnadiev. It was in this way that His Imperial Highness had the joy of finding you.

Amélie [*drily*]. How romantic!

Koshnadiev. Oh, His Highness is extremely romantic. I believe the reason His Highness has come back to Paris incognito is on your account. He is utterly besmitten with you.

Amélie. As much as all that?

Koshnadiev. When His Highness arrived this morning, he went at once to visit the President of the Republic. Within the hour he will be ready to see you.

Amélie. Ready to see me?

Koshnadiev. Oui, madame. His Highness is in love. He has the sweets for you very much indeed.

Amélie. He has the sweets, has he?

Koshnadiev. Something tremendous. He told me, "Koshnadiev, you run ahead and arrange things."

Amélie. Just like that?

Koshnadiev. Just like that.

Amélie. Is this your regular job?

Koshnadiev. Oui, madame.

Amélie. Don't you ever lead an army?

Koshnadiev. I am more like a diplomatist. You are not used to this sort of arrangements?

Amélie. I wouldn't say that. But they don't usually send a general.

Koshnadiev. Customs are so different in my country.

Amélie. Apparently.

Koshnadiev. Well, madame, when will you be able to receive His Highness?

Amélie. Now wait a minute. I hesitate to offend the Prince —but the fact is, I already have a gentleman who looks after me. He is the one I must consider.

Koshnadiev. Aha? Well, what does he want, this gentleman? Money is, of course, no object. Or a nice medal perhaps? An imperial decoration? We could make a knight commander of the Palestrian empire.

Amélie. Monsieur, you don't understand. I am faithful to my gentleman friend.

Koshnadiev [*scandalized*]. You don't mean you decline? You don't decline the advances of His Imperial Highness?

Amélie [*hesitantly*]. I'm not declining exactly—it's only that . . .

Koshnadiev. Think what it means to deceive your lover with a prince of the blood! This opportunity does not come often in a lifetime.

Amélie. It would definitely be something to tell one's grandchildren.

Koshnadiev. Of course, madame.

Amélie [*brightly*]. And as long as I didn't tell Étienne.

Koshnadiev [*hopefully*]. Ah?

Amélie. He's leaving town tonight for twenty-eight days' military duty.

Koshnadiev [*expansively*]. You see how Providence organizes these affairs for the convenience of His Highness.

Amélie. It would be, as you say, a prince of royal blood.

Koshnadiev [*murmurs in her ear*]. And the Prince is always very generous.

Amélie. My lover provides me everything I need!

Koshnadiev. With a woman, there are so very many little things she *doesn't* need.

Amélie. That's true.

Koshnadiev [*businesslike*]. Then everything is settled?

Amélie. I think so.

Koshnadiev. I believe I neglected to mention His Highness is in the habit, after each visit, of donating to the lady of his choice ten thousand francs.

Amélie. Ten thousand francs?

Koshnadiev. Ten thousand! [AMÉLIE *whistles.*] Therefore, I will be able to give you a total of nine thousand francs exactly.

Amélie. Nine?

Koshnadiev. Nine thousand.

Amélie [catching on]. Oh, yes, the usual ten per cent commission?

Koshnadiev. We understand each other completely. [*He makes a ceremonious bow.*]

Pochet [entering left]. I beg pardon. Here's the twenty francs you asked Adonis to get changed.

Koshnadiev. Ah, yes, thank you.

Pochet. Five, ten, fifteen, and five make twenty.

Koshnadiev [giving him a small coin]. That's *your* commission.

Pochet. Thank you. [*He pockets the coin.*]

Amélie. Father . . . let me introduce General . . . er, what was that name once more?

Koshnadiev. Koshnadiev.

Amélie. That's right. The General is aide-de-camp to His Highness, the Prince of Palestria.

Pochet. The Prince of Palestria! Well, well!

Koshnadiev. I am delighted . . . positively. [*He accompanies this with a wide gesture, which* POCHET *misinterprets. Thinking the* GENERAL *intends to shake hands,* POCHET *reaches out, but* KOSHNADIEV *continues his gesture in a sweeping movement toward* AMÉLIE. POCHET *stands a moment, hand outstretched, then with a sigh returns hand to pocket. Meanwhile, the* GENERAL *continues speaking.*] You have a very beautiful daughter. You deserve to be rewarded for your achievement. Would you like to be a commander of the military order of Palestria?

Pochet. Of course! But why?

Koshnadiev. Exceptional services. His Highness, the Prince, is in love with your daughter.

Pochet. Please do not speak of it. Consider my dignity as a father. [*He crosses down left.*]

Koshnadiev. Madame, I shall soon have the honor of bringing His Highness to see you.

Pochet [overhearing]. What?

Koshnadiev. You may expect him to call as soon as he is finished at the government palace.

Pochet [rushing upstage]. The Prince? The Prince coming here?

Koshnadiev. But certainly.

Pochet [placing chair for imaginary guest]. Sit down. Won't you be seated? [*Bows to left and right.*]

Koshnadiev [*accepting the chair*]. Thank you, you're very kind.

Pochet. No, not you, General. I'm talking to the Prince. Is it possible! Such an honor. Royalty coming to call. But I have no flags, no draperies, no trumpets!

Koshnadiev [*sternly*]. There must be no ceremony. His Highness is incognito.

Pochet [*agitated*]. What a pity! It would have impressed the neighbors!

MARCEL *enters hurriedly from down left.*

Marcel. Amélie! [*To* GENERAL.] Oh, pardon me, monsieur.

Koshnadiev. It is nothing.

Marcel. He's coming. I saw him through the window.

Amélie. The Prince?

Marcel. No. My godfather. Van Putzeboum!

Pochet. Who did you say?

Marcel. That's his name.

Pochet. Putzeboum?

Marcel. Yes—Van Putzeboum! [*Doorbell rings.*] There he is. He's here!

Amélie. You'd better go and welcome him.

Marcel. I will. [*To* KOSHNADIEV.] Monsieur, again I beg your pardon! [*He exits up left.*]

During the following, we see him cross behind partition. He returns at once, as ADONIS *is seen ushering* VAN PUTZE-BOUM *and* MARCEL *into adjacent room, then* ADONIS *withdraws.*

Koshnadiev. I shall return presently.

Amélie [*escorting him up right*]. Au revoir, General.

Koshnadiev [*to* POCHET]. Good-by, monsieur papa.

Pochet [*bowing*]. Good-by, General, and don't forget about my little decoration. A ribbon and a medal, I daresay?

Koshnadiev. And a certificate, too—signed by His Highness. [*He exits right and* AMÉLIE *follows.*]

Pochet. A certificate—signed by His Highness! What a distinction! [*He exits right, following* AMÉLIE.]

Marcel [*offstage up left*]. Come right in!

MARCEL *enters, followed by* VAN PUTZEBOUM.

Van Putzeboum. Well, here we are, Sonny. Ach, it is so nice here . . .

Marcel. Yes, godfather! [AMÉLIE *returns from up right*

entrance, followed by POCHET.] I should like to present you
to——

Van Putzeboum. Wait . . . wait, Sonny, let me guess. This
ought to be little Amélie, was it?

Amélie [*modestly*]. It was.

Van Putzeboum. Ach, I have guessed it!

Pochet [*aside*]. This fellow's a nincompoop.

Amélie. Marcel told us you were coming, monsieur. We've
been so excited.

Van Putzeboum. So?

Amélie. We didn't expect to meet you so soon, did we,
Papa?

Pochet. Just when you don't expect it, the unexpected always happens.

Van Putzeboum. Little Amélie! [*Aside to* MARCEL.] Got-
ferdeck, Sonny, she was a healthy-looking girl. Ain't you
lucky?

Pochet. She is my daughter.

Van Putzeboum. Ja? You was the father? You done a
beautiful construction job here, ja?

Pochet. With a little help from her mother. [*Nudges*
PUTZEBOUM.]

Van Putzeboum [*laughing heartily*]. Sure. Oh, I bet! [*Suddenly noticing* AMÉLIE.] Oh! In front of her, we shouldn't
say such things! Gotferdom!

Pochet. You're quite correct.

Van Putzeboum. Monsieur d'Avranches, is it not?

Pochet. My name's Pochet! [AMÉLIE *and* MARCEL *make
signs at him.*] Yes, Pochet-d'Avranches, that's my full name.

Van Putzeboum [*shakes hands with* POCHET *and turns to*
AMÉLIE]. Bride-to-be, here was an inhabitant from Holland
come to wish you good wishes.

Amélie. My new godfather-to-be.

Van Putzeboum. She calls me godfather. Little Amélie!
[*To* MARCEL.] Sonny, it is permitted a tiny smack? Just one?

Marcel [*giving* AMÉLIE *a little push*]. Go ahead—smack.

Van Putzeboum. You wouldn't mind being kissed?

Amélie. I'm used to it.

Van Putzeboum [*kissing her loudly on both cheeks*].
Mamzelle Amélie, was you sure a nice girl like you wants to
marry this no-good loafer Sonny of mine?

Amélie [*elegantly*]. I love him and he loves me. I shall
be proud to become his wife.

Van Putzeboum. Ha, you hear that, Sonny?

Marcel [*dramatically*]. All my life I have waited and now I have found my pure, sweet Amélie. [*He starts to embrace her.*]

Amélie. No, Marcel, you mustn't! We shouldn't even *touch* until the day we are married.

Van Putzeboum. Hear that? Ach, Sonny, ain't you lucky?

Marcel [*humbly*]. Forgive me, Amélie.

Van Putzeboum. Pure as the snow, she was.

Marcel. That's rare nowadays.

Pochet. What is, snow?

Marcel. No, purity!

Pochet. Snow is getting rare, too, when you think about it.

Van Putzeboum [*searching pockets*]. Where did I put it? I brought you something. Do you like diamonds, Amélie?

Amélie. Oh, I couldn't accept any expensive presents.

Pochet [*encouragingly*]. Do the gentleman a favor and try them on.

Van Putzeboum. Ja, accept, please, this little souvenir. [*Takes jewel case from pocket and opens it.*]

Amélie [*exclaiming*]. Now I'll have to kiss you properly. [*She kisses him with vigor.*]

Van Putzeboum [*in a daze*]. Oh, Sonny, you didn't know yet how lucky you was.

Amélie [*exhibiting necklace*]. Look, Papa. Look, Marcel.

Marcel. Charming.

Pochet. Are they genuine?

Amélie [*in a whisper*]. Quiet, Papa!

Pochet. A gift's a gift, but we don't want any phonies.

Van Putzeboum [*crosses back to* AMÉLIE]. This was in the family a long time. A collector's item. The big one, that's pear-shaped.

Pochet. Perhaps that's the only thing that's wrong with it.

Van Putzeboum. In Holland, diamonds is my business.

Pochet. You manufacture them?

Van Putzeboum. No, I sell them. Marcel will have lots of money when he comes into his papa's fortune.

Marcel. How soon will that be?

Van Putzeboum. The day when it gives out by you the marriage ceremonies.

Marcel. Oh, yes.

Amélie [*dangling the necklace in the air*]. A very practical gift. [*To* PUTZEBOUM.] I'm going to have to kiss you again.

Van Putzeboum. Sure, don't be bashful. [*She kisses him.*] You like it, ja?

Amélie. I'll be honest. I've always liked diamonds. I even prefer them to flowers.

Van Putzeboum. That reminds me. Did you get the basket?

Amélie. You sent me a basket?

Van Putzeboum. Of flowers, ja.

Amélie. Papa, did some flowers arrive?

Pochet. I haven't seen them.

Van Putzeboum. Ach! They didn't fetch up the flowers? What dummkopfs! Do you have a telephone machine so I could give them a few pieces of my mind?

Amélie. Yes, we do.

Van Putzeboum. It was the flower shop around the corner who makes up wreaths for funerals.

Marcel. Landozel.

Van Putzeboum. Ja, that was the name. So stupid! I told them, "This was for Amélie d'Avranches, the little girl who was going to marry Monsieur Courbois." They said to me, "The only Amélie we know was that floozy who was living with Monsieur Milledieu!"

Marcel. Good lord! ⎫
Amélie. Ah! Oh! ⎬ [*Simultaneously.*]
Pochet. Hum! ⎭

Van Putzeboum. "Lunkheads!" I told them. [*To* AMÉLIE.] Can you imagine? They had you mixed up with some no-good floozy—— [*Clapping hand over his mouth.*] Ach, what I said! I shouldn't mention floozies in front of such a nice young girl. Except this Monsieur Milledieu or Mildew——

Étienne [*entering from down left*]. Well, I changed my pants and——

All. Oh!

MARCEL *seizes* VAN PUTZEBOUM *by the shoulders and spins him to* AMÉLIE, *who performs same business, spinning him to* POCHET, *who propels him to right of center.*

Van Putzeboum [*whirling from one to the other*]. What was happening around here?

Marcel. Let me present . . . Monsieur . . .

Amélie [*thinking fast*]. Monsieur . . . Chopart.

Marcel. Yes, so it is—it's . . . Paul . . . Paul Chopart. How are you, Paul?

Étienne [*startled*]. What?

Amélie. Paul is my cousin.

Marcel. Her cousin.

Pochet. Amélie's cousin.

Van Putzeboum. How do you do, Monsieur Chopart. [*Shaking hands with* ÉTIENNE.]

Pochet. This is Marcel's godfather, Monsieur Van Schnitzelboum.

Van Putzeboum [*correcting*]. Putze—Putzeboum.

Étienne [*still puzzled*]. A pleasure to meet you, I'm sure.

Van Putzeboum. Chopart? Let me see. I knew a Chopart once in Rotterdam.

Étienne. That's a coincidence.

Van Putzeboum. Émile Chopart. Gin.

Étienne. Yes, but just a small glass, please.

Van Putzeboum. No, no. I mean that was his business. Gin.

Étienne. Oh, I see.

Van Putzeboum. You never was related to him, was you?

Étienne. My relatives drink gin, but none of them are in the business.

Van Putzeboum. It was very good gin. [*To the others.*] Now if you could excuse me, I want to telephone about the flowers.

Amélie. Certainly. Papa, show him the way.

Pochet. Follow me, monsieur. [*He escorts* VAN PUTZEBOUM *down left.*]

Van Putzeboum [*chuckling*]. Every time I think of that crazy flower shop talking about Monsieur Milledieu!

Étienne [*hears his name*]. What's that?

Van Putzeboum. This fellow Milledieu is living with some floozy! Ha, ha!

Étienne. Who is he laughing at?

Van Putzeboum. What a numbskull! [*He exits laughing, following* POCHET.]

Étienne. That Dutchman called me a numbskull!

Marcel. Not you. He meant the florist.

Étienne. What florist?

Marcel. The one who didn't deliver the basket.

Étienne. What basket?

Marcel. The basket of flowers for Amélie.

Amélie. What's the matter, Étienne? Can't you understand anything?

Étienne. No. Not today.

Amélie. It's simple. That nitwit of a florist told Marcel's godfather that Mademoiselle d'Avranches was living with Monsieur de Milledieu.

Étienne. Well, she is. Is that anything to be ashamed of?

Amélie. Yes. The fiancée of Marcel Courbois couldn't possibly be the same Mademoiselle d'Avranches.

Étienne. Ah, that's it?

Marcel. So we had to introduce you as somebody else.

Étienne. That's why I'm supposed to be Chopart?

Marcel. Exactly.

Étienne. Well, I don't think it's amusing.

Marcel. Don't worry, Étienne. As soon as my godfather leaves town, you can start using your own name again.

Étienne. That's very kind of you.

Pochet [*appearing down left*]. Amélie, come here. The telephone seems to be out of order.

Amélie. All right, Papa. [*Starts to cross, then comes back.*] Étienne, I didn't show you my new necklace.

Étienne [*crossly*]. I saw it without your showing it.

Amélie. Isn't it something?

Pochet. Come on. Don't keep the old goat waiting.

Amélie. I'm coming, Papa. [*To* ÉTIENNE.] Stunning, isn't it?

Étienne. Fanciest necklace I ever saw.

Pochet. Are you coming or not? [*He takes her wrist and leads her, down left.*]

Amélie [*dangling necklace*]. Look how it sparkles! You're not cross with me, Étienne?

Étienne [*furiously*]. Not at all! Not much! Not a bit! [POCHET *drags* AMÉLIE *off down left.*]

Marcel. Étienne, I'm afraid this is a nuisance——

Étienne. Never mind. I'll be leaving soon.

Marcel. I couldn't help myself.

Étienne. I don't mind your borrowing my girl if it'll help get your inheritance. But meantime, there's a favor you can do me.

Marcel. Anything.

Étienne. I'm terribly fond of Amy. Terribly jealous too. I'd take her with me if I could. But you know how it is around an army camp. All those officers in uniforms with an eye out for pretty girls.

Marcel. She's mad about you. She never looks at another man.

Étienne [*unconvinced*]. Maybe. But it's just as well not to put temptation in her path. With me out of town she's bound to get lonely. I'll be leaving her amongst friends. I mean, our chums—Boas, Bibichon, and the rest—a great gang of fellows. But when you stop to think of it, at heart they're all a bunch of bastards.

Marcel. That's true. Every one of them.

Étienne. You're the only one I can really trust. I know she'll be safe with you around. So while I'm gone, do me a big favor. Keep an eye on Amy!

Marcel. Me?

Étienne. Take her out to dinner. Take her to shows. Show her a good time.

Marcel. A good time?

Étienne. But not too much of a good time! Stay with her, so she doesn't get a chance to fool around with anybody else.

Marcel [*shaking hands*]. I appreciate your confidence in me, old man.

Étienne. I trust you absolutely.

Marcel. I'll keep an eye on her for you.

Étienne. Besides, I know she wouldn't touch you with a ten-foot pole.

Marcel. No wonder you trust me.

Étienne. Here they come back.

Van Putzeboum, Pochet, *and* Amélie *re-enter.*

Van Putzeboum. The telephone is kaput. It would be quicker if I run down to the flower store myself.

Amélie. That's the best way.

Van Putzeboum. Sonny, you come along with, ja?

Marcel. Where?

Van Putzeboum. To the flower store. We run down, then we run right back.

Marcel. All right, I'll come.

Pochet. It was a poor connection. The phone isn't working right at all.

Van Putzeboum. Somebody kept shouting to me, "This was the colonel speaking. I wish to talk with Monsieur Mildew."

Étienne. With *me*?

Van Putzeboum [*chuckling*]. No, not you, Monsieur Chopart. With Monsieur Mildew, the one with the floozy. [*Takes* Marcel's *arm and starts toward right.*]

Étienne [*grabbing* Putzeboum's *sleeve*]. You say it was the colonel calling?

Van Putzeboum [*amiably*]. Ja! Funny, ain't it?—"Important!" he said. So I said, "Get off the line, you crazy booby!"

Étienne. You didn't!

Van Putzeboum. Ja! I gave him some pieces of my mind. [*Étienne is speechless with rage.*] Auf wiedersehen! We come back soon! [*He exits with* MARCEL.]

Amélie. Papa, see them out. They might get lost. [POCHET *salutes and exits up right.*]

Étienne. The colonel was calling, and that Dutchman told him to get off the line!

Amélie. Never mind about the phone call. You have to go in twenty minutes. [*Crosses to sofa and sits beside him.*] Think about me for a change. Don't I mean a thing to you any more?

Étienne. You're right, Amy. Do you realize we haven't had a moment together all day long?

Amélie. You noticed that too, did you?

Étienne. Of course I did.

Amélie [*kissing him*]. You're going to miss me then?

Étienne. Miss you? Of course I'm going to miss you. When we're going to be separated for a month, we shouldn't just be sitting here. There are better ways to say good-by.

Amélie. That's what I was thinking.

Étienne. This isn't the proper place. No privacy.

Amélie. I know, Étienne.

Étienne. Let's go to your room where it's more comfortable.

Amélie. You think there's time?

Étienne. We'll make the time. [*They rise. He kisses her, leading her down left.*]

Pochet [*re-enters up right*]. Where are you two going?

Étienne. Why—er—we're going to telephone. [*He and* AMÉLIE *go out down left, closing the door.*]

Pochet. To telephone? Well, I hope they get a good connection. [*He shrugs.*]

Voices heard off right. ADONIS *is seen behind partition, crossing right to left, followed by* MARCEL, VAN PUTZEBOUM, *and two delivery boys carrying an immense basket of flowers.* ADONIS *enters up left, ushering them in.*

Adonis. This way, everybody! [*He goes to right center, moves card table, making room for the flowers.*]

Pochet. Who's coming now?

Adonis. It's the flowers. This way, boys.

VAN PUTZEBOUM *and* MARCEL *enter, followed by boys with basket of flowers.*

Van Putzeboum. Don't bump into nothing! Those posies was expensive.

The basket is carried down right.

Pochet. Stupendous.

Van Putzeboum. Such good luck we had. We descend to the lobby downstairs, and there we meet the flowers coming up.

Pochet. That's very good. [*Doorbell rings.*]

Adonis. Somebody at the door! [*Exits up right.*]

Van Putzeboum [*to delivery boys*]. Put it up above, over the table on top, ja? [*Boys put basket on card table.*] That's the best way, ja? [*To* POCHET.] But where is the little bride-to-be?

Pochet. She's in the bedroom with Chopart—they're making a telephone call.

Van Putzeboum. Ach, that telephone!

Adonis [*enters excitedly*]. He's here! He's arrived!

Pochet. Who has?

Adonis. His Imperial Highness! The Prince of Palestria!

Pochet [*in sudden frenzy*]. What? His Highness? You didn't leave him standing in the hall?

Adonis. No, but he's on his way up right now.

Pochet [*turns and pushes* MARCEL *and* VAN PUTZEBOUM]. Line up! Arrange yourselves! Stand at attention!

Marcel and Van Putzeboum [*bewildered*]. What's the matter? What's going on here?

Pochet [*shoving the florist's boys into position on either side of the basket*]. His Majesty is coming! Stand back! Farther, farther! [*Turns and runs up center.*] Where are the torches? [*To* ADONIS.] Light the candle. Quickly!

Adonis. Why, Papa?

Pochet. Do as you're told! His Majesty expects it! [*As* ADONIS *is lighting candle.*] Spread out, everybody! Give him air!

Van Putzeboum. Was he gone out of his noodle?

Pochet. Music! Music! Turn on the machine! [ADONIS *turns on gramophone, which plays* "La Marseillaise." POCHET *snatches up candlestick and holds lighted candle high, ready for the royal entrance. A pause. The* PRINCE *enters, followed by* KOSHNADIEV. *Everyone bows.* POCHET *is bent over with one arm upstretched holding candle.*] Your Majesty!

The Prince [*in a Slavic accent*]. So many people! [*Hearing music.*] Ah, they are playing the national hymn. [*He removes his hat. Others remain bent over.*]

Koshnadiev. Highness, permit me to present the father of Mamselle d'Avranches.

The Prince. This one? [*With a crisscross wave of his hand.*] Rise, Monsieur Commandeur!

Pochet [*making a curtsey and kissing the hand of the* PRINCE]. Welcome, Your Majesty!

The Prince [*noticing the candle*]. Why do you have this candle? Are you going to bed?

Pochet. No, Your Majesty. It is for you.

The Prince [*crossing down left*]. Yes, yes, I am going to bed. But I will not need this candle. [*Glancing about.*] Where is your daughter? She is waiting for me?

Pochet. She will come at once, Your Highness. Meanwhile, I can take her place.

The Prince [*shoots him a look*]. Oh, no! Not *you!*

Pochet [*backing away, bowing*]. I will bring her at once, Your Highness! [*Arriving down left.*] My Lord! Étienne's still with her! [*He opens bedroom door and reacts.*]

Amélie [*offstage left*]. Stay out of here! Don't disturb us!

Étienne. [*offstage*]. For God's sake, get out! Leave us in peace! [*Door is slammed in* POCHET's *face.*]

Pochet. I'm disturbing their peace. [*Shrugs.*] Your Royal Highness—step this way, if you please. There will be a short wait before you can see Madame. [*Holding candle aloft, he bows and beckons up left.*] Make way! Make way for His Majesty!

The PRINCE *makes a sweeping exit up left, followed by* KOSHNADIEV. *All others bow deeply.*

ACT TWO

Bedroom at MARCEL COURBOIS' *apartment. Down right, a window with recessed seat, velour curtains on a drawstring with tasseled cord. Up right, door to bathroom. Up center, a bed, footboard toward audience. To right of bed, a chair. To left of bed, a small table. Above table, switches for lights, and an electric bell to summon maid. Up left, an armchair.*

Left center, door to hall. Down left, a desk. Above it, a shelf. On shelf, among other articles, a vase which contains water. Up left, a wardrobe closet. On bedside table, a woman's hat, a grotesque carnival mask, a champagne bottle. On desk, a candlestick, writing materials, etc. On armchair, an evening gown.

At the rise of the curtain, scene is almost dark. Window curtains are drawn, and the night light provides the only illumination. MARCEL *is in bed, sound asleep. A pause. Then door left opens and* CHARLOTTE *enters, bringing pot of chocolate on a tray.*

CHARLOTTE [*putting tray on desk, then crossing toward bed*]. M'sieur. [*No answer. Raising her voice.*] M'sieur. [*Another pause.*] M'sieur!

Marcel [*turning over, without waking*]. Woof!

Charlotte. It's half-past twelve.

Marcel. Woof!

Charlotte. It's half-past twelve.

Marcel [*half sits up, eyes closed*]. Who gives a damn? [*He flops over on the other side.*]

Charlotte [*amiably*]. I'm sure I don't. But I brought you your chocolate. [*No answer.*] Your cho-co-late.

Marcel [*angrily*]. So what? What do you want anyway? Get out of here. [*He pulls covers up over head.*]

Charlotte [*politely*]. Whatever you say, sir.

Marcel [*head popping out again*]. What time is it?

Charlotte. It's twelve thirty-five.

Marcel. Who gives a damn? [*Retreats under covers.*]

Charlotte. You said that already. What time do you want breakfast?

Marcel [*crossly*]. Eight o'clock.

Charlotte. Eight o'clock this evening?

Marcel. Yes!

Charlotte. When M'sieur engaged me yesterday morning, you said breakfast at eight in the morning. Now you say eight in the evening.

Marcel [*mumbling*]. Now half-past twelve. Come back in seven hours.

Charlotte. Very good, sir. Eight this evening.

Marcel. Oh, shut up.

Charlotte. Yes, m'sieur. [*She exits.*]

MARCEL *sits up, rearranges pillows, and lies flat on his back.
A long pause. He tries to get back to sleep. Turns on his
left side. Pause. Turns on his right side. Pause. Sits up half-
way, punches pillows vigorously, then lies on stomach, bury-
ing face in pillow. Pause. Turns over on back.*

Marcel. I'm going to fire that maid. I'll kick her out.
She's got no business waking me up . . . especially when I'm
asleep. [*Yawns.*] I'm tired. It's half-past twelve. [*Yawns.*]
Now if this were China, it would be midnight . . . I could
sleep for eight hours and still get up early in the morning. . . . Who was the idiot that decided to put Paris on
this side of the globe? [*Putting his legs out of bed.*] I'd
better get up. [*He rises. He wears pajamas.*] My socks!
What did I do with my socks? Oh, there they are. [*Puts on
socks and slippers, leaning against bed to do so.*] My God,
half-past twelve! And I had an appointment at eleven. Oh,
well. It was with one of my creditors. He can wait. He's
been waiting for six months already, another hour won't hurt
him. Besides, I've nothing to give him anyway. So it'll be
soon enough for him. Courage, Marcel. [*Goes to the window
and opens curtains. Daylight streams in.*] The sun is up.
And it's only half-past twelve. [*Crossing back.*] Where the
hell is that maid? Why doesn't she bring my chocolate?
[*Rings bell and stands with finger to buzzer, which is heard
ringing offstage.* MARCEL, *leaning on bell, is half-asleep. Losing balance, he wakes with a start.*] What idiot is making all
that noise? [*Realizing.*] Oh, it's me . . . God, it's cold in
here. [*Taking off slippers.*] I think I'll have lunch in bed
and get up for dinner. [*Gets into bed without removing socks.
Stretches legs and encounters an obstacle under covers.*] Hey!
[*Moves feet about, and a horrified expression comes over his
face.*] What's going on, anyway? [*Kneeling on bed, he throws
back covers and gasps to see* AMÉLIE *across foot of bed,
sound asleep. He grabs her by wrists and pulls her up to
sitting position.*] Amélie!

Amélie [*smiling in her sleep*]. Brrrr! It's cold.

Marcel. What are you doing here?

Amélie [*still asleep*]. Woof!

Marcel. Wake up, you can't sleep here. [*Hearing* CHAR-
LOTTE *at door.*] Stay where you are. [*He lets go* AMÉLIE's
*wrists and she falls back. He claps a pillow over her face,
props elbows on it, and assumes a nonchalant air.*]

Charlotte [*entering*]. M'sieur rang?

Marcel. Yes, get out of here.

Charlotte. You rang for me to tell me that?

Marcel. Yes, get the hell out of here.

Charlotte. How unusual. [*She exits.*]

Marcel [*kneeling, removes pillow and shakes* AMÉLIE]. Amélie . . . Wake up, for God's sake.

Amélie [*asleep*]. Woof!

Marcel. Wake up. Snap out of it.

Amélie [*opening eyes*]. Marcel!

Marcel. That's right. Marcel.

Amélie. What are you doing here?

Marcel. What are *you* doing here?

Amélie. What?

Marcel. What are you doing at *my* house? in my bed? in my old nightshirt?

Amélie. I'm at your house? How did that happen?

Marcel. That's what I'd like to know.

Amélie [*struck by a thought*]. You don't mean to say that we . . . ?

Marcel. What?

Amélie. That we slept together? In the same bed?

Marcel. It's beginning to look like it. This isn't some trick you're playing? You didn't just get here?

Amélie. I don't think so.

Marcel. This is awful. We've been sleeping together.

Amélie. Apparently.

Marcel. And I was supposed to keep an eye on you. [*He gets up.*] What's Étienne going to say?

Amélie. What do you mean?

Marcel. I told Étienne I'd keep an eye on you! How will I explain?

Amélie. Well, we don't have to tell him.

Marcel. I know. But what about my conscience? I've got a conscience, haven't I? Amélie, what have we done?

Amélie. I don't remember.

Marcel [*hopping about as he puts on slippers*]. Étienne! My best friend! He told me when he left, "Look out for Amélie. You're the only one I can trust her with."

Amélie. That's nice. It shows he has a lot of confidence in me. What did he think I was going to do?

Marcel. Just what you *did* do, evidently.

Amélie. I don't know *what* I did, but he's got no right suspecting me in advance. So if we've done anything wrong, it serves him right.

Marcel. Speak for yourself. [*Sitting on bed.*] Lots of people wake up in bed together. Men and women both. [*Accusingly.*] But *you've* got no business being in *my* bed. I'm his best friend!

Amélie. He told you to keep an eye on me, did he?

Marcel. Yes, he did. He said not to let you out of my sight. So I didn't. [*Rising.*] You're right. It's his fault, after all!

Amélie. Of course. If he expected you to watch me day and night, something like this was bound to happen.

Marcel. Certainly. What did he expect? We're only human.

Amélie. He ought to be ashamed, putting us in a humiliating position like this.

Marcel [*getting back in bed*]. What did he take me for? I've got passions like anyone. And he said you wouldn't touch me with a ten-foot pole.

Amélie. He said that, did he?

Marcel. Yes.

Amélie. Well, phooey on him!

Marcel. Phooey! [*Silence while they think it over*]. All the same, we shouldn't have done it.

Amélie. No, we shouldn't.

Marcel. He trusted us. There's no excuse for what we did.

Amélie. What *did* we do, anyway? How do we know we did anything?

Marcel. That's right, too. How did we get here? What happened last night?

Amélie. First we went to the carnival at Montmartre with Yvonne and Bibichon and the gang.

Marcel. Yes, I remember that.

Amélie. We rode the merry-go-rounds and the Ferris wheel.

Marcel. And I got seasick.

Amélie. Then we went to the shooting gallery.

Marcel. That's right. And we put on funny masks.

Amélie. Then we went around scaring people. And we bought fireworks.

Marcel. The kind that give off sparks.

Amélie. After that, we drank champagne.

Marcel. Then we went to Pigalle and drank some brandy.

Amélie. Then we went to the Royale and drank some more champagne.

Marcel. And some more brandy.

Amélie. After that . . . I don't remember quite so well.

We went to some bars, the lights were flashing off and on, and everything started spinning around.

Marcel. I think we were getting a little tipsy.

Amélie. You're probably right.

Marcel [standing up]. You were kind of unsteady on your feet.

Amélie. I seem to remember I couldn't climb the stairs at my house.

Marcel. So I said, "Come over to my place and take a headache powder."

Amélie. Only when we got here you couldn't find the headache powder.

Marcel. So we had some more champagne. [*He picks up empty champagne bottle from bedside table and turns it upside down.*]

Amélie [sadly]. After that I don't remember a thing.

Marcel [slumping in chair]. I don't either. Not a thing.

Amélie. We *still* don't know what happened.

Marcel [rising]. Did we or didn't we? [*Taking* AMÉLIE *by wrists.*] Did we?

Amélie. The Lord only knows.

Marcel. Yes, the Lord knows.

Amélie. Well, as long as Étienne *doesn't!*

Marcel. Neither of *us* is going to tell him.

Amélie. So no harm done, is there?

Marcel [releasing her hands]. True, no harm done.

Amélie. Then we're all right?

Marcel. We're all right.

Amélie [lying in bed and pulling up covers]. I'm sleepy.

Marcel. No, you don't. You've got to get up at once.

Amélie. Now?

Marcel. Yes, now. I'll put your clothes in the bathroom and you get dressed right away.

Amélie. You're mean.

Marcel. Where's your dress?

Amélie. How should I know?

Marcel. Get up. [*Takes her hand and pulls her out of bed.*]

Amélie [with a laugh of surprise]. Look. I slept with my shoes on. [*She drops back on bed and kicks feet in air.*]

Marcel. Get up. No time for funny business.

Amélie. You're a grouch, that's what you are.

Marcel. Where's your dress? You must have been wearing one.

Amélie. I must have been.

Marcel [*crossing down left to desk*]. Here's your hat, and here's the mask you were wearing. [*Puts on mask, then claps her hat on his head.* AMÉLIE *laughs.* MARCEL *goes to armchair, finding dress.*] Here's your dress. [*Picks it up. A box falls to floor.*] What's that? [*He picks it up.*] Oh, the fireworks. What rubbish! [*To* AMÉLIE.] Come on. Get dressed. [*Goes out door right.*] Come on, I said.

Amélie. "Come on, come on, get up, get up!" What a pain he is this morning. All right, Amélie, get up. [*She walks about unsteadily.*] My legs don't seem to be working yet. Where did I put my slip? [CHARLOTTE *enters left with letters and papers.*]

Charlotte. Oh, I beg your pardon, madame.

Amélie [*confused*]. Oh! I was just looking for . . . I . . .

Charlotte [*equally flustered*]. Was it . . . were you looking for . . . Monsieur Courbois?

Amélie. Exactly. I'm glad to know I've come to the right house.

Charlotte. I'm not sure that M'sieur is up yet.

Amélie. Then don't disturb him, I'll come back later. [*She finds her slip on upstage chair, puts it over arm nonchalantly, and starts toward exit left.*]

MARCEL *appears at door right.*

Marcel. What's keeping you? [*Seeing* CHARLOTTE, *he quickly jumps between her and* AMÉLIE.] What are you doing in here?

Charlotte. The lady said——

Marcel. Lady? What lady?

Charlotte. She wanted to know if you were at home.

AMÉLIE *is leaning against* MARCEL, *back to back, trying to smother her laughter.*

Marcel. There's no lady around here. Who gave you permission to come in, anyhow?

Charlotte [*giving him a packet of letters*]. The mail just arrived.

Marcel. Is that any reason to run in and out as if this were a railway station? *Give* them to me. [*Snatches mail from her hand.*]

Charlotte [*holding out stationery and a ball of twine*]. Here is the stationery and the string you told me to buy.

Marcel. Well, put them down. Can't you see I have my hands full?

Charlotte [*puts articles on desk*]. Yes, m'sieur, you certainly have.

Marcel [*takes up champagne bottle, tossing it to* CHARLOTTE]. Take away this bottle.

Charlotte. Yes, m'sieur.

Marcel. Idiot!

Charlotte. Yes, m'sieur. [*She goes out left.*]

AMÉLIE, *bursting with laughter, collapses on window seat right.*

Amélie. Really, Marcel, I can't help thinking she *saw* me.

Marcel. That's all right, I'm going to fire her anyway.

Amélie. Why?

Marcel. I won't have her spying on me all the time. [*Goes to desk down left, puts down mail, and pours self a cup of chocolate.*]

Amélie. She's quite pretty, your maid.

Marcel. Is she? I never looked at her.

Amélie. What's her name?

Marcel. I never asked her.

Amélie. You never asked her name?

Marcel. No. I hired her yesterday morning before I woke up. We had a second talk this morning before I was awake. I've never even seen the girl.

Amélie. If I were Irène, I wouldn't let you have a pretty maid like that.

Marcel. You're *not* Irène—so go and get dressed. [*He pushes her toward bathroom.*]

Amélie. Now stop, Marcel. I *can't* get dressed.

Marcel. You can't? Why not?

Amélie. Because! I can't wear an evening gown in the middle of the day.

Marcel [*pushing her again*]. You'd damn well better!

Amélie. How will I get home?

Marcel. On the subway, of course.

Amélie. I'd look ridiculous. And what would the doorman say? No, I'll have to send a note to Papa. He'll bring me something suitable to wear. Your maid can take the message. She's seen me anyway.

Marcel. If you insist. But don't waste any more time.

Amélie [*rummaging about desk*]. Now let me see . . .

Marcel [*following her*]. What are you looking for? Don't mess up my desk!

Amélie. Paper and ink.

Marcel. Right under your nose.

Amélie. Thank you. [MARCEL *tosses down paper and envelopes.*] Thank you! [*She sits to write. He takes magazine from mailing tube and sits on bed to read.*] "Dear little Father: I am at Marcel Courbois' place at 27 Rue Cambon. He has given me lodging for the night. Please come at once and bring a dress for me to wear. Yours affectionately" —— [*To* MARCEL.] How do you spell "affectionately"?

Marcel. Spell it any way you like. Your father won't know the difference.

Amélie. "Yours truly, Amélie." [*Addressing envelope.*] "Monsieur Pochet, 120 Rue de Rivoli."

MARCEL *puts magazine aside and opens a letter. He reacts violently.*

Marcel. Oh, no! Not that!

Amélie. What's the matter now?

Marcel. My godfather. He's back in Paris.

Amélie. Who? Van Putzeboum?

Marcel. Yes, damn it! I thought he was halfway to America, and here he is back again.

Amélie. Do we have to go through *that* again?

Marcel. Listen to the old fool. [*Reading.*] "Dear Sonny"— he always calls me that. [*Reading.*] "Dear Sonny"—he was born in Dudelsackburg-am-Rhein——

Amélie [*finishing the sentence*]. But he lives in Holland.

Marcel. Oh, you know that, do you?

Amélie. Yes, I know.

Marcel [*reading*]. "Dear Sonny, I for you a little surprise have got. I will at Paris this morning arrive and you to see this afternoon hope. Love and kisses, your godfather." [*Rising.*] A little surprise for me he has got. Did you ever hear such madness?

Amélie. I never did.

Marcel. "P.S. Tonight it gives by me a dinner party for Amélie and her papa. Invite them for me, please."

Amélie. Tonight? I can't have dinner with him tonight.

Marcel. You must.

Amélie. But I *can't.* I've made other arrangements.

Marcel. Cancel them. You've *got* to.

Amélie [*sighs*]. All right, I'll cancel. I'll have dinner with you and old Putzy-bum. But you needn't expect me to enjoy it. [*Writing another letter.*]

Marcel. What are you doing now?

Amélie. Canceling my date.

Marcel. Good. Hurry up.

Amélie. This certainly messes up everything.

Marcel. Just when I thought I was rid of him. What could have happened? [*A thought strikes him.*] Maybe he's passing through Paris on the way to catch his boat. Of course, that's it. He's sailing from Cherbourg, so naturally he has to pass through town. Tomorrow he'll be on his way again.

Amélie. Of course. Tomorrow.

Marcel. That's a relief. Have you finished the letter?

Amélie [*addressing envelope*]. Almost.

Marcel. Do hurry up! God, but you're slow! [*Taking letters from her hand.*]

Amélie. Be careful, the ink's not dry.

Marcel [*handing them back*]. Then blow on them! [*Goes up left center and rings.* AMÉLIE *crosses down center, blowing on envelopes.*] All right, that's enough. Don't overdo it. [*Knock on door.*] Come in!

Charlotte [*putting head in door*]. I have permission to enter?

Marcel. Of course, of course.

Charlotte. You don't want me to come in so you can tell me to get out?

Marcel. Are you trying to be witty?

Charlotte. No, m'sieur.

Marcel. Then come in here.

Charlotte [*enters*]. Yes, m'sieur.

Marcel. Madame has an errand for you.

Amélie [*giving letters to* CHARLOTTE]. Would you deliver this letter to the porter at the Hotel Continental?

Charlotte. Yes, madame.

Amélie. And this one goes to the Rue de Rivoli.

Charlotte. Oh? That's not an errand.

Marcel. It isn't?

Charlotte. That's *two* errands.

Marcel. Will you get out of here?

Charlotte. Yes, m'sieur.

Marcel [*pointing to door*]. Then get *out*.

Charlotte [*as she goes*]. He said it again.

Marcel [*follows, shouting*]. And stay out!—That girl's a halfwit.

Amélie. Brrr! It's cold in here. [*Climbs into bed.*] That's better.

Marcel [*turns to where* AMÉLIE *had been standing*]. You've

no idea what I go through—— Where are you? [*Seeing her.*]
Come out of there!

Amélie. I'm freezing, and while I wait for Papa——

Marcel. Up, up! Wait for him standing up. [*Doorbell
rings.*] Good Lord, who's that? [*Both react alarmed.*] Someone's at the door!

Amélie. That's what *I* was thinking.

Marcel [*listening down left*]. Maybe they'll go away.

Charlotte [*off left*]. Whom did you wish to see, madame?

Irène [*off left*]. Is Monsieur at home?

Marcel. My God, it's Irène!

Amélie. What?

Marcel. Irène! Quick, get up!

Amélie. Madame la comtesse? [*She gets out right side of
bed as* MARCEL *gets in left side. He gives* AMÉLIE *a push from
behind, then pulls covers up to his chin.*]

Marcel. Damn it, woman, hide yourself! [*She starts right
toward bathroom.*] No, not in there. She *always* goes in
there.

Amélie. Where then?

Marcel. Under the bed! Quickly!

Amélie [*crawling under bed*]. This is a morning I'll never
forget.

Marcel. Hurry up! [*Leans over and swats her hind end as
it disappears. Seeing window curtains open, he leaps out of
bed, yanks them closed, and with one bound is back in bed.
At same instant,* IRÈNE *knocks and enters.*]

Irène. Yoohoo! May I come in?

Marcel [*sleepily*]. Who . . . Who is it?

Irène. Oh! It's so dark in here.

Marcel. What is it? Who's there?

Irène. Doesn't your heart tell you who it is?

Marcel [*quavers*]. Oh! You—Irène?

Irène. His heart told him. [*Groping blindly toward bed.*]
Cheri-baby, where *are* you?

Marcel. Here I am, sweetheart—— [IRÈNE *punches him
squarely in the face with her outstretched palm.*]

Irène. Oh, precious! Did I poke my finger in your eye?

Marcel. No, in my mouth.

Irène. Oh, my darling!

Marcel. My sweetie-pie. [*They embrace.*]

Amélie [*wriggles into view under foot of bed*]. Damned
uncomfortable under here.

Irène [*disengaging herself*]. But why are we in the dark this way? [*Searching for light switch.*]

Marcel. What are you looking for?

Irène. The lights! I like to *see* who I'm kissing. I have a handsome lover. I want to look at him.

Marcel. Not ugly old me! You're the beautiful one.

Irène. Marcel! You're only saying that.

Marcel. I'm the one that suffers when I don't see you.

Irène. You angel boy! [*Kisses him.*]

Amélie. What's going on up there?

Irène. Where's the light switch?

Marcel. Above the table.

Irène. Above the table . . . [*Groping about, she knocks ball of string from table, which rolls under bed.*] What have I done? I knocked something off the table! It must have rolled under the bed! [IRÈNE *gets down on all fours.*]

Amélie. My God, here she comes!

Marcel [*grabbing* IRÈNE]. It's nothing. Let it go. It's only a ball of string.

Irène [*half under bed*]. I can find it.

Marcel [*pulling her up*]. Let it go! I'll get it later.

Irène. Well, if you say so.

Amélie. That's too bad. I'd have enjoyed some company.

Irène. Let me see. Ah, here's the light. [*Switches on lamp above bed, illuminating room.*] And there's my sugarplum!

Marcel [*gestures in front of his eyes, as though dazzled*]. Ah, you found it.

Irène. Oh, lamb baby! Does it hurt your little eyes?

Marcel. It's because I just woke up.

Irène. And *I* woke you. How could I be so cruel!

Marcel [*starts to get out of bed*]. I'm glad you did. It's time I was up anyway——

Irène [*pouting*]. Don't you dare! I'm coming in there with you!

Marcel. What?

Amélie [*chin propped on hands*]. Olala! What next?

Irène [*prepares to undress*]. I don't object to your sleeping late, providing we sleep together.

Marcel [*uneasily*]. Er—— don't you, darling?

Irène. You'll be my hubby and I'll be your itty-bitty wifey.

Marcel. Oh?

Irène. Now, aren't you happy I came?

Marcel. Oh, yes . . . yes indeed . . .

Amélie. The party's getting hot.

Irène [*kneeling on bed*]. We'll be snug and cozy in a jiffy.

Amélie. This is above my head.

Irène [*hugging* MARCEL]. Lovey-dovey!

Marcel [*with forced enthusiasm*]. My pigeon!

Amélie. This is only the beginning.

Irène [*removing hat*]. I've nothing but time. We can spend the whole day in bed.

Amélie [*loudly*]. What?

Marcel [*terrified*]. Huh?

Amélie. I might be under here for weeks. [*She ducks out of sight.*]

Marcel [*weakly*]. Did you say all day?

Irène. You don't sound enthusiastic.

Marcel [*starting to get out right side of bed*]. I ought to take a bath. Come with me, if you like.

Irène [*runs around right, pushing his legs back*]. A bath? What a ridiculous idea!

Amélie [*pops head out left side*]. He'll have to think of something better than that.

Irène. A bed is more comfortable than a bathtub. [*Undoing back of her dress.*] Move over. I'll be right with you. [*Crosses down left center.* AMÉLIE *disappears again.*] I won't wait a minute longer.

Amélie [*pops out right side*]. These countesses don't waste much time.

Irène. Darn it. You'll have to help me. [*Sits on bed, back to* MARCEL. *He is muttering dementedly and doesn't notice her.*] *Well?* Marcel, aren't you going to unhook me? [*No answer. She turns to look at him.*] What's got into you today?

Marcel [*reacts*]. Uh?—Oh, yes. Why not?

Irène [*pushes his hands away*]. You've got something on your mind. Or somebody. You haven't been seeing Amélie d'Avranches again, have you?

Amélie. She means me.

Marcel. Me see Amélie? What put that in your head?

Irène. I didn't object to your being seen with her when your godfather was in town. But there's no need to continue behaving like a fiancé. You might get carried away.

Marcel. With Amélie? Impossible!

Irène. I was a fiancée myself. I know the hanky-panky that goes on.

Amélie. When it comes to hanky-panky, she's a past mistress. [*She turns over on her back, stretching out, half her body in view on right side of bed.*]

Marcel. You needn't worry. Amélie doesn't attract me. I don't know what Étienne sees in her.

Amélie [*reaching up, slapping the edge of the mattress*]. Look, old boy, don't lay it on so thick.

Irène. She has rather a pretty face.

Marcel [*slapping mattress to quiet* AMÉLIE]. Yes, her face is pretty. [AMÉLIE *grabs his wrist and does her best to pull him out of bed.*]

Amélie. You flatter me.

Marcel [*struggling to keep balance*]. Careful!—oops!

Irène [*grabbing him by the leg*]. Where are you going?

Marcel [*regaining balance*]. Nowhere. The mattress seems to be slipping.

Irène. It is? [*She rises and goes left center to examine mattress. Meanwhile,* AMÉLIE *has turned over on all fours.* MARCEL *takes this chance to put a foot on her neck and bears down hard.*]

Amélie [*flat on her face*]. Oooff!

Irène [*looks at* MARCEL]. What did you say?

Marcel [*pretending to yawn*]. Nothing. Oof . . . Just stretching. [IRÈNE *sits beside* MARCEL *again.*]

Irène. As I was saying, I know all about Amélie. She used to be my chambermaid. Of course, she's nothing but a trollop.

Amélie [*chin propped on hands*]. I'm listening. Go on.

Irène. She was always enterprising. In the old days, there wasn't a boy for miles around who was safe from her.

Amélie. Is that a fact?

Irène. At least, no boy over fourteen.

Amélie. A few of them slipped through my fingers.

Irène. At that time, she was in it for the fun. She still had her amateur standing.

Amélie. Fascinating. Tell us more.

Irène. Nowadays, she's just like all the other professional hustlers. Hard as nails.

Amélie. In another minute I'm going to let her have it.

Marcel [*trying to smooth things over*]. You exaggerate. Amélie's got good qualities too.

Irène. Actually I'm quite fond of her——

Amélie. Imagine how she'd talk if she didn't like me.

Irène. Although she's old enough to be my mother.

Amélie. That's all! [*Disappears under bed.*]

Irène. But never mind Amélie! We've better things to think about! [*Turns on night light and reaches for other switch.*]

Marcel. What are you doing now?

Irène. You were right. It's better with the lights off.

AMÉLIE *reappears at foot of bed, ball of string in hand.*

Amélie. This string will come in handy.

IRÈNE *snaps off overhead light.* AMÉLIE *pantomimes tying string to down right corner of coverlet.*

Irène [*on bed by* MARCEL]. Oh, lambie-doodle, how I've missed you!

Marcel. I missed you too!

Irène. I've been so lonesome I couldn't sleep. The other night I had a dreadful nightmare. I woke up, and there was a ghostly figure in white waving its arms and moving toward me.—Oh, Marcel, I do adore you!

Marcel. I adore *you.* My Reenie-Weenie. But what happened in your nightmare?

Irène. What? Oh, nothing. The vision turned out to be my husband putting on his nightshirt. But I've been *frightened* ever since—— [*Seeing coverlet slip off bed.*] Oh, the cover is on the floor.

Marcel. It doesn't matter.

Irène. I tell you I've been haunted. I see ghosts everywhere I—— [*Screams as she sees bedcover dancing about down left center with* AMÉLIE *underneath it.*] Eeek!!! [IRÈNE *vaults over* MARCEL *and cowers up right. The bedcover hops left to right, heading toward door.*] Aaaah!!!

Marcel [*on knees on bed*]. What's the matter?

Irène. That bedcover is bewitched!

Marcel [*to* IRÈNE]. I don't see anything.

Irène. Marcel, protect me!

Marcel [*joins her up right*]. If you mean the bedspread falling on the floor, that happens every day.

AMÉLIE *has gone out right, letting door stand open. Now the bedspread returns by itself, suspended on wire, jiggling crazily in midair.*

Irène. Help! It's coming back!

Marcel. My God, the place *is* haunted! [*Hides behind* IRÈNE.] Help! Police!

Bedcover settles to floor; now it hops up again. IRÈNE *screams, runs up over bed and cringes up left. Coverlet is again on floor.* MARCEL *ventures closer.*

Irène [*shrilly*]. Aaah! Marcel! Don't go near it!

Marcel [*reacts in panic each time she screams*]. Sh! Be quiet. This is man's work. [*Puts foot timidly on coverlet.*]

Irène [*screams*]. Aaak! Be careful!

Marcel [*reacts*]. Quiet! There must be an explanation. [*He stamps on the coverlet a couple of times, then jumps on it hard.*]

Irène. My hero! How brave you are!

Marcel. It's nothing. Silly girl. [*Picking up the bedcover, holding it for* IRÈNE *to see.*] Nothing to be afraid of.

The cover is snatched from his hand and flies back to foot of bed. Both scream and clutch one another in terror.

Irène. Let me out of here! I'm never coming back!

Marcel. Wait, Irène! Don't leave me!

At this moment, AMÉLIE *enters right, wearing a towel bathrobe with the hood up. On her face is carnival mask and in either hand she carries sparkler-type fireworks. She hops, then waddles toward the terrified lovers.* CHARLOTTE *enters left behind* MARCEL *and* IRÈNE. *She lets out a piercing shriek.* CHARLOTTE *and* IRÈNE *run out right.* AMÉLIE *pursues* MARCEL *around the room and over the bed, dodging back and forth. He grabs pillow and throws it at her. Finally he drops to knees center, clasping hands in front of him.*

Marcel. Spare me! Have pity! [*He salaams and presses forehead to the floor.*]

AMÉLIE *plunges fireworks into vase of water on down left shelf. Then, whisking off the robe and mask, she hurls them out right. She opens window curtains. Light streams in.*

Amélie [*innocently*]. Why, Marcel! What are you doing on the floor?

Marcel [*straightens, sees* AMÉLIE, *and rises*]. I might have known it was some of your monkey tricks!

Amélie. I did the best I could with what I had to work with.

Marcel. Those two women will keep running till they reach the Swiss frontier.

Amélie. Wasn't I clever to get rid of Reenie-Weenie? She might have stayed right through the Christmas holidays.

Marcel. How did you work that trick with the bedspread?

Amélie. Scared you, didn't I?

Marcel. Yes. How the devil did you do it?

Amélie. With a hairpin and this string, around the leg of the bed. [*Shows string and demonstrates, jiggling coverlet.*]

Marcel [*puts coverlet back on bed*]. Such antics!

Amélie [*laughing*]. Irène said I was a professional hustler, but nobody ever hustled like she did out that door.

Marcel [*goes to window*]. She may never come back.

Amélie. Serves her right, nasty old thing. I'm exhausted. [*She gets into bed again.*]

Marcel. Poor Irène! She didn't deserve to—— [*Turns to speak to* AMÉLIE, *looks about.*] You can't *do* that! Get up! Up on your feet!

Amélie. I refuse. [*Doorbell rings.*] The doorbell!

Marcel. I hear it! [*Rushes left and listens.*]

Putzeboum [*off left*]. I tell you I'm his godfather——

Marcel. It's him! My godfather! Get up! Get out! [*Pushes* AMÉLIE *out of bed, then dashes back to door.*] Hide yourself!

Amélie. But where?

Marcel. Under the bed!

Amélie [*sleepily, starts to obey*]. Oh, no! I've had enough of that! [*Gets back into bed.*]

Marcel [*seeing* AMÉLIE]. Get the hell out of there! No— too late! [*Leaps into bed and pulls cover up over their heads.*]

VAN PUTZEBOUM *enters in time to see his last maneuver.*

Putzeboum [*agape, facing front*]. Wait a second, please! What was it is coming off in here? [*Goes to foot of bed, lifts cover exposing two pairs of feet.* MARCEL *and* AMÉLIE *sit up.*]

Amélie. You can't come in. There's no more room in this bed.

Putzeboum. Gott in Himmel! It's Mamzelle Amélie!

Amélie. I just dropped in to say good morning to Marcel.

Marcel [*absent-mindedly*]. Nice of you to come by. How've you been? [*He and* AMÉLIE *shake hands.*]

Amélie. Oh, I can't complain.

Putzeboum. She says good morning to Marcel in bed already!

Amélie. We had a lot to discuss. Plans for the honeymoon, you know.

Putzeboum [*winks*]. Ja, plans! Better you should call it rehearsals! Oh, Sonny, you wasn't even married yet and you got all the advantages!

Marcel [*getting out of bed*]. I can explain everything——

Putzeboum [*chuckles*]. Don't you bother, Sonny. I got eyes, ain't it? Ach, what a couple of scalawags!

Marcel [*goes up left and puts on smoking jacket*]. Whatever you're thinking, godfather, I wish you'd stop!

Putzeboum. So you couldn't put it off no longer? Young people want to be in the hay while the sun is shining! [*Wagging finger.*] Amélie, when I think how innocent you was just two weeks ago!

Amélie [*laughs hoarsely*]. Me? [*Then, demurely.*] That's right. So I was.

Putzeboum. I know what a temptation it is for a girl when she grows up in Paris. Ach, Paris! You done fine to hold out so long.

Amélie [*pinching his cheek*]. You're a nice old "Putzi"!

Putzeboum. Ja! You call me "Putzi." I can call you "Amykins"! [*He bumps* MARCEL *playfully.*] What your poppa would say! [*Sudden thought.*] Donner und blitzen! Amélie's got a poppa! What was *he* going to say?

Marcel. He doesn't know. So don't say a word to him. Or to anybody else.—Especially, anybody else!

Putzeboum. Why not? It's a local custom, ain't it?

Amélie. Putzi, it was cold. We only got in bed to keep warm.

Putzeboum [*jocose*]. You was keeping warm all right! Forgive old Putzi. I was only busting in to make a susprisement.

Amélie. You succeeded.

Marcel. I expected you'd be passing through Paris on your way to the boat——

Putzeboum. Ja, but that's the susprisement. I ain't going no place.

Marcel. What?

Amélie. You're not?

Putzeboum. My partner is already on top of the ocean. He trips to America, so now I can stay stuck in Paris.

Marcel. You're going to s-s-stay?

Putzeboum. Ja, stuck! Out of respect to your poppa. He

would have liked it when the knot gets tied for me to watch the hitch-up.

Marcel. The huh-huh-huh?

Putzeboum. Ja, the hitch-up! Why was you stuttering so, Sonny?

Marcel. Hear that, Amy? He's going to stay for the wedding!

Amélie. Yes, that's the susprisement.

Putzeboum. Ain't you both happy?

Marcel [*mournfully*]. Delighted.

Putzeboum. Ha, ha. Look at Sonny's face! Whenever he looks so sad I know he must be feeling happy.

Amélie. Is that how you tell?

Putzeboum. Ja! I knew somebody who was just the same. Always made sad faces when he was happy! And when he was sad he just wagged his tail!

Amélie. Wagged his tail?

Putzeboum. Yes, he was a bulldog I used to have. [*Mechanically patting* MARCEL's *head.*] Such a good Sonny.

Marcel [*crossly*]. I'm glad I remind you of him.

Putzeboum. Here I was standing and talking when you and Amykins . . . Maybe I was intruding too soon?

MARCEL *dashes to desk, grabs up hat and cane.*

Marcel. You're not leaving? Don't rush away on our account!

Putzeboum. Ja, I got errands to do. Later I come back.

Marcel [*pushing him*]. Fine. Come back later.

Putzeboum. Amykins, don't forget to tell poppa we're going to have him for dinner tonight.

Marcel. Don't worry, she'll tell him. Good-by. [*Pushes* VAN PUTZEBOUM *off left and closes door.*] We're in a pretty mess now!

Amélie. *You* are. What are you going to do about it?

Marcel. It's a catastrophe. He's come to attend the wedding and there isn't going to be one!

Amélie [*leaves bed and goes up left*]. Don't worry, Marcel. It'll work out.

Marcel. You suggest something.

Amélie. How would it be if we pushed Putzi off the Eiffel Tower?

Marcel. Don't be facetious!

Amélie [*finds mailing tube and squints through it like*

telescope]. What's the difference between your Dutch god-father and this mailing tube?

Marcel. Do be quiet.

Amélie. One is a silly Hollander and the other's a hollow cylinder.

Footsteps off left.

Marcel. Look out, he's back again.

AMÉLIE *leaps back in bed.*

Putzeboum [*entering excitedly*]. Your poppa, Amykins! Poppa's coming the stairs up!

Amélie. That's good. About time, too.

Putzeboum. But he's up the stairs coming! Hurry, hurry! Hide yourself quick!

Amélie. Why should I?

Putzeboum. But, Amykins, you didn't want him to get suspicious, did you?

Marcel [*dragging from bed*]. He's right. Quick, Amélie. [*Shoving* AMÉLIE *off right into bathroom.*]

Amélie. Don't push! I'm going!

POCHET *enters left.*

Pochet. Gentlemen, good morning.

Marcel. Monsieur Pochet.

Pochet. Is my daughter here with you?

Marcel [*innocently*]. With me? Amélie?

Putzeboum [*interposing*]. No, certainly not she wasn't here.

Pochet. Not here?

Putzeboum. No, I was just looking for her all over and she wasn't here.

Pochet. Then where can she be?

Putzeboum [*hand on* MARCEL's *shoulder*]. Not here. Marcel is a good boy. He remembers not to forget himself with ladies—till after they get married.

Marcel. That's the truth.

Pochet. Well, it's you I want to talk to anyway. [*Goes down right.*]

Marcel [*escorting* VAN PUTZEBOUM *left*]. Godfather, it's too bad you have to go so soon.

Putzeboum. Was it? I was going?

Marcel. You said you had errands.

Putzeboum [*lowers voice*]. Ja, but be careful, Sonny! Shouldn't I stay better and guard the door? [*He points right surreptitiously.*]

Marcel. Leave it to me. I'll handle this.

Putzeboum. If you got to tell lies, make it good big ones. [*Eludes* MARCEL *and goes to* POCHET.] Poppa, you was going with us to have dinner tonight, ain't it?

Pochet. I am? Who said so?

Putzeboum. It was all fixed up here between us two and your little daughter.

Pochet. Oh! You did see her then?

Putzeboum [*flustered*]. Ach, no, I mean—I was just supposing she was coming! Don't she always take dinner with the fiancé?

Pochet. Ah, yes. I suppose she does. [*Goes back to down right window.*]

Putzeboum [*to* MARCEL]. My mouth got opened up by mistake. Better I should go away quick.

Marcel. Good-by.

Putzeboum. I come back later by and by after a while. Wiedersehen! [*He exits.* MARCEL *closes door.*]

Pochet. What's your godfather doing back in town?

Marcel. Here for a visit.

Pochet. Going to stay long?

Marcel [*nods*]. No, he's leaving right after the wedding.

Pochet. What wedding? Oh, that's bad. That's very bad. What do you plan to do?

Marcel. I don't know yet.

Pochet. Well, you can't go on being engaged to Amy. I won't permit it. She'll lose her good name.

Marcel. Her good name?

Pochet. You know what I mean. It's bad for business.

Marcel [*amused*]. Oh, I see.

Pochet. You won't believe this, but she didn't come home at all last night. I wish I knew where she was.

Amélie [*prankishly, peeking out*]. Bonjour, Papa.

Pochet. What are you doing here?

Amélie [*entering*]. Stop pretending. You knew very well I was here.

Pochet [*to* MARCEL]. But you said she wasn't.

Marcel. I didn't say so. My godfather did.

Amélie. You knew I was here because I wrote you.

Pochet. Wrote me?

Amélie. Yes. Did you bring the dress?

Pochet. I was supposed to bring a dress?

Amélie. Of course. All I have to wear is an evening gown.

Pochet. You call that an evening gown? Looks like a nightshirt to me. Anyway, I didn't get your letter. I went out early myself today.

Amélie. Then what are you doing here at all?

Pochet. Looking for you. I wanted to warn you.

Amélie. Warn me? About what?

Pochet. About Étienne.

Marcel and Amélie. Étienne?

Pochet. He's back in town.

Marcel. Already? It's only been two weeks——

Pochet. His regiment's disbanded. There was an epidemic of mumps.

Amélie. Mumps!

Pochet. He came home last night.

Marcel. Last night!

Pochet. I should say, three o'clock this morning.

Amélie. Where did you tell him I was?

Pochet. I said you'd gone out for a walk.

Amélie. At three in the morning? Very convincing!

Pochet. What could I say? You shouldn't put your father in such situations. Forcing him to tell lies.

Marcel [*sits on footboard of bed*]. How embarrassing!

Pochet. Isn't it? And me, a military man with a distinguished record to look back on.

Amélie. One lie isn't going to hurt you.

Pochet. The shame of it! Staying out all night!

Amélie. Papa, there's nothing to fuss about. I may have slept here, but we——

Pochet [*stopping her*]. That's enough. I don't wish to know the details. [*Severely, to* MARCEL.] I don't wish to know about it!

Marcel. I didn't say anything.

Pochet. You know, Amy dear, I never meddle in your affairs. There are occasions when it behooves a father to keep his distance. I never criticize. I've never attempted to reform your character. Have I?

Amélie. Not that I recall, Papa.

Pochet. But etiquette is one thing I've striven to impress upon your mind, ever since girlhood. If you call on a gentleman in the evening, stay a reasonable time, then get up, get dressed, and take a taxi home. *Never* stay out all night!

Amélie. Yes, Papa.

Pochet. When I was in uniform, I never slept away from home. Even when I was on night duty. [*To* MARCEL.] *Never!*

Marcel. I didn't say a word.

Pochet. You'd be better off if you followed your father's example. Confine your romances to the afternoon.

Amélie [*dutifully*]. That's right, Papa. It's safer.

Pochet [*gratified*]. You see?

Amélie [*taking Father's arm*]. I ought to tell you, the real reason I didn't come home was that we'd been drinking champagne and——

Marcel [*on the other side of* POCHET]. She was so intoxicated she couldn't stand up.

Pochet. Ah? If that was the case, I apologize. I should have known you had some excellent reason. [*One arm around* AMÉLIE, *other around* MARCEL. *Kisses* AMÉLIE *and turns instinctively to kiss* MARCEL, *stopping just in time.*] Wonderful!

Banging heard off left.

The Prince's Voice. Landlord! Where is the wretched fellow?

Marcel [*goes to left*]. Who's doing all that shouting? [*Opens door and closes it rapidly.*] My God, it's the Prince! Here in my vestibule!

Pochet [*running about excitedly*]. The Prince here!

Amélie. And me wearing Marcel's chemise! [*She hides behind curtain in window recess. At same time, she undoes drawcord and tassels and yanks them down.*]

Pochet. A candle! I must have a candle! [*He seizes candlestick down left.*]

Awestruck, MARCEL *lurks up left center. Door is flung open and* PRINCE *steps in.*

Prince. Oh! So many people!

Pochet [*holding candle aloft*]. Your Majesty! [*Backs away down center.*]

Prince. Ah, Monsieur Papa? Still with your candle, I see!

Pochet. Excuse me, Majesty. I didn't have time to light it.

Prince. What is this with you and the candles? Tell me, do they excite you?

Pochet. Your Highness?

Prince. Something ritualistic, I have no doubt. [*Crossing down right center and back again.*] You received the decoration I sent you?

Pochet [*at stiff attention*]. Yes, Highness! "Commander of Palestrian Cavalry"! I received the certificate and insignia!

Prince. It is a great distinction.

Pochet. I am honored, Your Highness, and may I say——

Prince. No, that's enough! Be quiet!

Pochet [*salutes*]. Yes, Highness! [*Puts candle back down left.*]

Marcel [*upstage*]. What's this Prince doing in my house?

The PRINCE *circles up left, brushing past* MARCEL, *but taking no notice of him.* MARCEL *flattens himself against wall.*

Prince [*coming down*]. Where is she? I do not see Mamzelle d'Avranches!

Pochet [*running down right*]. Amélie! Amélie! His Highness wants you!

Amélie [*hoarsely*]. No, no! Go away!

Pochet. Come out. When a Prince commands, you must obey. [*To* PRINCE.] She's hiding. She's a shy little thing.

Prince [*amorously*]. Mamzelle! I beg of you, come out!

Amélie [*behind curtain*]. Your Royal Highness!

POCHET *goes behind drape to bring her. Curtain billows as they struggle.*

Prince. Come out, Mamzelle, I implore you!

Amélie. But, sire, I am not properly dressed!

Prince. Not dressed? Ah, chérie, you have been waiting for me! [AMÉLIE *appears, led by* POCHET, *who holds her hand up high. She has wound curtain cords about her waist like a sash, another about her forehead. She curtseys.* PRINCE *advances, edging* POCHET *aside.*] You sent for me, my precious, and so I am here.

Amélie [*astonished*]. I sent for you?

Prince. General Koshnadiev is following with dresses for you to choose from. [*Regretfully.*] Not knowing your measurements, darling, I told him to bring all sizes.

Amélie. But, Highness, there's some mistake. I never sent for you.

Prince [*bridles*]. No? Why did you write me then this letter? [*Takes letter from pocket.* POCHET *approaches and looks over* PRINCE'S *shoulder. Latter turns and glares at him.* POCHET *pivots and retreats down left.* PRINCE *begins reading.*] "Dear little Father . . ."

Amélie [*aghast*]. You thought that was for *you*?

Prince. Why not? It is charming. In Palestria, that is what the Empress calls the Czar—"Little Father"—I *like* it! [*Reading.*] "I am at Marcel Courbois's place at 27 Rue Cambon. He has given me lodging." Courbois—what an amusing name!

Pochet. Isn't it? Ha, ha, ha.

Marcel. What's amusing about it?

Amélie [*indicating* MARCEL]. May I present him to Your Highness——

Pochet [*beckoning* MARCEL]. Hep!

Marcel [*runs down left, grabs candlestick, and bows*]. Your Majesty!

Prince [*shakes head sadly*]. Always with the candles, these people.

Amélie. This is Monsieur Courbois.

Prince. Aha! You are the landlord?

Marcel. Huh?

Prince. Very good. [*Turns back on* MARCEL.]

Marcel [*to* POCHET]. He called me the landlord!

Pochet. Sh! Don't argue!

Prince [*to* AMÉLIE]. Where was I? [*Reading.*] "Come and bring me a dress to wear."

Amélie. But I didn't mean for Your Highness to get that letter. That was intended for Papa.

Prince [*coldly*]. I do not understand.

Amélie. I must have mixed up the envelopes!

Pochet [*highly amused*]. Then I will be getting the letter you wrote to His Highness.

Prince [*reprovingly, as to a child*]. Ah!ah!ah!—Mamzelle will explain everything!

Amélie. I would never have dared to call you "Little Father."

Marcel. She wouldn't be so familiar with Your Highness.

Prince [*raising finger*]. Ah!ah!ah!

Marcel [*bows*]. Beg pardon!

Prince. What business is it of yours, landlord?

Pochet [*loudly, to* MARCEL]. Be quiet! Don't talk to the Prince unless he speaks to you first! [*In* PRINCE's *ear.*] Am I right, Prince?

Prince [*savagely*]. You seem to know so much about it!

Pochet. I was merely giving him advice——

Prince. Then do so!

Pochet. Ah?

Prince. Do not bother *me* with your advice.

Pochet. Good.

Prince [*turns back to* AMÉLIE *with a smile*]. On the contrary, darling, it is enchanting for you to call me "Little Father." It is tender, it is affectionate! It is Palestrian! I dislike formality.

Pochet [*to* AMÉLIE]. There, you see!

Prince [*to* POCHET]. *Ah!ah!ah!*

Pochet [*stepping backward*]. Good, good, good!

Prince [*to* AMÉLIE]. I am, after all, a simple fellow. I like to laugh, to make the little jokes. In Palestria, I am famous for my sense of humor.

Pochet [*approaches, laughing*]. I'll bet you are at that!

Prince [*brusquely, to* POCHET]. Ah! ah! [POCHET, *startled, spins about, jabbing* MARCEL *in stomach.*]

Marcel [*gasping, same tone as* PRINCE]. *Ah!*

Prince [*to* AMÉLIE]. You have heard perhaps of Patchnikoff?

Amélie. No.

Pochet. No, I never did.

Prince. I was asking Mamzelle.

Pochet [*nods*]. I was answering. Neither of us ever heard of him.

Prince [*fiercely*]. *Ah!ah!ah!*

POCHET *backs away, making deferential gestures.*

Marcel [*maliciously*]. Never talk to the Prince unless he speaks to you first!

Pochet [*to* MARCEL, *imitating* PRINCE]. *Ah!ah!ah!*

Prince. Patchnikoff was the court chamberlain. Well, one night, after dinner . . . [*He can hardly contain himself for laughing.*] I had four of my officers grab him by the arms and legs and throw him into a tub of iced water!

Amélie. No?

Prince [*roaring with laughter*]. Oh, he was furious. He didn't dare to say anything, you know, but he was *furious!* We laughed and laughed! [*Resuming natural tone of voice.*] He died the same night of convulsions.

Amélie. No?

Prince. Yes! Poor fellow. [*Shrugs.*] It was unfortunate. But it was amusing while it lasted.

Marcel. This Prince is a Palestrian idiot.

Pochet [*at the* PRINCE's *elbow*]. I bet you have lots of fun at court!

Prince [*turns to* POCHET, *who is directly under his nose*]. Listen, Papa! I made you a Knight Commander of the Empire. But now go away before I lose my temper! [*Doorbell rings.* PRINCE *speaks calmly.*] The bell. It must be the General. Landlord, let him in.

Marcel. He thinks I'm a muzhik or something.

CHARLOTTE *opens door, admitting* KOSHNADIEV, *who is followed by a shop assistant carrying a huge box.* KOSHNADIEV, *finding* MARCEL *upstage of door, hands him his hat and continues down left center.*

Marcel [*examines hat*]. Very funny! [*Puts hat on desk.*]

Prince. Good afternoon, General.

Koshnadiev [*making Palestrian salute*]. Highness.

Prince. You have brought the dresses?

Koshnadiev. Here they are, Highness. [*Sharply to* CLERK.] Put them down, Lieutenant. [*To* PRINCE.] I brought a selection on approval. [*Dismissing* CLERK.] Go back to your shop. You will be sent for when we need you.

Clerk [*bows*]. Oui, m'sieur. Au 'voir, messieurs, 'dame. [*Exits.*]

Prince [*offering hand to* AMÉLIE]. Would you like to see them?

Amélie [*gives* PRINCE *her hand and makes deep curtsey*]. Thank you, Your Highness. [*He leads her in a semicircle down left center. She curtseys again and trips backward over box.*]

All [*rushing to aid her*]. Oh!

Amélie [*regaining balance*]. Don't trouble yourselves.

Prince [*reading lid of box*]. "Madame Sophie—Boutique Magnifique—Creations by Royal Appointment to Queen Marie of Bulgaria, Princess Lidya Likoritinovitch, Grand Duchess Tamara, et cetera." Will these be all right, you think?

Amélie. It's not where I usually shop, but perhaps one of them will do.

Prince. Try them on anyway, chérie.

Amélie [*waves hand to right*]. Someone take them in there . . .

Prince [*seeing* POCHET, *who has lifted box*]. Ah!ah!ah! [POCHET *lets box fall with a bump.*] Koshnadiev! [KOSHNADIEV *picks up the box.*]

Amélie [*flattered*]. But, Highness, a General shouldn't carry boxes.

Prince [*contemptuously*]. Why not? A General should be good for something.

Koshnadiev. At your service, madame.

Amélie. This way, General. [*She precedes him into bathroom.* KOSHNADIEV *approaches door carrying box broadside. He halts, baffled.*]

Pochet. No, no. Like this. [*Turning box the long way.*] Now, forward.

Koshnadiev [*gratefully in Palestrian*]. Kolaschnick. Merci. [*Exits right.*]

Marcel [*whispering*]. Pochet, listen——

Pochet [*coldly*]. Kolaschnick! [*Exits right.*]

The PRINCE *has been surveying the room with a critical eye. He notices* MARCEL, *who is staring off through open door.*

Prince [*in a voice of thunder*]. What do you think you are doing, *you?*

Marcel [*whirling about*]. Nothing, Highness. I was just looking——

Prince. Do not look.

Marcel [*nervously*]. I hesitate to do so in your presence, but I was going to put on some clothes and—— [*He emits an unfortunate laugh.*]

Prince [*disdainfully*]. What possible interest do you think that would hold for me?

Marcel. But if Your Highness has no objection——

Prince [*flicking finger under* MARCEL's *nose*]. That face—it is very funny.

Marcel. Is it, Your Highness?

Prince [*repeats business*]. Where have I seen that face?

Marcel. Were you ever a private in the Twentieth Infantry?

Prince. No! Was it Monte Carlo? Hotel Monaco?

Marcel. Not me, Your Highness.

Prince [*accusingly*]. There was a waiter there who looked like you.

Marcel. I'm delighted—but it must have been someone else.

Prince [*glancing about*]. You rent rooms here, eh?

Marcel. Oh, yes. This is my place——

Prince. It is ugly.

Marcel. Oh?

Prince. Yes, very ugly.

Marcel. Well, when you consider the price, it's not too bad. The rent is cheap.

Prince [*crosses to him*]. How cheap?

Marcel. What?

Prince. What are the charges?

Marcel. You want to know how much?

Prince. Yes, yes. How much?

Marcel [*with a vague gesture*]. Well, let's see, it costs— eighteen hundred francs.

Prince. Per day?

Marcel. Per day. [*Correcting himself.*] Oh, no! Not per day. Per year.

Prince. Ah? Not bad!

Marcel. No, it isn't, is it? When you figure that in- cludes——

Prince. And what is it per *day?*

Marcel. What? Oh!—that's hard to say. The rent is pay- able every quarter. Each three months, I——

Prince. No, no, no! What is the price for *one day?*

Marcel [*dubiously*]. You really want to know?

Prince. Yes!

Marcel. Yes? [*Mutters.*] Is he ever nosey!

Prince. Well?

Marcel. I'll have to figure it out.

Prince. Well, *do* so! [*Crosses up left.*]

Marcel. "*Do* so!" Yes, well it should be very simple . . . [*Mutters.*] I had no idea these foreigners were so inquisitive. [*Commencing to figure.*] Eighteen hundred francs per year, what does that make it? As if I had nothing better to do than work out arithmetic! Eighteen hundred francs . . . If he wasn't a royal highness, I wouldn't bother . . . Now there are twelve months in a year. So if it were a hundred francs per month—that would make it—twelve months at——

Prince [*coming back*]. Go right ahead. Take your time.

Marcel [*interrupted*]. Yes, I'll get it.—Hum. If it was a hundred a month, that'd be a hundred times twelve. Clear enough! Twelve hundred! So I take twelve hundred francs and I put 'em here. [*Picks up imaginary francs and places them in pocket of jacket.*] Now we're getting somewhere. Good. Take eighteen from twelve, that leaves—er, leaves——

Prince. Eight!

Marcel. No, six!

Prince. Ah, twelve from eighteen. Yes, of course, six! six!

Marcel. Please, Your Highness. I'm fairly good at mathe- matics, but if you don't stop mixing me up, we'll never get to the bottom of this.

Prince. Don't distress yourself.

Marcel. It's not me that's distressing me. [*Starting again.*] Six. Good. We take six hundred and multiply. Six hundred times twelve makes——

Prince. Six hundred and twelve.

Marcel. Your Highness, please! *Please!*

Prince. Don't get so excited.

Marcel. Twelve hundred divided by two is six hundred, twelve hundred divided by twelve is one hundred, so divide by two again, half of one hundred is fifty. Fifty francs!

Prince. Did you do it?

Marcel. Almost. I take the hundred francs I put in my pocket. Add that to the fifty—which makes one hundred and fifty. That's it. That's the answer, Your Highness! One hundred and fifty francs! Whew! [*Sits exhausted but happy.*]

Prince. Per day?

Marcel. Per day. [*Correcting himeslf.*] No, per month.

Prince. Ah? And what is it per day?

Marcel. What is it? [*Discouraged.*] You want to know *that?*

Prince. Certainly. I don't care about the month.

Marcel. It's per *day* you want to know?

Prince [*crossing up left again*]. Certainly.

Marcel. He's only interested in what it costs per day. All right, so . . . [*Rises.*] My poor head!—Let's see, if it's a hundred and fifty francs per month, what'll it be per day? Very simple. Thirty days in a month, so that's a hundred and fifty divided by thirty.

Prince. Yes!

Marcel. Thank you. . . . Fifteen goes into thirty how many times? Two times. Two times fifteen equals thirty. So! I put down two—and I deduct thirty. No, something's wrong. It's difficult when you're out of practice. Two times thirty is sixty. From fifteen take away—*No,* sixty minus fifteen—— [*Continues to make calculations, writing in air with his right hand, counting off fingers on his left hand, transferring invisible sums of money from one pocket to the other, sketching imaginary figures on rug with toe of his shoe, erasing with sole, etc. Pantomime gets increasingly frantic.*]

Prince [*suddenly*]. Have you *got* it?

Marcel [*with a start*]. What? No! Don't *do* that! Now I've got to go all the way back to the beginning!

Prince. You still haven't found the answer?

Marcel. I was making progress. I nearly had it. Then you had to yell at me! Now I lost the thread again——

Prince. What thread?

Marcel. Sh! Wait a minute!—Five. Yes, *five.* Nine, seven, zero, zero . . . [*Resumes pantomime as before. Then:*] I've got it! Twenty-five thousand francs!

Prince. Twenty-five thousand francs! per *day?*

Marcel [*examines imaginary arithmetic on carpet, rubs it out with shoe*]. No. I made a mistake somewhere.

Prince. Absolutely.

Marcel. When I think how bookkeepers make a living at this sort of thing! They don't pay them enough. All they earn is a paltry hundred sous a day. A mere hundred and fifty francs a month for— [*With a victorious shout.*] Ah! I've got it. A hundred fifty francs a month is a hundred sous per day. A hundred sous is five francs! *Five francs per day!*

Prince. Five francs per day?

Marcel. Exactly. You see I got it right away. As soon as I quit using arithmetic.

Prince. You rent this place for five francs a day?

Marcel. Yes!

Prince [*looking around distastefully*]. Naturally, one wouldn't expect the Palace of Versailles for that price.

Marcel. No, and I wouldn't want to live there anyway. Too many visitors.

Prince [*crossing right*]. Five francs? Very well. I must tell the General as soon as he comes back.

Marcel. You think he'd be interested?

Prince. Of course. He concerns himself with all these matters.

Marcel [*shrugs*]. He must have nothing to do with his time.

Pochet [*entering*]. She's made her selection.

Prince. Ah, splendid. Koshnadiev!

Koshnadiev [*re-entering*]. Highness?

Prince. Moya marovna! Tetayeff polna koromyee momalak scrovno? (Come here! Has she found a suitable costume?)

Koshnadiev. Stichi! Aspanyay ko taneya, Monseigneur, ko rassa ta svalop! (Yes, a pretty dress, my lord, it fits her like a glove.)

Prince. Good. Good.

Koshnadiev [*at attention*]. *Svoya Altessia na bouk papelskoya mimi?* (Your Highness has further need of me?)

Prince. Nack. (No.) [KOSHNADIEV *makes bow and goes to get hat.*] *Voulia mavolak tvarla tschikopnay* to the landlord? (Would you give him some money?) [MARCEL *looks up.*]

Quantschi prencha. (Twenty francs.) [PRINCE *goes down right.*]

Koshnadiev. Oh! *Schti!* (Oh, yes!) [*He takes coin from purse.*]

Marcel [*to* POCHET]. What did he say? He was talking about me.

Koshnadiev [*gives coin to* MARCEL]. *Quantschi prencha.* There you are!

Marcel [*bewildered*]. What is this?

Pochet. Prenchi, prencha. It's a twenty-franc piece.

Marcel [*to* PRINCE]. But what's it for?

Prince. For the apartment.

Marcel. The apartment? His Highness is joking?

Prince. You said five francs. I am giving you twenty.

Koshnadiev [*sternly*]. We are giving you twenty.

Marcel. But I don't want it. What an idea!

Prince. What is the matter?

Marcel. This place is not for rent. Take your money back.

Prince [*scandalized*]. Koshnadiev!

Koshnadiev [*seizing* MARCEL *by the arm*]. Do not disturb His Highness——

Pochet [*seizing* MARCEL *by other arm and propelling him down left*]. Don't complicate things!

Marcel [*furiously*]. But I don't want his money!

Pochet [*taking coin from* MARCEL]. No need to make a fuss about it. Forgive him, Your Highness. He has no manners. [*Puts coin in his pocket.*] O-la-la!

Prince [*glowers at* MARCEL]. I am most displeased, you know. I will never rent your house again after today.

Pochet [*to* MARCEL]. You see?

Marcel. Well, that's good news.

Prince. Now, go away. I've seen enough of you.

Marcel. I'm supposed to go?

Pochet. Yes! Get out! You heard His Highness? *Out!*

Prince. Yes! And *you* go with him!

Pochet. Oh? Me also?

Prince. Go! *Both* of you!

Pochet. Good, good, good!

Marcel [*laughs shortly*]. All I needed was to get kicked out of my own house!

Pochet. Let us go. Since we're not required further. [*He escorts* MARCEL *right.*]

Prince [*shouts, startling them*]. *No!*

Pochet and *Marcel* [*echoing his cry*]. No?

Prince. Not that way. I have rented the bathroom also.

Marcel [*marching back left*]. Come along, Pochet.

Pochet. Where are we going?

Marcel. We'll go to the pantry and count the silver. [*They exit left.*]

Koshnadiev [*saluting* PRINCE]. *Svoya Altessia na jabo dot schalipp as madyay?* (Any further orders?)

Prince. Nack. (No.)

Koshnadiev. *Loyo, sta Svoya Altessia lo madjet, meh pipilski, terrahdyeff.* (Then if Your Highness will excuse me, I am leaving.)

Prince. Bonadya, Koshnadiev. (Good day.)

Koshnadiev. *Anahlouck, Mutcharyay!* (Au revoir, Sire.) [*He exits.*]

Prince [*pacing*]. She is very charming, this Amélie. But where did she find that stupid landlord? [*He sits on bed. Rap is heard left.* CHARLOTTE *enters carrying folded sheets.*] What do you want, little girl?

Charlotte. I was going to make the bed.

Prince. Were you? Advance a little, my darling. What is your name?

Charlotte. Charlotte.

Prince [*taking her hand*]. Do you know you are attractive?

Charlotte. All I know is, I can't make the bed when you're sitting on it.

Prince. I am Prince Nicolas! No?

Charlotte. I don't say yes, I don't say no.

Prince. Heir to the throne of Palestria!

Charlotte. It would still be difficult to make the bed——

Prince. Who cares about the bed? [*He takes sheets from her.*] Yes, yes! You are very pretty!

Charlotte [*laughing*]. You're comical!

Prince [*pulling her onto his knee*]. What do you like? [*He dances her up and down delightedly.*]

Charlotte [*laughing*]. He wants to play horsie. [*Patting his cheek.*] Giddyap!

Prince. That's right! I *love* informality! [*He jiggles her some more, then lies back on bed, drawing her with him.*]

AMÉLIE *enters wearing a smart frock.*

Amélie. Oh, Your Highness, I beg your pardon! [*She starts to exit again.*]

Prince [*sitting up*]. Not at all, my dear. I have been waiting for you. [*To* CHARLOTTE.] Run along now, sweetheart. Perhaps we will meet again later. [*He gives her a slap on the rear.*]

Charlotte [*as she exits*]. I never had a job like this before.

Prince [*extending hands to* AMÉLIE]. My beloved! Come to me!

Amélie. I'm afraid I interrupted you.

Prince. I was just filling in the time. You are the *pièce de resistance.*

Amélie [*takes step toward him*]. You've certainly picking up the language.

Prince. Let us speak only the language of love. [*Stretching out hand.*] I am waiting.

Amélie [*puts hand in that of* PRINCE *and makes curtsey*]. Yes, Your Highness.

Prince. Why did you put this on, this dress?

Amélie. Your Highness told me to. [*Pivots, displaying frock.*] Don't you like it?

Prince. I said to *try it on!* I expected you to take it *off* again at once! I liked better your other costume! [*Brightens.*] But it is no problem, taking off a dress! [*Pulls her onto knee, bouncing her up and down.*] What do you like? [*Both laugh.*]

POCHET *enters left followed by* MARCEL.

Pochet. Look out! He's coming!

Marcel. My godfather! He's back!

Amélie [*jumps up*]. Who?

Pochet. Putzeboum! He's on his way up!

Prince [*pulling* AMÉLIE *back*]. What is this about Putzeboum? Who is he? Is there no peace in this hotel?

Amélie [*on* PRINCE's *lap*]. How do you know he's coming?

Pochet. I saw him from the top of the stairs.

Marcel. He'll be here any second.

Amélie [*jumping up*]. He mustn't come in——

Prince [*pulling her back*]. Let him come, this fellow! What does it matter?

Amélie. No, Your Highness! He mustn't see you!

Prince [*showing alarm*]. Why not? Is he an anarchist? One of the Bolsheviki?

Amélie. No, no.

Prince [*trying to pull her back*]. Then I spit on him! [*Spits.*]

Marcel. He spits on my godfather! [*Doorbell rings.*]

Amélie. Look out, he's here!

Pochet. He's here! Come on!

Amélie. Quickly, Your Highness!

Marcel. This way! Through here! Down the fire escape! *[Simultaneously.]*

Prince. Fire escape! Where is there a fire? I do not like this!

Amélie. Come, Your Highness! Come with me!

Prince [*mollified*]. Ah, you are coming too, darling? That is different! [AMÉLIE *and* PRINCE *exit right.*]

Pochet [*goes off right and comes back. To* MARCEL]. You see what we go through for you! Sacrificing ourselves——

Marcel. Tell me about it later. [*Gives* POCHET *a vigorous push and follows him off, closing door.*]

Charlotte [*entering left*]. Come right in, m'sieur. [*Holds door open, then exits to vestibule.*]

Putzeboum. Thank you. [*Entering and finding stage empty.*] Ach! Where was everybody? [*Calling.*] Yoohoo! Amykins! Where was Sonny? Where was the poppa? [*Calling louder.*] Little girl, where was you?

Charlotte [*re-enters*]. You wanted me, m'sieur?

Putzeboum. Nobody was here.

Charlotte [*amazed*]. That's strange. There was a big crowd here a minute ago.

Putzeboum. But now they ain't.

Charlotte [*starts to cross right*]. I'll look in here. Maybe they're all in the bathroom. [*Doorbell rings.*] Oh, excuse me, someone's at the door. [*Turns and hurries out left.*]

Putzeboum. Yes, you go. [*Facing front.*] I bet you that no-good godson of mine is hiding someplace making hugs and kisses with his Amykins. [*Wags head and crosses down right.*]

Étienne [*heard off left*]. No need to announce me. I know the way.

Charlotte [*off left*]. But, m'sieur!

Putzeboum. Who is coming? I think I heard that voice someplace.

Étienne [*entering*]. Marcel! [*Seeing* VAN PUTZEBOUM *and not recognizing him.*] I beg your pardon . . .

Putzeboum. Ah, Monsieur Chopart!

Étienne [*puzzled*]. Who? [*Suddenly recalling.*] Ah, yes. The Dutch godfather.

Putzeboum. What was you doing here? I thought you was gone to the army.

Étienne. Company was dismissed. An epidemic of mumps . . .

Putzeboum. Oh, that's a shame.

Étienne. Not at all. It's a marvelous disease!

Putzeboum. And so you come right away to see your cousin-in-law!

Étienne. My what? Oh, yes, you mean Marcel! Isn't he here?

Putzeboum. He used to be, up to a little bit ago.

Étienne. What about you? I thought you were going to America?

Putzeboum. No, not yet. It was making me so sad not to see my Sonny getting married, so I come back to stay for the wedding.

Étienne. What's that? The wedding?

Putzeboum. From respect for his poppa, I fixed it up. So I am here to see the young folks tied in knots together.

Étienne. Oh? What did Marcel think of that idea?

Putzeboum. Marcel? Ach, he is so happy. Both him and Amykins was so glad I could be here.

Étienne [incredulously]. You don't mean it?

Putzeboum. Ja, so glad and so happy. And next week, it takes place the wedding maybe.

Étienne. Really? You amaze me.

Putziboum [chuckling]. Ja! And it ain't a minute too soon either, believe you me! Because . . . [*Breaks off laughing.*]

Étienne. Because what?

Putzeboum [finger to lips]. Oh, nothing! I promised I wouldn't say a word!

Étienne [suspiciously]. What do you mean, you promised?

Putzeboum. Ja, that's right, I promised I wouldn't tell nobody. So I got to keep it a secret.

Étienne. Surely you could tell *me?* After all!

Putzeboum. Ach sure, that's right. Ain't you Marcel's best friend? And Amélie, she's your cousin. I promised not to tell nobody . . . but you ain't nobody.

Étienne. Of course not, you can tell *me.* What has happened?

Putzeboum. Should I tell it? No, I couldn't!

Étienne [impatiently]. Of course you could.

Putzeboum [chuckles]. Give me your positive word of honor you wouldn't tell a soul?

Étienne. I promise!

Putzeboum. Good! Then this was the secret. It wasn't a minute too soon for the wedding!

Étienne. I know. You said that once. But why?

Putzeboum. Ach, those little turtledoves! What would you say if I was to tell you, when I come today and seen what I seen—— two little love birds sitting up in bed! Ja, that bed right here!

Étienne [*indignant*]. I'd say it was a lot of bunk.

Putzeboum. Well, *bunk, bed,* whatever you want to call it! I ain't been here in the country so long.

Étienne. You say you saw them both together in that bed?

Putzeboum [*pointing*]. Yah, that's the bunk!

Étienne. You didn't make this up?

Putzeboum [*looking at bed*]. *I* didn't. They must have made it up after I went out.

Étienne [*grabs him by the collar*]. You *saw* them? You're sure?

Putzeboum. Sure, I seen! Why was you so excited all of a sudden?

Étienne. You actually *saw* them sleeping together?

Putzeboum. When I saw them, they wasn't sleeping.

Étienne. But *in* the bed?

Putzeboum [*pushing* ÉTIENNE's *hands aside*]. In the bed here, sure! For what was you so upset?

Étienne [*raging*]. I'll kill them! I'll kill them both!

Putzeboum [*baffled*]. Why should you get so excited? Next week comes up the wedding and——

Étienne. When I think how I trusted that dog, Marcel! I said "Take care of Amy while I'm out of town!" He was taking care of her, all right!

Putzeboum. Gotferdom! Maybe I shouldn't never have told this fellow!

Étienne [*menacingly*]. I thought he was my friend! All the time, I thought he was my friend! [*Clenches fists.*] Wait'll I get my hands on him!

Putzeboum [*pleading*]. Chopart! Look here, Chopart!

Étienne [*with fury*]. And lay off that Chopart stuff! I've heard enough about Chopart! [*Pacing up and down.*] Damn those dirty double-crossers!

Putzeboum [*facing front*]. For goodness' sakes, such tantrums! You wouldn't never think he'd be so strict about his cousin! It isn't like it was his sister!

Étienne [*looking at the bed*]. I no sooner get out of town than they jump right in!—I'll beat 'em to a jelly! That's what I'll do! [*Leaps on bed and pummels pillows with his fists.*]

Putzeboum. Such a temper!—Wait, Chopart! You shouldn't take such attitudes! What right we got to judge others?

Étienne. Go away!

Putzeboum [*raising hands skyward*]. Which one of us was without sin? Who should throw rocks at glass houses? People who live in glass houses got to pull down the shades. We all done something wrong sometime.

Étienne. They certainly did! You caught them right in the act!

Putzeboum. Not in the act! Between the acts! [*Struck by a thought.*] Maybe they wasn't turtledoves at all! Ja, sure! They explained to me it was cold outside—that's why they got inside. And maybe they was tired.

Étienne. They'll be plenty tired before I'm through with them! [*He laughs, crosses down left, and circles upstage.* PUTZEBOUM *is making the same circuit on the opposite side, arriving below bed at same time as* ÉTIENNE.]

Putzeboum. No, no! That would make me a hot potato. You promised you wouldn't tell nobody what I told you! Besides, next week it's going to be the *wedding!*

Étienne [*seizes him and shakes him*]. Ha! Wedding! So you think there's going to be a wedding, do you? [*He gives* PUTZEBOUM *a twist which sends him spinning.*] Of course! Why not? Next week there's going to be a wedding—and *you'll* be there and *I'll* be there, to make sure *nothing* goes wrong.

Putzeboum [*trotting back*]. Chopart, listen, you wouldn't told nobody I told you.

Étienne [*with a grim smile*]. Certainly not. I gave my promise, so I won't tell a soul.

Putzeboum. I wouldn't either, any more.

Étienne [*sardonically*]. Probably you were right. They were tired. Or their feet got cold . . .

Putzeboum. Sure!

Étienne [*grinding his teeth*]. We shouldn't get angry at two little love birds!

Putzeboum [*fanning self with handkerchief*]. Ja, Chopart, I'm so glad to hear you say that. [*Crosses away, relieved.*]

Étienne. I'll get even with them for this. [*Punctuates remark by socking fist in palm of hand.*]

Putzeboum. That Chopart fellow's got a pleasant disposition, after all!

Marcel [*entering from right*]. Godfather, why didn't someone tell me?

Putzeboum. Oh, there you are, Sonny!

Marcel [*seeing* ÉTIENNE *and reacting*]. My word! Look
who's here now! [*With forced enthusiasm.*] Étienne! How
are you, dear fellow? [MARCEL *wedges himself between*
PUTZEBOUM *and* ÉTIENNE.]

Étienne. Marcel, old pal!

Amélie [*enters left, followed by* POCHET]. Étienne!

Pochet. You here?

Étienne. Yes, *me.* You're *all* so glad to see me, aren't you?

Amélie [*rushing to his arms*]. Étienne, darling!

Étienne. My *own* Amélie! [*Kisses her; then, aside.*] *My*
own—and everybody else's! [*To* MARCEL.] Marcel, how have
things been going?

Marcel [*shaking hands*]. I've nothing to complain about.

Étienne [*under his breath*]. Not yet, you haven't!

Pochet. Glad to be back, Étienne?

Étienne. Glad? To see Amélie and all my faithful friends?
I'll say I'm glad!

Marcel [*to* PUTZEBOUM, *aside*]. Especially *him,* you understand? Not a word to him! Don't tell him a thing!

Putzeboum. What? Me? How could you think it?

Marcel. Just remember!

Putzeboum. What kind of old blabberpuss must you take
me for!

Marcel. We can't be too careful. [*Aside.*] Well, that's a
relief! [*Returns to* ÉTIENNE, *who is chatting with* AMÉLIE.]

Étienne. Tell me, Marcel, she wasn't bored with me out of
town? You found her cooperative in every way?

Marcel. Oh, very cooperative.

Pochet. They were together all the time.

Étienne. Night and day, I suppose?

Pochet. They were never apart.

Étienne [*clasping* MARCEL *and* AMÉLIE]. Never apart!
[*Crosses to center.*]

Putzeboum. Listen, children, I came back to take you out
to dinner, but I see Marcel ain't even got dressed yet.

Marcel. Sorry—I had some unexpected guests who kept
stopping by.

Putzeboum. No hurry. I think maybe little Amykins would
like to visit with her cousin who she didn't see for two whole
weeks——

Amélie. That would be nice.

Putzeboum. So what was I standing here for? I couldn't help Marcel put on his pantaloons, and I ain't no use to the cousins, so maybe I better go——

All [*protesting overloudly*]. Oh, no. No, don't say that. Don't go. You mustn't.

Putzeboum. Ja, ja. I meet you all later, in an hour, at Amélie's house. It was good?

All. Au revoir. See you later then. Good-by, Putzi.

Putzeboum [*to* MARCEL]. Don't bother, Sonny, coming to the door. Better you should put on some pants, ja? Good-by, good-by.

All [*waving*]. Good-by. We'll see you. In an hour. Au revoir. Good-by.

PUTZEBOUM *waves and goes out.* MARCEL *closes door with a sigh and starts to cross to center.* PUTZEBOUM *pops in again.*

Putzeboum [*waving*]. Don't forget now, you should all come in an hour. Good-by.

All [*impatiently, waving him out*]. Good-by! Au revoir! We'll see you soon. Go on! Get out! [*He disappears again.*]

Marcel [*closing door*]. And don't come back! [*Crossing center.*] Well, Étienne, what do you think of the terrible thing that's happened?

Étienne. What do you mean?

Marcel. Putzeboum's come back!

Amélie. Yes, isn't it awful?

Étienne. I'll admit I was surprised.

Amélie. He's come back to attend the marriage.

Étienne. You don't mean it?

Pochet. And he won't go home till after the ceremony!

Étienne. That's too bad! [*To* MARCEL.] So your whole scheme goes up in smoke?

Marcel [*discouraged*]. Unless a miracle happens! [*Sits on foot of bed.*]

Pochet. Marcel will be back in hot water. Up to his ears this time.

Étienne. There must be some way out. Miracles do happen.

Marcel. I wish one would.

Amélie. Try to think of something, Étienne.

Étienne. I will! I'm not going to let Marcel go penniless. He's done a lot for me. It's time I did something for him. Right, Marcel? [*Shakes hands so hard that* MARCEL *winces.*]

Marcel. Good old Étienne! [*Massages his bruised fingers.*]

Étienne [*with a broad smile*]. I believe I've thought of

something. Yes, it might work. Only we'll have to go through with the marriage!

Marcel. What! You want me to marry Amélie?

Amélie. You want me to marry Marcel?

Étienne. Don't be alarmed! Do you think I'd ever give up my Amy who's been so *good* . . . so *faithful* . . . so *devoted!* [*On each of the adjectives he gives* AMÉLIE *a kiss and hugs her roughly.*]

Amélie. Come, I'm not so devoted as all that.

Étienne. Listen! What is it we want to do? Fool the old godfather! Pull the wool over his eyes, right? [*Taking* AMÉLIE *and* MARCEL *each by an arm.*] Now here's my idea . . .

All. What? What is it? Tell us!

Étienne. We'll go to City Hall with Putzeboum and let him see everything. Everything!

Marcel. You mean the whole ceremony?

Étienne. Certainly. We'll go through the whole ceremony!

Amélie. But then we'd be married!

Étienne. No! You two would go through the motions, all the formalities—just enough to satisfy your godfather. If we can convince him, he'll be satisfied and go back home.

Marcel. Yes? But how? How are you going to do it?

Pochet. Étienne's a genius. He'll figure it out. [*Chuckles.*]

Amélie. But how? How's it going to work?

Pochet. I don't know. He's going to tell us.

Étienne. We'll set the date, send out invitations, rent one of those rooms at City Hall for a private ceremony—I'll even give a banquet afterward. We'll have somthing to celebrate that day.

Amélie. Yes, but where does the trick come in?

Marcel. Yes, where?

Étienne. Well, you see, I've got this friend at the Exchange where I work—Toto Bejard, that's his name . . .

Marcel. Toto Bejard?

Étienne. Yes, you don't know him. [*To* POCHET.] You don't know him either.

Pochet. No, that's true, I don't.

Étienne. This Toto Bejard is terrific. He's the greatest practical joker in the world. I'll tell him "You act the part of the Mayor." And he'll dress up, pin on the sash, wear a false beard, and there right in front of your godfather and everybody, he'll perform the ceremony. Amélie d'Avranches will

be wearing a real bridal veil and carrying real orange blossoms
—but the wedding will be *phony!*

All [*jumping for joy*]. What an idea! Bravo! Hurrah for
Étienne! [MARCEL, AMÉLIE *and* POCHET *dance about.*]

Étienne [*nods and grins*]. I thought you'd like the idea.

Marcel [*clasping his hand*]. Étienne! You've saved my life!
You've made me rich!

Étienne. One good turn deserves another.

Marcel. How can I ever thank you?

Étienne. You can thank me later—after the wedding.

Marcel. I'll never forget what you're doing for me.

Étienne. You're getting your just deserts, Marcel! I'm giving you tit for tat! [*The others take hands and dance in a
circle around* ÉTIENNE.]

ACT THREE

SCENE 1

*Marriage chamber at City Hall. Right, a platform on which
is a high desk for the* MAYOR, *flanked by two tables for his
assistants. Up right, a door to* MAYOR'S *office. Facing* MAYOR'S
*desk, two armchairs for the bride and groom. Behind these,
upholstered chairs for relatives and guests. Behind them,
several rows of backless benches. A center aisle extending
diagonally from up left to right platform. On riser, extending
length of rear wall, two rows of chairs. Up left, a two-step
riser which leads to outer corridor. Above the* MAYOR'S *desk, a
bust of La Republique. On desk, an inkwell, a copy of the
marriage code, and official papers.*

*At rise, people are seated about the room, waiting for cere-
mony to begin.* GABY *is about to seat herself in front row.*
MOUILLETU, *an antiquated civil servant, is pussyfooting up
and down the aisle.*

MOUILLETU [*to* GABY, *in a reedy, singsong voice*]. Kindly
occupy the benches to the rear. Front seats are reserved for
the bridal party. Thank you very much.

Gaby. Sorry, I didn't know. [*Goes to first row of benches,
pushing past a couple seated on aisle.*] Pardon me, m'sieu.
[*Man gets up.*] Pardon me, madame. [*Lady gets up.*]

A Bearded Gentleman. The ceremony's set for three o'clock?

His Neighbor. If the bride and groom get here on time.

VALÉRY *and* MOUCHEMOLLE *have entered, arm in arm, and cross down aisle talking loudly.*

Valéry. I said, "That rat is cheating. Look at his cards."—
So the boys beat him up and threw him out.

Mouchemolle. He won't be back in a hurry.

Valéry. Hey, garçon! This where the Courbois wedding's going to be?

Mouilletu. That is correct, m'sieur.

GABY *is now seated at end of bench near footlights.*

Gaby [*wigwagging at* VALÉRY]. Hey! I see you boys made it!

Valéry. Look, here's Gaby! You saving that seat for me?

Gaby. You bet I am.

Mouchemolle. Hi, Gaby! [*Starts to go between first and second row of chairs.*]

Mouilletu. Front seats are reserved. Kindly occupy the benches to the rear.

Mouchemolle. Thanks, grandpa. I was just passing through.

Mouilletu. I'll have to ask you to go round the other way, please. Thank you very much.

Mouchemolle. You're welcome, my friend. [*Goes center, following* VALÉRY.]

Valéry [*disturbing the two persons on aisle*]. Pardon, m'sieur. Pardon, madame.

Mouchemolle [*sliding past, just as they are about to sit again*]. Pardon . . . pardon.

Valéry. Bonjour, Gaby.

Mouchemolle. How are tricks? [*Finding the row crowded, he climbs over and sits on bench behind.*]

Gaby. Bonjour, boys. You didn't want to miss the circus, huh?

Valéry. Not me.

Mouchemolle. You didn't either, eh, Gaby?

Gaby. It'll be the funniest show in town.

Valéry. Hard to believe it's on the level.

Gaby. How do you mean?

Valéry. I can't figure it out.

Mouchemolle. Why should Marcel marry Amélie?

Gaby. Haven't you heard? The whole thing's a put-up job.

Valéry [*laughing*]. That's what I thought, but now they're going through with it!

Gaby. Oh, no!

Valéry. They must be.

Gaby. No. Marcel was at the Tabarin last night, and he told us it was all a dodge. He's putting the bite on his godfather . . . so he can inherit some money.

Valéry. Listen, you're the one that's getting bit. How could they get away with a phony wedding in the City Hall?

Gaby. I don't know. But that's what he told me. [*They continue to talk sotto voce.*]

Cornette [*hurries in from up left entrance*]. Mouilletu! Mouilletu!

Mouilletu [*now on platform arranging* MAYOR'S *desk*]. There you are, Cornette.

Cornette. The boss didn't ask for me, did he?

Mouilletu. Oh yes, but you can thank me for saving you. I told him you were here already.

Cornette. Oh, thanks. I was held up longer than I expected.

Mouilletu. Having a drink at the café?

Cornette. I was down the hall talking to Jobinet.

Mouilletu. Jobinet?

Cornette. You know . . . the one that tells the funny stories. He does post mortems for the coroner's office.

Mouilletu. Ah, yes . . . I know the one.

Mayor [*putting head out door up right*]. Cornette!

Cornette [*hurriedly*]. Coming, m'sieur! Here I am! [*The* MAYOR *disappears.* CORNETTE *exits to office.*]

Valéry [*seeing* PAQUERETTE *and* GISMONDA *enter*]. Here's Paquerette. And Gismonda.

Gaby [*rising and waving*]. Yoohoo! [VALÉRY *and* MOU-CHEMOLLE *whistle.*]

Paquerette. Look, there are some of our pals.

Gismonda. Sure enough.

Gaby [*beckoning*]. Want to sit over here?

Paquerette. We'll be right over!

Mouilletu [*to the girls who have started to wriggle between the first two rows*]. Don't sit in the chairs. Occupy the back benches. Thank you very much.

Paquerette. We're going through, so shut your big trap.

Gismonda. Who does he think he is? [*Arriving down center.*] Now we got here, there's no room anyway!

Paquerette. We'd get a better view if we sat up back.

Mouchemolle. You think so?

Paquerette. I know so.

Valéry. Let's move, then. Excuse us, please . . . [*Group*

*starts toward rear benches, disturbing the people on aisle. As
they go, they ad lib noisily.*]

Gaby. Did you stay late last night?

Paquerette. Don't even mention it. Six o'clock in the morning.

Gismonda. We only left to get dressed for the wedding.
None of us ever got to bed.

Valéry [*who is up center*]. You mean, up here?

Paquerette. That'd be a good place.

Gismonda. It seems that this fellow Toto Bejard is going
to dress up like the Mayor.

Mouchemolle. Toto Bejard?

Paquerette. A pal of Étienne's from the stock exchange.

Gaby. Marcel told us, it's all a trick they're playing on his
godfather.

Paquerette. Of course.

Gaby. You see?

Valéry [*coming back*]. I still can't believe it.

A PHOTOGRAPHER, *camera under his arm, appears in rear
doorway, and comes down aisle. His passage is blocked by*
VALÉRY, GABY, PAQUERETTE, GISMONDA, *and* MOUCHEMOLLE.

Photographer. Pardon, messieurs, 'dames! [*Shoves past
them and arrives at platform right.*]

Mouilletu. Oui, m'sieur?

Photographer. Which way will the bridal party enter?

Mouilletu. Which way do you think? There's only one door.

Photographer. I'm the photographer from *Le Matin*.

Mouilletu. In that case, come with me. [*He and* PHOTOGRA-
PHER *go up left, pushing past the guests in aisle. Reaching
doorway, they meet another* PHOTOGRAPHER.

Second Photographer. Hullo! You here?

First Photographer. Aha! The competition!

Second Photographer. Who are you working for now?

First Photographer. Le Matin.

Second Photographer. I'm working for *Le Journal*.

First Photographer. You've got my old job.

Second Photographer. You've got mine! [*They chat together on steps.* MOUILLETU *crosses back, endeavoring to
clear the aisle.*]

Valéry. Tell me, young man?

Mouilletu. M'sieur?

Valéry. It starts at three o'clock?

Mouilletu. Oui, m'sieur.

Mayor [*putting head out door*]. Mouilletu!

Mouilletu. Coming, m'sieur! [*The* MAYOR *withdraws to office and* MOUILLETU *exits after him. closing door.*]

Mouchemolle [*looking at watch*]. It's three minutes to three right now.

Valéry. It shouldn't take long!

Gismonda. When we were passing their house, we saw the carriages lined up.

Valéry. They'll be here soon

A small brass band is heard from corridor playing the March from The Prophet.

Gaby. The music! They're coming!

Gismonda [*it strikes her funny*]. The bride and groom!—can you imagine?

All. The bride and groom are coming. Here they are. Make way.

MOUILLETU *hastens from* MAYOR's *office and runs up aisle.*

Mouilletu. Stand back, messieurs, 'dames. The bridal party is arriving. Stand back. Thank you very much.

The PHOTOGRAPHERS *come down steps and take positions either side of entrance.* MOUILLETU *hurries out to greet the procession.*

All. Here they come! The cortege! Make room! Stand back!

Gaby. Let's see them. Come on! [*She and her friends dash up steps and block the entire entrance. In the room, others of crowd stand on the benches, craning their necks.*]

Mouilletu [*returning from corridor and pushing crowd to one side*]. Make room, messieurs, 'dames! Make way for the bride and groom!

GABY, GISMONDA *and* PAQUERETTE *climb up on back bench. The two men stand in front of them and girls lean on them for support. Bridal party enters, led by* AMÉLIE *in bridal gown. She is on her father's arm.* POCHET *wears a frock coat and around his neck on a scarlet ribbon is the medal of Palestria. After them,* MARCEL, *escorting* VIRGINIE POCHET, *sister of* POCHET. *Behind them,* ADONIS, *smoking a cigar, and on his arm, a* LITTLE GIRL, *about six years old, dressed in white. After them, the four guests of honor:* ÉTIENNE, PUTZEBOUM, KOSHNADIEV, *and* BIBICHON. *Then* VALCREUSE, YVONNE, BOAS *and* PALMYRE.

Mouilletu [*on top step*]. This way, if you please. Thank you very much.

All. Isn't she lovely? . . . What a pretty dress!

The procession, led by MOUILLETU, *comes down left.* PHOTOGRAPHERS *explode flashlight apparatus. When* AMÉLIE *passes the bench where* GABY, PAQUERETTE *and others are standing, each has a compliment for her: "Oh! Charming! So sweet! . . . What a darling dress!" etc.* AMÉLIE *answers:* "Merci . . . Merci bien . . ."

Mouilletu [*crossing down right center*]. Step this way, messieurs, 'dames.

Amélie [*with* POCHET]. Are you crying, Papa?

Pochet [*choked*]. How can I help it? I cannot hide my emotion. I see my daughter in her bridal veil carrying a bouquet. I'm going to lose my little girl!

Amélie. Papa, you're not losing me. You know it's all a trick.

Pochet. I feel the emotion just the same. [*Blows nose.*] Marriage is a sacred institution!

Mouilletu [*seeing others have not followed*]. Messieurs, 'dames! This way, if you please! [*They cross down right, up past* MAYOR'S *desk to aisle.*]

Virginie [*to* MARCEL, *as they cross*]. It all depends. Now, at my house, I give a manicure for eight francs. But for my friends, I only charge half price.

Marcel. Amazing!

Adonis [*hauling* LITTLE GIRL, *who drags behind*]. Quit dragging your anchor. Come on!

Little Girl. I don't want to.

Adonis. What a great idea to pick the janitor's brat for maid of honor! Everybody's giving me the horse laugh!

Guests arrive right. Seats are pointed out to them by MOUILLETU.

Mouilletu. The bride, here. The groom, there.

Putzeboum [*to* ÉTIENNE]. Ach, I hope the young folks was going to be happy!

Étienne. This is the biggest day they'll ever have.

Mouilletu. The father, here. The mother, here.

Pochet. The mother? She has no mother.

Virginie. I am the aunt.

Mouilletu. Well then, Madame sits here!

Koshnadiev [*to* BIBICHON]. The Prince commanded me to

represent him at the wedding. I am here to lend a note of dignity.

Bibichon. I am here to lend a note of mediocrity!

Mouilletu. Guests of honor, kindly be seated here. Thank you very much. [*They take places.*] Guests of the bride, here . . . Guests of the groom, there . . . [ADONIS *and* LITTLE GIRL *have taken seats in second row.*]

Putzeboum. You children go out of there, please! Out! Out!

Yvonne [*to* BOAS, *seated with her in third row*]. Doesn't this suggest to you that maybe *we* should get married?

Boas. You starting that again?

Yvonne. Think it over. Someday you might lose me.

Boas. I'll keep on thinking.

Palmyre. Any time I wanted to get married, I could, couldn't I, chéri?

Valcreuse. Maybe so, but not to me.

Palmyre. You promised me only the other night——

Valcreuse. People say things at night they regret the next day.

Mouilletu. Monsieur le garçon, mademoiselle?

Adonis. Come on, that's us.

Little Girl. You're supposed to look after me all day!

Adonis. What time do I give you your bottle?

Mouilletu [*ushers them to seats in third row, downstage side*]. This way——

Little Girl. You won't give me no bottle!

Adonis. I'll give you something to shut you up! [*Showing the flat of his hand.*] I'll give you this across the mouth!

Little Girl. Oh!

Adonis. Don't say I didn't warn you!

Mouilletu [*to other guests*]. Take your places, if you please. The Mayor will be with you in a moment. [*Goes on platform and exits to office. Muted conversation from guests.*]

Marcel [*to* ÉTIENNE]. Well, how about it?

Étienne. About what?

Marcel [*with a wink*]. Your friend, Toto Bejard, he's still the Mayor, huh?

Étienne [*winking back*]. Toto Bejard. He's our boy!

Marcel. Hear that, Amélie?

Amélie. What?

Marcel. Toto Bejard—he's going to be the Mayor.

Amélie. I know.

Pochet. What was he saying?

Amélie. Toto Bejard, he's going to be the Mayor . . .

Pochet. Ah, yes! [*Turning to* VIRGINIE.] His friend, Toto Bejard, he's the Mayor.

Virginie. I don't care what his name is.

Putzeboum [*to* ÉTIENNE]. What was the name from the Bourgemeister? Toto Bejard?

Étienne. Forget it. It doesn't matter.

A burst of laughter from YVONNE, PALMYRE, BOAS *and* VAL-CREUSE.

Yvonne [*laughing*]. You idiot!

Boas. Get the idea? Pretty good, huh?

Amélie [*leaning toward them*]. What is it? Tell us.

Boas [*laughing*]. Nothing, nothing!

Palmyre. Boas again . . . with one of his naughty stories.

Amélie. Well, what? Tell us.

Pochet [*rising*]. Who told the story? Where do you think you are? Have a little respect for the occasion! Who told it?

Amélie. Boas did.

Pochet. Oh? [*Pointing a finger at* BOAS.] Remember. Tell it to me later. [*He seats himself.*]

Adonis [*to* LITTLE GIRL, *who is whispering in his ear*]. Huh? What are you talking about? [LITTLE GIRL *whispers again.*] What? . . . Not now! Just when things are getting started.

Amélie [*turning around*]. What's the matter?

Adonis. Nothing.

Amélie. I want to know.

Adonis. It's the brat here . . . [*Whispers in* AMÉLIE's *ear.*]

Amélie. Well, then, *take* her there.

Adonis. Now? In front of everybody? No, thanks!

Pochet. What is it? What's the trouble?

Amélie. It's the little girl, Papa. She . . . [*Whispers in his ear.*]

Pochet. Why not? It's only human.

Adonis. Oh, yes! Now we're going to tell everybody. Oh, fine!

Amélie [*going to* MOUILLETU, *who is in middle of platform*]. I wonder if you could tell me . . .

Mouilletu [*leans forward as she murmurs in his ear*]. Mademoiselle? . . . Certainly, mademoiselle.

Adonis. Let Adonis do it! He doesn't mind! He'll enjoy the trip!

Mouilletu. No trouble. Nothing could be more simple. Is it for the young gentleman?

Adonis [*mimicking*]. "*No!* It's not for the young gentleman!"—Old fishface! [*Grumbles under breath.*] It's a plot to humiliate me. They had the whole thing planned.

Mouilletu. It is for the young lady? [*Coming down from platform.*] Come this way, petite mam'zelle. [*Takes* LITTLE GIRL's *arm and guides her up aisle.*]

Little Girl [*notices* ADONIS *hasn't budged*]. Adonis! [*Runs back and grabs him.*] Adonis!

Adonis. Beat it, will you? [*Yanks hand away.*] What am I *doing* here anyway? [*Cringes as* LITTLE GIRL *begins jumping up and down.*]

Amélie. Go with her.

Adonis. Me?

Pochet. A gentleman never deserts a lady in distress.

Adonis. Now, stop . . . I mean, have a heart——

Amélie. It won't hurt you. Poor little thing, she's frightened. You can't let her go alone.

Adonis [*furiously*]. Why don't *you* take her? It's your wedding! If anybody asks, I'll tell them where to find you. [LITTLE GIRL *is dragging him up the aisle. All spectators are giving full attention.*] How do you think *I* feel?

Mouilletu [*clearing path*]. Make way! Make way for the demoiselle of honor!

Marcel [*waving good-by*]. Hurry back, little sunshine!

Adonis. Oh, go to blazes!

Mouilletu. Step this way, if you please.

Adonis. You should have taken precautions before you left home!

Mouilletu [*twirling his finger*]. First corridor to the left, second to the right . . .

Adonis. We'll find it. We can read the signs. [*Giving* LITTLE GIRL *a push.*] Go on, if you're in such a hurry! [*They go out.*]

PUTZEBOUM *has risen, mystified. He turns to* ÉTIENNE, *who has risen to stretch legs.*

Putzeboum. Where was they going, the little ones?

Étienne. They'll be back.

Putzeboum. What a day! So far it was perfect. Just like weddings in Paris ought to be.

Marcel [*looking at watch*]. He's keeping us waiting, this Toto Bejard.

Amélie. I wish he'd get it over with. I feel sorry for the Prince. I made a date with him this afternoon . . .

Marcel. You did? Where?

Amélie. At my apartment. Étienne is host at the reception. So it's my first chance to see the Prince alone.

Marcel. You mean you've kept him waiting all this time?

Amélie. What could I do with Étienne around the house? It makes it difficult.

Marcel. While Étienne's at the reception, you'll be seeing the Prince. Ha, that's a good one.

Mouilletu [*on platform*]. Silence, messieurs, 'dames. Thank you very much. [*Takes seat at downstage table.* MAYOR *enters and seats himself behind desk.*] May we have it quiet, please? Thank you very much.

The MAYOR *nods affably to the wedding guests.* CORNETTE, *who has followed him, goes to upstage table. The* MAYOR *is imposing, portly, and majestic in manner. He wears a frock-coat and the sash and ribbons of his office. On his forehead is a large growth or protuberance. He indicates for all to be seated. The group sits, with the exception of* POCHET, *who stands with back to the* MAYOR, *gazing toward up left entrance.*

Mayor [*hand extended toward* POCHET, *indicating he sit down*]. Monsieur!

Amélie [*to* POCHET, *indicating* MAYOR]. Papa!

Pochet. Oh, excuse me! [*Thinking the* MAYOR *wants to shake hands.*] Enchanted.

Mayor [*snatching hand away*]. I want you to sit down.

Pochet [*seating himself*]. I beg your pardon.

The MAYOR *sits down and leans over to consult with* CORNETTE.

Marcel [*to* ÉTIENNE]. That's him? Your friend, Toto Bejard?

Étienne [*winks*]. That's him. That's Toto Bejard!

MARCEL *stands and goes up close to look at* MAYOR.

Mayor [*turning*]. What do you want?

Marcel [*chuckles*]. Nothing, nothing! [*To* ÉTIENNE, *as he sits.*] The make-up is marvelous! He won't make any slip-ups?

Étienne. Don't worry. He'll do the job right.

Mayor [*rising, to* MARCEL]. And now, if you please . . . [*Seeing that* MARCEL *is not listening.*] Monsieur, the groom.

Amélie [*giving* MARCEL *a jab with her elbow*]. Marcel!

Marcel. Huh! *me?*

Mayor [amiably]. You, of course. Only one groom, isn't there?—Your full name, if you please.

Marcel [to ÉTIENNE, *as he rises].* This guy's terrific!

Étienne. Didn't I tell you?

Marcel [holding brim of his hat up to mouth to conceal smile]. Joseph-Marcel Courbois. *[Splutters with laughter.]*

Mayor [disturbed]. What are you laughing at?

Marcel [chuckles]. Go right ahead. You're doing fine.

Mayor [stares at him blankly, then turns to AMÉLIE*].* And you, mademoiselle?

AMÉLIE *rises to answer.* POCHET *with a gesture waves her back to chair and he advances to* MAYOR'S *desk.*

Pochet. Amélie-Clémentine Pochet!

Mayor. No, not you! I was asking mademoiselle.

Pochet [going back]. Beg your pardon.

Amélie [rising]. Amélie-Clémentine Pochet. *[Sits down.]*

Pochet [returning]. Isn't that just what I said?

Mayor [beginning to be alarmed]. Well, yes, it is.

Pochet. You understand, of course, that I *gave* her those names. She's *my* daughter. I knew the names before she did.

Mayor [glances toward heaven and takes deep breath]. Thank you very much, monsieur!

Pochet. That's all right, your lordship. Please continue. *[Resumes seat.]*

Putzeboum [to ÉTIENNE*].* Why "Pochet"? I thought the name was "D'Avranches"?

Étienne. Oh, yes. It's . . . it's an honorary title bestowed by the Pope. That's why it can't be mentioned in a civil ceremony.

Putzeboum [impressed]. Ah? Oh!

Mayor. You will now hear the marriage contract read. Cornette, if you please. *[Seats himself, elbow on table, hand shading his eyes.]*

Marcel. What a performance! You'd think he'd been doing it all his life.

Cornette [begins to drone text of marriage contract]. In the year nineteen hundred and eight, on this fifth day of July, at three o'clock post meridian, appearing before us, Mayor of the Eighteenth District in the city of Paris, to be united in marriage, the party of the first part, M. Marcel Courbois, bachelor, residing at 27 Rue Cambon . . . *[Lowers* *voice gradually to monotone, giving impression of speaking full voice, but not distracting from ensuing dialogue.*] . . . age twenty-eight years, unmarried . . .*

Amélie [*in a low voice, to* MARCEL]. Did you notice, Marcel . . . that lump on his forehead?

Marcel. What lump?

Amélie [*tapping forehead*]. That lump on the Mayor's brow.

Marcel. Ah, yes. I should say.

Amélie [*to* POCHET]. You saw the bump, Papa?

Pochet. Huh?

Amélie. That bump on the Mayor.

Pochet. Oh, I know. Enormous!

Amélie. Big as a pigeon's egg.

Marcel [*to* ÉTIENNE]. You didn't tell me Toto Bejard had a lump like that!

Étienne. That's a fake. It's part of his make-up.

Marcel. No? [*To* AMÉLIE.] Hear that, Amélie! That bump—it's phony.

Amélie. Oh, no!

Marcel. So help me!

Amélie [*to* POCHET]. Oh, Papa, that lump on his forehead! it's part of the make-up.

Pochet. It *is?* [*Getting up.*] That's a *good* one! [*Takes spectacles, fixes them on nose, and goes to have a closer look.*]

Mayor [*looking up suddenly*]. What is it you want?

Pochet [*recoiling*]. Nothing, nothing! [*Makes a nudging gesture and winks broadly. Then goes and sits down. The* MAYOR *shrugs and resumes former position.*]

Pochet [*to* AMÉLIE]. You'd swear it was the real thing!

Virginie. What's the real thing?

Pochet. The lump on the Mayor. They say it's a false one.

Virginie. No? [*To her neighbors.*] The lump on the Mayor's head—it's a false one!

Koshnadiev [*indifferently*]. Ah?

Palmyre [*leaning forward*]. What is it that's false?

Pochet. That lump on his forehead, it's just stuck on.

Palmyre [*and her entire row*]. No! It can't be! Impossible!

Yvonne [*passing the news to the third row*]. That bump on the Mayor—it's a fake!

* Full text of marriage contract is given at end of scene.

The Third Row. No?!
The Second Row. Yes!
The Fourth Row. What is it? What's the matter?
The Third Row. That bump on the Mayor—it's false!
Man in the Fourth Row. You mean the bump on his fore-
head? Aha!

*The news is whispered: "That lump on his forehead is false
. . . it's a fake bump . . . it's a phony!" Everyone wants
a better look. They crane their necks. Front row—with the
exception of* PUTZEBOUM, *who is dozing—gets up and advances toward* MAYOR's *desk. Second row has risen and is
leaning forward. Several in other rows climb on benches.*
MAYOR *suddenly looks up and finds himself surrounded. He
begins to rise, very slowly, out of his chair. As he does so,
the crowd starts shrinking back in opposite direction. By
the time the* MAYOR *has attained full height, they are back
in their places looking innocent.*

Mayor [*in loud voice*]. What is it? What's going on here?

Everyone is seated, except KOSHNADIEV *who remains standing, looking* MAYOR *in the eye.*

Mayor. What's the matter?
Koshnadiev [*who has understood nothing*]. It appears that
it is false.
Mayor. What is?
Koshnadiev. I don't know! [*He sits down.*]
Mayor [*to* MOUILLETU]. What a wedding! My God, what
a wedding!
Cornette [*raising voice as he reaches end of contract*].
. . . have therefore publicly pronounced that M. Joseph-
Marcel Courbois and Mademoiselle Amélie-Clémentine Pochet
are united in marriage.
Koshnadiev. Bravo!
Mayor. Quiet! [*To* POCHET.] Rise, please. [MARCEL,
AMÉLIE, POCHET *stand up. To the couple.*] Be seated! [*All
three sit down. To* POCHET.] No! Rise, please! [*All three
rise. To* MARCEL *and* AMÉLIE.] Be seated! [*All three sit
down. To* POCHET.] Will you please stand up! [*All three
stand up.*]
Marcel. I wish he'd make up his mind. [*To* MAYOR.] Do
you want us to stand up or sit down?
Mayor [*to* MARCEL]. I am speaking to M. Pochet. Sit
down!

All Three [*sitting down*]. Ah, good!

Mayor [*to* POCHET]. Well? Why are you sitting down?

Pochet. Pardon me, but you just said, "I am talking to M. Pochet. Sit down!"

Mayor. I meant, "I am speaking to M. Pochet. You, the bridal couple, sit down. And you, M. Pochet, remain standing."

Pochet. Ah! Good!

Mayor. Well then, stand up! [POCHET *stands up.*]

Marcel [*to* AMÉLIE]. Why couldn't he say so in the first place?

Mayor [*to* POCHET]. Monsieur Amédée Pochet——

Pochet. That's me.

Mayor [*with a sigh*]. Yes, I know. Do you consent to give in marriage your daughter, Amélie-Clémentine Pochet?

Pochet. From the bottom of my heart!

Mayor. You needn't say that.

Pochet. I always say what I think.

Mayor. That's very possible, but I am not interested in your personal reactions. Say "Yes or no."

Pochet. Absolutely.

Mayor. No, not "absolutely." Would you be willing to answer yes or no?

Pochet. Certainly. After all, that's what we've come for.

Mayor [*exhausted*]. All right. That will do. I will now read aloud to you . . .

ADONIS *and* LITTLE GIRL *make their reappearance in archway and start down aisle. They are greeted by "Ohs" and "Ahs" from the crowd, nodding and smiling approval.*

Amélie [*to* ADONIS]. Did she find it all right?

Adonis [*as he and* LITTLE GIRL *resume places*]. Yes. Just in time, too. I don't know why *I* have to take her out!

Mayor [*trying to make himself heard*]. With your permission, I'd like to read . . .

Pochet. That Adonis! If she were ten years older, he'd be *glad* to take her out.

Mayor. I would like to read . . .

Bibichon [*coming forward*]. If she were five years older, *I'd* take her out!

Koshnadiev [*laughing*]. Ha! ha! ha!

Mayor [*banging his fist on desk*]. When you have finished with your conversation!

Bibichon [*hastening back to seat*]. Oh!

Pochet [*rising and addressing guests*]. Come, friends! Show a little respect! Remember where you are!

Mayor [*brusquely*]. I'd like you to bear in mind . . .

Pochet [*to the guests*]. Now, bear this in mind, every-body——

Mayor. Will you please be quiet?

Pochet [*emphasizing each syllable*]. Re-mem-ber that! Quiet! [*To the* MAYOR.] That ought to hold them!

Mayor. *You* be quiet!

Pochet [*sitting*]. Oh, certainly.

Marcel. He's a natural, this Toto Bejard. What a character!

Mayor. I am going to read you articles from the civil code pertaining to the rights and duties of husband and wife.

Pochet [*half-rising and turning to crowd*]. Now listen to this, all of you.

Mayor [*quietly*]. Silence!

Pochet [*who was already sitting down again, rises and holds up hand*]. Silence!

Mayor [*loudly, to* POCHET]. *Silence!*

Pochet [*to* MAYOR]. Just what I told them. [*To crowd.*] Silence!

Mayor [*pointing his finger at* POCHET]. *You!*

Pochet. Ah? Me! [*To himself, putting finger to lips as he sits down.*] Silence!

Putzeboum [*muttering*]. That poppa was a dummkopf!

Mayor [*reading from code*]. Article 212: The husband and wife are united in law for their natural lifetime and must discharge to each other and the community the duties legally imposed.—Article 213: The husband must provide a home, support the wife and children, and protect them and her from injury and insult.—Article 214: The wife is obliged to live with her husband, to aid in the maintenance of the family by such reasonable labor as the domestic requirements and financial position demand.—Article 226 . . . [*As* MAYOR *begins to read Article 213,* MOUILLETU *tiptoes to where* LITTLE GIRL *is seated and hands her collection plate.*]

Mouilletu. Young lady, I wonder if you would kindly oblige?

Adonis. Oh, no! They're not going to let her take up the collection!

Beckoned by MOUILLETU, ADONIS *and* LITTLE GIRL *start up aisle with plate.*

Mouilletu [*following and chanting refrain*]. A small con-

GLENDALE COLLEGE LIBRARY

tribution for the poor of the district! Thank you very much! . . . A small contribution for the poor! Thank you very much! . . .

At moment MAYOR *pronounces: "Article 226 . . ." LITTLE GIRL trips over PUTZEBOUM's foot and falls to floor, scattering money.*

Adonis. I knew this would happen.

All. What is it? What's the trouble? Who fell down?

Mayor [*endeavoring to be heard above tumult*]. Article 226: The wife is not permitted under law to sign binding documents without the authorization of her husband . . .

Simultaneously, the following dialogue.

Adonis. It's the brat here. She took a header, that's all.

Yvonne. Oh, the poor little thing!

Amélie [*who has risen*]. Adonis, what have you done to her? I hope you didn't push her.

Yvonne. You didn't hurt yourself?

Little Girl [*back on her feet*]. No, no. I'm all right.

Mayor [*rapping several times on desk*]. Messieurs, 'dames! I must insist . . . I won't allow . . .

Adonis. Naturally she fell down! She didn't look where she was going. [*Cuffing the* LITTLE GIRL.] Why don't you look where you're going? [LITTLE GIRL *begins to cry. During above, various guests have scurried about retrieving the money, which* MOUILLETU *gathers into plate.*]

Mayor [*furiously*]. I won't put up with this! You, boy, what have you done?

Adonis [*hauling* LITTLE GIRL *back to seat*]. It wasn't me. It was this kid here. She fell down with the collection plate.

Mayor [*severely*]. That is no reason to interrupt the ceremony!

Adonis [*to* LITTLE GIRL]. There! See what you've done. You interrupted the ceremony!

Little Girl. Let go of me!

IRÈNE appears in entrance.

Irène [*addressing photographer*]. Is this where the weddings take place?

Photographer. Yes, madame, it is.

Mayor. Are we ready to proceed? The bride and groom will rise. [MARCEL *and* AMÉLIE *stand facing the* MAYOR.]

Mayor. Monsieur Marcel Courbois!

Marcel. I am here, your honor.

Amélie [glances about and sees IRÈNE]. Ah! Your friend is here.

Mayor. Do you take this woman . . .

Amélie. Look, Marcel! Irène is here!

Mayor. Mademoiselle Amélie-Clémentine . . .

Marcel [turning around]. Who? Irène?

Mayor. . . . Pochet?

Marcel [clasping his hands with joy]. No!

All [as MARCEL *and* AMÉLIE *wave to* IRÈNE]. What? What did he say? What was that?

Mayor [grimly]. What do you mean, *"no"?*

Marcel [startled, turning to MAYOR]. What? Oh! Well naturally . . . as long as she's here . . .

Mayor. "As long as she's here"! Do you consent to marry her or do you not?

Marcel. Oh, yes! *Yes,* of course! *[Turns again, fluttering fingers at* IRÈNE.]

Mayor. Mademoiselle Amélie-Clémentine Pochet!

Amélie [not hearing MAYOR]. She came to your wedding. That means she still loves you. *[Smiles and nods to* IRÈNE.]

Mayor [seeing he is ignored]. Mademoiselle Amélie! Amélie-Clémentine! Mademoiselle Pochet!

Pochet [tapping her shoulder]. Amélie!

Amélie [startled]. Right here!

Mayor [to MOUILLETU]. What is the *matter* with all these people?

Pochet. Pay attention to what you're doing!

Amélie. It's only because Madame is here . . . Comtesse de Premilly!

Pochet. Ah? Madame la comtesse! So it is! *[Turns and makes repeated bows to* IRÈNE.] Bonjour, madame! Pray be seated! *[*POCHET, AMÉLIE *and* MARCEL *are giving full attention to* IRÈNE, *bowing, waving, and saluting.]*

Mayor. Well, Mademoiselle Pochet, perhaps you'd prefer to come back tomorrow?

Amélie. Ah, no, your honor! *[Indicating* IRÈNE.] Only Madame la comtesse is here, and——

Mayor [cutting her off sharply]. Never mind! *[Reverting to his affable tone.]* Mademoiselle Amélie-Clémentine . . . do you take this man, Monsieur Marcel Courbois, to be your lawful wedded husband?

During this, IRÈNE *takes seat in rear row.*

Amélie [*shrugs*]. That goes without saying.

Mayor. That's not a proper answer.

Amélie. Sorry, monsieur. I mean, yes.

Mayor [*quickly*]. Therefore, I, by virtue of the authority vested in me, hereby declare you man and wife. [*Mops his brow.*]

Koshnadiev [*loudly*]. Bravo!

All [*following his example and applauding*]. Bravo!

Mayor [*pounding desk energetically*]. Messieurs! Please! This is not a vaudeville theatre.

Étienne [*rising*]. Not much it isn't! [MARCEL *and* AMÉLIE *have embraced.* MARCEL *turns round and begins blowing kisses to* IRÈNE.]

Marcel [*to* ÉTIENNE]. He's a *genius*, this Toto Bejard.

Étienne. A great comedian.

Marcel. Great! [*Turns to* IRÈNE *and agitates his hat in air.*] What a clown, huh? [*Points to* MAYOR *with his thumb.* IRÈNE *smiles and nods.*]

Mouilletu. Messieurs, 'dames, if you would care to come forward to witness the documents? Thank you very much.

First Row rises and goes upstage to sign register on CORNETTE's *table.* POCHET *and* AMÉLIE *go downstage to sign at table of* MOUILLETU. ADONIS *goes to occupy seat vacated by* PUTZE-BOUM. LITTLE GIRL *goes and sits on lap of* PALMYRE.

Mayor [*indicating* AMÉLIE]. If you would care to sign there . . . Thank you, madame! [*While* AMÉLIE *signs at downstage desk,* MARCEL *has finished signing upstage. He crosses* AMÉLIE *en route downstage.* POCHET *signs downstage register and hands pen to* MARCEL. *He then goes up to sign* CORNETTE's *book.* MAYOR *leans toward* MARCEL, *baring his teeth.*] I can't say I admire the behavior of your acquaintances, M. Courbois!

Marcel [*as he signs*]. You'll have to forgive them. They can't keep a straight face the way you do.

Mayor. What say?

Marcel. Oh, Toto! You ought to be on the stage! You're a great comic. [*He turns away, leaving the* MAYOR *dumbstruck.* PUTZEBOUM, *en route to downstage table, passes the* MAYOR.]

Mayor. Toto? He called me Toto! Who is Toto?

Putzeboum. I have never heard of him!

MARCEL *hurries back to warn* MAYOR

Marcel [*finger to lips*]. Sssh! That's my godfather! Ssssh!

Mayor [*taking offense*]. I don't understand what you're saying.

Marcel [*nervously*]. Not so loud. He might hear you!

Mayor [*insistently*]. What's this about your godfather?

Putzeboum [*looking up*]. You was speaking to me?

Marcel [*seizing* PUTZEBOUM *and whirling him around*]. It's nothing, godfather! Come on——

Mayor [*mumbling*]. They belong in a madhouse, the whole lot of them!

Marcel [*to* ÉTIENNE]. Your pal, Bejard! He certainly plays it straight!

Étienne. He's famous for it.

Marcel [*fretfully*]. He nearly gave us away just now.

Mouilletu. Would the bride and groom step forward, please, to receive the compliments of the Mayor? Thank you very much. [*Closes his book and crosses up left. Wedding guests return to seats.* MARCEL *and* AMÉLIE *once more stand facing* MAYOR.]

Mayor. Monsieur and Madame Courbois . . .

Marcel [*urgently, leaning toward him*]. Don't overdo it now.

Mayor [*shocked*]. What?

Marcel [*in an irritated whisper*]. I said, don't overdo it.

Mayor [*considers this for a moment, then decides to proceed*]. Monsieur and Madame Courbois! It may be that I have detected in you and your companions . . .

All. What's that? What does he say? What?

Mayor. . . . a lack of respect which should attend an occasion of this kind.

All. Oh! Did you hear that? Ah!

Mayor. I will not, however, refrain from following my usual custom. I intend to spare you, Monsieur and Madame Courbois, the tedium of listening to a long speech——

Koshnadiev. Bravo!

Mayor [*shooting him a glance*]. I offer you my felicitations and I trust you will be very happy.

All. Bravo!

Amélie. Thank you, your lordship.

Marcel. I want to thank you too. [*Leaning forward.*] While you're at it, say a few words in tribute to my godfather. He's the one that's getting swindled! Ha, ha——

Mayor. Yes, yes, I'd be glad to . . . [*A pause.*] Swindled?

Marcel [*jocosely, whacking him on stomach with his hat*].
Go ahead! You know what to say!

Mayor. How dare you! [MARCEL *returns to seat, laughing.*
AMÉLIE *grabs* MAYOR's *hand and pumps it enthusiastically.*]

Amélie. Toto, I love you! [*She glances about to make sure
no one is behind.*] And you know what nearly finished me?
That thing! [*She points, almost touching the lump on his
forehead. She makes a couple of twisting gestures as though
she were going to tweak it, then staggers back to seat, chor-
tling with laughter.*]

Mayor [*purple and apoplectic*]. Messieurs, mesdames . . .
[*Words fail him.*] Bonsoir! [*Followed by* CORNETTE, *he
stomps off to his office. A smattering of applause from crowd.*]

Mouilletu [*in doorway up left*]. The ceremony is concluded. The procession will kindly pass this way, thank you
very much. [*He signals to offstage musicians, who play*
Mendelssohn's *march rapidly.*]

Marcel [*marshaling his forces*]. Line up now, everyone.
Amélie, be careful of your train.

Amélie. Papa, don't tread on my skirt.

Pochet. Have no fear, I shall keep my distance.

Members of immediate family embrace the bride and groom.
ADONIS *and* LITTLE GIRL *bring up the rear.*

Amélie. You take care of her, Adonis. And if she wants to
go anywhere . . .

Adonis. If she does, she can shift for herself. It's my turn
now.

The procession goes up the aisle. As AMÉLIE *and* MARCEL
reach upper step, MOUILLETU *places them in position to
shake hands with the passers-by.*

All [*moving slowly past, kissing and hugging the bride and
groom*]. Bless you, children! . . . Darling, you looked marvelous! Your dress is a dream! . . . I know you'll be very
happy! [*Other responses are left to the discretion of the
artists. It is important, however, that the crowd does not
exit to corridor too quickly.* POCHET *is down left of archway, bidding guests to attend the reception.*]

Pochet. You're coming to the luncheon? No? Chez Gilet.
You'd enjoy it . . . Do come to luncheon. Not far. Around
the corner . . . Chez Gilet. Come if you can!

Wedding guests filter out left. ÉTIENNE *has watched departure with interest. Hands in his pockets, he strolls and stands near right proscenium.*

Irène [*at the end of line of guests*]. Bonjour, Marcel.

Marcel. So there you are, sweetheart?

Irène. Yes, darling. I enjoyed your wedding.

Amélie. Bonjour, Madame.—Papa, you see who's here?

Pochet. Madame la comtesse, we are honored! You will come to the luncheon?

Irène. No, Pochet! Really I couldn't!

Pochet. We are serving strictly buffet. Right around the corner at Chez Gilet. Surely you will come for a glass of wine and some cake?

Irène. I am desolated, my dear Pochet. But I shan't be free!

Marcel [*an arm about* AMÉLIE]. You saw us united in marriage, didn't you, Irène?

Irène. I did. I laughed and laughed.

Marcel. Comical, wasn't it?

Irène. It was so *funny!* [*All totter about, laughing and embracing.* ÉTIENNE *is equally amused.*]

Irène. But your godfather! Did he swallow the bait?

Marcel. He certainly did! Hook and line!

Irène. Nothing went wrong?

Marcel. Not a thing. It was very convincing. I've never seen a trick that was better planned. [*Sardonic laugh from* ÉTIENNE.] Look at Étienne! He's still laughing!

Irène. He deserves a lot of credit.

Marcel. It was his inspiration.

Irène. And now you are rich!

Marcel. In more ways than one. [*Starts to embrace her.*]

Irène. Marcel!—Not in public!

Marcel. It's a wedding. Everybody can kiss anybody!

Irène. I forgot! [MARCEL *kisses her passionately.*]

Amélie [*seeing* PUTZEBOUM *returning from hall, gives* MARCEL *a hindward kick.*] Here comes Putzi!

Irène. I'll wait for you outside, chéri. We'll go straight home together. [*She exits, passing* PUTZEBOUM *in doorway. Dazzled, he backs down the steps, watching her off.*]

Putzeboum. My, that was a humdinger! Who was that, Sonny?

Marcel. Er—just an old playmate from my school days.

Pochet. He and Irène have done lots of homework together.

Putzeboum. I bet she was head of the class. Well, now the crowd is out, I come to wish my compliments.

Pochet. You will be at the luncheon, I suppose?

Putzeboum. Why don't we all go together, ja?

Marcel. Oh, no! I'm afraid that Amélie and I may not stay long.

Putzeboum [*waggishly*]. Ach, you shouldn't have to mention it. Couldn't get home fast enough, didn't I know! But first I take a smack from Amykins.

Amélie. Darling old Putzi! [*Kisses him.*]

Mouilletu [*coming from* MAYOR'S *desk with paper*]. Here is your marriage certificate.

Marcel [*looking worried*]. My marriage certif—— [*With a grin.*] He's really got this organized! [*Brandishes certificate at* ÉTIENNE.]

Mouilletu. May I offer my congratulations?

Marcel [*giving him a coin*]. We're very grateful.

Mouilletu. Thank you very much. [*He pussyfoots back to right, fussing around desk.*]

Marcel [*calling to* ÉTIENNE]. You're a devil. You really thought of everything.

Étienne [*calls back*]. Everything!

Putzeboum. How was that? Everything what?

Marcel. Er—*everything's* just dandy! Never spent a happier day! [*Crosses past* PUTZEBOUM *to left.*]

Koshnadiev [*reappears carrying* AMÉLIE'S *cloak*]. If Madame is ready?

Amélie. Yes, of course. [*As she passes* MARCEL; *lowering voice.*] I'm off now. His Highness is waiting.

Marcel. Run along then.

Amélie [*with a curtsey*]. I have my husband's permission?

Marcel. Don't hesitate on my account.

Amélie. This is an unusual marriage.—Coming, General?

Koshnadiev. At your command. [*He offers his arm and they start to exit.*]

Putzeboum [*trotting after them*]. You was leaving?

Amélie [*waving*]. Yes. Good-by, everyone. [*She and* KOSHNADIEV *exit.*]

Marcel [*delaying* PUTZEBOUM]. She's going on ahead. I'll join her later.

Putzeboum. Ach, good.—You know, Sonny, what I should be doing now maybe? Since you was married, better I should go to my hotel and get the check so you can have your money. Ja?

Marcel [*pushing* PUTZEBOUM *out door*]. Ja, ja! That's a fine idea! Don't waste a minute!

Pochet. Well, if nobody else is going to the luncheon, I'll go myself. You're not coming, Marcel?

Marcel. No, but good appetite!

Pochet. Merci. I might as well celebrate. A man's daughter doesn't get married every day. Au revoir! [*He exits.* ÉTIENNE *strolls to center.* MARCEL *crosses to meet him.*]

Marcel. Ah-hah!

Étienne. Ah-hah!

Marcel. That's it!

Étienne. That's it!

MARCEL *and* ÉTIENNE *laugh uproariously and exchange slaps on the shoulder.*

Marcel. Étienne, I just can't thank you enough.

Étienne. You're happy, are you?

Marcel. Happy! Am I ever happy? It couldn't have gone better.

Étienne. That's what I've been thinking.

Marcel. He fell for it. My godfather swallowed the bait. What a day! What a day! [*Each time he says "What a day!" he thumps* ÉTIENNE *on the back.*]

Étienne [*same business, thumping harder*]. What a day! What a day! [*They laugh again hilariously.*]

Marcel. There couldn't be a better joke—than to make that godfather of mine think this marriage was on the level!

Étienne. I can think of a better one.

Marcel. Oh, no! Oh, no! [*Laughs hysterically.*]

Étienne. Oh, yes! [*Joins in laughter.*] And that would be to make *you* think it *wasn't* on the level!

Marcel. Yes, ha, ha, that would be . . . ha, ha—— [*Stops laughing.*] What's that you say?

Étienne. You don't really think you're still a single man, do you? Because you're not. No, you're *not!*

Marcel. Huh?

Étienne. Thought you could play around with my Amélie while I was gone? Now you've got lots of time to play!

Marcel. You mean you know about—?

Étienne. Oh, yes, I know!

Marcel [*clapping hand to brow*]. Ouch!

Étienne. It might have been embarrassing to be seen in bed with my girl. But you needn't be embarrassed from now on. It's perfectly legal.

Marcel [*leaping for* ÉTIENNE's *throat*]. Why, you traitor!

Étienne [*ducks under* MARCEL's *arm, dashes upstage left, and turns in doorway*]. Bonsoir! Have fun! And keep an eye on Amy! [*He exits.*]

Marcel [*stumbling after him*]. Étienne! Étienne!

Étienne's Voice [*heard from distance*]. Keep an eye on Amy!

Marcel. Étienne! Come back! [*He staggers back down steps like a drunken man.*] Oh, my God! Married! [*Seeing* MAYOR *emerge from office, hat on head and pulling on his gloves.*] Ah! Toto Bejard! [*Lurches toward him.*] Come here! Quick! [*Meets* MAYOR, *clutching him by lapels.*]

Mayor [*flabbergasted*]. Stop! Hands off!

Marcel [*shaking him*]. How much truth is there to this?

Mayor [*breaking free*]. What ails you, anyway?

Marcel. This marriage—was it on the level?

Mayor. On the level? Of course it was.

Marcel. You mean I'm married?

Mayor. What do you think we've just been doing?

Marcel. But I don't want to be married! I want a divorce!

Mayor [*crossing toward left*]. Divorce? That's not my department. Go to Room 210 upstairs.

Marcel [*grabbing his coat tails*]. You *are* Toto Bejard, aren't you?

Mayor [*haughtily*]. Monsieur! I am the Mayor of this district.

Marcel [*feeling ill*]. The Mayor! *ah!* [*Topples forward into* MAYOR's *arms.*]

Mayor. Look out! What is this?

Irène [*arriving in doorway*]. Marcel, are you coming—— What's happened?

Marcel [*haggardly*]. Irène! I'm married to Amélie.

Irène [*running toward him*]. What are you saying?

Mayor [*struggling to be rid of* MARCEL]. Monsieur . . . Stand up, I say!

Marcel. Étienne double-crossed us! I'm married to Amélie d'Avranches!

Irène. You mean you're—— *ah!* [*She swoons, falling over* MAYOR's *other arm.*]

Mayor [*trying to hold them both up*]. Help! Somebody! Cornette! Mouilletu! Help! [*Hearing the* MAYOR's *cries and the screams of the lovers, people have begun to enter from both sides.*]

All. What's the matter? What happened? What's going on?

Marcel [*wailing*]. I'm married to Amélie!

All. What's that? What is it? What does he say?

Marcel. I'm married to Amélie d'Avranches!

Bibichon. You can't be!

Putzeboum [*enters, running*]. What happened to you, Sonny?

Marcel [*staggers free of* MAYOR, *collapsing into arms of* PUTZEBOUM]. Godfather! I am married to Amélie!

Putzeboum [*beaming*]. Ja, I know! Ain't it vunderbar?

Text of marriage contract to be read by CORNETTE, *as indicated in this scene:*

Cornette. In the year nineteen hundred and eight, on this fifth day of July, at three o'clock post meridian, appearing before us, Mayor of the eighteenth district in the city of Paris, to be united in marriage, the party of the first part, Monsieur Marcel Courbois, bachelor, residing at 27 Rue Cambon, eldest son of Pierre-Joseph Courbois, banker, deceased, and his wife, Caroline-Émilienne Toupet, likewise deceased; and the party of the second part, Mademoiselle Amélie-Clémentine Pochet, born at Paris on the twentieth day of March, 1886, living in Paris at 120 Rue de Rivoli, only daughter of Auguste Amédée Pochet, aged fifty-four years, formerly brigadier and officer of the peace, same address, and of the late Marie-Thérèse Laloyau, his wife. The father being here present and giving his consent; after having received before this bench the contracting parties, each in turn, declaring their intention to wed, we have this day publicly pronounced, in the name of the law, that Monsieur Marcel Courbois and Mademoiselle Amélie-Clémentine Pochet are therefore united in marriage.

SCENE 2

AMÉLIE'S *bedroom. Down right, door to salon. Below door, a chair. Up right, set slantwise, an elegant bed. Against foot of bed, a small settee. Up left, at an angle, a window. Left, door to bathroom. Above door, a dressing table and mirror. Other furniture and decor as needed. On settee, a negligee belonging to* AMÉLIE.

At rise, the PRINCE *is pacing impatiently back and forth. He is in shirtsleeves, having removed his coat, vest, and trousers, revealing long woolen underclothing. His trousers are on down right chair. The bed shows signs of disorder, the pillow rumpled, as though he might have been lying down in it. After pacing two or three times the breadth of the scene, he halts suddenly, at center.*

PRINCE. By God the Father! What can be keeping her? I had no idea that it took so long to get married. [*Doorbell rings.*] The bell. It is perhaps she. It must be she. [*Goes to open door and stops astonished to see* KOSHNADIEV *enter alone.*] Well! Where is she?

Koshnadiev [*making the Palestrian salute*]. Your Highness, here comes the bride.

Prince. At last.

Koshnadiev [*holding door*]. Mademoiselle d'Avranches, if you please? [*Bows as she enters on the run.*]

Amélie. Your Highness, I beg your pardon for being so—— [*Stifling a cry.*] Ah!

Prince. What is the trouble?

Amélie. It's the costume Your Highness is wearing. I wasn't prepared for it.

Prince. It is only to save us time. When one is bored, it is necessary to do something. Leave us, Koshnadiev.

Koshnadiev. Yes, Highness. [*Salutes and exits.*]

Amélie. But, Your Highness . . . In my house, surely you don't think it looks right . . . What if someone had come in and seen you?

Prince. But it is all arranged. No one is coming.

Amélie. I know. But one must think of appearances!

Prince. Darling, I have been waiting an eternity for you to come. Take off your dress.

Amélie [*startled*]. So soon?

Prince. On the wedding day, one is in a hurry. [*Reaches out to embrace her.*]

Amélie [*stepping aside*]. Your Highness! First let me remove my bridal veil. [*Goes to dressing table and sits, taking off her headdress.*]

Prince [*stands close behind her*]. If you but knew with what impatience I have been counting the minutes. I tried to sleep while I was waiting. I lay down inside your bed——

Amélie [*with a gasp of surprise*]. Not with your boots on?

Prince [*not the least disturbed*]. Certainly with boots. I couldn't sleep. Love kept waking me up.

Amélie. Look at my hair.

Prince. You are adorable. I would like to see you with hair down your back like golden fleeces. I wish to wander barefoot through your hair.

Amélie [*rising*]. That's an idea! But it's seldom done even in Paris. [*She crosses to foot of bed.*]

Prince [*seeing she is about to unhook her dress*]. Permit me to help you.

Amélie. Thank you, Your Highness.

Prince [*unhooking* AMÉLIE]. This is exciting! It makes *me* seem to be the bridegroom.

Amélie. Well, he gave us his permission.

Prince. I am Louis XV—and you are Madame Pompadour!

Amélie. They were never bride and groom.

Prince [*sucking thumb*]. Oh! I am bleeding!

Amélie. It must have been a pin.

Prince. I am so glad you told me. [*Continues to unhook her.*] And everything went well?

Amélie. How do you mean?

Prince. Your marriage to the landlord?

Amélie [*laughing*]. I've told you, Highness, he isn't my landlord.

Prince. I always think of him that way. Was it a success?

Amélie. The marriage?

Prince. The joke. The little godfather, did he walk into the trap?

Amélie [*holding up arms for* PRINCE *to help her out of sleeves*]. Yes, he walked into the trap.

Prince [*pulling off sleeves*]. I find it funny. This landlord pretending to be married with you. I adore little comedies, so I sent the General to the wedding.

Amélie [*letting gown fall to floor and stepping from it*]. You were very kind. [*She crosses down left.* PRINCE *gathers up dress and puts it on settee.*]

Prince. You found him helpful, the General?

Amélie. Enormously!

Prince. He is decorative. I do not know how he would be in a war . . . but as a pimp he is perfect! [*Sees* AMÉLIE *in her slip, half-turned away with hands crossed modestly over her bosom.*] Ah! Lovely! Like a Madonna! [*Hands behind back, he advances, and leaning forward kisses the back of her neck.*]

Amélie. Oh, Your Highness, you tickle me!

Prince. And you tickle me. Darling! [*Leads her to the bed, pulls her onto his lap, and dances her up and down.*] What do you like?

Amélie. Here we go again. [*Doorbell rings.*] The door!

Prince. Who is it?

Amélie. I don't know. My maid is there. She will send them away.

Prince. Splendid. How I love you! [*He kisses her ardently on the throat.*]

Marcel [*heard off right*]. Amélie!

Prince. Stay out!

Amélie. You can't come in! [*They leap away from one another.*]

Marcel [*entering like a whirlwind*]. Amélie!

Prince. Aha! the bridegroom!

Marcel. Something terrible has happened!

Prince. What has happened?

Marcel. We're married! Legitimately, positively married!

Amélie. What are you saying?

Marcel. Toto Bejard wasn't Toto Bejard. He was really the Mayor!

Amélie. You're joking!

Marcel. Étienne was joking! He knew all along about us— that day at my house.

Amélie. He didn't?

Marcel. He did!

Amélie. Well, I'll be damned!

Marcel. This was his revenge. Now we're married, married for good!

Amélie [*not believing*]. Both of us?

Marcel. Yes, both of us. The ceremony was genuine. The Mayor was genuine. Everything was genuine. I'm your husband and you're my wife.

Amélie [*clutching her throat*]. It can't be! Then *I* am Madame Courbois!

Marcel. Yes!

Amélie [*unexpectedly*]. Ah, chéri! My chérie! My own dear husband! [*Throws herself into* MARCEL'S *arms.*]

Marcel [*stupidly*]. What's this?

Prince [*with a gracious bow*]. Monsieur, my felicitations for a happy marriage.

Marcel. Huh?

Amélie. Your Highness, I want you to meet my husband.

[*Looking at* MARCEL *tenderly.*] My *husband!* May I introduce His Highness, the Prince of Palestria?

Marcel [*agog*]. What?

Prince [*shakes hands cordially*]. Enchanted, monsieur.

Marcel [*passing a hand across his brow*]. I'm going mad. I must be out of my mind.

Amélie [*cosily, to* MARCEL]. You'll see what a tidy little wife you have, faithful, domestic, devoted to your comfort——

Marcel. How do you mean, "my tidy little wife"?

Amélie [*suddenly modest*]. Oh, what you will think of me! Here I am only half-dressed . . . Forgive me! [*Gets negligee from foot of bed.*]

Prince [*to* MARCEL, *as he assists* AMÉLIE *into negligee*]. What you must think of us! Excuse it, monsieur.

Amélie. Thank you! [*Crossing down right.*] And now, Your Highness, you may stay here no longer.

Prince. Beg pardon?

Amélie. I apologize, but my new station in life does not permit me to entertain gentlemen.

Prince [*disbelievingly*]. But no! I have come here to . . . [*Makes a sweeping gesture in direction of bed.*]

Amélie [*going to* MARCEL *for protection*]. Sir! How dare you!

Prince. It does not suit me to go!

Amélie [*utterly respectable*]. I implore you to leave this house. Remember, you are in the presence of my husband!

Marcel [*stupefied*]. What's going on around here?

Prince [*pauses, then bows submissively*]. You're quite correct, madame. Believe me, monsieur, it is not in my nature to do anything that would compromise the honor of a lady. [*Walks with elegance to upstage table for his bowler hat and gloves. He takes them up, hat under one arm, cane under other. As he pulls on his gloves, he returns downstage.*] Madame, it has been a pleasure making your acquaintance.

Amélie [*making deep curtsey*]. Your Royal Highness. [*The* PRINCE *puts on hat and swinging his cane, starts toward door, forgetting that he has no coat or trousers on.*]

Marcel [*hypnotized by the scene he has witnessed, suddenly snaps out of it and runs down right, barring the* PRINCE's *way*]. Oh, no! Do you think for a minute that I intend to put up with this marriage?

Amélie. What can you do? You said it was genuine.

Marcel. I won't stand for it. I want a divorce.

Amélie. A divorce?

Marcel. Right away too.

Amélie [*determinedly*]. Oh, no. I am strongly opposed to divorce. And so is Papa.

Marcel. I don't care. This marriage isn't valid, because I didn't consent——

Amélie. You consented when you answered yes!

Marcel. Because my confidence was abused.

Amélie. You answered yes all the same.

Marcel. It's an outrage!

Prince [*tapping* MARCEL's *shoulder*]. Listen to me, my unfortunate landlord.

Marcel [*whirling about angrily*]. What do you want, Prince? Kindly have the decency to shut up! [*He crosses down left.*]

Prince [*with dignity*]. Take care! I am the Prince of Palestria!

Marcel. Not around here you're not! [*Recrossing down right.*] I'm the boss around here, the husband of Amélie d'Avranches!

Amélie [*encouraged*]. And I am your wife, isn't that so, Marcel?

Marcel [*ignoring her*]. Amélie d'Avranches, who has more lovers than any woman in Paris.

Amélie. Marcel!

Marcel. A woman that I find on the day of her wedding disrobing in her boudoir with the Prince of Palestria!

Prince. Ah, but with honorable intentions!

Marcel [*scornfully*]. This is the hussy to whom I have given my name!

Amélie [*shakes a finger under* MARCEL's *nose*]. That will be enough of that kind of talk, or something will happen that you don't expect!

Marcel. Something will happen, eh?

Amélie [*putting hand on* PRINCE's *shoulder*]. His Highness is here, you know!

Prince [*in no mood for fighting*]. Me?

Marcel [*a gleam in his eye*]. The Prince is here? How appropriate! I may never again have such an opportunity. I'll show you both what's going to happen. I said I wouldn't stand for it. You'll both be sorry before I'm done. [*Rushes upstage to window and flings it open.*]

Prince. He is crazy!

Amélie. What are you doing? Stop! [*She and the* PRINCE *run after* MARCEL, *seizing him.*]

Marcel [*struggling*]. Let go!

Prince. Would you throw yourself out the window?

Marcel. Ah, no! Not *me!*

Prince [*lets go his hold and backs away*]. No, please!

Amélie. Not *me?*

Prince. Not *us?*

Marcel. No, these! [*Runs downstage, snatches up the* PRINCE's *coat, vest, and trousers, dashes to window and flings them out.*]

Prince and *Amélie.* Ah! Oh! Ah! [MARCEL *dashes out door right as* PRINCE *leans out window, looking for his lost garments.*]

Prince. He has thrown my clothes out of the window.

Amélie [*running right*]. Marcel!

Prince [*turns and runs right*]. You! Landlord! [*They find the door closed and locked from outside.*]

Amélie. He has locked us in! [*Crosses down left.*]

Prince [*trying the door*]. He dares to lock up the Prince of Palestria!

Amélie. The beast!

Prince [*hurrying to door left*]. We can go through here.

Amélie. No, that's my bathroom. There's no way out.

Prince. In Palestria, I would have him whipped and sent to the salt mines.

Amélie. Unfortunately we are in Paris. [*Goes to window and looks out.*]

Prince. By God the Father! Imprisoned without trousers!

Amélie [*seeing* MARCEL *below*]. There he is. [*Calling.*] Marcel!

Prince [*joins her at window*]. You see him?

Amélie. He's gone into the police station across the street.

Prince. Police station?

Amélie. The office of the Commissaire.

Prince. So much the better. Let him bring the Commissaire. I will have him arrested. No one is permitted to lock up the Prince of Palestria.

Amélie. Don't forget, Your Highness, he is my husband.

Prince. It is a trap.

Amélie. He wants to prove misconduct, damn him!

Prince. This is horrible. There will be a scandal. And in my high position. [*Harshly.*] Is there no way out?

Amélie. Only the window. You could jump.

Prince. From the third floor? No, thank you.

Amélie. The floor below doesn't count. It's only a mezzanine.

Prince. If you are jumping, it counts.

Amélie. The street's macadamized.

Prince. Is that preferable?

Amélie. I believe so.

Prince. You should go to the window and scream. Make signs to the people passing by. Tell them we need help.

Amélie. Fine. And they'd run right into the police station and tell their story. What good would that do?

Prince. What shall we do then?

Amélie [*raising her arms skyward*]. We must hope for the best.

Prince. What will my great-aunt, the Czarina, have to say?

Voices are heard off right.

Amélie. Listen!

Prince. Who is that?

Amélie [*at door*]. It's Marcel coming back!

Prince. He's back?

Amélie. And not alone. There are people with him.

Prince. Oh! [*He hurries into bathroom, closing door behind him.*]

Key is heard in lock of door. MARCEL *appears.*

Marcel. Sorry, Amélie, it had to be done. Come in, monsieur.

Commissaire [*speaking to his men outside*]. You two guard the entrance! [COMMISSAIRE *enters, hat on his head, his hand on saber hilt.*]

Amélie. What do you wish, monsieur?

Commissaire [*surprised, seeing* AMÉLIE *and removing hat*]. A lady! Pardon me, madame, but monsieur said . . . [*To* MARCEL.] Well! Where is the burglar?

Amélie. Burglar? What burglar?

Commissaire. I don't know, but monsieur told me——

Marcel. I had to tell you that or you wouldn't have come. The thief is the one who is stealing my honor.

Commissaire [*frowning*]. What's this?

Marcel. I want you to witness that my wife, this woman here, has been entertaining a lover on the very day of our marriage.

Commissaire. You mean madame?

Marcel. The same! Witness, monsieur. This bed has been slept in. Witness also, the seductive garment she has on. [*Picking up marriage dress from settee.*] Her bridal gown is here—still warm!

Commissaire. Is this true, madame?

Marcel. Dare she deny it?

Amélie. Marcel, you've used your head for once in your life. The only way to get divorced is to go through with this. And at least when it's over, we'll be rid of each other. [*Sits at foot of bed.*] Sir, everything this man has said is absolutely true.

Marcel [*triumphant*]. You see.

Commissaire. And madame's accomplice, where is he?

Amélie [*jerking a thumb over her shoulder*]. In the bathroom. [*As* COMMISSAIRE *crosses to door left.*] Marcel, you're brilliant.

Commissaire [*puts on hat, then pushes open the door with his fist*]. Come out, monsieur. We know you are there. [*He and* MARCEL *stand back, giving the culprit room to emerge. A pause. The* PRINCE *enters wearing his trouserless ensemble. He has tilted his derby down over his forehead and tucked the flaps of his cravat under the hat brim to hide his face.*]

Prince. Very well. I am here.

Marcel. Witness the interesting costume of this gentleman.

Prince. Permit me to say, this fellow threw my trousers out of the window.

Commissaire [*thundering*]. If he threw your trousers out, it stands to reason that you didn't have them on— Your name? [*Producing notebook and starting down right.*]

Prince. I cannot tell you. I am here incognito.

Commissaire [*taking this for a wisecrack*]. Another clever remark of that sort and I'll put you in jail.

Prince. You cannot do it.

Commissaire. We'll see about that. Who is he?

Marcel. This roué, this wrecker of homes, is His Imperial Highness, Prince Nicolas of Palestria.

Commissaire. What's that? [*Instinctively he whips off his hat.*]

Prince [*vexed*]. Marakasch! [*Shoves his bowler back, letting his necktie fall.*]

Marcel. Remember that face, officer.

Commissaire [*who has heard enough*]. Oh! no! I'm getting out of here. [*Hurries to door down right.*]

Marcel [*confused*]. Where are you going?

Commissaire. I don't want to start a government crisis!

Marcel [*crosses to* COMMISSAIRE, *firmly*]. What do you mean? This man has been flagrantly misbehaving in——

Commissaire. I don't care what he did or whom he did it to. That's your lookout. No affair of mine.

Prince [*delighted*]. Of course.

Marcel. But I am the husband. I found this man here——

Commissaire. What do you expect me to do? How do you think I could testify? Where is the evidence?

Marcel. Evidence? Look at Madame! Look at him! His pants are missing——

Commissaire [*shouting, nose-to-nose with* MARCEL]. And why? Because you threw them out the window! That's why!

Prince [*shouting too*]. He threw them out! That's why!

Marcel [*flustered*]. That proves that he didn't have them on at the time!

Commissaire [*waving his arms*]. You call that proof?

Marcel. Madame has confessed. What more do you want?

Commissaire [*thrusting out his chest like a bantam rooster*]. Not another whisper! I don't need lessons from you on how to do my job.

Marcel. Huh?

Prince. Bravo.

Commissaire [*circles about* MARCEL *in cockfight style*]. Consider yourself lucky if I don't bring you before a magistrate.

Marcel. Me?

Commissaire. Yes, you. Where is your burglar, eh? Where is he?

Marcel [*completely befuddled*]. But I . . . but . . .

Commissaire. Don't you dare let it happen again!

Prince. Bravissimo!

Marcel [*stunned*]. I'm getting it from both sides.

Commissaire [*bowing low*]. I hope Your Highness will accept my apologies.

Prince. Rise!

Commissaire. It was all the fault of that simpleton.

Prince [*waving his forefinger under the nose of the* COMMISSAIRE]. I make you Commander of the Order of Palestria.

Commissaire [*bowing and scraping*]. What an honor! How shall I ever be able to express to Your Highness?

Prince [*dismissing him*]. That will be all. Go! [*Turns on his heel, taking no further notice of the* COMMISSAIRE.]

Commissaire. Yes, Highness. [*Bowing low.*] *Your Highness!* [*A backward step.*] Madame! [*Another step. Addressing* MARCEL *in the same worshipful tone.*] *Simpleton!*

Marcel. What?

Commissaire [*stands erect, about faces and marches out*]. Come, men. That burglar must have slipped through our fingers. [*Door is heard closing.*]

Marcel. It's my usual run of luck, that's all!

Amélie [*to* PRINCE, *who is pacing nervously*]. Your Highness, I am mortified that I should be the cause——

Prince. Yes, yes. Enough. [*To* MARCEL.] I hope you are satisfied, you!

Marcel. I was wrong, Your Highness. You have all the rights, all the privileges. I should have known.

Prince [*still pacing*]. I shall complain tomorrow to the President of the Republic.

Marcel. Go ahead, complain. Why not?

Prince. Back in Palestria, I could deal with such a case. I am sorry not to have you there.

Marcel. I'm sorry, too, Your Highness.

Prince. I would send you to the torture chambers.

Marcel. Home is best, isn't it?

Amélie. Your Highness, calm yourself.

Prince [*with a demoniac scream*]. I am perfectly calm! [*Continues pacing.*]

Marcel. I hope Your Highness realizes that I meant nothing personal.

Prince. That is no excuse.

Marcel. I needed a divorce. You happened to be here. It wasn't your fault.

Amélie. It's Étienne's fault, the whole mess.

Marcel. Yes, Étienne! If I could think of some way to pay him back!

Amélie. Couldn't we send him on a long vacation? A tour of Palestria, all expenses paid——

Prince [*stalks over to* MARCEL]. Do you think I wish to be here the rest of my life with no pants? Go and find me some clothes!

Marcel. Where?

Prince. I do not care where. Find them— Why not give me yours? [*Plucks at* MARCEL's *coat.*]

Marcel. If I gave you my clothes, I'd have to stay here——

Prince. Go then, and—— [*Door slams off right.*] Who is it now?

Marcel. Ssh! [*All listen.*]

Étienne's Voice. Are the newlyweds at home?

- *Marcel.* It's Étienne.

Amélie. He's got a nerve to come here!

Marcel. I can't tell you how glad I am to see him!

Étienne [*appears, hat on head, hands in his pockets*]. How are the happy honeymooners?

Amélie. Weasel!

Marcel [*advancing slowly*]. What are you doing here?

Étienne [*whimsically*]. Calling on the newlyweds. Are you enjoying married life?

Amélie. You fiend!

Marcel. Come in, Étienne! You're more than welcome! [*Grasps* ÉTIENNE *by arm and hurls him down left.*]

Étienne. What are you donig?

Marcel. His Imperial Highness needs a pair of pants!

Prince. Yes, I do.

Marcel. Étienne, give him yours!

Étienne [*laughing*]. Don't be silly!

Marcel [*taking revolver from pocket*]. Your trousers, or I'll fire!

Prince [*in the line of fire*]. Wait! Not yet! Don't shoot yet! [*Crosses quickly to far left.*]

Étienne. You're joking. You wouldn't dare!

Marcel. Joking, am I? [*He shoots the gun at ceiling.*]

Étienne [*jumping back*]. Ah!

Amélie [*dropping behind settee at upstage end of bed*]. Ah!

Prince [*cowering*]. Ah!

A piece of plaster drops from the ceiling and lands on the floor.

Amélie. My beautiful ceiling!

Marcel. To hell with your ceiling. [*To* ÉTIENNE.] Off with your pants! Or I'll shoot you down like a dog!

Étienne [*pleading*]. Marcel!

Marcel [*brandishing his revolver*]. Hurry up!

Étienne. Yes! Yes! [*Unbuttoning suspenders.*]

Marcel. Faster than that!

Étienne [*leaping out of his trousers*]. Here they are! [*Throws them at* MARCEL, *who tosses them over shoulder to* PRINCE.]

Marcel. Catch!

Prince. A thousand thanks! [*Slipping on the trousers.*] It'll be a tight fit.

Marcel. Now your coat and vest.

Étienne. Marcel, have pity!

Marcel. For you? After what you did to me! [*He laughs eerily.*]

Étienne [*whipping off coat and vest*]. He's gone mad. [*Gives coat and vest to* MARCEL, *who flings them over shoulder.*]

Marcel. While we're at it, Your Highness, would you like his underwear?

Prince. No thanks, my own is prettier.

Étienne [*appealing to* AMÉLIE]. Amelie, for old times' sake, don't let him do this!

Amélie. I don't care what he does. I hope he shoots you.

Marcel. Now, Your Highness, I have a project in mind which does not require your presence. I'd be grateful if you'd get out from underfoot.

Prince. I understand. This gentleman is my substitute?

Marcel. Exactly.

Prince. Splendid. I am going. Good luck. Au revoir, my charming lady.

Amélie. Au revoir, Your Highness.

Prince [*pausing in doorway*]. *Kahkvee boronzhnoff! Lyahppettick lakrarsh!*

Étienne. What does he say?

Prince. Yahmarleck, grobouboul! [*He exits.*]

Étienne. First he takes my clothes, then he swears at me. Wait!

Marcel [*holding him at gun point*]. Take another step and I'll blow your brains out.

Étienne [*backing away*]. What do you want *now*?

Marcel [*taking* AMÉLIE'S *hand*]. I want to apprehend you *in flagrante delicto* with my wife.

Étienne. What!

Amélie [*beaming*]. Isn't he clever? [MARCEL *and* AMÉLIE, *hand in hand, advance on* ÉTIENNE.]

Marcel. You have been guilty of intolerable lewd and lascivious conduct! You're my wife's lover!

Amélie. What's more, you found us together, didn't you, my husband?

Étienne. Huh?

Marcel. In the bridal chamber . . . in his underwear.

Amélie. And me in my chemise! Shocking, isn't it?

Étienne [*distrait*]. They've both gone crazy.

Marcel. Now, if only the Commissaire were here.

Amélie. If only he were! [*Knocking at door right.*]

Marcel [*cocking an ear*]. Who is it?

Commissaire [*off*]. The Commissaire!

Amélie [*curtseys to* MARCEL]. He's here!

Marcel [*goes and opens door*]. Come in, Monsieur le Commissaire! We were just speaking about you.

Commissaire [*entering with* PRINCE's *garments*]. About me? Where is His Highness? Isn't he here?

Marcel. He had an appointment elsewhere.

Commissaire. But I brought back his clothes. They were turned in at the station.

Marcel [*taking clothes*]. I'll see that he gets them. [*Tosses them on settee.*]

Commissaire [*noticing* ÉTIENNE, *who is cringing down left*]. Monsieur!

Étienne [*bowing*]. Monsieur!

Commissaire [*alluding to his costume*]. The heat wave . . . no doubt?

Étienne. Yes, it's been stifling, hasn't it?

Marcel [*politely*]. I haven't introduced you. Monsieur Étienne de Milledieu, my best friend. Monsieur le Commissaire. [ÉTIENNE *and the* COMMISSAIRE *bow to one another.*] I ask you to witness that this man is guilty of adulterous misconduct with my wife.

Commissaire. Again so soon?

Amélie. I'm afraid so, Commissaire.

Étienne [*outraged*]. Marcel!

Marcel. Quiet, you! [*To* COMMISSAIRE.] I was mistaken a little while ago. My wife's lover was not the Prince, it's this scoundrel here! [*Levels a finger at* ÉTIENNE.]

Commissaire [*delighted to have a substitute*]. How fortunate for you!

Étienne. But it isn't true.

Amélie. Of course it's true. I recognize this man. I'd know him anywhere. *He* is my lover.

Étienne. Oh! you baggage!

Amélie. Furthermore, almost anyone in Paris will tell you the same thing.

Étienne. Oh!

Commissaire. The proof is sufficient.

Marcel. You will sign a statement?

Commissaire. Certainly. Where is pen and ink?

Amélie [*opening door left*]. Here in my dressing room.

Commissaire. Good, follow me.

Étienne [*endeavoring to block the way*]. This is an outrage! I'm a patriotic citizen!

Commissaire. That will be taken into consideration. [ÉTIENNE *puts his hat on head. When he had taken off suspenders, he had put them in hat. They now hang down like pigtails on his neck. He exits following* AMÉLIE *and the* COMMISSAIRE.]

Marcel. Revenge is sweet! [*Before he can exit,* PUTZEBOUM *enters right.*]

Putzeboum. Ach, Sonny, here you was! I received just now a telegram which announces it I should leave tonight. So I have with me brought the check.

Marcel. The check?

Putzeboum. You have filled out all the requirements of your poppa's will, so here was the money: twelve hundred thousand, plus interest: two hundred seventeen thousand ninety-three francs and five sous.

Marcel [*disconcerted by this flood of figures*]. How much?

Putzeboum [*handing him the check*]. That's right. I counted it myself.

Marcel [*glancing at check*]. Plus ninety-three francs and five sous. Yes, it couldn't be more perfect!

Amélie [*appearing left*]. Ah! It's your godfather. How are you, Putzi dear?

Putzeboum [*sentimentally*]. My little Amykins! [*She goes and kisses him, then stands beside* MARCEL.]

Marcel. Now, we have a little announcement to make about a coming event.

Putzeboum [*jumping to conclusions*]. Ach, so soon? That's wunderbar!

Marcel. No, no. You misunderstand me.

Putzeboum. How, Sonny?

Marcel. I wish to announce my forthcoming divorce from Madame Amélie Clémentine d'Avranches Pochet Courbois, who today was apprehended in adultery with my close friend, Étienne Milledieu.

Putzeboum. I wasn't sure I understood all of this?

Marcel [*to* AMÉLIE]. True, isn't it, Amy?

Amélie [*amiably*]. Truer words were never spoken.

Putzeboum [*reaching for the check in* MARCEL's *hand*]. In that case, it would be better——

Marcel [*snatching hand away and putting check in pocket*]. Sorry, godfather. The conditions were fulfilled! You said so yourself!

Putzeboum. Ja, that's so. They was filled a week ahead of time, eh, Sonny?

Marcel. So the money's legally mine!

ÉTIENNE *and* COMMISSAIRE *re-enter.*

Étienne. But, monsieur, after all it's not as if——

Commissaire. The matter is entirely out of your hands. The divorce will undoubtedly be granted.

Marcel. Come along, godfather! [COMMISSAIRE *crosses to right.* VAN PUTZEBOUM *follows, escorted by* MARCEL. *They are about to exit, but are stopped by voice of* ÉTIENNE.]

Étienne. I'll get even with you someday!

Marcel [*laughs*]. Au revoir, Amélie. [*Comes back and kisses her good-by.*]

Amélie. Au revoir, Marcel. It was a nice marriage while it lasted!

Étienne [*feeling left out*]. What am I supposed to do from now on?

Marcel. You? I'll tell you what you're supposed to do. Amélie, you tell him . . . [*Whispers in her ear, then turns her around by shoulders and pushes her toward* ÉTIENNE.] Bon soir. [*He exits, preceded by* PUTZEBOUM *and* COMMISSAIRE.]

Étienne [*slumping on settee*]. What did he say to you, the scoundrel?

Amélie [*sits on his knee*]. He said you had better keep an eye on Amy! [*Playfully tweaks his nose.*]

Étienne [*smiles*]. Aha! [*He kisses her.*]

A United Family

(*La famille tuyau de poêle, ou Une famille bien unie*)

by

JACQUES PRÉVERT

English version by J. D. Allen

Copyright © 1958 by J. D. Allen.

CHARACTERS

GASPARD-ADOLPHE BÂTONNET, *a young lawyer*
A PLUMBER
GERTRUDE, GASPARD-ADOLPHE'S *housekeeper and former nursemaid*
JACQUELINE DESGAMESLAY, *the Colonel's daughter*
LIEUTENANT COLONEL ARMAND DESGAMESLAY
CLAUDINET, *the Colonel's "nephew"*
MATHILDE DESGAMELSLAY, *the Colonel's wife*

A United Family

PROLOGUE

An actor in costume steps before the curtain and addresses the audience.

Ladies and Gentlemen:
French plays these days are wonderfully bold and brainy. They are also—who can deny it?—a bit scabrous. With such models as the Paris theatre is now providing, how could we here at the Fontaine des Quatres Saisons keep from raising the torch ourselves—to offer a play which braves the winds, clouds, and storms of modern life to probe the hidden and unspoken secrets of futility?

And though we think it better in our day to weep than to laugh—it is ever so much more healthy, austere, and true— we hope you will not be so rigorous as to demand a play that is too *afflicting*, too *despairing*.

The scenery represents a Paris lawyer's living room, which is quite proper when you stop to think that the action takes place *in a Paris lawyer's living room.*

So prepare to see, in fearsome confrontation, souls in torment and bodies in distress! Get ready to make an effort to enter the realm of Ideas!

The curtain rises on a studio with doors and windows, furniture and bric-a-brac.

A WORKMAN, *dressed in the impeccable blue of the French workman's blouse and wearing a Basque beret, is doing something to a radiator. He is whistling a bright, catchy little tune.*

The MASTER OF THE HOUSE *enters in a dark, elegant smoking jacket. He gives the* PLUMBER *an annoyed look, the look of a man who is waiting for someone and has been disturbed. Drawing back the light muslin window curtains, he looks onto the street and then retraces his steps.*

Observing a flower in a vase, he takes it, puts it in his buttonhole, and inspects himself in a mirror. Then, seeing the empty vase and deciding it doesn't look right, he puts the flower back into the vase and picks a book from the bookcase.

MASTER OF THE HOUSE [*reading aloud*]. "We shall have beds full of light odors, And divans as deep as the grave . . ."

[*But since the* PLUMBER *goes on whistling his catchy little tune, he breaks off reading to speak to him.*] Are you going to be much longer?

Plumber. I'll be finished in a minute.

Master of the House [*resuming his reading*]. "We shall have beds full of light odors . . ."

Plumber [*shaking his head disapprovingly*]. Oh! Beds full of light odors! [*Still whistling, he starts to leave.*] I'm going to the kitchen now. Frankly, it's a mess. [*Exit.*]

Master of the House [*picking up the book and holding it behind his back, he tries to recite by heart the verses already repeated so often*]. "We shall have beds, divans, deep beds, light odors . . ." [*He grows bored, closes the book, throws it on the divan, moves toward the window, retraces his steps, stops suddenly, takes a coin from his pocket, and looks at it anxiously.*] Heads, she'll come; tails, she won't. [*He tosses the coin, stoops to pick it up, and looks in vain for it on the carpet.*] Oh! Where d'you suppose it could have rolled to? [*He gets up suddenly and rings for the maid. She enters. She is an ordinary-looking old servant except for a strange glimmer in her eye.*]

Gertrude. You rang, sir?

Master of the House. What a thing to ask, Gertrude. Of course I rang!

Gertrude. You never can tell, sir, when somebody's ringing and when they aren't. It's those bells. When they ring, they're stronger than me. And I'm going to give in to them. You never can tell, sir, when somebody's ringing and when they aren't.

Master of the House. You needn't bother me about your bells. I was tossing a coin and it rolled off somewhere. Look for it!

Gertrude. Very well, sir.

Master of the House. Don't touch it. Look at it very carefully. If it's heads, run off to the kitchen, open a bottle of port, light the grate in my bedroom, and put my pink slippers under the bed.

Gertrude [*interrupting him*]. And if it's tails?

Master of the House [*looking out the window*]. If it's tails . . . [*The possibility wearies him.*] If it's tails . . . [*He absent-mindedly pulls on the curtain, making it fall.*] Here, Gertrude. Do something about the curtain! It just fell down.

Gertrude [*on all fours and facing the audience, she speaks in the voice of an inspired idiot*]. But the curtain hasn't fallen. I see people in the room, and lights, many lights——

Master of the House. I'm talking about the window curtain, stupid!

Gertrude. Stupid! An old servant! The curtain. How's a body to know what curtain he's talking about? [*She gets up painfully, clambers awkwardly onto a chair, and tries to rehang the curtain, all the while talking as though in a dream.*] It's like it was with the plumber, not like it is with the others, that plumber, and so well brought up—for a plumber. A moment ago the two of us were talking about bells, and what he said to me about them touched me to the heart. [*Suddenly transported with joy.*] You'd have said if was my youth rang out to me so passionately. [*She loses her balance and falls to the floor, wrapped in the flimsy muslin curtain.*]

Master of the House [*rushing to her*]. Oh! You aren't hurt, are you, Gertrude? [*He stoops down to help her up, but the old servant, still wrapped in the curtain, grabs her master round the neck and kisses him on the mouth.*]

Gertrude. Oh! Gaspard-Adolphe!

Gaspard. Oh! Gertrude, my Gertrude!

Gertrude. Rock-a-bye, baby, in the tree top . . . Who is this? Why, it's little Gaspard, the little sleepy-head with his Gertrude. [*Pathetically.*] Ah! Gaspard-Adolphe, my Gaspard? For thirty years I've worked for you, and all that time I've been waiting for this happy day! Oh! My Gaspard! what a life I've led. When you were tiny and I gave you my breast, I used to say to myself, "You'll love me, Gaspard, you'll love me!" It's been a martyrdom. Always having to make beds, change them . . . for others! [*She weeps.*] For others! And time rolled by, and my poor breasts sagged! And you loved me in silence, Gustave-Adolphe!

Gaspard. "Gaspard-Adolphe!"

Gertrude [*with a jollying sort of laugh*]. All right, all right, my little bear! Just look at me, I'm in my bridal gown. At last the old troubles are over. A new life is about to begin! [GERTRUDE, *less and less herself, draped in the softening and dilapidated "bridal gown" and as impulsive as at twenty, takes* GASPARD-ADOLPHE *in her arms. One can't tell whether she's attempting to rock him to sleep or simply trying to make him dance.* GASPARD-ADOLPHE *doesn't much know what's happening either.*]

Gaspard [*sublime and enraptured*]. It's mad. I love my nurse, practically my mother! [*The bell rings.*] Somebody's ringing, Gertrude!

Gertrude [*regretfully taking off her bridal veil*]. Very well, sir. I'm going.

Gaspard [*straightening his tie and the hang of his trousers*]. If only it's she!

Gertrude [*she comes back and speaks in a grave and tortured voice*]. A young lady who wouldn't give her name! [*She crosses herself and bows out before a very pale young woman in a mink coat.*]

Gaspard. You, Jacqueline!

Jacqueline. Weren't you expecting me?

Gaspard. Yes, of course I was.

Jacqueline. Well?

Gaspard. Yes, of course. [*He makes a grand, expansive gesture.*] Well?

Jacqueline [*very chic, sophisticated, and self-possessed*]. You are very strange, Gaspard. You've begged me to come often enough, and one fine day I promised I would. Today I keep my promise, and you act surprised, so very surprised.

Gaspard. It isn't surprise, Jacqueline. It's joy which . . . which . . .

Jacqueline. Which *what?*

Gaspard. Which leaves me speechless. [*He makes a great lyrical gesture.*] Your presence so long awaited . . . to see you here, with me, and me with you, and the two of us together. After all, it's marvelous. After all, you've come!

Jacqueline [*she looks dreamy, but her voice has an edge to it*]. I've come because I swore to myself I would belong to you.

Gaspard. Jacqueline!

Jacqueline. Swore to belong to you, and a Desgameslay never goes back on her word.

Gaspard. You can trust me. [*They have gradually reversed positions, so that* JACQUELINE *is now standing about a yard from* GASPARD-ADOLPHE *with her back to the audience.*]

Jacqueline. I came because I promised I would the other night in the café. Look at me, Gaspard-Adolphe! Under my coat I'm naked! [*She opens her coat.*]

Gaspard [*stammering*]. Please, Jacqueline, stay covered. No, I mean to say, take off your coat . . . It's so terribly hot . . . Oh! I don't know what I'm saying any more. I love you, Jacqueline. I love you! [*He rushes to her and takes her in his arms, just as* GERTRUDE, *sublime in self-sacrifice, appears in the doorway. She has a bottle of port in each hand*

and waves them to catch GASPARD-ADOLPHE'S *attention. Finally he notices her.*]

Gertrude [*waving the bottles and whispering*]. Red port or white?

Gaspard. You really look after me, don't you? Red port! Red! I've told you a thousand times, you bungling fool! [GERTRUDE *retires, crossing herself.* JACQUELINE *begins to sob.*] Don't cry, Jacqueline, I love you.

Jacqueline [*murmuring as though in a dream*]. Oh! I should never have come, but I have. I couldn't do anything else, and it's dreadful being here. Oh, Gaspard-Adolphe, if only you knew what drove me to you! [*During this speech* GERTRUDE *brings in a tray containing a bottle of port and glasses, and then retires, moving all the while like a sleepwalker.*]

Gaspard [*pouring and drinking several glasses in quick succession*]. You came because you love me, Jacqueline! [*He moves toward the window. The wine has made him lyrical, carrying all his literary rubbish to his head.*] Ah *how* I love you! Ah, Jacqueline, what a glorious thing love is! Look out of this window, look at the people, all those others down there in the street. Look how they come and go. They're leaving their offices, their factories—all that poor mass of silly, unhappy people, without souls and without love! Ah, Jacqueline, we aren't like the others. We're . . . we're . . . [*He stammers.*] We're . . . "We shall have beds full of light odors,/Deep davenports full of depths . . ." We shall have . . . We shall have . . . beautiful love, majestic music. Oh! My jewel, my treasure, my honeybear, my delight, my little owl! [*He tries to take off her coat.*] Take off your coat!

Jacqueline [*raising her arms to heaven*]. Oh, this is frightful, perfectly frightful!

Gaspard. But you can trust me!

Jacqueline. As if I cared about that! [*She moves closer to him.*] Listen to me very carefully, Gaspard-Adolphe. The only reason I came here was to escape an even greater danger. Pay attention now, Gaspard-Adolphe. [*She pauses.*] I love my father! Well, now you know!

Gaspard. But that's nothing at all!

Jacqueline [*acting all the while as though unaware of her state of undress*]. Nothing at all. He doesn't understand a thing. He doesn't see how pale I am, how my hands are trembling, how my heart is beating like a drum! [*She shakes him by the shoulders.*] I love my father. Yes, I love my father,

Lieutenant Colonel Desgameslay. I'm in love with him!
[*Weakening.*] It's a guilty love!

She is about to faint. GASPARD-ADOLPHE *throws open the window. Its draft blows one wing of the double door open, to show* GERTRUDE *crouched at the other wing, eye to keyhole. She gets up, enters, and takes* JACQUELINE *in her arms.*

Gertrude [*motherly*]. How very well I understand you, my
poor darling!

Gaspard. Somebody's ringing, Gertrude!

Gertrude. If you'll look after the young lady, sir, I'll see
what it is. [*As* GASPARD-ADOLPHE *takes* JACQUELINE *in his
arms,* GERTRUDE *wantonly chucks him under the chin.*] You
little rascal, you! [*She laughs fatuously and runs to the door,
repeating:*] You never can tell when somebody's ringing and
when they aren't.

Gaspard [*he shakes* JACQUELINE]. Wake up, darling, wake
up!

Gertrude [*returns and announces gravely*]. Lieutenant
Colonel Desgameslay.

Jacqueline [*comes to with a start, frees herself, pulls her
coat around herself tightly, and shouts*]. Heavens! My father!

Gaspard [*badly frightened*]. Heavens! Your father! Heavens! Her father!

Gertrude. Our Father Who art in Heaven!

Jacqueline [*shaking* GERTRUDE]. Save me! Hide me, you old
fool!

Gertrude [*she shows* JACQUELINE *into the next room and
closes the door after her*]. Oh, that ungrateful girl! That hateful thing! After all I just did for her! You work yourself to
the bone for people, you make sacrifices for them! She's
wicked! Spoiled rotten!

Gaspard [*with trembling dignity*]. Show our visitor in,
Gertrude!

Gertrude [*suddenly becoming calm*]. Very well, sir.

*She leaves the room and then immediately shows in the visitor.
He is in mufti, distinguished-looking, and probably retired.
With him is a somewhat effeminate soldier in the swashbuckling uniform of a Zouave regiment.*

Lieutenant Colonel [*in a honeyed voice to the Zouave*]. Be
seated, Claudinet!

Gaspard [*more and more frightened*]. I give you my word
of honor that Miss Jacqueline——

Lieutenant Colonel [*without listening to him and speaking with great authority*]. Are you Mr. Gaspard-Adolphe Bâtonnet, the lawyer, sir?

Gaspard [*still more frightened, he jerks himself into a military posture and even clicks his heels*]. Yes, Colonel!

Lieutenant Colonel [*casting a brief glance about the room*]. Are we quite alone here?

Gaspard. Yes, Colonel!

Lieutenant Colonel [*weighing his words*]. What I have to say to you——

Gaspard. Colonel, I swear to you on my honor that I'm ready to give you my word that——

Lieutenant Colonel [*without listening and even without hearing him*]. What I'm about to say to you— [*Lowering his voice.*] —or rather confide to you, is something damnably annoying, or to be more precise, something deucedly delicate.

Gaspard [*frightened, but a little reassured now*]. I'm at your service, Colonel.

Lieutenant Colonel. Very well, then, here it is. I don't beat about the bush. I'm an old soldier, you know. Dash the technicalities and red tape and all that rot. I don't go all round the barn. When I have something to say, I say it! I don't mince words. I let fly. They can't put the muzzle on me. I'd as soon let 'em cut off my leg. I go straight to the point— without hesitation or fear. Camouflage, complications, subtleties—they're for civilians. I look the enemy straight in the eye. D'you understand what I'm talking about?

Gaspard. Perfectly, Colonel, perfectly. But if you'd be so kind as to supply a few more details . . .

The Zouave takes the flower from the vase and contemplates it rapturously.

Lieutenant Colonel. Quite so. But you know, when I have something to say . . . [*He lowers his voice.*] Are we quite alone?

Gaspard. We are, Colonel.

Lieutenant Colonel. All right, then! You must be aware, Mr. Bâtonnet, that a military career isn't always amusing. And if a man didn't have a bit of fun now and again . . . So you see, if I'm an old soldier, I'm not the less a true Parisian. Like anyone else, I have my little amusements, my little eccentricities, my little vices. [*He grins.*] What the devil! A man's not made of wood, is he? D'you see what I'm talking about?

[Gaspard-Adolphe *shakes his head, and the* Colonel *continues.*] Well, dash it all, the honor of the French army's at stake, and we must defend it . . . [*Lowering his voice.*] So, to be brief about it, they took us by surprise, Claudinet and me . . .

The Zouave demurely lowers his eyes and drops the flower.

Gaspard. May I ask you a few questions, Colonel? Is Claudinet the Zouave?

Lieutenant Colonel. He's not a Zouave. He's only eighteen. He's my nephew. [*Confidentially.*] In a manner of speaking.

Gaspard. Forgive me, but I thought . . . the uniform . . .

Lieutenant Colonel. You're forgiven, Mr. Bâtonnet. I gave Claudinet the uniform myself. It's so dashing, so masculine— the fez, the trouser legs stuffed into the boots. I'm an old Parisian, all right, but still a colonel with a good bit of dash!

Gaspard. You were saying just now that you'd been caught. Where were you caught, Colonel, and who was it caught you?

Lieutenant Colonel. In a . . . behind the Jardin des Plantes. There was a raid.

Gaspard. Of course, this could be extremely awkward, but I rather imagine, Colonel, that we'll be able to clear it all up without too much fuss. And it may not take so very long, either. What kind of world would it be in this day and age if honest folk having their bit of fun were to get into hot water over mere trifles?

Lieutenant Colonel [*enthusiastically clicking his heels*]. Splendid, sir, splendid! It was a lucky star that led the two of us here. [*Indicating* Claudinet, *who is holding a rose and sniffing it indifferently.*] You realize, sir, the reason why I came to see you about this business was that I absolutely refuse to have any of my friends, no matter how influential, interfere in the matter.

Jacqueline, *still dressed in nothing but her fur coat, bursts into the room. She is magnificent in a kind of pained stupefaction.* Claudinet, *no less stupefied, rises to his feet, while the* Colonel *remains frozen in his chair.*

Jacqueline. I've heard everything, Father. How very shameful! So all your indifference and coolness toward me was Claudinet's fault! I should have guessed it after all those mornings the two of you had breakfast in bed together! Oh, how blind I was! [*Pointing an accusing finger at him, she moves toward her father.*] You preferred a fake Zouave to your own daughter. You're my father no longer. Get out! I'm through with you!

Claudinet. Oh! You ungrateful girl!

GERTRUDE, *who has been standing aside, creeps up behind* JACQUELINE *and opens her coat as wide as possible, grinning all the while.*

Gertrude. Missy ought to take off her coat. It's very warm in here.

Lieutenant Colonel. My daughter! Stark naked in the house of a damned little nobody of a lawyer!

Claudinet [*trembling*]. Oh! Dirty slut! Whore!

Gaspard. Colonel, I give you my word of honor that it's all a misunderstanding!

The COLONEL, *ignoring them all, looks long and hard at his daughter as though sizing her up.*

Lieutenant Colonel. But where were my eyes? How beautiful my daughter is. Beautiful and surprising. [*He snaps his fingers briskly.*] And there's something . . . something . . . about her. [*His voice becomes dreamy, and his hands go through the motions of describing a woman.*] Ah, I can just see her, yes, I can just see her in a hussar's tunic . . . yes, nothing but a tunic and boots. Yes, little polished boots, black silk stockings, and— [*Clicking his heels.*] —spurs!

Claudinet [*jealous and upset*]. Oh, Uncle Armand, don't be like that!

Lieutenant Colonel. "Don't be like that"? [*He shrugs his shoulders.*] What d'you mean, "Don't be like that"? I've discovered her at last, seen her for the first time as she really is. [*To his daughter.*] Oh, Jacqueline, I was blind too!

Jacqueline [*deeply moved*]. No, you weren't blind. How *could* you have seen me? Mother was always coming between us.

Lieutenant Colonel. Alas! [*He sinks back into the chair and talks piteously to himself.*] All that time lost— [*Indicating* CLAUDINET.] —for fu-til-i-ties. If I'd known in time, I wouldn't be here tonight with this mess on my hands. Alas! It's too late. Destiny has spoken.

Jacqueline. Father, it's never too late to love!

Gertrude [*taking her affectionately by the neck*]. How very true that is! [*Tenderly indicating* GASPARD-ADOLPHE.] It's also taken my master a long time to discover he was in love

with me. [*The doorbell rings.*] So long, so very long . . .
[*She sobs as the bell goes on ringing.*]

Gaspard. Someone's at the door, Gertrude, and they sound
pretty insistent.

Gertrude [*in a voice choked by sobs*]. Very well, sir, I'm
going. [*She goes out sobbing as the bell continues to ring.*]
You never know when somebody's ringing . . .

Gaspard. I'll excuse you, Gertrude, from that stuff about
bells.

Long silence. They all look at one another without speaking.

Jacqueline [*simply to say something*]. Well, what do you
know? I just saw a falling star.

Gaspard [*magnanimously*]. Let it fall. [*Aside.*] This will
give me a bit more time.

Gertrude [*distressed, but resigned too*]. Another lady who
wouldn't give her name, and probably for the same reasons.
[*She points a furtively vindictive finger at* JACQUELINE.]

Jacqueline [*coldly, to* GASPARD-ADOLPHE]. Very nice, very
delicate. Thanks very much.

Gaspard. Jacqueline! You can't possibly suppose . . . [*To*
GERTRUDE.] What kind of woman?

Gertrude. Between young and middle-aged. How can I tell?
And distinction itself. [*A deep sigh.*] Ah, sir, you choose them
well. She's mad with impatience and very excited. She
doesn't just stand there: she positively paws the ground! You
little rascal! There's one thing I'm sure of: if you don't let
her in straightaway she'll break the door down, even if it *is*
locked.

Gaspard [*nervous again*]. Go tell her, Gertrude, that—that
—— Tell her I'll take care of her in a moment.

Gertrude. Take care of her? He even brags of it! [*Shrilly.*]
And what's more, she's a lady reporter.

Gaspard. What?

Gertrude. She kept talking about the *Journal.* It had something to do with that when she asked if the Colonel was still
here.

Lieutenant Colonel [*shouting*]. A newspaper woman? You
hear that, Claudinet? [*Without waiting for him to answer.*]
But it's the end of everything: dishonor, scandal, ruin!
[*Weakly.*] What shall I do? My God, what shall I do?

GASPARD-ADOLPHE, *like a shepherd sensing a storm and herd-
ing his flock together, manages to get his visitors off into
another room.*

Gaspard. This way. I'll take care of things. [*As he closes the door, he meets the* PLUMBER, *whistling quietly and gaily the same little tune.*]

Plumber [*looking very beatific and otherworldly*]. I was about to give you an account of my mission, sir. [*Suddenly brightening.*] God be praised! The sink has been altogether unstopped, and it's truly a marvel to see it working.

Gaspard [*losing patience*]. You! I *beg* your pardon, but couldn't you——

Plumber [*looking to Heaven*]. It is not of me you should beg pardon.

Gertrude [*who has been holding back*]. That lady's getting impatient, sir.

Plumber. One must never keep a lady waiting. [*Going through the door.*] I'm going to the bathroom. [*Smiling, and making a wide sweep with his arm.*] The bathtub and— [*Lowering his hand closer to the floor.*] —the smaller vessel. Humble things, perhaps, but with great missions to fulfill all the same.

On the way out he collides with a LADY *who, quite out of her head with impatience, stampedes into the room without waiting to be shown in. The encounter is quick but violent. The* LADY, *very much the* grande *dame, makes resolutely for* GASPARD-ADOLPHE, *utterly ignoring the lowly Workman, who mutters his excuses and, painfully pulling himself together, disappears.*

The Lady [*preemptorily*]. Mr. Bâtonnet?

Gaspard [*bowing*]. Your servant, madam.

The Lady [*pale and anguished*]. What complaints did he make against me?

Gaspard [*at a loss*]. But, madam . . . to whom have I the honor of speaking?

The Lady [*in a voice dolorously worthy*]. All questions deserve answers, Mr. Bâtonnet. [*Lowering her voice.*] You have, alas! the honor of speaking to the Colonel's wife.

Gaspard [*suddenly disconcerted*]. The Colonel's wife?

The Lady [*lugubriously*]. I am Mathilde Desgameslay! [*Sadly hanging her head.*] Alas! You ought to have guessed it. He just this moment left, didn't he?

Gaspard [*embarrassed*]. Oh, that I can't say.

Mathilde. Yes, of course—professional ethics. [*She half-collapses onto the sofa and begins wringing her hands feverishly.*] Oh! I'm sure he's read my journal.

Gaspard [*stupefied*]. The journal?

Mathilde. Come now. Don't pretend you don't know what I'm talking about. He's asking for a divorce! A divorce! Why else would he have come here? When I heard him ask for your address, I knew what was up, for he was dreadfully upset, pained, and angry. [*She falls silent for a moment, and* GERTRUDE, *increasingly sublime in sacrifice, discreetly offers from a distance the red port and the white. With a curt gesture,* GASPARD-ADOLPHE *stops her signaling.* GERTRUDE *retires, while the* COLONEL's *wife continues with her mournful plaint.*] It's perfectly obvious that he's read my journal. Yes, my private diary where I laid bare my secrets and fondled them. [*Getting up and suddenly becoming aggressive.*] Dare to tell me, Mr. Bâtonnet, that he was not reading it, day after day, behind my back!

Gaspard [*with great simplicity*]. Madam, I believe I may, without being indiscreet, give you my word that your husband was *not* here because of that book.

Mathilde. Thank you, sir. You have lifted a great weight from my breast. [*Suddenly pacing around distractedly, her movements jerky.*] My journal is where it should be. Nothing has been broken open. Is it my fault I had to go and lose the key? [*Suddenly mistrustful.*] All right, why *did* he come to see you?

Gaspard. He was in the neighborhood and just dropped in for a friendly chat.

Mathilde. A friendly chat?

Gaspard. Yes, he regards me as a friend of the family. His daughter and I are friends. No more than friends, of course.

Mathilde [*hoarsely*]. My daughter!

Gaspard [*apologizing*]. I should have said "your daughter."

Mathilde [*bitterly*]. Oh yes, quite so. I have a daughter "too," a little idiot— [*Shaking her head and smiling bitterly.*] —an idiot daughter. [*Then suddenly.*] Give me your word that you have not been lying to me!

Gaspard. Far be it from me, madam, even to think of such a thing.

Mathilde. Your words are reassuring. But the Colonel has been acting so strange these past few years. [*Speaking harshly and more to herself than to* GASPARD-ADOLPHE.] To be quite frank, he has never taken much interest in love, alas! He's a man of duty. Only friendship has much meaning for him. Manly friendship, the comradery of the field, narrow escapes with his men—that kind of thing. [*A sigh.*] Ah! It's not easy to be married to a hero! [*She grabs the vase of flowers and dashes it to the floor.*] Oh! Something tells me he came for a divorce even—if you were telling me the truth—even if he didn't dare bring himself round to mentioning it. I'll be frank with you, Mr. Bâtonnet. He was talking in his sleep one night, and I heard him cry out that he wanted to be single again. I was worried, I thought he was sick, so I was listening outside the door. We have separate rooms, you know.

Gaspard. Yes, so I gathered.

The PLUMBER *can be heard, at first faintly and then more and more loudly, whistling his catchy little tune in a nearby room.*

Mathilde [*beside herself*]. Divorced! How dreadful! I who have always dreamed of a sweet widowhood—with my only son! [*Suddenly half-crazed and shouting.*] My only son, whom I loved!

Gaspard. Ah!!

Mathilde. Ah! You may well say "Ah!" It's enough to drive one mad! And sometimes I wonder what made the Good Lord—— For do you know whom he gave me up for? For God Himself!

Gaspard [*understandingly*]. He took Orders?

Mathilde. Yes . . . and he'd never given me the least sign of such a thing. [*Shaking her head.*] He must have been reading my journal—the journal of my most intimate life, where I confessed, without a shred of shame, in full detail and— [*Lowering her voice.*] —even with some drawings, the great and fatal love I bore for him.

Gaspard. Oh, madam!

Mathilde. Oh! You may well say "Oh!" [*Suddenly becoming intensely nostalgic.*] A boy so fascinating, but also so— I would not say savage, no, but taciturn—yes—restless, feverish, secretive. [*Her voice increasingly distant and troubled.*] In his teens, his only pleasure was solitude.

Gaspard [*shaking his head*]. Curious, very curious!

Mathilde. No, not in the least. He was curious only about himself. And ceaselessly setting himself soul-searching problems. [*A deep sigh.*] He was perfectly indifferent to his needs, but not in the least egotistical, not at all. No, simply in love.

Gaspard. In love?

Mathilde. Yes, with himself!

Gaspard. But that's perfectly natural at that age. Just a stage of narcissism that all boys go through.

Mathilde [*raising her voice*]. You call that just a stage? Oh, you are very understanding, Mr. Bâtonnet! [*Suppressing deep sobs.*] One evening I found him in front of a mirror. He was plucking petals from a daisy and saying, "He loves me, he loves me not." And what's more, he was jealous! He used to have frightful scenes with himself over mere trifles. He'd even—and this is hard to believe—send himself anonymous letters. You should have seen him—worried, distraught, standing by the window, watching for the postman . . .

There follows a painful silence, during which one can hear, growing louder, the PLUMBER *now singing the words to the tune which till now he has been content to whistle.*

Pumber's Voice.

> How lovely a day, how touching a spectacle,
> Let's shake with love, O happily!
> Lord Jesus emergeth from his tabernacle
> And setled forth, triumphantly!

Mathilde [*hand clutching her breast, she shouts*]. Ah! [*The voice stops.*]

Gaspard. What is it, madam?

Mathilde [*passing her hand across her forehead*]. Nothing at all, sir. A slight indisposition, and, as in a dream— [*A gesture of great weariness.*] —I thought I heard . . . [*A long, sad sigh.*] Joan of Arc heard voices, too. [*Suddenly radiant.*] But what voices! [*Then, with immense bitterness.*] While in my misery I hear only one voice, the voice of my own bad conscience! [*Raising her voice.*] Ah! I am accursed!

Gaspard [*annoyed*]. Come now, madam! Don't let's be morbid.

Mathilde. Morbid! Ah, sir! If you had on the robes you wear in court, I would speak to you as to a confessor. [*Deliriously.*] Yes, as to a confessor—my confessor. And I would shout to him, through the little grill in the box, my sin and my pain! [*Approaching* GASPARD-ADOLPHE.] And you would hear Mathilde Desgameslay say to you— [*A prolonged sigh.*] Yes, I, Mathilde Desgameslay, would say to you, "I have committed the most horrible, the most frightful, the most unspeakable of adulteries!"

A door opens and there appears, flanked by his daughter and his "nephew," sublime with stupor and charged with rightful indignation, LIEUTENANT COLONEL DESGAMESLAY.

Lieutenant Colonel [*deeply wounded but still dignified. He speaks coldly*]. Oh, Mathilde, the most unspeakable of adulteries! [*Sadly shaking his head.*] And you cry it to the housetops.

Mathilde [*stupefied*]. Are you here, Armand?

Claudinet [*darkly*]. Armand's here, all right.

Jacqueline [*casually*]. And I was with him.

Mathilde [*wounded and humiliated*]. So you've been here with him all the time, Armand—hiding, spying! [*Pointing a trembling and scornful finger at* GASPARD-ADOLPHE.] And this miserable wretch let me go on talking while all the time you were spying on me. Oh! You've caught me in a trap.

Lieutenant Colonel [*alternately red with rage and pale with shame*]. I want to know his name, Mathilde! This instant!

Mathilde [*surprised*]. His name?

Lieutenant Colonel. I have a right to know the name of the man with whom you have committed— [*Lowering his voice.*] the most unspeakable adultery.

Mathilde [*with a gleam of hope*]. Armand, haven't you read the journal?

Lieutenant Colonel [*exploding*]. The *Journal.* How disgusting. So it's already in the *Journal.* With photos, no doubt. What a mess. [*Threatening her with trembling hands.*] I don't know what keeps me from——

Jacqueline. Father!

Claudinet [*stopping her with a gesture*]. Stay away from him! Let him alone!

Lieutenant Colonel. What keeps me from . . . It would teach you a good lesson! [*Then, suddenly magnanimous, with a simple but effective gesture, he threatens himself.*] What keeps me from killing myself!

Jacqueline [*running toward him*]. Oh, Father! My darling father!

Claudinet [*also frightened*]. Don't do it, Uncle Armand!

Gaspard [*intervening in his turn*]. Come now, Colonel, a man of your worth——

Mathilde. And of such greatness of soul——

Gaspard. ——should never even think of such a thing.

Lieutenant Colonel [*wearily*]. Yes, of course, I'm not that sort. [*Defeatedly.*] But what to do? My God, what am I to do? Such a scandal! I'm at my wits' end.

A long silence, during which one can hear the PLUMBER *whistling and then singing his little tune. After a moment, the* PLUMBER, *in a state of rapture and with eyes far too much on*

Heaven to pay the slightest heed to the people around him, enters.

Plumber [*ecstatically*]. God be praised! Everything is in working order. [*A broad gesture.*] The big vessel and— [*He stoops down and holds one hand nearer the floor.*] —the little one!

MATHILDE *freezes, like a woman just turned into a pillar of salt, and then lets out a terrible cry.*

Mathilde. André-Paul!

Plumber [*discovering her as he straightens up*]. Mother!

Lieutenant Colonel. My son!

Jacqueline. My brother!

Claudinet [*to the Colonel*]. Your son, Uncle Armand!

Mathilde [*to her daughter*]. Your brother!

Gertrude [*coming forth now, eyes ablaze*]. My brother, too! A moment ago he called me his sister.

Plumber [*at first stupefied and then radiant*]. My family! My parents! My home!

Lieutenant Colonel [*rather aggressively*]. But I thought you were a priest, André-Paul!

Plumber. I still am, but I'm a workman, too.* [*Modestly.*] The workman of the eleventh hour.

Gaspard [*looking at his watch*]. On the nose!

Eleven o'clock sounds in the deep silence. MATHILDE *uses this silence to say to her son, in a trembling and half-whispered voice.*

Mathilde. André-Paul, answer me! Have you read the journal?

Plumber [*innocence itself*]. I never read the papers, Mother. [*Taking a book from his pocket.*] I read only my breviary and— [*Taking out another book.*] —the plumber's manual.

Mathilde [*in raptures*]. God be praised!

---

* The PLUMBER is a worker-priest (*prêtre-ouvrier*), a member of the clergy who works with and among the workers in order to effect their conversion. Training of such priests, begun shortly after World War II, was discontinued in 1953 after it had become clear that the influence of the workers on the priests was perhaps greater than that of the priests on the workers.

The notion of a "worker-Zouave" (soon to come up in the play) is entirely the PLUMBER's. There are no worker-Zouaves.— Tr.

Plumber. Yes, God be praised. Let us thank Divine Providence for having—and by a miracle—brought us all together again. [*He gathers them together, and they stand there hypnotized, pressed against one another while he lavishes his joyous affection upon them.*] I shall not leave you. I shall never abandon you again. And you will be able to celebrate the return of the Prodigal Son. [*Music from offstage, distinct at first, then almost inaudible, and then growing louder and clearly recognizable as the* PLUMBER's *tune. The* PLUMBER, *raising his voice, addresses them all, but especially his father.*] Forgive me, but since I belonged to a model family, I felt unworthy of it. So I left it to be, in my own modest way, a model myself. [*Lyrically.*] So I sought out the promiscuity of the little people, of the disinherited, and I cast myself headlong into the bottomless abyss of vulgarity. At first, I must admit, it was terribly dangerous.

Lieutenant Colonel [*clicking his heels*]. It was dangerous? Good for you! Splendid!

Plumber. Yes, in the underworld, on the docks, in looking for work, I almost lost my faith.

Mathilde [*deeply moved*]. Oh, André-Paul!

Plumber. Rest easy, Mother. I work in private homes now. My employer is humble and so is my salary. And then to find all of you again—here! What an inspiration, what a lesson! One doesn't often find a united family nowadays. [*Then, surprised at finding* CLAUDINET *there.*] But who is this young man? So far as I know, he doesn't belong in the family. [*With a bright smile to* JACQUELINE.] Your fiancé, perhaps?

Jacqueline [*bitterly*]. In a manner of speaking.

Plumber [*placing an affectionate hand on* CLAUDINET's *shoulder*]. How sad you look! Yes, sad and uneasy. [*Delicately indicating his uniform with his finger.*] Your trade, perhaps, is a soldier's? You've had doubts too, maybe? Believe me, you really should become a worker-Zouave.

At first softly and then insistently, the bells ring out offstage, and GERTRUDE *reappears, once more draped in her "bridal veil." Smiling ecstatically, she wildly waves her two bottles.*

Gertrude [*deliriously*]. Red port and white port. Why hold back, why be stingy? [*To* GASPARD-ADOLPHE.] Something told me things were going to happen. [*Then turning to the* PLUMBER.] I had a feeling from the first that you were something more than a common plumber. Oh, marry us, Father, marry us! All of us here now, just as we are! Marry each of

us to all the rest! But first of all, marry Gaspard-Adolphe and
me! [*Mad with joy.*] It's been so long, so very long since I've
waited to be called Mrs. Bâtonnet, Gertrude Bâtonnet!

*The bells irregularly mingle their bronze splendor with the
bright, catchy, triumphant, and edifying melody of the*
PLUMBER.

Gaspard [*to say something*]. Somebody's ringing, Gertrude.
Somebody's ringing!

Gertrude [*increasingly enraptured*]. But those are bells that
are ringing!

Gaspard [*bewildered by what has been happening, but with
a generous and fastidious gesture*]. Quite so, Gertrude. Go let
them in.

Gertrude. Very well, sir, I'll go do it. [*She leaves the bottles
of port with* GASPARD-ADOLPHE, *who stands there bewildered,
bottles in hand.*]

Gaspard [*as the curtain falls*]. You never can tell when
somebody's ringing and when they aren't!

NOTES

A TRIP ABROAD was first performed at the Théâtre du Gymnase in Paris on September 10, 1860. One notes that between Francisque Sarcey's first review of it at that time and his review of a revival in 1879 it had become a classic. (It is time, says Sarcey, differing sharply from those who think a play's fate is settled at once, that makes masterpieces.) The play has long had a safe place in the repertoire of the Comédie Française, but in Anglo-Saxon countries has suffered from being merely the sauce to French grammar as served up in schools. Several times translated into English, it seems never to have been widely available in any book either in Britain or in the United States.

The editor was tempted to print here Clyde Fitch's adaptation of the play, *Uncle Billy,* produced in 1905 on Broadway by Charles Frohman, and now preserved in manuscript at the New York Public Library, but, since Fitch made Perrichon a native of Scranton, Pennsylvania, and applied his own dramaturgic skill to the script, *Uncle Billy* is an example of American, rather than French, farce. When Mr. Ward's version came along—so much lighter in touch than other "straight" translations of the play—that decided the matter. It is here printed for the first time, and has not yet been produced in the United States.

CÉLIMARE was first performed at the Théâtre du Palais Royal on February 27, 1863. In his admirable book *Eugène Labiche: sa vie, son oeuvre,* Philippe Soupault remarks that, while *A Trip Abroad* won success after a rather unsuccessful debut, *Célimare* had so much initial success that, later on, it could only decline in favor. One might add that the qualities that made it the rage of Paris for a while have prevented this play from ever being heard of in England and America. At the center of it is adultery. And while certainly adultery is not absent from the Anglo-American stage, it is never handled, either, with this degree of combined suavity and aggression.

Sarcey's own curious discussion of the theme, as mentioned above (page xi), is to be found in his review of another Labiche play, *The Happiest of the Three.* Here is an extract:

"I had often complained that they bored us constantly with this question of adultery, which nowadays is the subject of three-quarters of the plays. Why, I asked, take pleasure in painting its dark and sad sides, enlarging on the dreadful consequences which it brings with it in reality? Our fathers took the thing more lightheartedly in the theatre, and even called adultery by a name which awoke in the mind only ideas of the ridiculous and a sprightly lightheartedness. . . . Chance brought it about that I met Labiche. 'I was very struck,' he said to me, 'with your obser-

346

vations on adultery and on what one could derive from it—even with a present-day audience—for farce. You think one would find lots of material for laughter in that area; I agree. You want the play; I shall try to do it for you.' I had all but forgotten this conversation when I saw the title posted outside the Palais Royal: *The Happiest of the Three*. It was my play; it was adultery treated lightheartedly . . ."

CÉLIMARE was translated especially for inclusion in the present volume. The music for the lyrics (which is taken from Offenbach's *Les Brigands*) may be borrowed from Samuel French Inc. whenever the play is in production. (The idea of setting all the lyrics to Offenbach tunes was prompted by the note "Air d'Offenbach" on one of the songs in the French original.)

LET'S GET A DIVORCE! was first performed at the Théâtre du Palais Royal on December 6, 1880, and had its American première at Abbey's Park Theatre on March 14, 1882. It was a huge international success and has remained so. Among the actresses to play Cyprienne are Réjane, Niemann-Raabe, Duse, Mrs. Fiske, Grace George, Käthe Gold, and Uta Hagen. There have been various English versions, at least two of which have been published, though only in acting editions and with a curious distribution of credits: these are *Divorçons* as published by the Dramatic Publishing Company (Chicago, 1909) with no translator listed, and *Cyprienne* "by Margaret Mayo," as currently distributed by Samuel French Inc., which does not even give Sardou and Najac primary credit for authorship. Uta Hagen and Herbert Berghof tried out a rather free adaptation by Dorothy Monel in Madison, Wisconsin, in 1955. The Goldsby version was commissioned for inclusion in the present volume. Further facts may be found conveniently in *Sardou and the Sardou Plays,* by Jerome A. Hart (Philadelphia, 1913).

THESE CORNFIELDS was first performed on February 7, 1898, at the Grand Guignol theatre in Paris. In the original, the title is *Les Boulingrin,* for the married couple in the play were called Boulingrin, a French word which derives from the English "bowling green." The visitor is called Des Rillettes, which, as every tourist knows, is an hors d'oeuvre consisting of cooked pork. When he tells Félicité his name, she replies, "That's nothing: where I come from—Saint-Casimir near Amboise—we had a neighbor called Piédevache"—meaning cow's foot. The translator concluded that he must anglicize the names. And, if the result was to remain farce, no literal anglicizing would suffice. Names must be chosen which, rather, might have a roughly equivalent effect. Once the names Cornfield and Herring were used, references to exclusively French things in the dialogue began to seem absurd. It seemed best to transport the whole action to New York. The changes required were few and small. Very unlike

Courteline's famous satirical pieces, this little play does not depend for its main effect on nuance or the exact notation of local custom. For that matter, if any producer disagrees, all the French names and references can be reinstated, and that in about a quarter of an hour.

One or two Courteline plays have been produced in New York: for instance, *Boubouroche,* adapted by Ruth Livingstone, in 1921; *A Private Account (La Paix chez soi),* adapted by Edward Goodman, in 1917. Several of the one-acts, translated by Jacques Barzun, are available from Mr. Barzun (Columbia University, New York 27, New York). *These Cornfields,* which is not known to have been Englished before, was translated for inclusion in the present volume.

KEEP AN EYE ON AMÉLIE! was first performed at the Théâtre des Nouveautés on March 15, 1908. It was produced on Broadway under the title *Breakfast in Bed,* adapted by Willard March and Howard Booth, in 1920. Many of us today know it either from the French film distributed in the United States as *Oh, Amelia!* or from the production of the Compagnie Jean-Louis Barrault-Madeleine Renaud. Mr. Duffield's version, believed to be the first Feydeau play ever printed in English,* awaits its first production. Marcel Achard's essay on Feydeau appears in this volume as an appendix.

A UNITED FAMILY was first published in Jacques Prévert's book *La pluie et le beau temps* (1955). No production has been reported, and this is its first appearance in print in English. Perhaps it is more of a skit than a farce—partly a skit *on* farce, but even more, a skit, in the manner of farce, on some modern ways of thinking and behaving. Mr. Allen writes: "This play combines the forms of farce with materials that are not altogether characteristic of it. Such an extension of subject matter would be of little importance if there were not also a shift from the celebration of the accepted to the celebration of the unaccepted." In this Mr. Allen seems to the present editor both right and wrong. It is true that farce rarely *confesses* its commitment to impropriety as M. Prévert's little play does: but the *existence* of such a commitment seems to the present editor of the very essence of the matter. A UNITED FAMILY was chosen as a kind of epilogue for the present collection just because M. Prévert blurts out so much that the others say only in the symbolic language of farcical action. Strictly, Prévert does not belong in the world of Labiche, Courteline, and Feydeau; but he makes a comment on it with something of their intelligence and their imaginative extravagance.

* *Hotel Paradiso* by Georges Feydeau and Maurice Desvallières, English adaptation by Peter Glenville, was published in London after the present book went to press.

Mr. Allen's version is the first thing of Prévert's to appear in English except for a thin sprinkling of poems in little magazines.

An alternative title suggested by Mr. Allen is: "The Family That Plays Together Stays Together." On the stationery of the Magistrates' Court of the City of New York, the editor of this collection finds another slogan that might serve as a title for Prévert's play: "When Family Life Stops—Delinquency Starts."

APPENDIX

GEORGES FEYDEAU

by

Marcel Achard [1]

GEORGES FEYDEAU, the greatest French comic dramatist after Molière, was born in Paris on December 8, 1862, a direct descendant of a Marquis de Feydeau de Marville.

His father, Ernest Feydeau, was a writer of some repute under the Second Empire, and a friend of Flaubert and Théophile Gautier. He used to remark casually: "Myself and Flaubert . . ."

Fanny, a spicy and rather daring book by the elder Feydeau, incurred the wrath of the Archbishop of Paris, who denounced its licentiousness from the pulpit. The book was having a poor sale, and the prelate's thundering diatribe had an interesting result. Within the week, the first edition was all the rage, so much so that the author quite fittingly dedicated the subsequent editions to "the most reverend Archbishop of Paris, in grateful acknowledgment."

Ernest Feydeau's only vanity was literature. He made himself known in a select company by studies of a highly serious, almost scholarly nature. So it was that, in 1862, *The History of Funeral Customs and Burial Rites of Ancient Peoples* and little Georges, future biographer of *la môme Crevette*,[2] both by the same author, saw the light of day.

Georges Feydeau's mother, Lodzie Zelewska, was Polish, as her name indicates, and almost arrogantly beautiful.

According to the Goncourts, in their *Journal,* Georges was an enchanting child—and a lazy one. The indefatigable worker who produced thirty-nine plays was, above all else, a great sluggard. He tells in his own words how he found his vocation:

> How did I come to write comedies? Very simple! Through pure indolence. Does that surprise you? Are you not aware that

---

[1] Originally the introduction to Feydeau's *Théâtre Complet,* copyright by Éditions du Bélier, 1948; here translated by Mary Douglas Dirks.

[2] In *La Dame de chez Maxim.* "La môme Crevette" has no English equivalent, since the character, Crevette, is both a "kid" and a bit of a trollop.—M.D.D.

indolence is the miraculous mother of industry? I say miraculous, for the father is quite unknown. I was a mere child—six or seven, I can't remember exactly. One evening, I was taken to the theatre. The play? I have forgotten it. But I came home full of enthusiasm. I was infected. The evil had entered into me. Because of it, I did not sleep all night: the next morning, at dawn, I went to work. Biting my tongue, fiercely tugging at my hair which was tangled from a sleepless night, I was writing a play—just like that. My father surprised me.

"What are you up to?" he asked.

"I am writing a play," I confidently replied.

Some hours later, the governess, whose task it was to instill in me the first elements of all the knowledge in use at that time—a very nice young lady, but, oh, how dull!—came to fetch me.

"Come, Monsieur Georges, it is time . . ."

My father intervened.

"Let him be," he said gently. "He has worked quite hard enough this morning. He has written a play."

Instantly, I beheld the road to salvation. From that blessed day on, whenever I forgot to do my homework or to learn my lessons (believe me, this sometimes happened) I flung myself upon my notebook of plays, and my governess, nonplused, left me in peace. People are not sufficiently aware of the uses of dramaturgy."

* * *

The laziness which determined his vocation was unlimited. One day, many years later, he was sitting at a table with Marcel Simon, his friend and favorite actor. Enter a ravishing woman.

"Ah," said Simon, "Turn around—a sublime woman, quite possibly the prettiest I have ever seen."

"Describe her to me," said Feydeau.

Happily for us, this indolence was productive. When he was at the Lycée Saint Louis, he wrote a few crackling heroic dialogues; but, according to him, his teacher pilfered them from him as fast as he turned them out, so that he was unable to preserve a single souvenir of his academic work.

In 1883, when he was twenty-one, his first comedy, *Amour et Piano,* was produced at the Athénée. It had a *succès d'estime* and was nothing less than decisive; for at that time, it would have taken very little for this master of laughter to become an actor instead of a playwright. He had shown remarkable talent as a comedian in amateur theatricals. Deslandes, then director of the Vaudeville, wanted to engage him, and made an appointment with him to sign the contract.

Deslandes was late. Feydeau waited a few minutes for him, then left. And that is how he cut short his career as an actor.

"That day," he said, "I realized the advantages of unpunctuality. I therefore took an oath to be late for the rest of my life. Up to now, I have kept my word."

* * *

While he was serving with his regiment in the Seventy-fourth Division he wrote his first full length play, *Tailleur pour Dames*. It was a triumph.

Alas, [he recalls] I had not yet arrived, as I naïvely supposed. I was forced to come down a peg or two. I came to know the agony of half-successes. Of course, in those days I was philosophical, because I hadn't the experience that came later. So I came down a peg, but I did not lose heart. On the contrary, I sought the answers within myself—and, because I am obstinate, I found them. If one is obstinate and lazy, one is always sure to get somewhere. I remember, when the curtain came down on the opening night of *Tailleur pour Dames,* I ran into Jules Prével, who said: "They gave you your triumph tonight, but they'll make you pay for it."

And pay for it he did. He came to know the horror of: "*Monsieur le directeur* is out, come back tomorrow." And: "Your play isn't bad, but it's not suitable for our theatre." And: "This one doesn't quite hit the nail on the head, but make another play out of it."

Then, on the eve of the winter of 1892, when he timidly asked the porter whether the director of the Palais Royal had happened to read the two comedies he had left with him six months before, he was stunned to be told: "*Monsieur le directeur* will see you."

"I am going to produce *Monsieur Chasse,*" this gentleman informed him. "Not right away, of course—in April or May, for the summer season. As for your other manuscript," (meaning *Champignol malgré lui*) "you would do well to relegate it forever to your desk drawer—it is absurd. It hasn't the slightest chance of success."

Such is, always has been, and ever will be, the discernment of theatrical directors.

Feydeau would have disowned almost all the rest of his works as long as *Monsieur Chasse* was accepted; and he readily agreed that *Champignol* was a ridiculous play.

Whistling happily, he left to take his daily walk along the

boulevards. At the door of the Théâtre des Nouveautés, he
saw Micheau, the director—a wan and exhausted Micheau.
His last production had been disastrous, his creditors were
merciless, and his mother had just taken to her bed, declaring
that their fortunes had been squandered. In short, Micheau
was in the precise position when every theatrical director
takes to heart the words of Grisier: "When one has suffered
what I have suffered, one no longer owes anything to anybody."

"What's that under your arm?" he asked Feydeau.

"Oh, a play they just turned down at the Palais Royal."

"Let me read it."

"No, thanks. It's idiotic."

At that moment, Feydeau was sincere. It seemed to him
that a director shrewd enough to take *Monsieur Chasse* was
incapable of being wrong.

Micheau was flabbergasted.

"I never heard an author say anything like that before.
Let me read it anyway."

"It's idiotic!"

"I'll be able to tell. In my position, I have nothing to
lose."

An expeditious gentleman, Micheau retired to his office
with the manuscript. After the first act, his eyes sparkled. He
exclaimed "Oh, oh," and "Ah, ah!" Feverishly, he finished
the second act, then dashed up the stairs, four steps at a time,
to his mother's room.

"You can get up now," he told her. "Here," he said,
throwing the manuscript on the bed, "is our fortune." He
was right. *Champignol malgré lui* was performed over a
thousand times. Three times more than *Monsieur Chasse*.

"I shall not attempt to describe the audience," wrote
Francisque Sarcey. "It was exhausted, dead from laughter—
it could laugh no more. Toward the end of the play, the wild
laughter which seized and shook the whole theatre was so
thunderous that the actors could no longer be heard—the act
was finished in pantomime."

*   *   *

An era of uninterrupted triumphs began: *Le Système
Ribadier, Un Fil à la Patte, L'Hôtel du Libre-Échange, Le
Dindon, La Dame de chez Maxim,* made the audiences, more
numerous and enthusiastic than ever, scream with laughter.

I have taken the following delightful description by Robert

de Flers from that precious little book which Léon Treich devoted to *The Spirit of Feydeau:*

I can see Georges Feydeau still—his elegance, his physical refinement, his gentle, attractive expression, his manner, so full of ease and sincerity, never marred by a mediocre thought or a vulgar word. He was all grace and charm, the gift of effortlessness. Never was a man so utterly unself-conscious as he. There are some personalities that develop little by little, painfully and rigorously, by dint of concessions, sacrifices, and patient will-power. Feydeau's individuality lay in the fact that he owed everything to nature, and surrendered himself entirely to her counsel. That is why he was a poet: for who knew better than he the wealth of fantasy, as well as disenchantment, that hovers in the smoke rings of a cigar? Through this gossamer cloud, he observed people, as it were, with an attentive absence of mind. He dreamed constantly. And, because the stars seemed too far away, the moonlight too pale, and the ideal a bit weary, he dreamed of life—and that is why he seldom smiled. Quite naturally, in fact, it pleased him to be a living, charming paradox. He was exceedingly cordial, though somewhat cool; extremely sensitive beneath an apparent indifference; ambitious but modest; a carefree worker; at once merry and melancholy.

Robert de Flers has described him magnificently—and here are a few anecdotes to give weight to his sketch:

Cordial, though somewhat cool. An actor asks him, "Dear Master, did you happen to see me in the play at the Variétés?" "Of course, of course, my dear friend. And I earnestly hope you will forgive me for having done so."

Extremely sensitive beneath an apparent indifference. "I say," says a friend, "I've noticed you have a weakness for deaf-mute beggars." "Oh, I'm like everyone else—I give them money because I'm afraid they'll give me hell."

Ambitious but modest. He is about to be made an officer of the Legion of Honor, and fourteen francs are demanded of him for chancery fees. He does not agree to pay them: "Either they are giving me this rosette because I deserve it, or else they're selling it to me, and in that case I don't want it. Not even for fourteen francs."

A carefree worker. He rehearses the first two acts of *Occupe-toi d'Amélie* (*Keep An Eye on Amélie*) for six weeks. Then, after driving the actors to distraction, he writes the most famous scene in the play, the marriage in the town hall, between eight o'clock at night and midnight.

At once merry and melancholy. Lajeunesse and he are

discussing one of their associates: "That character is good for nothing but being cuck—— cheated on!" "And, what's more," replies Feydeau, "his wife will have to help him!"

That was Feydeau at the peak of his career. The press accorded him rapturous reviews—and not only Sarcey. The poets of the period, Catulle Mendès and Jean Richepin, were possibly even more enthusiastic. Finally, supreme consecration, other writers imitated him. Better still, they borrowed from him—his colleagues, the vaudeville writers, pilfered his situations, his characters, even his lines.

One day he had had a charming idea. Seeing an enormously tall woman escorted by a wee little man, he remarked: "She certainly makes a better man than he does a woman." One of his habitual plagiarists, a third-class playwright, who had heard this quoted, came to him and said, "My dear fellow, that was very funny—is it original?" "Yes," replied Feydeau, "but it won't be much longer."

*   *   *

With success came money. Then, alas, to his sorrow, Feydeau began to play the stock market. From the little restaurant where he used to eat, on the Rue Vivienne, he haphazardly gave orders to buy and sell. At first, Fortune smiled upon him. He made a few substantial killings. Then, one fine day, after an unexpected panic, he found himself several millions in debt—Feydeau experienced the agonies of Dostoievsky and Balzac. Just as they were forced to write novels and more novels, so he was forced to contrive plays and more plays.

It is to material preoccupations that we owe these masterpieces: *La Puce à l'Oreille, Mais n'te promène donc pas toute nue, Feu la Mère de Madame, On purge Bébé, Je ne trompe pas mon mari, Léonie est en avance, Le Bourgeon*, etc. Just as we are thankful that Marcel Proust was wealthy, perhaps we ought also to be glad that Feydeau had reverses on the stock market: they kept him from going to sleep after his first taste of glory. At the end of life, he declared gloomily: "They tell me I earned millions. I never saw fifty thousand francs." And he added: "Rich people assure us that money can't buy happiness. We'd better take their word for it quick, or they might give us some."

Conversations on this topic often found him irascible. An industrialist, who had made his fortune in the war of 1914, having announced that a true artist ought to be poor, was told by Feydeau: "That's like saying an industrialist ought not to have brains."

*　　*　　*

He had few friends, but of great quality—Desvalliers, his first and best collaborator, who used to polish the silverware while he patiently waited for the night-owl Georges to get up; Courteline, the other giant (the two men admired each other enormously); Capus, in Feydeau's opinion the wittiest of them all; Tristan Bernard, the exquisite Tristan, twitted by Feydeau for his dilettantism:

"Now, take Tristan. He is like the architect from whom you commission a six-story house to be completed in three or four months. You don't lay eyes on him again for two whole years. Then he says: 'I have found a little knickknack that will look perfectly enchanting on the drawing room mantel.' "

And there was Lucien Guitry, who invited Feydeau and Simon to dine one day.

"Georges," he begged, "write a play for me. I am longing to act in one of your plays."

"My dear Lucien, in comedy, there are two leading characters."

At these words, a shadow passed over the great actor's face.

"Two leading characters," Feydeau went on, remorselessly. "The one who delivers the kicks to the backside and the one who receives them. The one who delivers them never gets the laughs—only the one who receives them. And you, my dear Lucien, cannot receive them."

Lucien Guitry was overwhelmed by this great lesson in theatre. And they talked of other things.

*　　*　　*

I have said that Feydeau was the greatest French comic dramatist after Molière. That was an imprudent statement. Imprudent, not exaggerated. It was imprudent, because it is my intention to convince you of this fact—and yet what the quintessence of Feydeau is I cannot tell, for he is a mathematician, an astronomer, a chess player, and an inventor. He is Galileo, Pythagoras, Vaucanson, Philidor, and Denis Papin. He is the Galileo of a world which spins in reverse, the Pythagoras of an implacable theorem, the Vaucanson of a hundred delicately mechanized automatons, the Philidor of a stratagem by which the spectator is left checkmated, the Denis Papin who discovers steam pressure at the end of a series of explosions of laughter.

In a Feydeau play, the events are linked together with the precision of a well-oiled machine. The *qui pro quo* precedes the imbroglio. Unexpected *coups de théâtre* superabound, follow one upon the other, and frequently become entangled. That is generally why the critics give up when they attempt to recount Feydeau's plots. They begin their review in fine spirits, joyously setting down events and characters; but they soon realize that they have covered sixteen single-spaced pages and aren't even halfway through the first act. So they complete their article by saying:

"But go and see it."

Of course they are right. And, obviously, I cannot hope to succeed where they have failed. Even Francisque Sarcey, the best of them all, gave up when it came to Feydeau.

"Allow me to stop here in my analysis," he writes, in his review of *La Dame de chez Maxim*. "All farces congeal when they are transferred from the stage to a cold description of them. I merely wished to convey some idea of the author's marvelous agility and firmness of touch."

I am not more cunning than Sarcey; and not being a professional critic, I lack the ability to deal in generalities. Unfortunately, it is not enough simply to say that everything is regulated by an infallible geometry which marks the point of departure and traces the graph of the action. I still must prove it. I must try to assemble the pieces of this puzzle. And this is somewhat like being in the position of the clockmaker who has to dismantle the carillon on the Strasbourg cathedral.

* * *

It is impossible to cut anything in Feydeau's plays. The most amazing thing about them is the infallibility with which all things are regulated, explained, and justified, even in the most extravagant buffoonery. There is not a single incident, once introduced, of which we cannot say: "Yes, that's true—it could not have happened in any other way."

There is not a single detail, not one, which is not necessary to the action as a whole; there is not a single word which, at a given moment, does not have its repercussion in the comedy—and this one word, I have no idea why, buries itself in our subconscious, only to issue forth at the precise mo-

ment when it must illumine an incident we were not antici-
pating, but which we find entirely natural, and which delights
us because it sounds improvised—and because we realize that
we should have foreseen it.

As I said before, it is quite impossible to cut anything
from a Feydeau play. Students in drama classes have often
mentioned this to me. Those who shamelessly cut a scene
of Musset, or Beaumarchais, or Marivaux, dumbfoundedly
agree that Feydeau's comedies will not stand up under their
sacrilegious blue-penciling; and they see the precise mechanism falling to pieces before their eyes. That is because the
author of *La Main passe* brought to his choice of situations
the same relentless discrimination that Paul Valéry used in
selecting each word of his poems. There is a kind of Mal-
larmé-like strictness in Feydeau's discovery of poetry—the
comic poetry of a logarithmic table.

Feydeau knows all the arts of comedy, but, in particular,
he is a great master of the comedy of the technician. When
Richemont, director of the Théâtre Femina, was rehearsing
Mais n'te promène donc pas toute nue, he begged Marcel
Simon (whose friendship with Georges exposed him to all
the unpleasant chores) to intervene with Feydeau to cut at
least ten minutes from the play. Simon screamed like an
osprey: "You're out of your mind. Ten minutes! He'll an-
nihilate me. Not even two minutes. Not even thirty seconds!"

"Look, Marcel, buck up—the show is too long."

"Do your cutting in the curtain-raiser."

"It's already been done, you know that. Take out another
twenty-five lines and there won't be anything left of it."

Marcel Simon, good sport that he was, gave in.

"You know very well I never add anything that doesn't
have a point," Feydeau told him. "If I cut something, even
I won't be able to understand it."

"I know that. But they're beside themselves. The show
will run overtime."

For a moment, Feydeau was silent. Then, icily:

"How much time do they need?"

"Uh . . . ten minutes."

"And how many pages for ten minutes?"

"Uh . . . Well, pardon me . . . twenty pages."

"Very well. Tell them to start on page twenty-one." *Mais
n'te promène donc pas toute nue* was played without cuts.
Which was as it should be. It was not easy to be clockmaker,

engineer, chess player, mathematician, and comic author all at once.

Feydeau decreed Draconian laws; and, paradoxical as always, he obeyed them.

*   *   *

At least everyone knew his first and most important commandment:

"When two of my characters should under no circumstances encounter one another, I throw them together as quickly as possible."

A splendid rule—indispensable to any good dramatist. Sophocles, Shakespeare, and Molière followed it instinctively. Feydeau had the gumption to formulate it. And he never repudiated it.

"The audience is greatful to you for not cheating it. I want no applause on false pretenses."

*   *   *

We all know the supreme drama of the playwright: he imagines one play and writes another; the actors play a third; and the audience sees a fourth. Not so with Feydeau. He imagined a play, and wrote it; the actors played it as it was written; and there was no possible misunderstanding out front.

His stage directions are as inviolable as his plots. The masters of *mise-en-scène*—Jean-Louis Barrault, Pierre Dux—are the first to acknowledge that it is quite impossible to alter Feydeau's staging. He leaves no room for difference of opinion. The manuscript of one of his plays always contains a hundred pages more than other men's plays—a hundred pages of stage directions. The movement of each scene, every nuance, is thoroughly noted. The actors' positions are always numbered; their gestures, even their inflections, are always indicated.

It happens, in *Occupe-toi d'Amélie,* that two actors have to say, in relation to each other and twice over:

"Ah-hah! That's it!"

Obviously, "Ah-hah! That's it!" can be said in any number of different ways, any one of which may be funny.

But we have reached the third act of a Feydeau play. By this time the audience is convulsed with laughter. It is now a question of getting bigger laughs than ever. Feydeau has no intention of leaving this problem to the possibly faulty inspiration of the actor.

There is a way of saying: "Ah-hah! That's it!" The right way—the only way—Feydeau's way. And I beg you to realize that it is not exactly the easiest way. He gave directions for it. He wrote it down—on a stave—with notes: he made his "Ah-hah! That's it!" into music.

*   *   *

When one demands that kind of precision from actors, it goes without saying that the plays must be rehearsed long and carefully. Feydeau rehearsed his for three months. Besides, he almost always used the same actors, the three leading roles going to Marcel Simon, Armande Cassive, and Germain. Simon and Germain alternated in the best role—the one who receives the kicks in the rear. Cassive was always the catastrophe, a blonde catastrophe—sensual or shrewish, depending on the part.

Famous actors like Signoret and Gémier, to mention only two, were suffocated under Feydeau's characters, because in order to act his comedies as they should be acted it was necessary to put oneself entirely in his hands. He insisted on sincerity. When an actor is not sincere, he maintained, the audience doesn't reject the actor—it leaves the play. And he would not have that at any price. He also had the greatest scorn for "artistes" and their initiative. He was inclined to look upon them as intelligent and unruly phonographs. He cut out their work for them; and he was ferocious when they didn't grasp it quickly enough.

At a revival of one of his plays, which he was forced to see performed without his favorite actors, he strode up and down, his cigar belching smoke, his hat set at a pugnacious angle on his head. One of the actors, aware that a storm was brewing, remarked sourly, "What's the matter, Master, isn't it going well?"

"Oh, yes indeed. It's going fine. The only trouble is that every one of you is giving his cues to an idiot."

But there was something that infuriated him even more than stupidity, and that was bad acting. In the text of *La Dame de chez Maxim,* there occurs the following interesting admonition, addressed to the various actresses who portrayed *la môme Crevette,* with particular reference to their interpretation of the ballad, "La Marmite à Saint-Lazare:"

Author's note. Having observed that many actresses have a tendency to sing the above ballad facing the audience, rather than the guests (on stage), I would remind them that they are indulging in utter nonsense, to the detriment of what is happening on stage. At this moment, the wench is supposed to be singing for the General's guests—therefore she should face *them,* and not come downstage. I am counting on the actresses who play this role to take this advice into consideration.

And he adds with crushing contempt: "When I am forced to deal with a third-rate actress, I naturally authorize her to act in her own best interests."

*   *   *

There are three periods in Georges Feydeau's work, and all three are ruled by the female character. When the heroine changes, the style, pace, and quality of the comedy change too.

The first period is dominated by middle-class ladies. They have not sinned—yet—but they dream about it all the time. They are charming, unstable, and a bit mad. They are despotic mistresses and rather uncommendable wives. As Feydeau says: "They breathe virtue, and are forthwith out of breath." They are more emancipated than the heroines of Labiche, but not unlike them. They say: "What a pity one cannot take a lover without deceiving one's husband!" Though they are all smiles at the idea of sin, they cannot stand being themselves deceived—their only recourse is to apply the law of retaliation. It is only in those fleeting moments when they give no thought to what they are saying that we can be sure of what is really going on in their heads. Still, they know what's what. "One may doubt the man who says, 'I love you,' but one can be sure of the man who does all he can to conceal his love."

This is the period of *Monsieur Chasse, La Main passe, Dindon, La Puce à l'oreille* and *l'Hôtel du Libre-Échange.*

*   *   *

The second period deals with the *cocottes,* or *dégrafées* as they were called at the time—Amélie, Bichon, *la môme Crevette.* These girls have character. They are amusing, aggressive, ridiculous. A whole cosmopolitan menagerie, a whole rich fauna of rakes, weaklings, refugees, and deadbeats follow in the wake of these ladies. Standards are rising.

And because these girls are given to all kinds of lunacy, the author can profit from them in the multiplication of his own. They are likely to say anything—but they say it so well that they are quoted by a duchess, the wife of a subprefect, twelve society ladies, and a priest. When one of their set marries and becomes the Duchesse de la Courtille, they say, quite reasonably:

"That makes one less chippy, but not necessarily one more lady."

They are trollops, but good trollops. They are as nice to their brother as they are to the *valet de chambre*.

Their chief preoccupation is jewels; but, if their lovers object, they attempt to appease them: "Look, I had that diamond he gave me set into a ring—just for you." They frolic gaily in the midst of situations that are excruciating for everybody else. Because they are pretty and have nothing to lose, they are amiably content to be the cause of all catastrophes.

They do not complain of their condition. One of them, who had been a lady's maid, is questioned by her former mistress:

"Then, you became a ———"

"Cocotte, yes, madame."

"But how could you?"

"Ambition."

This is the era of sparkling successes—*La Dame de chez Maxim, Je ne trompe pas mon Mari,* and *Occupe-toi d'Amélie.*

* * *

The last period is the reign of the untamed shrews: it is also the period of his masterpieces, his one-act plays. Feydeau has now given up cataclysmic encounters, disguises, pistol shots, conditional threats, brawls, booby-trapped rooms, apparitions, magnetism, spiritualism, anesthetizing ecstasy. He abandons all his accessories, concentrating on nothing but his excruciating buffoonery, which he will bring to bear upon a married couple—a weak and rather stupid man in the clutches of a terrible, fascinating, and pitiless shrew.

The names of the characters change: in *Mais n'te promène donc pas toute nue,* they are Ventroux and Clarisse; in *On Purge Bébé,* Follavoine and Julie; in *Léontine est en avance,* Toudoux and Léonie; in *Feu la Mère de Madame,* Yvonne and Lucien. But only the names are changed. Feydeau planned to publish this series of comedies in a single volume, to be called *Du Mariage au Divorce*. What we find in these four plays are the irritations, the interminable wranglings, the small, horrible catastrophes in the lives of a man and woman who are united only by habit. If the author had not made these ill-mated couples pass before fun-house mirrors that warp and magnify, they would be Strindberg characters.

The language in which they express themselves has been the subject of much discussion. Obviously it is not "the elegant French of Labiche, nor the delicately shaded language, full of scintillating color, which illuminates the dialogues of Meilhac." Nor is it a revival of the solemn grandiloquence of Bossuet parodied by Georges Courteline.

It is an abrupt and chaotic language, marked by an abundance of absurd and stupefying notions. It is a conjurer's raiment: from the sleeves, the pockets, the collar, come fish, flowers, an omelet, a rabbit, soap bubbles, a cannon ball, or a display of fireworks. The speech changes with the milieu, the class, the occupation of the characters; it runs with the action, keeping up with its antics and its perilous leaps. It is the *maillot* of the acrobatic clown, the skin on the muscles.

*   *   *

Georges Feydeau was indeed a great master of comedy. The greatest after Molière. The miracle of Feydeau is the brilliant animation by means of which the unfortunate Pinglets and Petypons are stirred up, carried off, and swept away. Feydeau's plays have the consecutiveness, the force, and the violence of tragedies. They have the same ineluctable fatality. In tragedy, one is stifled with horror. In Feydeau, one is suffocated with laughter. We are occasionally given some respite by the heroes of Shakespeare and Racine, when they melodiously bemoan their fate in beautiful poetry. But Feydeau's heroes haven't got time to complain. It is characteristic of their destiny to make us laugh, while the small catastrophe, which barely manages to come off, paves the way for an immense vexation, which, we know, will be only the first in a whole series of new ones. Jean Cocteau believes the gods create highly perfected infernal machines for the annihilation of the human race. The god Feydeau controls his infernal machine from a practical-jokes-and-novelty shop.

But an infernal machine it is, for it turned itself on its creator.

Jean Richepin expressed amazement that a brain could

give birth to so many buffooneries, so much sensible nonsense, without bursting. The fears which Feydeau transmuted into laughter were prophetic; and the hour came when the creator of so many luminous delights suddenly entered the night of eternity.

Georges Feydeau's light was extinguished on June 5, 1921, at dawn. He died from his desire to make us laugh, killed by his own genius.